Ville Mäkipelto
Uncovering Ancient Editing

Beihefte zur Zeitschrift für die alttestamentliche Wissenschaft

―

Edited by
John Barton, Reinhard G. Kratz, Nathan MacDonald,
Carol A. Newsom and Markus Witte

Volume 513

Ville Mäkipelto
Uncovering Ancient Editing

Documented Evidence of Changes in Joshua 24
and Related Texts

DE GRUYTER

ISBN 978-3-11-071053-3
e-ISBN (PDF) 978-3-11-060224-1
e-ISBN (EPUB) 978-3-11-060011-7
ISSN 0934-2575

Library of Congress Cataloging-in-Publication Data
Names: Mäkipelto, Ville, 1988- author.
Title: Uncovering ancient editing : documented evidence of changes in Joshua 24 and related texts / Ville Makipelto.
Description: 1 [edition]. | Boston : De Gruyter, 2018. | Series: Beihefte zur Zeitschrift für die alttestamentliche Wissenschaft ; Band 513 | Includes bibliographical references and index.
Identifiers: LCCN 2018026146 (print) | LCCN 2018029553 (ebook) | ISBN 9783110602241 (electronic Portable Document Format (pdf) | ISBN 9783110598117 (print : alk. paper) | ISBN 9783110602241 (e-book pdf) | ISBN 9783110600117 (e-book epub)
Subjects: LCSH: Bible. Joshua, XXIV–Criticism, Redaction. | Bible. Joshua, XXIV–Criticism, interpretation, etc. | Intertextuality in the Bible.
Classification: LCC BS1295.52 (ebook) | LCC BS1295.52 .M35 2018 (print) | DDC 222/.2066–dc23
LC record available at https://lccn.loc.gov/2018026146

Bibliographic information published by the Deutsche Nationalbibliothek
The Deutsche Nationalbibliothek lists this publication in the Deutsche Nationalbibliografie; detailed bibliographic data are available in the internet at http://dnb.dnb.de.

© 2018 Walter de Gruyter GmbH, Berlin/Boston
This volume is text- and page-identical with the hardback published in 2018.
Typesetting: Integra Software Services Pvt. Ltd.
Printing and binding: CPI books GmbH, Leck

www.degruyter.com

Preface

This book is a slightly revised version of my doctoral dissertation, completed at the University of Helsinki in March 2018. This work could not have been accomplished without the help, support, and inspiration of numerous people. My supervisor Dr. Juha Pakkala has constructively guided me through the research process, and introduced me to the international community of biblical scholars. The support and encouragement I received from Pakkala has been a constant companion, beginning already with my Master's thesis – for this I will ever be grateful. I have also had the privilege of receiving supervision from two brilliant textual critics, Prof. Anneli Aejmelaeus and Dr. Tuukka Kauhanen. Their critical comments and input, especially concerning section 3 of this book, have been invaluable. I have learned much from my team of accomplished supervisors. As for the remaining disagreements and possible errors, I of course take full responsibility.

My research was conducted as part of the Finnish Academy's Centre of Excellence *Changes in Sacred Texts and Traditions* (CSTT), directed by Prof. Martti Nissinen. The Centre provided full funding for my work, as well as an excellent working environment. Before the advent of my academic career there, I had never expected that research could be pursued in such a diverse and innovative community. I am very grateful for this opportunity, for Prof. Nissinen and all the members of CSTT. The members and collaborators of our team *Literary Criticism in the Light of Documented Evidence* – Prof. Reinhard Müller, Dr. Mika Pajunen, Prof. Francis Borchardt, Prof. Urmas Nõmmik, Dr. Anssi Voitila, Timo Tekoniemi, Prof. Sara Milstein, and Prof. Christoph Levin – deserve special recognition for our many discussions on texts and methodology. Moreover, the University of Helsinki and its Faculty of Theology provided many other fruitful contexts for my work. The postgraduate seminar in Old Testament studies, assisted at the time by Dr. Jessi Orpana, was an especially important forum.

During my doctoral research, I spent two longer periods abroad as a visiting scholar. Prof. Müller deserves my warmest gratitude for hosting my visit of ten months at the *Westfälische Wilhelms-Universität* in Münster (Germany). I also wish to thank Prof. Jan Joosten and the staff at the *Oxford Centre for Hebrew and Jewish Studies* for making my five months visit to Oxford (UK) possible. During these stays, I received important input from my hosts and other resident scholars, for which I am ever so grateful. Special thanks goes to Prof. Reinhard Achenbach, Dr. Sofia Salo, Dr. Jonathan Robker, Dr. John Screnock, and Jelle Verburg.

I am grateful to Dr. Seppo Sipilä for frequently letting me use his personal library, and for helpful comments on my work. Along this journey, I have also visited several international conferences, where I have had many discussions with people who are too numerous to list here separately. I am very thankful to you all! A big thanks also to Dr. Christopher TenWolde for revising the English of my study.

Finally, thank you Jenna, my best friend and dear wife, for your constant love, support, and inspiration!

In Helsinki, April 2018,
Ville Mäkipelto

Contents

Preface —— V

1	**Introduction —— 1**	
1.1	Documented Evidence of Editorial Processes —— 1	
1.2	Current Trends in the Study of Editorial Processes —— 4	
1.3	The Outline and Aims of This Study —— 14	

2	**Textual Witnesses to the Book of Joshua —— 16**	
2.1	The Plurality of Joshua Texts in Second Temple Judaism —— 16	
2.2	The Masoretic Textual Tradition —— 16	
2.3	The Septuagint of Joshua —— 17	
2.3.1	Reconstructing the OG —— 18	
2.3.2	Aspects of the Translation Technique —— 24	
2.3.3	The Relationship of MT and OG Joshua —— 29	
2.3.4	Interim Conclusions on the Septuagint of Joshua —— 39	
2.4	Biblical Joshua Texts from Qumran —— 40	
2.5	Other Joshua Texts —— 42	
2.5.1	Rewritten Joshua Scrolls —— 42	
2.5.2	The Samaritan Joshua Texts —— 43	

3	**Documented Evidence of Editing in Joshua 24 —— 49**	
3.1	Introductory Remarks —— 49	
3.2	Joshua 24:1–13: Text and Apparatus —— 51	
3.2.1	Text-Critical Analysis of the OG —— 56	
3.2.2	Evaluation between the OG and the MT —— 63	
3.3	Joshua 24:14–27: Text and Apparatus —— 92	
3.3.1	Text-Critical Analysis of the OG —— 97	
3.3.2	Evaluation between the OG and the MT —— 101	
3.4	Joshua 24:28–33: Text and Apparatus —— 118	
3.4.1	Text-Critical Analysis of the OG —— 122	
3.4.2	Evaluation between the OG and the MT —— 125	
3.5	Text-Critical Conclusions —— 156	
3.6	The Samaritan Farewell Speech of Joshua —— 163	

4 Literary and Redaction Criticism of Joshua 24 in the Light of Documented Evidence — 170

- 4.1 Introduction — 170
- 4.2 A Complex Web of Literary Connections — 172
- 4.2.1 Joshua 24 and Genesis — 172
- 4.2.2 Joshua 24 and Exodus — 176
- 4.2.3 Joshua 24, Numbers, and Deuteronomy — 180
- 4.2.4 Joshua 24 and Joshua — 183
- 4.2.5 Joshua 24 and Judges — 188
- 4.2.6 Joshua 24 and Samuel-Kings — 191
- 4.2.7 Joshua 24 and Other Historical Summaries — 194
- 4.2.8 Three Interim Conclusions for Literary and Redaction Criticism — 197
- 4.3 Literary and Redaction Criticism of Joshua 24 — 198
- 4.3.1 Introductory Remarks — 198
- 4.3.2 A Late Literary Unity — 202
- 4.3.3 A Basic Commitment Narrative Expanded in Several Stages — 206
- 4.3.4 Deuteronomistic Redactions — 220
- 4.3.5 The Transition from Joshua to Judges — 225
- 4.4 Literary and Redaction Critical Conclusions — 239
- 4.4.1 Joshua 24 – A Gradually Evolving Late Nomistic Text — 239
- 4.4.2 Literary and Redaction Criticism in the Light of the Documented Evidence — 242

5 Evidence of Editorial Techniques Used by Ancient Scribes — 246

- 5.1 How and Why Did Scribes Edit Texts? — 246
- 5.2 Editorial Processes at the End of a Book — 247
- 5.3 Additions — 249
- 5.3.1 Harmonizing Additions — 250
- 5.3.2 Small Additions and Marginal Glosses — 253
- 5.3.3 Small Addition to Smooth Out Tensions Created by an Earlier Large Addition — 256
- 5.4 Omissions — 258
- 5.5 Rewriting — 260
- 5.6 Transpositions — 264
- 5.7 Editorial Techniques and the Creativity of Ancient Scribes — 268

6 Conclusions and Discussion — 270

- 6.1 Documented Evidence of Changes in Joshua 24 — 270
- 6.2 The Literary Prehistory of Joshua 24 — 271

6.3   Documented Evidence of Editorial Techniques —— 273
6.4   Signposts for the Text-historical Study of the Hebrew Bible —— 274
6.5   Issues for Future Research —— 276

Abbreviations —— 279

Bibliography —— 281

Index of Ancient Sources —— 297

Index of Modern Authors —— 303

1 Introduction

1.1 Documented Evidence of Editorial Processes

The aim of this study is to reconstruct the textual and editorial history of Josh 24 and related texts as a test case for understanding the ancient editorial processes that produced the Hebrew Bible. First, I will undertake a text-critical analysis of all the extant textual witnesses. This analysis illuminates the latest stages of the textual and editorial history. Second, I will offer an outline of the editorial history of Josh 24 that is not visible in variant versions, in the light of patterns observed in the text-critical evidence. This twofold analysis is then complemented with a collation and examination of various editorial techniques utilized by Second Temple Jewish scribes in creating Josh 24. This offers tools and guidelines for studying the editorial history of the Hebrew Bible in a more reliable way. Moreover, it offers an opportunity to discuss the methodological relationship of textual, literary, and redaction criticism.[1] Therefore, although focusing on a single text, this study has several implications for the basic methodology of biblical criticism.

The Hebrew Bible is a product of an ancient creative scribal culture.[2] Most of the texts of which it is comprised are not the work of one author, but have gone through several stages of successive editing.[3] For ancient Near Eastern

---

1 In this study, literary criticism refers to the German *Literarkritik*, which is also known as source criticism. Literary criticism aims at understanding the prehistory of a text. It examines the unity or disunity of a given text and seeks to reconstruct the various sources and layers visible in its editing. Redaction criticism, on the other hand, focuses on the redactors responsible for creating the text out of the assumed sources. It seeks to describe their ideological motives and workings.
2 See, for example, Van der Toorn 2007, 8: "Being a product of the scribal workshop, the Bible owes its existence to generations of scribes, each new one continuing the work of previous ones."
3 The term "editing" is not unproblematic. In this study, I speak about "editing" to refer to intentional changes made by ancient scribes during the creation, updating, and transmission of texts. Thus, it is understood in a rather broad sense. These scribal changes may differ considerably in size and intent. For example, both the change of a verbal form from third-person to first-person and the addition of a whole verse in the copying of a text count as editing. Editing is not necessarily connected to the creation of "editions" of a text – I am not sure if the term "edition" is helpful at all when speaking about ancient compositions. Therefore, "editing" is also different from "redaction" which refers to a wider and more systematic editorial effort to unify texts guided by a specific theological stance. One problem with the term "editing" is that it carries various modern connotation (this is also the case with terms such as "book" and "Bible"). These modern connotations should not affect the analysis; the evidence itself should lead to the conclusions. For a helpful discussion of issues related to the term "editing", see Brooke 2017, 23–39.

https://doi.org/10.1515/9783110602241-001

compositions, this seems to have been the norm rather than the exception.⁴ Despite this, is it possible to uncover the editorial processes at play in the birth and transmission of the texts in the Hebrew Bible? How can a modern scholar reach methodologically sound conclusions on the complex histories behind these texts? Is the reconstruction of the earlier developmental stages of a given text viable if differing versions are not preserved in the textual witnesses?

Recently, there has been a surge of literature focusing on the editorial processes related to the Hebrew Bible in the light of documented or "empirical" evidence.⁵ It has traditionally been peculiarities – such as repetitions, contradictions, and inconsistencies – observed in single texts that have led scholars to assume the presence of editing and the usage of different sources.⁶ The proponents of focusing on documented evidence of editing have rightly noted that since we possess variant versions of the same texts this is where we should start. Such variant versions include parallel passages within single textual traditions (e.g. 2 Sam 22 and Ps 18 or 2 Kgs 18 and Is 36 in the MT) and variant versions between different textual traditions (e.g. the LXX and MT versions of Jeremiah). This endeavor has been greatly fueled by the full publication of the evidence from Qumran, a newfound appreciation of the "rewritten" and Samaritan sources, developments in the textual criticism of the LXX and other ancient translations, and a growing awareness of the editorial processes of other texts from the ancient Near East.

Meanwhile, many have questioned the validity of studying editorial processes altogether, especially when the assumed prehistory of texts is in question. Some argue that the concept of an ancient "editor" or "redactor" is not useful at all.⁷ Others accept that biblical texts have a long editorial history but argue

---

4 This study focuses mainly on the Hebrew Bible and other ancient Jewish texts. To name a few studies concentrating on the editorial and compositional processes of other ancient Near Eastern literary works see, for example, Tigay 1982 & 1985 on the Gilgamesh Epic, Abusch 1990 on the Akkadian witchcraft text *Maqlû*, Odorico 1994 on the annalistic texts of Tiglath-pileser III, and Milstein 2016, 76–146 on the use of "revision through introduction" in the Adapa Myth and Gilgamesh Epic.
5 See the survey below. I prefer to speak about documented evidence, since it conveys more clearly the nature of our textual evidence. The term "empirical" – as used in several publications – is somewhat misleading, since it usually refers to experimental research.
6 In German literature, these are called *Kohärenzstörungen* ("coherence disturbances"). See, for example, Becker 2011, 55–63. For a brief English summary of literary-critical criteria see Steck 1998, 54.
7 For example, Van Seters (2006, 297, 398–401) claims that the concepts "edition", "editor", and "redactor" are anachronistic when dealing with the scribes of the antiquity. These concepts are, according to Van Seters, based on an analogy drawn from the editorial activities of the European scholars of the Renaissance. Therefore, one should avoid these concepts when dealing with ancient history. Van Seters allows that there have been several additions and interpolations

that this history cannot be reconstructed due to the complexity of the editorial processes.⁸ Furthermore, many argue that the study of the "final text" should be at the center of critical research. This "final text" is usually the diplomatically chosen Masoretic version of the Hebrew Bible (MT). This approach results in the application of various synchronic and literary methods.⁹ Finally, some proponents of the importance of orality in the transmission of the Hebrew Scriptures have questioned the validity of studying text-related scribal practices as such.¹⁰

---

in the history of biblical texts, but he would not label these scribal interventions as "editing". Instead, Van Seters argues for a model of "ancient historiography" highlighting the creativity of authors. The criticism by Van Seters is partly valid but exaggerated. See, for example, the critical notions by Pakkala 2013, 63–66. Textual witnesses to the Hebrew Bible clearly illustrate that biblical texts were repeatedly changed by the ancient scribes. It is perhaps interesting to ponder whether the scribes responsible for these changes should be called authors, editors, redactors or something else. However, the analysis must go where the evidence leads. In many cases, the evidence reveals creative changes which can, in my opinion, be called "editing". Nevertheless, learning from the valuable work by Van Seters, one must keep in mind that "editing" is an *etic* term with anachronistic connotations, and the analysis should be guided by the textual evidence instead of modern meanings.

8 See, for example, Ben Zvi 2005, 6; Lemche 2008, 379–392; Carr 2011, 4.

9 Jan Fokkelman, for example, advocates a synchronic and narrative approach to the text of the Hebrew Bible. In his study of Genesis, he argues that diachronic methods have been greatly overemphasized in biblical studies. One should begin with a synchronic analysis focusing on the relationship between the text and the reader (or listener). After such an analysis, diachronic questions may turn out to be less necessary than often imagined (Fokkelman 1991, 2–3). A complete rejection of diachronic processes is perhaps limited to conservative scholars. For instance, Eugene H. Merrill (2008, 24–28) argues that modern theories on the editorial history of the Hebrew Bible rest "on the most tenuous, subjective evidence, all of which is based on the assumption that only religious developmentalism can account for the present shape of the Old Testament phenomena". Merrill's treatment of the textual witnesses to the Hebrew Bible reveals that his approach does not adequately consider all of the evidence. He argues that differences between the textual witnesses are due to late production of translations and copies from a well-preserved Hebrew original. He dismisses without any textual arguments the fact that the witnesses from Qumran and the LXX often witness to earlier textual forms than the MT (Merrill 2008, 23–24).

10 For instance, Ivan Engnell (1960, 17, 21–24) argued that "the anachronistic literary-critical method is out of date". According to Engnell, this endeavor should be replaced with the Scandinavian traditio-historical method, which seeks to analytically discern tradition unities and complexes behind the texts of the Hebrew Bible and their *Sitz im Leben* in an oral culture. The inconsistencies in the written sources, according to this view, are not due to editorial activities but a result of fusing different traditions together already in the oral stage. It is noteworthy that Engnell seemed to place a high value on the MT (1960, 20–21), and was negative towards the text-critical value of Qumran and the LXX in uncovering the textual history of the Hebrew Bible. In the light of modern text-critical research, this negativity should not be upheld. Even though orality plays a

This study participates in this discussion with a fresh examination of Josh 24 and related texts. The book of Joshua was chosen since it offers a wealth of documented evidence of editorial processes. The principal textual witnesses reveal that in the Late Second Temple Period the book was circulating in various forms and was being edited by different scribal circles.[11] The last chapter of the book is important since it offers a plethora of textual variants between the MT and the LXX, and it has been used as evidence for various competing models for the wider editorial processes related to the composition of the historical books. For this reason, Josh 24 allows us to discuss editorial processes ranging from minor scribal changes to larger compositional issues. Josh 24 is also related to many other texts – e.g. Judg 2:6–9 and Josh 5:2–9 – which allows textual analyses of editorial phenomena beyond this chapter. Moreover, Josh 24 illuminates the phenomenon of editing the ending of an ancient composition.

Even though Josh 24 has been the subject of many studies, scholarly opinions on the nature, date, and character of this theologically important text vary greatly, justifying a fresh examination. Josh 24 has also not yet been examined with a focus of integrating textual evidence of changes closer into the literary- and redaction-critical discussion. Furthermore, the evidence from the LXX has not been adequately analyzed and utilized in the discussion. The focus of this study, which is to better understand editorial techniques in the light of text-critical evidence, is also new in relation to Josh 24.

1.2 Current Trends in the Study of Editorial Processes

The traditional methodology of biblical criticism makes a clear distinction between textual criticism ("lower criticism") and literary/redaction criticism ("higher criticism"). In this traditional framework, the textual development of biblical books is envisioned as a process with two distinct phases: the composition of the text, followed by the transmission of the text. Textual criticism deals with the latter, and seeks to recover the original form of a text as it left the hands of the final author or redactor. In other words, the textual developments studied in textual criticism are explained as secondary developments that have emerged – often accidentally – in the later copying of the manuscripts. Literary and redaction criticism, in turn, aims at reconstructing the earlier prehistory of a

---

role in the work of the scribes, the plea to abandon literary criticism altogether is problematic, since our textual evidence witnesses to editorial activities.
11 See section 2.

text. Its task is to find out what sources were used, and how and why they were put together in the composition of a text. This traditional view is seen in several books on methodology.[12] Many early theories on the history of the book of Joshua also rely on this traditional view.[13]

Two current trends are confronting the traditional view and challenging the way in which the editorial history of the Hebrew Bible is being researched. First, the methodological boundaries of textual, literary, and redaction criticism have been revealed by many as being artificial.[14] This is due to the existence of large-scale editorial differences in the textual evidence of the Hebrew Bible. For instance, LXX Jeremiah preserves a version of the book which is approximately 15% shorter than MT Jeremiah. Their differences cannot be explained in any other way than by assuming that they present two distinct phases in the editorial development of the book of Jeremiah.[15] Further large-scale editorial differences are witnessed, most notably, by the Dead Sea Scrolls and the Samaritan sources. Since textual criticism illuminates the latest literary development of such texts, it is not possible to make a clear distinction between textual and literary/redaction criticism.[16] Second, as already mentioned above, several scholars argue that the study of the editorial history of the Hebrew Bible should begin with an evaluation of textual evidence from variant versions. These documented cases of editing provide guidelines and controls for using the methods of literary and redaction criticism in outlining the literary prehistory of texts. These two trends should be kept in mind when examining recent studies on ancient editorial processes.

The strongest plea to integrate documented evidence of editing closer to the study of the literary and redaction history of the Hebrew Bible was put forwards by Jeffrey Tigay in the edited volume *Empirical Models for Biblical Criticism*. When parallel versions of the same text exist, Tigay referred to these versions as

---

12 See, for example, Steck 1998, 16, 18–20: "the task of text criticism is to confirm the 'original text of the Old Testament' – by critically sorting out the Hebrew text form which exists in the Old Testament at the conclusion of the process of productive, written formation." See also the characterization of the traditional view by Van der Meer 2004, 7–9.
13 This becomes evident especially in section 4.3, dealing with literary and redaction criticism of Josh 24.
14 Some of this criticism is explored later in this section.
15 Tov 2012, 286–293. Large scale differences between the LXX and the MT can be discerned at least in the Pentateuch, Joshua, Samuel-Kings, Jeremiah, Ezekiel, Proverbs, Esther, Daniel, and Ezra-Nehemiah.
16 See, for example, De Troyer 2003, 127–128; Schenker 2003; Trebolle 2008, 437–463; Tov 2012, 283–326; Aejmelaeus 2012, 3; Lemmelijn 2012, 203–207; Ausloos 2014, 358–375; Kratz 2016, 501–524 & 2017, 163–188. More studies challenging the separation between textual and literary/redaction criticism are surveyed later in this section.

empirical evidence of editorial processes. Several such instances can be found in the Hebrew Bible and ancient Near Eastern literature. The articles in the collected volume focus on the editing of, for example, the Pentateuch, 1 Samuel, Joshua, Jeremiah, Neo-Assyrian Royal Inscriptions, and specific editorial techniques or traces of editing (e.g. conflation, assimilation, and the stylistic criterion for uncovering various sources). The overall aim of studying empirical evidence in the volume is to help in uncovering changes in the literary and redaction history of texts; that is, the editorial processes that have usually been studied based on clues within the single MT.[17]

To be sure, Tigay was not the first scholar to integrate textual evidence into the study of literary and editorial processes. Julius Wellhausen is often mentioned as one of the early pioneers who integrated textual evidence from the LXX to his literary and redaction critical models. In his study on the books of Samuel, for example, he often noted that the LXX holds earlier readings than the MT. In this manner, his reconstruction of the literary and redaction history of Samuel was preceded by a thorough analysis of the textual evidence.[18] In the case of Joshua, one could also mention the 1955 study *Shechem: A Traditio-Historical Investigation* by Eduard Nielsen. When Nielsen analyzed texts from Joshua and other historical books, he began with a thorough analysis of the changes visible in the textual witnesses (MT, LXX, and Peshitta). Only after the evaluation of these changes did he continue to the reconstruction of other layers and the dating of texts.[19]

After the publication of Tigay's volume, however, the amount of studies focusing on documented evidence of editing has seemingly increased. One can already speak of a new paradigm in the field of text-historical studies. Several studies have examined textual evidence of editing in single texts, compared the editorial processes visible in different texts, or focused on specific editorial techniques. Meanwhile, they have also discussed the relationship of textual, literary, and redaction criticism. To create the backdrop for my study, I will next introduce and evaluate the claims of some of these studies.

In *The Kings – Isaiah and Kings – Jeremiah Recensions* Raymond F. Person seeks to illuminate the redactional processes of the book of Kings with "the use of text critical controls." The focus of the study is on 2 Kgs 18:14–20:19 and 2 Kgs 24:18–25:30. The textual evidence consists of the MT and LXX versions of these passages, as well as their parallel versions in Isa 36:1–39:8 and Jer 52:1–34 in the MT, the LXX, and 1QIsa^a.[20] Person's conclusions have great implications for

---

[17] Tigay 1985, 1–20.
[18] Wellhausen 1871.
[19] Nielsen 1955.
[20] Person 1997, 5.

redaction criticism. According to his analysis, the MT versions of both passages in Kings seem to be late in relation to the other versions. Since most models of Deuteronomistic redactions have ignored the LXX and Qumran versions, they "all fail methodologically". Person posits that the earliest version of the accounts, recoverable with the help of textual criticism, and the latest version present in the MT present two distinct Deuteronomistic redactions of Kings. He also contends that it is not enough to argue for redactions based on language and themes, but that there must be a "significant difference between the redactional layers in order to distinguish one redactor from another."[21] Without commenting on the details of Person's textual analysis, it is important to highlight the methodological steps taken in the study. First, one needs to compare all the textual evidence and make conclusions on the editing that can be directly observed. Only then should one discuss the possible editorial developments not discernible by comparing different textual witnesses.[22]

This methodological order stands in stark contrast with the methodology employed by Michaël N. van der Meer in his analysis of texts from the book of Joshua. His study *Formation and Reformulation. The Redaction of the Book of Joshua in the Light of the Oldest Textual Witnesses* seeks to clarify the relationship of textual, literary, and redaction criticism through the analysis of three case examples (Josh 1, 5:2–13, 8:1–35). Van der Meer refers to the recent trend of seeking an "empirical basis" for the diachronic study of texts, but argues that there are several problems with this approach.[23] The main methodological question in his study is what the implications of the textual evidence for methodology should be: "Should theories concerning the development of the biblical books be made dependent upon the often scanty and ambiguous textual evidence? Or conversely, should the diffuse variety of textual data be explained on the basis of a well-tested theory of literary developments leading up to their final form?" Van der Meer seeks to follow a third path in which both textual criticism and literary/redaction criticism are first kept apart and undertaken in their own right, and only the results are compared at a second stage.[24] In practice, he turns to "generally accepted theories concerning the redaction history of Joshua" and compares these theories with his analysis of the LXX and Qumran material.[25] There might

---

[21] Person 1997, 7.
[22] Although Person does not take the second step far in his study, instead focusing only on the documented editorial layers.
[23] Van der Meer 2004, 13–14.
[24] Van der Meer 2004, 16, 155–159.
[25] According to the analysis of Van der Meer, the texts of Joshua in LXX and Qumran are generally secondary in relation to the MT. Therefore, according to him, they do not function as

be some heuristic merit for this methodological order; it is certainly good to evaluate the results of literary and redaction criticism by comparing them with the analysis of textual evidence. However, the model of Deuteronomistic redactions proposed by Van der Meer as the "generally accepted theory" is ultimately based solely on the MT.[26] There is no longer any excuse for prioritizing the MT over other textual witnesses as a starting point for a historical analysis.[27]

So, to answer the questions posed by Van der Meer on the methodological priority between "ambiguous textual evidence" and a "well-tested theory of literary developments" I would suggest that these should not be juxtaposed. One should always begin with an analysis of all the available "hard" evidence. In this analysis, literary and redaction critical observations already emerge. Literary and redaction critical considerations should not be made apart from the analysis of textual evidence, but should be integrated into the analysis from the beginning. Rather than upholding a dichotomy of textual evidence and theories on literary development, these should be regarded as a continuum of textual development. Ultimately it is the nature of the evidence that dictates the methods. In this regard, it is easy to agree with Van der Meer that "the situation differs from composition to composition."[28]

Indeed, with regard to the book of Joshua several scholars have noted the need to begin the study of the editorial history by first assessing textual evidence. In this process, literary and redaction critical issues are already present. The work of these scholars show that keeping the methods apart, as Van der Meer seems to do, leads in inadequate results. For example, working with Josh 10, Kristin De Troyer argues that the latest editorial stages of the text are visible in textual evidence, since the Hebrew *Vorlage* of the OG attests to an Old Hebrew text which was later transformed into the MT. Thus, the MT in relation to the OG attests to the "final redaction of the book of Joshua."[29] This redaction consists of minor changes that are ideologically meaningful. For instance, through small alterations the editor created a concept of a "highly unified" Israel and highlighted the role of Joshua as the leader of this Israel.[30] If the analysis by De Troyer is correct, in Josh 10 this redaction is characterized by so small editorial changes that one

---

documented evidence for the prehistory of the book of Joshua. See section 2.3.3. I will evaluate some of his textual arguments critically in section 3.4.2.
26 Van der Meer 2004, 119–121.
27 Dozeman 2011, 189–190: "The tendency among redaction critics is all too often to privilege or even limit research to the MT in determining the final form of Joshua or any book for that matter."
28 Van der Meer 2004, 17.
29 De Troyer 2017, 224.
30 De Troyer 2017, 240–243.

could not possibly reconstruct them if working only with the MT. Therefore, the latest redaction of Joshua is lost if one does not begin with an analysis of the textual evidence. Another example of this approach can be seen in a short article by Adrian Schenker. Schenker argues that the Old Latin of Josh 22 preserves the earliest recoverable textual form of the chapter. In this earliest recoverable text, for example, Josh 22:27b–28 was missing, and it was only secondarily added to the text witnessed by the OG and the MT with the help of a *Wiederaufnahme*.[31] Schenker notes that earlier literary and redaction critical research did not notice the variant version preserved in the Old Latin, and therefore did not take into account the latest editorial trajectories visible already in textual evidence.[32] The examples analyzed by De Troyer and Schenker strongly suggest that starting with textual evidence is the correct way of proceeding when examining the editorial processes of the book of Joshua and conducting literary and redaction criticism.[33]

This way of working is furthermore corroborated by the work of several textual scholars, some of which have already been mentioned in footnote 16. In his influential introduction to the textual criticism of the Hebrew Bible, Emanuel Tov devotes a whole section to the relationship between textual and literary criticism. He presents evidence from books that exhibit large-scale editorial differences between the textual evidence from LXX, MT, and Qumran. According to Tov, the last stage in the development of several books is visible in the textual evidence.[34] In addition to this introduction, Tov has convincingly illustrated in two articles that this is also the case in the book of Joshua.[35] The research by Eugene Ulrich should also be highlighted in this regard. Much of his influential work has been synthesized in *The Dead Sea Scrolls and the Developmental Composition of the Bible*, which offers a model of the developmental history of the Hebrew Bible in the light of the pluriform textual evidence from Qumran. The volume contains a chapter on Joshua which, in my opinion, demonstrates clearly that the editorial history of Joshua cannot be written without taking the documented evidence of editing into account.[36] Finally, one should also mention the multifaceted research by Julio Trebolle Barrera in which one overarching theme has long been "the joint application of textual, literary, and redaction criticism".[37] Trebolle has analyzed the textual evidence pertaining to several

---

31 Schenker 2008, 419–421.
32 Schenker 2008, 424.
33 For other examples and studies see section 2.3.3.
34 Tov 2012, 283–326.
35 Tov 1999c and 2015b.
36 Ulrich 2015, 47–65.
37 Piquer Otero & Torijano Morales 2012, ix–x.

books in the Hebrew Bible. Several articles also deal with Joshua, showing that the textual evidence of editing in Joshua needs to be at the center of the study of editorial processes.[38]

In addition to analyses of specific texts and compositions, there have been some general studies focusing on the phenomenon of editing and specific editorial techniques in the light of documented evidence. In *Evidence of Editing: Growth and Change of Texts in the Hebrew Bible,* Reinhard Müller, Juha Pakkala, and Bas ter Haar Romeny explore fifteen passages from the Hebrew Bible of which variant versions have been preserved. The aim is "to demonstrate that substantial editing took place in the history of the Hebrew Bible."[39] In a way, the study is a response to the skepticism of scholars who argue that the editorial history of biblical books cannot be reconstructed.[40] While defending the possibilities of literary and redaction criticism, however, it also reminds that literary and redaction critical models are hypotheses, and that it "would be a mistake to assume that literary-critical reconstructions are evidence of the same caliber as preserved textual witnesses".[41] The case examples presented in the study focus particularly on different editorial techniques that can be discerned with the help of textual criticism. The study then offers evidence on how the techniques of addition, omission, rewriting, and relocation functioned. This information on editorial techniques can further be applied to cases where editing has supposedly taken place but textual evidence has not been preserved.[42]

Documented or "hard" evidence of a specific editorial technique is at the core of *Tracking the Master Scribe: Revision through Introduction in Biblical and Mesopotamian Literature* by Sara J. Milstein. Milstein focuses on the scribal technique of "revision through introduction" in which a scribe inserts a new frontal introduction to an earlier text. When a new introduction is added, it changes the way that the text is interpreted by subsequent readers. The bulk of the study consists of four complex case studies from both Mesopotamian and Biblical literature. The Mesopotamian evidence presents the clearest documented cases of revision. When the Assyrians transmitted the Sumerian Adapa myth, in one instance a long introduction was omitted and in another instance a prologue was

---

[38] Trebolle 2005, 401–413; 2008, 437–463; 2014, 231–256; 2016, 231–256.
[39] Müller, Pakkala & Haar Romeny 2014, 1.
[40] Müller, Pakkala & Haar Romeny 2014, 9–15.
[41] Müller, Pakkala & Haar Romeny 2014, 15, 220–225.
[42] The study of editorial techniques in the light of documented evidence is at the core of the current research by Juha Pakkala and Reinhard Müller. See, for example, the recent collection of articles Müller & Pakkala 2017. They are also currently working on a handbook of ancient editorial techniques (http://blogs.helsinki.fi/sacredtexts/teams/litcrit).

added.⁴³ Different tablets of the Gilgamesh Epic also attest to frontal additions and omissions.⁴⁴ The case examples from the Hebrew Bible derive from the book of Judges which, according to Milstein, "is replete with examples of revision through introduction", with the method having been used in almost every narrative of the composition.⁴⁵ In the case examples from Judges, Milstein does not rely directly on variant versions of the same text, but does discuss her findings in the editorial continuum which finds its latest developments in "hard" evidence.⁴⁶ The importance of the work by Milstein in the study of editorial processes lies in two features. First, it combines various kinds of evidence from the ancient Near East and the Hebrew Bible, illustrating that the editorial processes of the Hebrew Bible are not unique in the ancient world. Second, it is among the few complete studies focusing on specific editorial techniques, which allows for tracing the use of the scribal method in other texts.⁴⁷

Another study focusing on a specific editorial technique is *God's Word Omitted. Omissions in the Transmission of the Hebrew Bible* by Juha Pakkala. Pakkala demonstrates that in much literary and redaction critical scholarship it has been the implicit or explicit assumption that texts have been edited only through the addition of new material. It has been supposed that since the transmitted texts were considered ancient and sacred, the deletion of material was not permitted.⁴⁸ Through the examination of several documented cases of editing, chosen from canonical and non-canonical sources, Pakkala illustrates that sometimes ancient editors deleted or rewrote parts of the material they were transmitting. According to Pakkala, documented evidence suggests that often the traditional assumption is true, and that texts have been edited mainly or almost entirely through expansions (e.g. the Samaritan Pentateuch and the book of Jeremiah). Addition seems to have been the most common editorial technique. However, the evidence also points in the other direction: even radical editorial processes are visible in the textual evidence. This is especially true of the later books in the Hebrew Bible (e.g. Esther and Ezra-Nehemiah). Pakkala suggests that conservative editorial processes were related to editing within an ideological paradigm, while radical editorial processes took place when there was a considerable paradigm shift

---

43 Milstein 2016, 76–109.
44 Milstein 2016, 110–146.
45 Milstein 2016, 37.
46 See, for example, Milstein 2016, 171–173.
47 The scribal method of "revision through introduction" may have been used in the literary history of Josh 24, when the historical summary (24:2–13) was secondarily added at the beginning of the chapter. See section 4.3.3.
48 Pakkala 2013, 16–17, 88–91.

(e.g. the destruction of the temple).⁴⁹ The study of omissions turns out to have major implications for the study of the textual history of the Hebrew Bible. If ancient editors could omit and rewrite material, one cannot automatically assume that we can recover all the ancient textual forms, or that there was a continuation of ideas in the history of ancient Israel. In this way, the examination of a single editorial technique in the light of textual evidence turns out to have far-reaching conclusions.

Finally, one should note the recent edited volume *Empirical Models Challenging Biblical Criticism*, which aims at "correcting discussion on the efficacy of source and redaction criticism" with an assortment of articles devoted to documented cases of editing in Mesopotamian and Biblical literature. The articles themselves represent divergent views, having been written by different authors on various kinds of material. In the introduction by Person and Robert Rezetko, however, the editors note that much of recent scholarship has focused on the positive force of Tigay's argument; that is, scholars have frequently used Tigay's work as a confirmation for the possibility of sustaining as complex models of the editorial history of texts as the Documentary hypothesis of the Pentateuch. The editors themselves emphasize that they wish to take the cautionary side of Tigay's work further. Specifically, they argue that the complex composite textual history of the texts in the Hebrew Bible can only be uncovered when traditional traces of literary activity are "paired with text-critical variants and other empirical data." For instance, while textual evidence demonstrates that *Wiederaufnahme* or resumptive repetition can be a trace of earlier editing in a text, *Wiederaufnahme* "by itself cannot be understood as reliable discernible trace" of editing. According to the authors, this also applies to other traces of editing such as grammatical problems and inconsistencies. Therefore, Person and Rezetko propose that in the future source and redaction criticism "must accept much more limited goals and objectives". Scholars of textual history should focus on the extant texts and their plurality, since in the explanation of this evidence alone there are already dissenting voices and competing models.⁵⁰

If the argument by the authors is followed strictly, scholars should not build models on the editorial history of texts when there is no supporting "hard" textual evidence. This would, according to these authors, be crossing the line of plausibility. However, two objections should be made. First, would it not be possible to build a cumulative argument on the prehistory of a text even if "empirical" evidence does not directly support the model? Much of the criticism by Person

---

49 Pakkala 2013, 351–369.
50 Person & Rezetko 2016, 14–35.

and Rezetko focuses on using single literary-critical criteria exclusively. This is certainly valid criticism. Nevertheless, literary and redaction critics often base their conclusions of editing on multiple criteria; if several traces are visible together, the argument for editing is stronger.[51] If the assumed editorial processes are also known from other documented cases of editing, the argument is even stronger. Second, the authors do not discuss the degrees of probability of different solutions. Textual scholars should be more explicit in evaluating the degrees of probabilities of their models. For instance, when extant textual witnesses corroborate editing, the probability of a model is high. This seems to be the level at which Person and Rezetko are willing to work. If, however, the literary-critical solution is based on multiple traces in a single text and a well-known editorial technique witnessed by documented evidence elsewhere, I would argue that the probability of the model is lower but still acceptable. A scholar of history should not abandon proposing solutions on this lower level of probability, since the preservation of our textual evidence is random. In statistics, this lower level would probably be equated to a p-value greater than 0.05, which would certainly not be acceptable if, for example, the effectiveness of a medicine would be in question. However, since scholars of history cannot generate more evidence or design new experiments, it is important to propose even bold solutions on how to best explain the existing evidence. These objections aside, the criticism by the authors is valid, especially in relation to exceedingly complex models of the prehistory of the Hebrew Bible.[52]

To sum up, current trends in the study of the editorial history of the Hebrew Bible clearly point towards the necessity of examining documented evidence of editing. The comparison of extant differing witnesses of the same text provides the best possible basis for examining the editorial processes used in the creation and transmission of texts in the Hebrew Bible. This is especially clear in the book of Joshua. While scholars focusing on documented evidence of editing agree on this point, there are some differences of opinion in how far we should proceed. Van der Meer was introduced as a proponent of implementing a text-critical evaluation of the evidence, but keeping it separate from a literary and redaction critical analysis based on the MT. In my opinion, this position cannot be preferred, since it essentially upholds the artificial separation between textual, literary, and redaction criticism. Since all these methods deal with similar scribal

---

51 For instance, Becker (2011, 56) emphasizes that the argument for literary disunity is often based on the interaction of many observations from various levels of argumentation (e.g. syntactical, linguistic, and theological tendencies).
52 This point is discussed further in section 4.4.2.

changes, it seems that they should rather "be implemented hand in hand."[53] To be sure, it is pragmatic to keep the working stages of a textual analysis separate to some degree, but even in such an approach the processes of textual, literary, and redaction criticism should be simultaneously kept in mind. The other point of disagreement relates to how far beyond documented evidence of editing the scholar should go. Person and Rezetko are skeptical of literary-critical solutions which assume editing without any documented evidence. Adopting their view completely would hinder the possibility of going beyond the latest stages of formation of a text. This would also mean that the Hebrew Bible could not be used critically as a source when reconstructing the history of ancient Israel beyond the last centuries of the Second Temple period. In my opinion, scholars should be open to building models of the prehistory of a text even when direct documented evidence of editing is missing. There is enough external evidence to assume that, when used critically, the Hebrew Bible could also provide some information deeper into the history of ancient Israel. However, arguments concerning editorial history should be based on trajectories visible in textual evidence elsewhere, and be cumulative in nature. The models should be evaluated on the basis of their explanatory power: how well does the assumption of earlier editing explain the extant evidence?

1.3 The Outline and Aims of This Study

In the light of the growing trend towards studying documented evidence of editorial processes, it is necessary to turn the focus on single important texts in the Hebrew Bible. This study is centered on an in-depth examination of the editorial interventions visible in Josh 24 and related texts. In section 2, I will introduce the evidence used in the text-historical study of the book of Joshua and examine the key problems related to each type of evidence. Here LXX Joshua will take up the biggest part of the discussion, since many questions related to its usage are still under debate. Next, the text-critical analysis of OG and MT Josh 24 in section 3 takes up a major part of this study and builds the backbone for further sections. This results in a model of the latest editorial developments of Josh 24. In section 4, I will sketch the editorial prehistory of Josh 24 in the light of the results of the text-critical evaluation and literary and redaction critical arguments. In this context, I will also discuss the role of Josh 24 in some key models related to the composition of the historical books. Finally, in section 5, before the conclusions and

---

[53] Müller, Pakkala & Haar Romeny 2014, 225.

discussion, I will ask how and why different editorial techniques were used by ancient scribes involved in the editing of Josh 24. This section will offer guidelines for recognizing these techniques in other texts.

The main research question of this study can be formulated as follows: *How has the end of the book of Joshua been edited in the light of documented evidence, and what does this tell about the ancient editorial processes that produced the Hebrew Bible?* The specific aims and questions of each section are:

- What kind of editorial processes can be observed from the documented evidence (MT, LXX, Qumran, SamJosh) pertaining to Josh 24 and related texts (e.g. Josh 5:2–9)? What is the earliest textual form of Josh 24 inferable from textual evidence, and how and why has it been subsequently edited? (= documented textual history, section 3)
- What is the most probable model explaining the literary and redaction history of Josh 24 in the light of documented evidence? How does this model correlate with wider theories on the composition of the Pentateuch and the historical books? (= editorial prehistory, section 4)
- What is the relationship of textual, literary, and redaction criticism? What are the strengths and challenges of integrating documented evidence into literary and redaction critical models? To what extent should the diachronic study of biblical texts even be done, and how accurate can it be? What kind of methodological implications can we draw from Josh 24 for future text-historical studies? (section 4)
- How and why did ancient scribes edit texts? Is it possible to discern the use of various editorial techniques without direct documented evidence? (section 5)

2 Textual Witnesses to the Book of Joshua

2.1 The Plurality of Joshua Texts in Second Temple Judaism

There was no single book of Joshua in Second Temple Judaism. The extant textual witnesses reveal that the composition was circulating in various biblical and rewritten textual forms.[1] The preservation of various textual forms for the use of modern scholars is largely due to the fortunes of history. The MT usually serves as an easy starting point for scholars of the Hebrew Bible. However, many scholars do not go further. Several commentaries privilege the MT when interpreting the book of Joshua.[2] Most literary and redaction critical models have also been built based solely on the MT.[3] In the post-Qumran age of textual criticism, this Masoretic privilege is not a sustainable position. The starting point of all text-historical studies should be the analysis of all the available textual evidence.

There are different questions and issues related to various pieces of evidence witnessing to the book of Joshua. Therefore, in this section I will introduce the basic types of evidence and examine the central problems related to their usage in the text-historical study of the Hebrew Bible.

2.2 The Masoretic Textual Tradition

The MT is not a single and stable text, but refers to a stream of textual tradition that began in the Second Temple period and continued developing throughout antiquity and the middle ages. The MT of Joshua is best preserved in the Leningrad Codex, dating from 1008 CE, which serves as the basis for the modern edition of the Hebrew Bible, and which is the *Biblia Hebraica Stuttgartensia* also utilized in this study. Other notable partially preserved manuscripts attesting to the MT

---

[1] This point was most recently explicated by De Troyer 2016, 330–346. The terms "bible", "biblical", and "rewritten" are problematic when discussing the Second Temple period, since they anachronistically project a modern concept of canon to ancient times. See, for example, Zahn 2011, 93–120. For pragmatic reasons, I will use the terms "Bible" and "biblical" for the textual forms that later became accepted as canon for various communities (MT, LXX). Therefore, the so-called rewritten and Samaritan Joshua texts are not included in these categories. This represents purely conventional *etic* terminology and should not be considered a statement on the priority, authority, or popularity of different textual forms in Second Temple Judaism.

[2] For instance, Soggin 1972 and Woudstra 1981 generally regard the variants in the LXX as later developments.

[3] See section 4.3.

are the Aleppo Codex (10th century CE) and the Cairo Codex (9th century CE).[4] In the 18th century, Benjamin Kennicott and Giovanni Bernardo De Rossi collected Hebrew variants from various medieval and Renaissance manuscripts. Their collections – although not free from errors – may at times contain interesting variants, especially when supported by other textual witnesses.[5] The fragmentary manuscripts from the Cairo Geniza (600–900 CE) also have a prominent role in uncovering the variants within the MT traditions. However, these fragments, along with those pertaining to the book of Joshua, remain understudied until this day.[6] The *Biblia Hebraica Quinta* edition of the Hebrew Bible, based on the Leningrad codex but containing a substantially better apparatus than the *BHS*, is still not finished in the case of the book of Joshua.[7]

Even though the best manuscripts of the MT date from medieval times, the Dead Sea Scrolls demonstrate that a textual tradition close to the MT was already in use at the end of the Second Temple period.[8] This text is referred to as the proto-MT text.[9] We do not know the exact wording of this textual form, but for pragmatic reasons it is usually assumed that it was close to the text of *BHS*, although without vocalization. The textual forms of the Aramaic Targums, the Syriac Peshitta, and the Vulgate also generally follow the MT.[10] These versions will be consulted in this study only when their text markedly differs from the MT.

2.3 The Septuagint of Joshua

The oldest Greek translation of the book of Joshua (OG Josh) presents a textual form substantially different from the MT. Before a text-critical analysis of the differences between the MT and the OG of Joshua can be executed, however, three aspects of the LXX tradition of Joshua needs to be discussed. First, since a critical *Göttingen* edition of the OG text of Joshua is not yet complete and published, the textual witnesses, their groupings, the most important recensional qualities, and

---

4 See, for example, Würthwein 1994, 10–13.
5 Kennicott 1776 and De Rossi 1785. See Fox (2015, 17–18) on the usage of these editions in textual criticism.
6 There are several fragments in the Cambridge Genizah collections witnessing to the book of Joshua (including Josh 24) which await closer scrutiny. See the catalogues of the MSS in Davis & Outhwaite 2003a, 469–470 and 2003b, 518.
7 https://www.academic-bible.com/en/home/current-projects/biblia-hebraica-quinta-bhq/
8 See, for example, Tov 2012, 24–25.
9 Most variants in the Qumran scrolls conform to the proto-MT text, but also witness other traditions. See section 2.4.
10 Würthwein 1994, 79–90; 95–99.

modern editions pertaining to the LXX will be examined to carry out the analysis with the best possible approximation of the OG text.[11] Second, aspects of the translation technique of OG Joshua will be investigated. For this, I will rely mostly on past research. Considering that many text-critical arguments rely on the supposed literalness or flexibility of the translator, I will specifically ask how the translator handled his source text. Third, previous research on the relationship of the MT and the Hebrew *Vorlage* of OG Joshua will be critically surveyed in some detail. This will allow me to relate my conclusions to earlier scholarship.

2.3.1 Reconstructing the OG

The Sources
When studying the Greek version of Joshua, one is confronted with a wealth of ancient sources. There are eight known majuscule manuscripts and some 100 minuscule manuscripts. These manuscripts date from between the 3rd century and 16th century.[12] In addition, the variant readings found in the quotations in patristic literature and the daughter translations (chiefly Sahidic, Old Latin, Ethiopian, Armenian, and the Syrohexapla) have to be considered.[13]

The important preliminary work of collating and grouping the manuscripts of the LXX was done by Max L. Margolis already in the first half of the 20th century. He distinguished five families of manuscripts, which he named after the areas in which they were, according to him, preserved and revised: the Egyptian (*E*), the Syrian (*S*), the Palestinian (*P*), and the Constantinopolitan (*C*) group. In addition, there was a fifth Mixed (*M*) group of manuscripts. According to Margolis, the OG of Joshua is often best found in the Egyptian group, which includes the earliest extant version of LXX Joshua, the Codex Vaticanus (B) dating from the 4th century. Other manuscripts in this group include 120 707 129 946, and three translations (Coptic-Bohairic, Coptic-Sahidic, and Ethiopian).[14]

---

11 The editing of a critical Göttingen text of LXX Joshua was in progress by Udo Quast, who sadly passed away before the work was completed. As of the date of the writing of this study, a new editor has not been announced. An earlier critical version was finished by Max L. Margolis, and has now been fully published in five fascicles (Margolis 1931–1938, 1992). Margolis' edition is not without problems, however. These are explored later in the present section.
12 See, for example, Den Hertog 1996, 3.
13 Margolis 1927; Bieberstein 1994; Van der Meer 2004, 23–24. In this study, I will use the numbering of manuscripts developed by Rahlfs (1914) and used in the Göttingen edition. For an easy comparison with the designations used in the Brooke-McLean edition, see Jellicoe 1993, 361–369 (Appendix II).
14 Margolis 1927, 307–323; Den Hertog 1996, 5–6.

Later research has in many respects confirmed two aspects of Margolis' research. First, the text of B and other manuscripts close to it are usually held to be the best representative of the OG. It is, however, not free from revision or errors, and cannot be used without taking the other manuscripts into account.[15] Second, the groups established by Margolis are mostly sound, and the main features of the relationship of these groups have been corroborated by numerous scholars.[16] The groups correspond closely with what in current Septuagint scholarship are called the Old Greek text (*E*), the Lucianic or the Antiochene recension (*S*), the Hexaplaric recension (*P*), and the Catena groups (*C*).[17] Some problematic aspects of Margolis' grouping include the identification of these groups with certain geographical localities, and some details of the recensional activities. To give one example of the latter, Pretzl and Bieberstein have rejected the idea that the manuscripts in the *C* group are purely post-Hexaplaric, and have identified them with much earlier pre-Hexaplaric revisional activities.[18] Moreover, in many instances it is clear that Margolis assumed too readily that the translator of Joshua was translating a text similar to the MT.[19]

Thus, while Margolis' grouping of the witnesses is a good starting point, his conclusions cannot be accepted uncritically. In later times, scholars have significantly refined his work. I will now look more closely at some of the most important recensions and manuscripts that need to be considered when evaluating the readings of LXX Joshua. These are the *Kaige*, Hexaplaric, and Lucianic or Antiochene recensions. Finally, I will also discuss the significance of the oldest Greek witness of LXX Joshua manuscript 816.

The *Kaige*-Theodotion readings in the Joshua material have been collected and thoroughly analyzed by Leonard J. Greenspoon in *Textual Studies in the Book of Joshua*. In his careful study, Greenspoon first analyzes the 171 readings in the Greek Joshua material attributed to Theodotion, most prominently found in manuscript 344, and compares them to the OG, on the one side, and to the MT on the other. These readings are then placed into six distinct categories. The overall conclusions are, first, that Theodotion revised the OG to a form of

---

[15] Margolis 1927, 316; Pretzl 1928, 419–420; Greenspoon 1983, 1–6; Den Hertog 1996, 9; Sipilä 1999, 18; Van der Meer 2004, 23; De Troyer 2005b, 129.
[16] Pretzl 1928; Smith 1978; Bieberstein 1994; and Den Hertog 1996, 3–23. Bieberstein (1994, 15) notes: "Die Einteilung der Gruppen selbst wurde von Smith geprüft und bestätig und kann daher übernommen werden." Pretzl (1928, 377–427) used his own designations for the separate groups. The groups by Margolis and Pretzl have been compared by Den Hertog 1996, 5–6.
[17] Van der Meer 2015, 75.
[18] Pretzl 1928, 412–421; Bieberstein 1994, 32–36.
[19] For a concise summary of the criticism of Margolis' grouping see Van der Meer 2004, 30.

the Hebrew that is almost identical to the MT.[20] Second, he clarifies the relationship of Theodotion with Aquila and Symmachus, concluding that Aquila used Theodotion rather than the OG as a basis of his revisions towards the Hebrew. In addition to using Theodotion as one source, he also knew the OG independently of Theodotion.[21] Third, in consideration of the 96 characteristics of the *Kaige* recension, Greenspoon concludes that 37 of the typical *Kaige* characteristics are not relevant to the book of Joshua, and that Theodotion in Joshua forms a part of the general *Kaige* recension.[22] In addition, Aquila applied these characteristics with an even greater consistency.[23] There are some minor details in Greenspoon's analysis that have been contested,[24] but overall it is an important study to take into account when analyzing the readings in the Greek manuscript material. It also reveals that the B-text in the book of Joshua does not contain as strong *Kaige* tendencies as is the case with Judges and parts of Samuel-Kings.

To the Hexplaric group, Margolis included manuscripts G 19 108 376 426 and the Syrohexapla. This recension is characterized by corrections towards the Hebrew text attributed to the hand of Origen.[25] The designation of these manuscripts as the Hexaplaric group for the book of Joshua can be characterized as "scholarly consensus" even today.[26] Margolis divided the group into two subcategories. Subcategory **P₁** included the first four manuscripts, and subcategory **P₂** included 426 and the Syrohexapla. He claimed that the latter subcategory reflected the Tetrapla. Sipilä, however, has shown that Margolis' hypothesis differentiating between the Hexaplaric and Tetraplaric material is unnecessary.[27] He concludes: "I cannot show that the Tetrapla never existed in the traditional sense of the word, and I do not think that anyone can. But it seems to me quite

---

[20] Greenspoon 1983, 7–218.
[21] Greenspoon 1983, 219–267.
[22] Greenspoon 1983, 275–276. There is, for example, no recension or tradition that would consistently use καιγε to translate the Hebrew גם. As Greenspoon notes, this is, of course, no reason to abandon the existence of the *Kaige* revision in Joshua altogether. No one characteristic can be named as the most important feature of the revision. In addition, גם does not occur in Joshua as often as it does in many other books of the same length.
[23] Greenspoon 1983, 269–377.
[24] Auld 1986, 135–136.
[25] Den Hertog 1996, 10–12.
[26] Sipilä 2014, 261: "That we can now speak about the consensus is seen by the fact that the late Udo Quast also followed the similar understanding about the Hexaplaric text in his work on the Göttingen edition of the book".
[27] Sipilä 1998a, 16–38.

clear that the Tetrapla is not needed when explaining various readings in the manuscripts of Joshua".[28]

One of the disputed issues in the study of LXX Joshua is the existence of a Lucianic or Antiochene recension for this book. Manuscripts 44 54 75 106 134 314 are usually seen as belonging to a Lucianic group of manuscripts in the book of Joshua.[29] According to Margolis, these manuscripts belonged to the Syrian group. The Old Latin version as preserved in the *Codex Lugdunensis* (La^{100}) can also be included in this group.[30] The major characteristic of this recension is not first and foremost correcting the text towards the proto-MT Hebrew text, but the aim of making the Greek style better. The typical secondary elements in the Joshua MSS correspond to those in other books. There is a tendency to stylistically improve the Greek language; in many cases, the language is corrected towards the standard Attic Greek dialect.[31] In addition, among the secondary elements one encounters substitutions of unfamiliar words with more familiar ones, omissions of repetitive pronouns and unnecessary prepositions, harmonization, conflations, and clarifications of the text with minor additions.[32] The Lucianic MSS, however, have also adopted several secondary Hebraizing readings, probably from the Hexaplaric text.

On the other hand, the existence of a Lucianic recension for Joshua has been questioned altogether. The criticism against identifying a distinctly Lucianic text for the book of Joshua – and the whole Octateuch, for that matter – is voiced by Natalio Fernándes Marcos. According to him, no groups of manuscripts of the Octateuch bear distinctive features of this recension, and no external evidence, that is quotations from the Antiochene fathers, support a Lucianic recensions for these books.[33] Sipilä explores in two articles the Joshua quotations from the Antiochene fathers John Chrysostom and Theodoret of Cyrrhus. The analysis seems to strengthen at least the latter part the argument by Fernándes Marcos.

---

28 Sipilä 1998a, 38.
29 This was already observed by Hautsch 1910. The Lucianic MSS are different in the Octateuch than in Samuel-Kings.
30 Margolis 1927, 312–313; Sipilä 1997, 331. The *Codex Lugdunensis*, dating from the second half of the 6th century, is the only Old Latin manuscript that contains the book of Joshua. For basic information of the manuscript see Gryson 1999, 159–160. In addition to witnessing to Lucianic readings, this manuscript often goes its own way and contains several radical differences. See, for example, Schenker 2008, 417–425 and Sipilä 2014, 257–272. In the future, there should be a study focusing on the readings found in this manuscript and their importance for the textual criticism of the LXX and the history of the Hebrew text.
31 Margolis 1927, 313. However, the issue is not always that clear. See Sigismund 2016, 30–35.
32 Van der Meer 2004, 27.
33 Fernández Marcos 1994, 12.

According to Sipilä, there are no traces of typical Lucianic improvements in these quotations, and Chrysostom's citations should not be used as a source when studying the Lucianic text in Joshua.³⁴ Elsewhere, Sipilä has concluded that "the L text in Joshua is not preserved, if it ever existed in the proper sense of the word."³⁵ However, recently Sigismund has challenged the evaluation of the external evidence and concluded through a qualitative and quantitative analysis that the text used by Theodoret of Cyrrhus was Antiochian more than anything else.³⁶ Resolving the issue of a Lucianic Joshua-text is beyond the scope of this research. This debate should, however, be considered when dealing with the manuscripts in this group.

Whether or not there was a distinct Lucianic recension, these manuscripts exhibit many unique readings. Most of them seem to be secondary qualities. At times, however, one cannot escape the idea that the Lucianic manuscripts might have preserved Old Greek features in its unique readings. In such cases, it seems that the B-text may have been influenced by early Hebraizing secondary revision.³⁷ In the textual history of LXX Joshua, this is a relatively unexamined possibility.³⁸ Many such readings will be dealt with in the textual notes of Joshua 24, and in two instances I will follow the readings in the Lucianic manuscripts and Old Latin instead of the B-text.³⁹

The oldest extant Greek Joshua manuscript 816 should also be mentioned here, since it is an important text reflecting mostly Old Greek readings. The text was edited and analyzed by De Troyer. From the study of this manuscript, an important reservation arises: namely, one should be careful when attributing revisional elements to recensions. Even though the text is independent of the Hexaplaric and *Kaige* revisions, it revises in several parts the Greek text towards a Hebrew text.⁴⁰ When analyzing the Greek sources, one should therefore be alert

---

34 Sipilä 1997, 353–354.
35 Sipilä 2014, 267. See also Sipilä 1998b, 167–168.
36 Sigismund 2016, 13–36.
37 De Troyer 2005b, 148 notes: "…although I strongly believe that even Codex Vaticanus already contains prehexaplaric corrections toward the MT."
38 In the case of the book of Joshua, this possibility has been recently explored by Sigismund 2012, 626–634 and 2016, 13–36. In the study of the textual history of the four books of Reigns, the situation is different. In the so-called *Kaige* sections and sometimes even in the non-*Kaige* sections (Aejmelaeus 2017a, 169–184), the B-text is affected by early Jewish Hebraizing revision (*Kaige* or "*Kaige*-type") and the Old Greek text is found in the Antiochene manuscripts. This line of research carries on the legacy of Dominique Barthélemy. See, for example, Kreuzer 2009 and Law & Kauhanen 2010.
39 See section 3.2.
40 De Troyer 2005a, 89–145.

against too easily attributing revisions to for example Origen. De Troyer herself, in her edition, uses the term "(pre-Hexaplaric) revision" for certain elements.[41] Manuscript 816 and its contribution for the study of LXX Joshua will be dealt in more detail below, in section 2.3.3.

Lastly, it should be highlighted that I share the methodological conviction voiced by, for example, Timothy M. Law and Tuukka Kauhanen in their article on the textual history of the Septuagint versions of the book of Reigns. Namely, readings found in the different LXX manuscripts should always be assessed on a case by case basis. Even though the *E*-group of Margolis is usually held to be the best representative of OG in Joshua, I think the assertion of Law and Kauhanen should be extended to Joshua: "No single manuscript or manuscript group contains the OG 'in general'. That is a fact." Before arriving at text-critical conclusions, the possibility that each manuscript could preserve the oldest reading of the LXX should be explored.[42] In this study, the most important conclusions of this critical work will be presented in the text-critical notes in conjunction with the Greek text in section 3.

Modern Editions

In practice, scholars have three modern critical editions to operate with: the diplomatic Cambridge edition by Brooke-McLean, the semi-critical edition by Rahlfs-Hanhart, and the critical edition by Margolis. Brooke-McLean presents the text of B with minor corrections in obvious misspellings. The apparatus of Brooke-McLean, recording most of the important variants, is of immense help. Rahlfs, on the other hand, offers an eclectic edition based mainly on A and B, occasionally considering other witnesses.[43] In three chapters involving obscure place names (15, 18 and 19), it simply presents the texts of A and B in parallel columns. Margolis, in turn, offers a critical reconstruction of OG based on all manuscripts available to him. The apparatus of Margolis' edition is also helpful (albeit confusing as it uses unprecedented markings) since it also includes his observations on the technique of the translator.[44]

The main texts of Brooke-McLean and Rahlfs are very similar, and only rarely differ.[45] The differences between Rahlfs and Margolis, in turn, have been

---

41 De Troyer 2005a, 130.
42 Law & Kauhanen 2010, 78.
43 The Book of Joshua is absent in S.
44 For example, Tov (1999b, 21–30) and Sipilä (1993, 17–21) have written on the usage of Margolis and his peculiar apparatus.
45 Sipilä 1999, 18.

systematically compared in a study by Den Hertog. They differ in circa 270 passages, and in most of these cases, according to Den Hertog, preference should be given to Rahlfs.[46] Otherwise, these versions agree with each other to a high degree.[47]

Finally, it should be highlighted that the main text of Margolis cannot be taken as it is as a starting point for textual criticism. This is mostly because some of its choices are guided by the assumption that the translator worked with a text like the MT.[48] This is to the extent that he could sometimes reconstruct Greek readings based on the MT not preserved anywhere in the Greek manuscript material.[49] The edition is, however, an important attempt to describe the original Greek text of Joshua, and the work of Margolis should not be dismissed in research. The classification of the Greek sources, already mentioned earlier, is regularly utilized in the study of LXX Joshua.[50]

In this study, the edition of Rahlfs will be the starting point for the analysis, however the variant readings in other modern editions and ancient manuscripts will be carefully evaluated and considered. I will deviate from Rahlfs in some minor cases. Finally, it should be highlighted that there are no significant disagreements between the best LXX manuscripts on major text-critical differences, namely larger plusses, minuses, transpositions, and rewritings between the OG and the MT of Josh 24.[51] Therefore, the large-scale variants attesting to text-historical developments in the Hebrew text of Josh 24 are not dependent on text-critical details in the LXX manuscript material.

2.3.2 Aspects of the Translation Technique

In Thackeray's classic grouping, the OG translation of Joshua was placed in the category characterized as "good κοινή Greek".[52] Joshua was situated in the same

---

[46] Den Hertog 1996, 30–109.
[47] Den Hertog 1996, 109.
[48] On this, Margolis was already criticized by Orlinsky (1968, 187–195). See also the criticism by Van der Meer (2004, 25–30).
[49] See, for example, the textual notes on Josh 24:5 in section 3.2.1.
[50] Sipilä (1998a, 24–25) has noted, accordingly: "I think that his text is in many respects the best attempt to describe the 'original' wording of the Septuagint. I do not accept his conclusions in every detail, but in general his text seems to be more reliable than the text of Rahlfs's Septuaginta".
[51] For example, the longer ending of Josh 24 is illustrative of this. See section 3.4.2.
[52] I am fully aware of the problematic nature of the concept "translation technique". It is a modern term which might suggest that the translator was always systematic in his approach to the translation process. Since the term has become so central in LXX studies I will use it, however,

2.3 The Septuagint of Joshua — 25

group with the Pentateuch, and was seen as forming "a kind of link between the Pentateuch and the later historical books".[53] This means that Thackeray did not consider Joshua to be the most literal translation (like Jeremiah or Ezekiel) in the LXX, but neither did he consider it to be a free or paraphrasing translation (like Job or Proverbs). While Thackeray's study forms the basis for later scholarship, his conclusions were based on an overall view of the different translations, and not on a thorough linguistic analysis.

Many details of the translation of OG Joshua have been further examined by the Finnish scholars of the Septuagint. Their line of study was started in Soisalon-Soininen's influential study on the infinitive translations in the LXX, which placed Joshua among the most freely translated books.[54] Sollamo later, in her study on the Hebrew semiprepositions in the LXX, refined this view and concluded that Joshua does not belong among the freest translations, but in the second most free category, together with Genesis, Leviticus, Numbers, and Deuteronomy. To be more precise, the translator uses free translation equivalents in one third of the semiprepositions, but should in about 44% of all semiprepositions be characterized as literal, even slavish.[55] The translator's freedom can be seen in that there is no strong tendency to always translate the same semiprepositions with the same equivalents. For example, וְעָבְרוּ לִפְנֵי הָעָם ... וַיֵּלְכוּ לִפְנֵי הָעָם in Josh 3:6 is translated with the Greek equivalent καὶ προπορεύεσθε τοῦ λαοῦ ... καὶ ἐπορεύοντο ἔμπροσθεν τοῦ λαοῦ in which προπορεύομαι is a good example of the degree of freedom the translator could take. While the translation here does not slavishly follow the Hebrew structure, it does not change the meaning of the source text.

The most comprehensive work on the translation technique of Joshua by a Finnish scholar has been carried out by Seppo Sipilä. In his study, he employed the theoretical framework set forth by Anneli Aejmelaeus, who has illustrated that the translation of Hebrew clause connectors including the most common conjunctions ו and כי are useful in determining the translation technique of different books.[56] The careful analysis by Sipilä reveals that out of the 807

---

understanding it vaguely as translation "style" or "practice". More room should be given, for example, for the possibility of ad hoc translation decisions. For more about the terminology, see Aejmelaeus 2001.

[53] Thackeray 1909, 13–14. For some reason, Thackeray added "part" in parenthesis. He does not elaborate on this at all.

[54] Soisalon-Soininen made this classification based on the translation of the ב-preposition + infinitive construct -structure. Soisalon-Soininen 1965, 176–190.

[55] Sollamo 1979, 280–286.

[56] Aejmelaeus 1982 and 2007, 43–57.

occurrences of the ו-conjunction, 716 (88.7%) have been translated with the Greek equivalent καί.[57] In this respect, the translation of Joshua can be characterized as fairly literal, since genuine Greek far more often uses, for example, δέ as a connector.[58] In the case of כי, the translator shows a greater degree of freedom, as he often employs the conjunction γάρ, which is more idiomatic than the more literal equivalent ὅτι.[59] The overall picture emerging from Sipilä's study, when focusing on the translation of these most common Hebrew conjunctions, is that compared to the literal translation of Judges the Greek translation of Joshua can be situated "between literalness and freedom". This is generally in line with the previous observations by Sollamo.

While the Finnish scholars of LXX Joshua have concentrated mostly on the translation of key Hebrew syntactical features, Den Hertog has written a monograph on other important aspects, namely the origins of the translation and the lexical choices made by the translator. In *Studien zur griechischen Übersetzung des Buches Josua*, Den Hertog gives evidence for the traditional assumption that LXX Joshua was translated right after the Pentateuch, and is dependent on that translation.[60] He also finds features in the translation that point at an Egyptian – not Palestinian – place of origin.[61]

The most important contribution of Den Hertog's study is the analysis of some lexical aspects of the translation. Through several examples, Den Hertog shows that the translator of Joshua did not merely mimic the Hebrew of the source text, but gave intentionally varied renderings of the Hebrew words. Take for example מזבח, in Josh 22, which is first rendered as βωμός when the legitimacy of the altar built by the Eastern tribes is questioned (22:10, 11, 16, 19, 23, 26), and later translated with θυσιαστήριον when the legitimacy of the altar as a memorial to the works of YHWH has been established (22:28, 29).[62] While the interpretive variation introduced here by the translator is possible, I do not agree

---

[57] Sipilä 1999, 74–82.
[58] Den Hertog (2011, 609) agrees, and introduces this phenomenon as an example of how the translator usually follows the Hebrew word order and aims at giving an equivalent for every element in his source text.
[59] Sipilä 1999, 140–192; 198–199.
[60] Den Hertog (1996, 110–144) arrives at a third century dating, which means that LXX Joshua was dependent on LXX Pentateuch but preceded LXX Judges.
[61] According to Den Hertog (1996, 142–144), the deficiency in the translator's knowledge of Palestine geography is apparent in e.g. the confused designation παραλίους Χαναναίους ἀπὸ ἀνατολῶν (Josh 11:3), the unknown area of Μαδβαρῖτιδις (Josh 5:6, 18:12), and the rare use of Hellenized Greek toponyms. In addition, the choice to designate Hebron as μητρόπολις (Josh 14:15, 15:13, 21:11, cf. 10:2) reveals that the translator had the Egyptian administrative system in mind.
[62] Den Hertog 1996, 180–183.

that the translator worked as a "theologian",⁶³ since the differentiation of a legitimate and non-legitimate altar is not systematic. A case in point is the last reference to the altar in verse 22:34, where the legitimacy of the altar as a witness is established but it is still translated with βωμός. The phenomenon of variation in the name of the altar is also known from the Pentateuch, and the translator could have taken his cue from there.⁶⁴ In addition, it has also been proposed that the variation might have already been present in the Hebrew *Vorlage* of the translator.⁶⁵

Harry Orlinsky has analyzed how the translator dealt with anthropomorphism and anthropopathisms – that is expressions where God is ascribed human traits or emotions. His conclusion is that the few anthropomorphisms in the book of Joshua are generally avoided by using more innocuous equivalents. For example, the word פֶּה "mouth" in the expression עַל־פִּי יְהוָה "according to the word (mouth) of YHWH" is regularly translated διὰ προστάγματος κυρίου "by the command of the Lord". Anthropomorphisms are, however, never left out or distorted. In the case of anthropopathisms (e.g. "to destroy Israel", "to deliver Israel to the hands of", "to wage war for Israel", "to rebel against the lord"), the translator renders the Hebrew faithfully. According to Orlinsky, these conclusions, together with studies by scholars before him, "cannot but indicate that the fidelity of the translator to his Hebrew text can be questioned only on the basis of other cogent arguments to the contrary ... such argument is in fact lacking."⁶⁶

One final observation should be made on how the translator made his translation. Both Soisalon-Soininen and Den Hertog agree that the translator probably worked by first dividing the text into very short segments (sometimes even single clauses), which he then translated separately.⁶⁷ This phenomenon of segmentation explains some of the variation in, for example, rendering similar Hebrew structures in varying ways. As for Joshua, Den Hertog points out the sparse use of Greek subordinate or conditional clauses introduced with ἐπεί, ἡνίκα, ὅταν, and ὡς which could be explained through segmentation.⁶⁸ Segmentation, thus, might account for some cases of variation in the translation of similar Hebrew structures that would otherwise be harder to explain.

---

63 As concluded by Van der Meer (2004, 83), working on Den Hertog's observations.
64 Den Hertog 2011, 607–608.
65 Auld (1986, 136) has proposed that the differentiation could go back to a variation between במה and מזבח in Hebrew. The MT could be the result of a revision that favored the western altar tradition and changed the altar to מזבח throughout the chapter.
66 Orlinsky 1969, 193–194.
67 Here Den Hertog (1996, 179–180) is dependent on the work of Soisalon-Soininen 1987.
68 Den Hertog 1996, 179.

From this brief evaluation of the research on the translation technique of OG Joshua, it seems apparent that the translator should generally not be credited for introducing radical changes such as large omissions, expansions, or rewritings in relation to the source text.[69] The translator was generally not in the business of changing the meaning of the Hebrew source text.[70] This overall view is nicely crystallized in a quote from the conclusions of Greenspoon's study on the recensional features in LXX Joshua:

> The OG translator rendered, to the best of his considerable abilities, the Hebrew text that lay before him. His knowledge of Hebrew and his fidelity to that Hebrew are to be rated far higher than the derogatory comments of some previous scholars would allow.[71]

Samuel Holmes has appropriately concluded that if the translator is a reviser, the overall conception of him would be peculiar. In Josh 19, the translator would seem to be a skillful redactor, while in Josh 6 he would be missing any redactor skills. In Josh 5 and 18, on the other hand, he would have smoothened out many subtle contradictions to create a coherent entity, while in Josh 6 and 7 many apparent contradictions would have gone unnoticed.[72]

The translator did, however, enjoy some degree of freedom. This is visible mostly in the flexibility of using different translation equivalents for recurring Hebrew expressions and structures.[73] In other words, while being faithful to the Hebrew text, the translator also aimed at producing good Koine Greek. Therefore,

---

69 Thus also Tov 2015b, 133: "The translation is somewhat free, but not free enough to ascribe shortening, expansion, and large-scale changes to the translator. Studies of various areas of the translation technique establish the translator's faithful representation of grammatical categories."

70 In a 2002 article, Rösel voiced an opposing view. He argues that the translator could have introduced some long plusses to the text (Josh 6:26; 16:10; 21:42; 24:31; 24:33) to bring Joshua into closer conformity with the later historical books. This would have been necessary since the other former prophets were not yet translated. The suggestion is improbable, since such a redactor-translator would have probably been more systematic. As Van der Meer (2004, 90) pointed out, he would have somehow hinted towards such key figures as David and Solomon, as the redactor of 4Q522 has done. Moreover, this is not a phenomenon that is otherwise known in the study of the LXX translations.

71 Greenspoon 1983, 379.

72 Holmes 1914, 2.

73 Moatti-Fine (1996, 42–66) has also noted the translator's tendency to ascribe different translation equivalents for the same Hebrew words. One descriptive example of this is the translation of the verb עבר which has 16 different equivalents in the Greek translation: ἀπέρχομαι (10:29, 31, 34), διαβαίνω (1:2, 11, 14; 3:1, 11, 14, 17; 4:1, 7, 10–13, 22–23; 5:1; 24:11), διεκβάλλω (15:7), διέρχομαι (3:2; 18:13, 18), εἰσέρχομαι (1:11), ἐκπεριπορεύομαι (15:3), ἐκπορεύομαι (15:3), ἵστημι (3:16; 18:5), παραβαίνω (7:11, 15; 23:16), παραπορεύομαι (6:7, 15:6), παρέρχομαι (15:10, 11; 16: 2, 6; 24:17),

the possibility that the translator might have introduced changes in relation to the source text needs to be considered when evaluating single textual variants. There needs to be, however, exceptionally good arguments when ascribing radical changes to the process of translation. Based on past research, one can justifiably hold to the assumption that the translator was rather faithful to his source text.

2.3.3 The Relationship of MT and OG Joshua

Scholarly views on the relationship of the OG and the MT versions of Joshua can be divided into three categories.[74] These three views differ especially in the way they understand the nature of the OG Joshua translation.[75] First, the view highlighting the priority of the MT assumes that MT Joshua generally represents the more original version of Joshua. According to this traditional view, changes present in OG Joshua are mainly due to editorial activity by the translator or an editor of the Hebrew *Vorlage* behind the translator. Second, the intermediate view claims that the priority of MT or OG Joshua cannot be generalized to the whole text. In some cases, the MT presents the earlier readings and in some the OG. Quite often this cannot even be decided. The intermediate view usually highlights the nature of the OG translator as altering between a literal and a free translation technique. Third, the view arguing for the priority of the OG holds that OG Joshua mostly reflects a different and an earlier Hebrew text of Joshua. MT Joshua represents a version in which either this *Vorlage,* or a common Hebrew version from which this *Vorlage* and proto-MT once split, has been edited. This view highlights the relative literalness of the OG translation and holds that the translator would not have introduced any major changes to his source text.

I will now proceed to evaluating some aspects of these major views as they have been articulated by different scholars. I do not plan to give a comprehensive review of the research history. The aim is, rather, to find and evaluate the most common arguments used in the discussion so that they would benefit my own textual analysis.

περιέρχομαι (6:7, 19:13), πορεύω (3:4; 15:4), προσάγω (4:5), προπορεύω (3:6), χωροβατέω (18:9). For more cases, see Den Hertog 2011, 609.

74 The categorizing used here is my own. It should be noted that while categorizing scholarly views helps in outlining and evaluating the field in question, the different scholarly voices inside one category do not always fully coincide. There are more nuances to each and every view.

75 The different proponents of these views will be introduced further below.

Early Research

One of the earliest studies to address OG Joshua and its relationship to MT Joshua was Johannes Hollenberg's *Der Charakter der alexandrinische Übersetzung des Buches Josua und ihr textkritischer Werth*.[76] The focus of Hollenberg's study is on the translation technique of the Greek translation, through which it also addresses the differences between the OG and the MT. This brief study is an early proponent of the intermediate view, and has had a major impact on the study of the Greek Joshua, even in the 21st century, as is evident from the positive appraisal by Van der Meer in his recent study.[77]

Hollenberg's research leans a bit more towards the traditional view, in the sense that it considers the OG Joshua as often representing a vulgar text that is in many cases inferior to the MT.[78] According to Hollenberg, the differences present in OG Joshua in relation to MT Joshua are due to three factors: (1) a translation technique that aims at an eloquent and non-repetitive Greek style, (2) the limitations in the translators ability to understand the Hebrew source text, and (3) some late additions to the Greek text.[79]

In some instances, Hollenberg concludes that the translator occasionally had in front of him a *Vorlage* differing from the MT. These cases are explained either as scribal errors behind the MT, or as late intentional additions behind the Hebrew *Vorlage* of the OG. An example of the former is the significant OG plus in Joshua 13:7, which elaborates on the land about to be divided.[80] According to Hollenberg, this was dropped out of the MT due to a *homoioteleuton* caused by the second occurrence of וַחֲצִי הַשֵּׁבֶט הַמְנַשֶּׁה in the *Vorlage* of OG Joshua 13:8.[81] The latter

---

[76] Hollenberg 1876.
[77] Van der Meer 2004, 32–37.
[78] Hollenberg 1876, 20.
[79] Hollenberg deals with a multitude of cases in his short study of 20 pages. The first factor is seen, according to Hollenberg, in instances where the translator deals differently with the same Hebrew expression. For instance, in Josh 10:10 the expression וַיַּכֵּם מַכָּה־גְדוֹלָה "and (YHWH) he slew them with a great slaughter" is translated καὶ συνέτριψεν αὐτοὺς κύριος σύντριψιν μεγάλην "and the Lord shattered them with a great destruction". However, in Josh 10:20 the same Hebrew verb (albeit in the infinitive construct form) is translated with another verb κόπτοντες αὐτοὺς κοπὴν μεγάλην "smiting them with a great slaughter" (Hollenberg 1876, 5). He also points out several contextual translation equivalents. For instance, in Josh 24:9 וַיִּלָּחֶם "he fought" is translated with the more nuanced καὶ παρετάξατο "he arrayed for battle". According to Hollenberg, an example of the second factor is the expression עַד־הַשְּׁבָרִים "as far as Shebarim" (Josh 7:5) which is missing from the LXX because the translator did not understand its meaning. Unfortunately, Hollenberg's study is so brief that he did not discuss alternative explanations for these examples.
[80] "From the Jordan as far as the great sea toward the setting of the sun you shall give it; the great sea shall be the boundary. But to the two tribes and to the half–tribe of Manasse..." (NETS)
[81] Hollenberg 1876, 13–14.

2.3 The Septuagint of Joshua — 31

phenomenon, in turn, is the best explanation for plusses in the OG such as 6:26a and 21:42a–d.[82] This, in my view, is the most problematic dimension of Hollenberg's study. To simply name plusses in OG as late additions to the Hebrew *Vorlage*, and not consider the possibility that they could be omissions of more original material in the proto-MT, is one-sided. To be sure, Hollenberg's study is too short to be able to consider all the possible explanations. Hence, while it is easy to agree that this is a "pioneer study", I must disagree with it being "well balanced and exhaustive", as Van der Meer puts it.[83] The study is simply too concise to adequately consider all the possible explanations for the divergences between OG and MT Joshua.

While Hollenberg occasionally affirmed the priority of the OG text, a more negative view on the text-critical value of OG Joshua was voiced by August Dillmann in *Die Bücher Numeri, Deuteronomium und Josua* published in 1886.[84] The results of his verse-by-verse analysis is typical of the traditional view. Whenever he considers the variant readings in the OG, he regularly contends that those readings are secondary, as they reflect the translator's tendency to abridge his source text and create intentional changes and additions based on other biblical books. In many cases Dillmann does not consider other possibilities, as for example when analyzing the longer ending of OG Josh 24. There he simply states that this is added material that is partly apocryphal and partly taken from the book of Judges.[85] Moreover, Dillmann argues that whenever there are disputable cases concerning the priority of the MT or the OG, it can be reasoned from the several obvious cases of the priority of the MT that the OG is also secondary in the uncertain instances.[86] This kind of logic depends on an argument from a supposed tendency which is problematic in itself, but also especially since the "certain" cases of shortening in the OG are not that certain.[87]

---

82 Hollenberg 1876, 17–18.
83 Van der Meer 2004, 36.
84 Dillmann 1886, 437–590.
85 Dillmann 1886, 590. The longer ending in OG Josh 24 is further discussed in section 3.4.2.
86 "Im allgemeinen ist der LXX-Text der kürzere; dass darum auch der ursprünglichere, versteht sich nicht von selbst. Bedenkt man, dass in 2:15b, 6 … diese Kürze entschieden fehlerhaft ist, so wird man auch in andern Stellen, wo man zweifeln könnte (wie 2:15 …), fast eher das System des absichtlichen Kürzens vermuten müssen." Dillmann 1886, 690.
87 On this, see the criticism against Dillmann's analyses by Holmes 1914, 10–16. In Josh 2:15, for example, MT has a plus, nowhere to be found in the OG, that localizes the position of Rahab's house as being connected to the city wall (כִּי בֵיתָהּ בְּקִיר הַחוֹמָה וּבַחוֹמָה הִיא יוֹשָׁבֶת). Dillmann lists this as one of the cases where an omission in the OG is certain (Dillmann 1886, 448, 690). There are, however, good reasons to suspect that this might be a late addition in the proto-MT tradition that was missing from the earlier Hebrew text attested by the OG. Holmes (1914, 10–11) points out that

Lastly, even in the early scholarship there have been proponents of the view arguing for the priority of the OG. Samuel Holmes was one of the earliest scholars to propose the priority of OG Joshua. He formulated his hypothesis, and gave an extensive critique of Dillmann's analysis, in *Joshua: The Hebrew and Greek Texts*, published in 1914. In addition to a thorough (but admittedly concise) analysis of all the variants between OG and MT Joshua,[88] Holmes gives several reasons to assume that the text represented in OG Joshua is generally earlier than that of MT Joshua. First, he notes that there are several minuses in the OG of the same word or expression. This makes it improbable that these are accidental omissions and points towards a pattern. Second, in the majority of the cases where the two texts differ from one another, they are consistent with themselves. This points to a systematic revision which cannot be ascribed to a translator, but must be the work of a Hebrew reviser. Third, the shorter text in OG Josh 5:4ff. can be easily retroverted into Hebrew, and is demonstrably earlier that the equivalent longer text in the MT. This passage is especially important, since it is where the OG translator is often assumed to be highly creative by those arguing for the priority of the MT. Fourth, Holmes demonstrates that the cases of alleged deliberate shortening in the OG are based on disputable arguments. Finally, if the Greek translator is claimed to be a reviser, his work would be highly inconsistent, since in some passages he would have eliminated subtle discrepancies while many obvious contradictions would have gone uncorrected.[89] Throughout his study, Holmes gives numerous textual examples supporting these arguments.

Holmes' study is impressive, and many of his conclusions are still supported in modern research. The importance of his work is well-reflected in the words of Orlinsky referring to the thorough inspection of each plus and minus in the OG: "Nothing like it had been done on Joshua previously, and certainly nothing since."[90] This evaluation is correct even today, since no thorough word-for-word analyses have been published evaluating all the differences between the Hebrew and Greek texts of Joshua.

One of the problems with the study of Holmes is, however, that he does not consider the possibility that the *Vorlage* of OG Joshua might have gone through editing, and thus also include secondary elements. Take for example Holmes' view that the radical differences between OG and MT Joshua in chapter 20 are

---

there are no reasons why the translator would omit this. Moreover, the clause can be understood as an "explanatory insertion" which is added by using the connecting כִּי-preposition.
88 Holmes 1914, 17–80.
89 Holmes 1914, 1–16.
90 Orlinsky 1968, 190.

fully explained by assuming that the text of the OG is the more original text.[91] Already the small amount of space (10 lines, in other words, one third of a page) devoted to such a complex text should alert the reader that these variants might not be as easily explained. In fact, recent scholarship has shown that while OG Josh 20 contains early elements, it also probably reflects secondary developments in its Hebrew *Vorlage*. Thus, at some points the MT version of Josh 20 is the earlier text.[92]

There are also other important studies, in early research, addressing extensively or in passing the relationship of OG and MT Joshua. It is not expedient to introduce them all here. Some of them will, however, be considered during this study.[93] Next, I will turn to later research that builds on earlier studies but also has the benefit of considering the evidence from Qumran.

Before and After Qumran

Before the findings from Qumran, in the first part of the 20th century, there were several scholars who defended the priority of the MT and regarded the OG as secondary.[94] The popularity of this view was, at least in part, due to the solutions made by Margolis in his critical reconstruction of OG Joshua.[95] At the bottom of every page in his edition, Margolis added notes in which he compared the reconstructed OG text to the MT. There he notes repeatedly that the Greek text omits references found in the MT ("G om").[96] The tendency to favor the priority of MT Joshua was apparent already in the article announcing the publication of a critical edition in 1927. There he notes e.g.: "He (the translator) was apparently given to curtailments –".[97] This view was adopted by Martin Noth, who was responsible for the text of Joshua in Kittel's *Biblia Hebraica*. This is apparent

---

91 Holmes 1914, 71. In OG Joshua, chapter 20, which elaborates on how the cities of refuge should be arranged in the new land, is missing verses 4–6 altogether. There are also other plusses and minuses in relation to the equivalent chapter in MT Joshua.
92 See the recent analysis in Müller, Pakkala & Haar Romeny 2014, 45–58.
93 Some of the most important ones are Bennett 1895; Wellhausen 1899, 352–353; Steuernagel 1900, 131–248; Ehrlich 1910, 1–66.
94 As shown by Orlinsky 1968, 190–192; Auld 1975, 96–97; Auld 1998, 7–8; Noort 1998, 48. An exception is the commentary by Cooke (1918, ix) which embraces the view of Holmes: "The LXX of Joshua ... often presupposes a more correct type of Hebrew Text than the MT ... Apparently the Hebr. Text of Joshua was once current in two forms; the one which lay before the Greek translator and perhaps was generally accepted in Egypt; the other which is represented by the MT, and perhaps was best known in Palestine".
95 Margolis 1931–1938, 1992.
96 Thus also Orlinsky 1968, 191.
97 Margolis 1927, 318.

from his commentary, in which he states that in several occasions the Greek has shortened and simplified the original Hebrew text.[98] Thus, in the first part of the 20th century, several scholars followed the traditional view.

However, along with Holmes, some early 20th Century commentaries defended the priority of the OG in some variants.[99] After Qumran, this view was significantly amplified, as illustrated by Harry M. Orlinsky's paper at the Rome Congress of the International Organization for the Study of the Old Testament in 1968. Orlinsky's paper, published in print in 1969, was a brief but powerful formulation of the view highlighting the priority of the OG.[100] Orlinsky argued for the priority of OG Joshua against MT Joshua in most of the cases where these two texts diverge. In addition to his own textual observations, Orlinsky's argument is based on the earlier work by Holmes and the publication of the Qumran scrolls of Jeremiah and Samuel, which corroborate some of the readings in the OG versions of those books. At the time of Orlinsky's paper, the evidence from Qumran pertaining to Joshua was, however, still not fully available, and he thus concludes: "Whether such a text will show up among the Dead Sea Scrolls, I do not know."[101]

Before turning to the evidence from Qumran, the dissertation by A. Graeme Auld should also be noted as an important proponent of the priority of the OG. In this 1976 dissertation, *Studies in Joshua: Text and Literary Relations*, Auld took a crucial step in bringing the text-critical data from Joshua into the literary-critical discussion. Building partly on arguments from Holmes and Orlinsky and partly on his own analyses,[102] Auld concludes that literary-critical observations on the "editorial processes affecting the text of Joshua" should not be made based on the MT alone, since OG Joshua more frequently contains the earlier form of the text. This necessary interplay of methods is illustrated for example in Auld's analysis of the land division material in chapters 13–19.[103] In several later articles, Auld has further defended and illustrated the priority of OG Joshua and the need for taking this text into account when doing literary and redaction criticism.[104]

Later, the evidence from Qumran has also been integrated into the text-critical discussion of Joshua. The evidence is scarce and debated. From Qumran

---

98 Noth 1938. See also the brief comments concerning Noth's treatment of the LXX by Orlinsky 1968, 191–192.
99 For example, in his analysis of Josh 5:4–7 and Josh 24, Steuernagel (1900, 167–168, 241–247) favors in many instances the shorter text of the LXX as the earlier version. See also Cooke 1918, ix.
100 Orlinsky 1968, 187–195.
101 Orlinsky 1968, 195.
102 Auld 1975, 95–150.
103 Auld 1975, 169–234.
104 A collection of these articles has been published in Auld 1998.

Cave 4, two scrolls have been found that represent the text of the biblical book of Joshua. These have been named 4QJosh[a] and 4QJosh[b] and they include parts of chapters 1–5, 7–8, 10, and 17.[105] These scrolls mostly reflect proto-MT readings, but also those found in the OG and those not found anywhere else. Tov has demonstrated that 4QJosh[a] supports the OG text in the minus of Josh 8:11b–13. In fragment 15, line 10 has parts of verse 10b. The text continues with verse 11 on line 11, but jumps to verse 14 on the next line 12 (in fragment 16). The longer version present in the MT could not fit in the lacuna, thus the fragments support the shorter version in the OG. In addition, the ends of lines 10–13 agree twice with the OG against the MT in their vocabulary.[106] Moreover, it has been argued that 4QJosh[a] agrees with the OG minus present in 10:14b–17.[107]

In addition to relying on the evidence from Qumran, Tov has put forth several arguments supporting the assumption that the OG reflects a different and often an earlier Hebrew text. First, Tov argues that while the translator of OG Joshua is in some respects free, his faithfulness to the Hebrew *Vorlage* is so high that he would not introduce significant changes to his source text.[108] Second, there are so many Hebraisms in the long pluses of OG Joshua that these could not be elements introduced by the translator.[109] Third, in addition to the Qumran scrolls of Joshua, there is additional external evidence supporting the shorter readings in OG Joshua. The Samaritan Joshua traditions support the absence of 8:11b–13 in OG Joshua,[110] and the longer ending in OG Joshua 24:33a–b seems to be known to the author of the Damascus Document.[111] Fourth, Tov has given in several publications analyses of textual elements that in majority of the cases support the priority of OG Joshua over MT Joshua.[112] Accordingly, Tov argues that there is textual evidence for two different literary

---

105 For further details see section 2.4.
106 Tov 2015b, 134–135.
107 See Tov 2015b, 134–135. A skeptical treatment concerning the suggested support of 4QJosh[a] to the OG text was given by Van der Meer 2004, 93–114.
108 Tov 2015b, 133. According to Tov (1999a, 153–163; 2012, 85), however, there are some instances of "Midrash-type exegesis" in the OG translation of Joshua. Some of these elements are already present in the Hebrew *Vorlage* of the translator, but some are introduced by the translator. For example, in Josh 5:2, the translator adds an element (OG: μαχαίρας πετρίνας ἐκ πέτρας ἀκροτόμου, MT: צֻרִים חַרְבוֹת) explaining that the flint knives with which Joshua circumcised the people were made of sharp stone. This element was apparently already in the OG text, and the omission of πετρίνας in manuscripts A 19 29 82 426 121 is due to later revision towards the MT.
109 Tov 2015b, 136.
110 Tov 2015b, 136–137. For the Samaritan Joshua texts see section 2.5.2.
111 Tov 2012, 298.
112 Tov 1999c, 385–396; 2012, 294–299; 2015b.

strata of Joshua, the earlier being represented by the OG and 4QJoshᵃ and the later by the MT.

Finally, the dissertation of Mazor has made a necessary refinement to the view arguing for the priority of the OG. The arguments of Mazor are like those of the earlier scholars, arguing for the general priority of OG Joshua based on translation technique, the Hebraistic style of the OG pluses, Qumran scrolls, and a text-critical analysis of minor and major variants between the OG and the MT versions of Joshua.[113] The refinement of this view, made by Mazor, is the argument that MT Joshua is not based directly on the Hebrew *Vorlage* of OG Joshua. Instead, MT Joshua and the Hebrew *Vorlage* of OG Joshua have both diverged and developed independently from a common source.[114] This highlights the observation that, while OG Joshua most commonly reflects the earlier version of Joshua, both MT and OG Joshua contain secondary elements. Such a refinement is probably needed, since many scholars positing the priority of OG Joshua still argue for the priority of MT Joshua in some instances. The clearest of these instances is the priority of Shechem (MT) over Shiloh (OG) in Josh. 24:1, 25.[115]

Recent Scholarship

In past research, many scholars have worked within all the above paradigms as part of their analyses of various texts in the book of Joshua.[116] Here, it suffices to present three views from the 21st century as exemplars of the various paradigms. The traditional view arguing for the priority of the MT is extensively defended by Van der Meer in a monograph. The intermediate view is most clearly taken by Thomas Dozeman in his recent commentary on Joshua 1–12. The view positing the priority of OG Joshua, in turn, has been developed by De Troyer in several articles focusing on numerous text-critical details.

In *Formulation and Reformulation*, Van der Meer explores the textual history of the book of Joshua as a test case for formulating the methodological relationship of textual criticism and literary/redaction criticism.[117] In addition to an extensive survey of past research, he analyzes three passages (Josh 1, 5:2–12, and 8:1–35) in the oldest witnesses to the text of Joshua, mainly the LXX and Qumran

---

[113] Mazor 1994, 31–33.
[114] Mazor 1994, 38.
[115] Holmes 1914, 78–79; Tov 1999a, 161; Pakkala 2013, 197. If one credits this interchange to the translator, it is of course possible to argue that MT Joshua was edited from the Hebrew *Vorlage* of OG Joshua.
[116] See, for instance, Rofé 1982 (LXX-priority); Bieberstein 1995 (MT-priority); Rösel 2002; Müller, Pakkala & Haar Romeny 2014, 45–58 (intermediate view).
[117] Van der Meer 2004, 115–118; 17–19. See also section 1.2.

scrolls, and relates this data to a redaction-critical model of the textual growth of Joshua. As was noted above, Van der Meer aims at keeping the analysis of individual textual witnesses and a redaction-critical analysis of the MT separate for as long as possible.[118] The reasoning behind this order of procedure is that if the textual data of a certain passage points to editorial activity, a redaction-critical analysis of the same passage should result in similar conclusions about the work of the editors. Thus, in an ideal case textual, literary, and redaction criticism reinforce each other.

In the text-critical analysis of all the three passages, Van der Meer concludes that the MT presents the earliest attainable form of the book of Joshua. The minuses in the OG in comparison to the MT are a result of "a conscious attempt to streamline the redundant and layered Hebrew text for the sake of a coherent and stylized Greek–".[119] Some changes are a result of the translator's conscious attempt to smoothen contradictions and problems in the text. In Van der Meer's analysis, the translator is characterized as one who takes "literary initiatives" quite freely.[120] In the end, Van der Meer ends up concluding that the proto-MT version of the book of Joshua was quite like the modern-day MT. It included all the redundancies and roughness of a text that has been redacted in at least three separate phases (DtrH, DtrN, and RedP). The OG version of Joshua, as well as the texts found in Qumran, represent reformulated texts that include for the most parts later readings.

Several aspects of Van der Meer's study have been criticized. Steven L. McKenzie, for one, wrote in a review of Van der Meer's monograph that he "essentially proves what he assumes".[121] Van der Meer assumes that a particular redactional theory, namely one version of the redaction theory of the "Göttingen School", is the best alternative, and concludes that the text-critical material does not support this theory. In my opinion, the main problem in Van der Meer's text-critical analysis is that too much freedom is ascribed to the translator. While many observations on the freedom of the translator made in the study are certainly correct, the assumed large-scale changes from the hand of the translator are far more problematic. I will return to some of these arguments in section 3.4.2.

The 2015 commentary on Joshua 1–12 by Dozeman, belonging to the Yale Anchor Bible series, deals with the LXX in an exceptionally broad fashion when compared to many other commentaries, which often privilege the MT. In the text-critical introduction of his commentary, Dozeman notes that both the view

---

[118] Van der Meer 2004, 155–159.
[119] Van der Meer 2004, 246.
[120] Van der Meer 2004, 408.
[121] McKenzie 2005.

arguing for the priority of the MT and the view arguing for the priority of the OG are present in modern research, and that they are often contrasted with each other. He then explicitly states that his aim is to "draw on both approaches to interpret the textual history of the book of Joshua". In addition, he highlights the pluriformity of texts circulating of the book of Joshua during the late Second Temple period. In line with this approach, some variants in the MT are seen as secondary editorial changes made even as late as in the Hasmonean period, while some variants in the LXX are part of the "creative process of the interpretation of the book of Joshua in the Hellenistic period."[122] In accordance with this intermediate methodological approach, in the actual commentary the LXX, the MT, and other sources (most notably 4QJosh[a]) are consistently commented upon. The intermediate nature of the commentary is seen in the observation that often the variant editions are simply described on their own, but no text-critical preference is given to either one of the differing accounts. While Dozeman does in these cases present the arguments used to defend either one of the traditions, he often leaves the question of text-critical priority open.[123] Finally, the appendices of the commentary give a helpful synoptic translation of both traditions and an extensive comparison of the different geographical terms between the LXX and the MT.[124]

Finally, De Troyer has in several contributions argued that the OG reflects a Hebrew version earlier than the MT. In a 2013 article dealing with Josh 10, she discovers through a text-critical analysis that three distinct concepts were not yet as developed in the Hebrew text underlying the OG as they are in the MT version of Joshua. These are: the idea of a "highly developed joint collaboration" between Joshua and Israel, the stress on the camp of Israel, and the importance of Gilgal as the location for Israel's camp. These ideas were only later developed by the proto-MT redactor.[125] Elsewhere, De Troyer dates this proto-MT redaction to the second century BCE based on the importance given to Gilgal.[126]

In addition to a careful text-critical comparison between the OG and MT versions of Joshua, De Troyer's contribution has been the publication of additional external evidence for the reliability of reconstructing the OG text of Joshua.

---

[122] Dozeman 2015, 33–34.
[123] A case in point is, for example, the analysis of the conquest of Ai. See Dozeman 2015, 366–367. A similar intermediate approach can be observed in an article written by Dozeman (2011) on the various functions of the book of Joshua in the canons of the LXX and the MT.
[124] Dozeman 2015, 501–555.
[125] De Troyer 2013, 1; 7–33. See also De Troyer 2006, 105–118; 2017, 223–265.
[126] De Troyer 2003, 57–58. The addition of Gilgal as the camp of Israel was done by a redactor who had the importance of Modein in Maccabean times in his mind. De Troyer argues that Modein is in a way an alternative Gilgal.

De Troyer has published an edition of the Greek papyrus which has been given the Rahlfs number 816.[127] This papyrus probably originates from the Oxyrhynchus area in Egypt and has been dated to 210–215 CE, making it the oldest remaining fragment of LXX Joshua. The readings in 816 are independent of the Hexaplaric revision, and it has also helped in discovering some recensional elements in B.[128] In the text of 816, there are also some marks of revision towards the MT. While this papyrus has no direct influence on the text-critical evaluation between the OG and MT Joshua, it gives overall confirmation for the task of reconstructing the OG. This is especially important in the minuses in OG Josh 10 in relation to the MT which are corroborated by 816.[129]

Finally, it should be noted that both Van der Meer's and De Troyer's studies are limited to certain selected passages from Joshua. Their overall conclusions on the relationship of the OG and MT versions of Joshua should therefore be considered with caution, since the situation may differ depending on the passage in question.

2.3.4 Interim Conclusions on the Septuagint of Joshua

In this section, I first surveyed the available modern editions and ancient sources pertaining to LXX Joshua. As observed in this critical survey, the usage of LXX Joshua in reconstructing the textual history of the Hebrew Bible is challenged by the absence of a high quality critical edition. Nevertheless, the manuscripts of LXX Joshua and their recensional qualities have been thoroughly researched for well over a hundred years. With the help of this research and the three modern editions of LXX Joshua, the OG text can be constructed with a good degree of probability. In the case of Josh 24, this work is carried out in section 3 of this study.

Second, I analyzed the translation technique of the OG translator of Joshua. The translation technique varies. The translator alternates between rendering the source text literally and being flexible in finding different translation equivalents for recurring Hebrew words and expressions. The translator did not merely mimic the Hebrew of the source text, but gave creative and varied translations. This is seen especially in the usage of different Greek equivalents for the same Hebrew words. The translator probably did not, however, introduce

---

[127] De Troyer 2005.
[128] De Troyer 2003, 105–106.
[129] De Troyer 2003, 115: "Manuscript 2648, the Schøyen Joshua papyrus, is a valuable tool to construct an OG text without v. 15, 17, and 42."

substantial changes in relation to his source text. Attributing rewritings, additions, omissions, and relocations to the translator would in most cases be improbable, since the translator generally seems to be quite faithful to the Hebrew source he used. This has been corroborated by several scholars working with various details in the translation of OG Joshua. One should therefore be careful in not attributing major differences between OG and MT Joshua to the translator. Nevertheless, when evaluating single textual variations, every possibility needs to be considered.

Third, I analyzed some of the arguments used in earlier studies addressing the relationship of OG and MT Joshua. In the history of this research, there can be seen three basic paradigms for explaining the differences: the traditional view claiming for the priority of the MT, the view postulating the priority of the OG, and the intermediate view situated somewhere in between. Based on this survey, it seems necessary to take all the options into account when analyzing Josh 24. There might well be original material in both the MT and the OG readings. After a careful analysis, it might be possible to make conclusions that contribute to the discussion pertaining to the whole book of Joshua.

In section 3, I will further analyze the primary sources of Josh 24, keeping in mind the threefold results of this section. The comparison between OG and MT Joshua will take a prime place in this analysis.

2.4 Biblical Joshua Texts from Qumran

The biblical Joshua material from Qumran is sparse. Only two manuscripts pertaining to the book of Joshua were found in Cave 4; these are 4QJosh^a and 4QJosh^b.[130] 4QJosh^a is dated to the Hasmonean period and contains parts of Josh 5:2–7; 6:5–10; 7:12–17; 8:3–11a, 14a, 18; 10:2–8, 8–11. 4QJosh^b, in turn, is dated to the late Hasmonean period and contains parts of Josh 2:11–12; 3:15–4:3; 17:1–5; 11–15. In addition, in the Schøyen collection there is the fragment MS 2713 of unknown provenance, often called XJosh, which is dated to 40 BCE–68 CE and contains parts of Josh 1:9–12, 2:4–5.[131] According to the calculations by Van der Meer,

---

130 The so-called rewritten Joshua texts are discussed below in section 2.5.1.
131 On the biblical Qumran fragments see, for example, García Martínez 2012, 145–147 and Feldman 2013, 15–16. The biblical Qumran Joshua scrolls are easily available in Ulrich 2010, 247–253. Regarding XJosh one should be extremely careful, since lately there has been increasing evidence that some of the fragments discovered post-2002 in the Schøyen collection could be forgeries. XJosh has not been closely examined, but it was acquired to the collection together with MS4612, whose authenticity has been seriously doubted on good grounds (Davis et al. 2017, 14–15).

these scrolls together attest only to less than 0.5% of the whole book of Joshua.[132] Josh 24 is not attested in the Dead Sea Scrolls.

The textual alignment and implications of the Joshua texts from Qumran is debated. Most of the textual material accords with the MT. In addition, there are readings according with the OG and unique readings. 4QJosh^b could be called "semi-Masoretic" since it contains 18 readings agreeing and 9 readings disagreeing with the MT, but only 2 readings agreeing and 26 readings disagreeing with the OG.[133] The textual alignment of 4QJosh^a is more complicated. As mentioned already above in section 2.3.3, 4QJosh^a aligns with the OG in the likely shorter textual form of Josh 8:11b–13 preserved in fragment 15 along with some minor textual details. This being noted, however, one should also consider that for Josh 5:2–7 and 6:6–7, 4QJosh^a does not reflect the shorter textual form present in the OG.[134]

The most notable discussion in relation to 4QJosh^a pertains to the different location of the reading of the law (MT Josh 8:34–35) at the beginning of Josh 5 in 4QJosh^a. In the MT, the building of the altar and reading of the law is located after the conquest of Ai at the end of Josh 8, while in the OG, it is situated two verses later in 9:2a–e. In the light of this varying location, it is interesting that in 4QJosh^a parts of this scene are located after the crossing of Gilgal. According to Eugene Ulrich, 4QJosh^a preserves the earliest location for the whole altar scene, while the MT and the OG reflect later revisions.[135] However, many have pointed out that 4QJosh^a might not have contained the whole altar scene, but only the reading of the law (Josh 8:34–35) at the beginning of Josh 5.[136] The building of the altar has to be reconstructed, since the scroll is fragmentary. Moreover, the location of the altar scene in 4QJosh^a seems to reflect a later harmonization of the events in Joshua to accord with Deut 27:1–8, which commands that an altar should be built immediately upon entering the Promised Land. Thus, 4QJosh^a probably does not preserve a lost ancient sequence of events, but a later harmonization towards Deuteronomy.[137] In any case, 4QJosh^a is an interesting witness since it contains MT, OG, and unique readings.

In sum, the Joshua texts from Qumran are scant, but they certainly illuminate that at the end of the Second Temple period the text of Joshua was not yet

---

132 Van der Meer 2004, 21.
133 Lange 2009, 187.
134 Tov 2015b, 134.
135 Ulrich 2015, 48–49.
136 Van der Meer 2004, 513; Feldman 2013, 117.
137 For a more detailed argumentation of this view see also De Troyer 2005, 141–164 and Tov 2015b, 147–153.

consolidated. The composition was being used in different textual forms. The evidence also corroborates that the late text of the MT and the variant readings attested in the OG both have a long history extending to the Second Temple period.

2.5 Other Joshua Texts

2.5.1 Rewritten Joshua Scrolls

Four scrolls from Qumran Cave 4 (4Q123, 4Q378, 4Q379, and 4Q533), one from Cave 5 (5Q9), and two from Masada (Mas 1039-211) contain rewritten versions of the book of Joshua. These texts are dated to the Hasmonean and Herodian periods. They are often referred to as the Apocryphon of Joshua, in accordance with the suggestion by Tov that these scrolls are copies of the same composition.[138] However, given the fragmentary state of the manuscripts, one should probably refrain from making conclusions as to whether these scrolls attest to a single or different composition.[139] Even though these scrolls have been sporadically discussed from the 1950s, the first exhaustive reconstruction, commentary, and study of these texts is *The Rewritten Joshua Scrolls from Qumran. Texts, Translations, and Commentary* by Ariel Feldman.[140] It represents the best available starting point for the study of these texts.

Although the rewritten Joshua scrolls do not contain parallels to Josh 24, three points should be made concerning the implications of the texts for the research questions of this study. First, the scrolls attest to important variants. For instance, 4Q379 contains two minor readings differing from the MT that are supported by the OG and partly also by 4QJosh[a].[141] In several other cases, one must assume a different Hebrew textual form for the rewritten Joshua text diverging from all the known textual witnesses.[142] This strengthens the assumption that the Hebrew *Vorlage* of the OG differed from the MT, and that the text of the book of Joshua was still circulating in different forms at the end of the Second Temple period. Second, the rewritten Joshua texts provide documented evidence of

---

138 Tov 1998, 233–256. However, Feldman (2013, 187–193) disagrees: "– it seems that in their present state of preservation the five RJ scrolls are better served if treated as five separate compositions."
139 Van der Meer 2004, 113.
140 Feldman 2013.
141 Feldman 2013, 115, 119–125, 194–195.
142 See, for example, Feldman 2013, 70–71.

various editorial techniques being used at the end of the Second Temple period. For instance, there are several harmonistic expansions in relation to the biblical text.[143] An example of this editorial phenomenon can be found in 4Q378 fragment 3 line 2, where an allusion to Exod 34:16 is expanded with the language of Deut 7:3. There are also several other allusions to Deuteronomy in 4Q378 which attest to the editorial technique of harmonizing texts to accord with Deuteronomy.[144] This editorial technique is also visible in the evidence of this study.[145] Third, it is noteworthy that 4Q123 is written in a paleo-Hebrew script. This brings into mind the Samaritan Joshua texts as already noted by Ulrich in the first published edition of this text.[146] However, since 4Q123 only consists of some twenty words that are hard to identify, one cannot draw any conclusions about the relationship of 4Q123 with Samaritan sources.

2.5.2 The Samaritan Joshua Texts

The canon of the Samaritans is limited to the Pentateuch. In recent scholarship, the text-critical value of the Samaritan Pentateuch has become increasingly obvious.[147] Joshua is the greatest hero of the Samaritans after Moses.[148] There are several Samaritan texts that parallel with the biblical book of Joshua. These are most notably the Arabic and Hebrew versions of the book of Joshua and a part of the Samaritan Chronicles or *Sepher Hayamim*.[149] These texts, their transmission history, and especially their value in reconstructing the textual history of the book of Joshua, are still open and contested. In my opinion, however, it is necessary to integrate them more closely into the critical study of the book of Joshua, keeping in mind that their place in the textual history of the book of Joshua is not yet clear.[150]

---

143 Feldman 2013, 194–195.
144 Feldman 2013, 70–72.
145 See section 3.5.
146 Ulrich 1992, 201.
147 See, for example, Anderson & Giles 2012, 3: "…the SP is once again moving toward the center stage in text-critical discussion of both the Hebrew Bible and the Christian New Testament."
148 Macdonald 1969, 3.
149 The name is based on the title given at the beginning of the best manuscript זה ספר הימים בו דברי הימים מאז מובא יהושע בן נון אל ארץ כנען עד היום הזה "This is the book of Days, containing the events of the days from the entry of Joshua the son of Nun into the land of Canaan up to the present day".
150 Recently Tov (2015a, 215–216; 2015b, 136–137) has pointed out that the Samaritan Joshua texts might in fact be valuable in textual criticism. Other scholars have also argued that the

The Samaritan book of Joshua, initially known from a 14th century CE Arabic manuscript,[151] was edited and published in 1848 by Theodor W. J. Juynboll, with a Latin translation and comments.[152] The Arabic Samaritan book of Joshua narrates a long era from the appointment of Joshua as the successor of Moses to the times of the Samaritan high priest Baba Rabba (4th century CE). The material parallel to the biblical book of Joshua is found in chapters 9–25, which paraphrase most of the book of Joshua. This rewritten biblical text was likely the earliest core of the work, which later grew in several steps through the addition of other legends.[153] The Hebrew version of the Samaritan book of Joshua (SamJosh) was acquired from the Samaritans and published by Moses Gaster in 1908.[154] He considered it to be a version of a composition dating ultimately to the exilic or early Second Temple period, which had also served as the Hebrew source of the Arabic version.[155] The manuscript itself is a modern copy of an earlier text, and dated to 1904. It parallels largely with the Joshua part of *Sepher Hayamim* whose earliest MS is, according to John Macdonald, from 1616.[156] The nature of the text, however, cannot be deduced from the age of the manuscript: the challenge of working with Samaritan material is that Samaritans usually sell scholars only modern copies of older manuscripts. The possible earlier manuscripts are not easily given over to the scrutiny of scholars.[157]

Samaritan Joshua texts should be examined more carefully. See, for example, Nodet 1997, 200 and Feldman 2013, 1.
151 The MS was acquired by Joseph Justus Scaliger to the Leiden university library. For more information on the MS see, for example, Gaster 1930.
152 Juynboll 1848.
153 A helpful introduction of this material is found in Farber 2016, 223–274. The best English translation of the Arabic text is Crane 1890.
154 Gaster had formed a personal relationship with Samaritans, and with the high priest Jacob ben Aaron (1841–1916), who had a special interest in making Samaritan history and customs known to western scholars. During his interactions with the Samaritans, Gaster acquired approximately 80 manuscripts of various Samaritan works. On how he discovered SamJosh and the character of the manuscript, see Gaster 1908, 210–212.
155 The Hebrew and Arabic versions are clearly connected but differ in several aspects. For details see Gaster 1908, 215.
156 However, this date has also been contested, and it has been suggested that it should rather be dated to 1908. See Cohen 1981, 185–187. All in all, including the larger work *Sepher Hayamim*, there are six known modern manuscripts preserving the Hebrew version of the Samaritan book of Joshua. However, it has not been possible to assign the date of some of the MSS. These MSS are kept in the John Rylands Library in the University of Manchester. See Macdonald 1969, 69–72.
157 See, for example, Gaster 1908, 534: "Aus Erfahrung wußte ich, wie schwer es überhaupt ist, bei ihnen eine alte Handschrift außer Bibelhandschriften aufzutreiben." See also the responce received by Joseph Scaliger in 1598 when he was trying to acquire manuscripts from the

2.5 Other Joshua Texts — 45

The publication of SamJosh and claims made by Gaster sparked immediate opposition and critique. Scholars such as Paul Kahle,[158] Abraham S. Yahuda,[159] and Alan D. Adler[160] claimed that the manuscript is either a forgery or a late compilation from the Arabic sources and the MT. Gaster responded to the criticism and defended the authenticity and antiquity of SamJosh. He based his argument on several detailed observations and comparisons of various textual traditions. First, according to him, whenever the MT has a *paseq* the parallel text in SamJosh, if there is one, offers a differing reading of the MT which is often close to the LXX in its minor details. Therefore, according to Gaster, *paseq* is a pre-Masoretic marking which allows us a glimpse into the workings of the ancient Hebrew editor. Whenever he used the *paseq*, the proto-MT editor compared his text to the proto-Samaritan version in use.[161] Unfortunately this conclusion cannot be substantiated, since Gaster did not publish the promised new critical edition of SamJosh, including the analysis of the texts with *paseq*. Second, a comparison with the LXX reveals that SamJosh and LXX agrees in several textual variants against the MT.[162] According to Tov, the most significant of these agreements are the absence of MT Josh 20:4–6 from both the LXX and SamJosh and the additions in LXX 10:12 and 24:33 which are partially reflected in SamJosh.[163] Third, SamJosh presents some information together with Josephus that is not found anywhere in the MT.[164] For example, the succession of the priesthood to Phinehas is reported after the death of Eleazar (SamJosh 23:16 / Ant 5.119).[165] Fourth, the division of the land in SamJosh follows more closely the one presented in Josephus and Ezekiel (Ezek 47:15ff.) than the one presented in MT Joshua.[166] Even though Gaster was too quick to date the provenance of SamJosh to the exilic or postexilic period, especially the relationship of

---

Samaritan community: "We are not allowed to sell you the book of Joshua or the Writing when you are not Samaritans." Nodet 1997, 195–196.
158 Kahle 1908, 550–551.
159 Yahuda 1908, 887–914.
160 Adler 1908, 1143–1147.
161 Gaster 1925, 135–136. Gaster built on the work of Kennedy (1903, 19–21) who argued that *paseq* is an ancient sign that preceded the work of the Masoretes.
162 Gaster 1909, 115–127; 1925, 137.
163 Tov 2015a, 216.
164 Gaster 1925, 137.
165 See also Nodet 1997, 199: "...since it is really improbable that Josephus had sought Samaritan sources, or that the Jewish Antiquities would have had any influence on the present JosS, it must be concluded that one as well as the other, despite their reputation for inaccuracy, had drawn a common source..."
166 Gaster 1908, 220–222; 1925, 138–139.

SamJosh with the LXX makes it hard to dismiss it merely as late medieval reception history of MT Joshua.

A somewhat mediating position was presented by Alan D. Crown, who showed that, on the one hand, much of the early criticism of SamJosh was either unfounded or too hasty and, on the other hand, the claims made by Gaster were too extreme. According to Crown, Gaster did not, for example, consider the possibility that while the core of SamJosh might be ancient, the composition as it stands may have gone through several changes along its long transmission process.[167] Crown himself argued that a text like that found in SamJosh probably served as a source of the Arabic version, and was written utilizing earlier sources which may even reflect traditions from the third and fourth centuries CE.[168] According to his analysis of several textual details, it is more probable that a Hebrew text like SamJosh was the source of the Arabic version rather than the other way around.[169]

The merit in the analysis by Crown is that he allows for a long transmission history for the Samaritan Joshua texts: while much of it is indeed probably late reception history and Samaritan interpretations, one cannot dismiss the possibility that it might build upon older traditions. Indeed, as is seen in the pluriformity of the early textual material (MT, LXX, and Qumran) and the rewritten Joshua scrolls, we simply do not know all the textual forms of the book of Joshua present in the Second Temple period. Interestingly, Feldman has noted that there are parallels between 4Q378 and 4Q379 and the Arabic and Hebrew Samaritan Joshua traditions; for example, both claim that the crossing of the Jordan took place during the year of Jubilee.[170] Therefore, it is heuristically interesting to entertain the possibility that SamJosh might, in fact, "have a longer history than currently allowed by western scholars".[171]

In addition to the independent books of Joshua, a major part of the Samaritan Chronicles or *Sepher Hayamim* is devoted to the events that took place during the time of Joshua. As for the biblical books, it contains material parallel to the books of Joshua, Judges, Samuel, Kings, II Chronicles, and Psalms. The work is extant in several manuscripts. The most accessible edition was published by John Macdonald in 1969, following in its main text a modern manuscript which was copied by Tobiah ben Phinehas in Shechem. In addition, Macdonald presents

---

[167] Crown 1972, 86–87.
[168] Crown 1964, 79–100.
[169] Crown 1972, 86–111. As agreed also by Stenhouse 1989, 220.
[170] Feldman 2013, 195–197.
[171] Crown, Pummer & Tal 1993, 42.

variant readings from other manuscripts in an extensive apparatus.[172] Even though Macdonald cautions strongly not to confuse *Sepher Hayamim* with the independent SamJosh published by Gaster,[173] the work overlaps in many instances with SamJosh and both should therefore be considered together when analyzing the Samaritan Joshua traditions. While *Sepher Hayamim* is often judged as representing merely late reception history of Joshua, Macdonald himself notes: "But even if the ST is a later work *in extenso*, it may contain genuinely ancient traditions which antedate some polemical MT passages."[174]

As for MT Josh 24, SamJosh 22 contains the closest parallel combining elements found from Josh 23 and 24. There, Joshua gathers the people on Mt. Gerizim before his death (vv. 1–6). The people swear that they will serve YHWH alone, Joshua makes a covenant with the people, and gives them the law (vv. 6–17). The law is written in a book which is given over to the Levites (v. 17). Then the altar is established on Mt. Gerizim (vv. 18–22), the kingship is lotted (v. 22), and Joshua dies and is buried to Mt. Gerizim (vv. 22–24). Also, SamJosh 23 parallels partly with the end of Josh 24, recalling in a longer form the priesthood of Eleazar and the succession of the priesthood to Phinehas, who renews the covenant and authors the calendar.[175] *Sepher Hayamim* contains a similar text differing only in some textual details.[176] I will return to an analysis of this text in section 3.6.

The Samaritan Joshua texts contain readings that are far too interesting to be bypassed without an examination.[177] Therefore, I propose that the text should be approached without *a priori* expectations, while also keeping in mind the uncertainty relating to its character and the fact that the earliest witnesses for this text are medieval. In this study, I will analyze the Samaritan text parallel to Josh 23–24 utilizing internal criteria for evaluating its readings. In practice, I will compare the text of SamJosh with textual evidence from the OG and the MT that we know for sure stems from the Second Temple period. In addition, SamJosh might shed light on some textual and literary questions. Hence, I will offer a fresh analysis on SamJosh 22 in section 3.6 after having examined the primary textual evidence.

---

[172] For the Joshua part of Sepher Hayamim, Macdonald (1969, 9–10) utilized six different manuscripts.
[173] Macdonald 1969, 5.
[174] Macdonald 1969, 89. See also Stenhouse 1989, 222–223 and Hjelm 2000, 98–99.
[175] Gaster 1908, 214–215.
[176] Macdonald 1969, 98–99; 29–31.
[177] Nodet (1997, 195–201) has argued briefly that the book of Joshua originally came to the Judeans from the Samaritans. In his opinion, SamJosh is not derived from the MT. Thus, he also argues that the Samaritan Joshua material and its position in the textual history of the book of Joshua needs to be evaluated anew.

I wish to emphasize that such an analysis is exploratory in nature. My textual and literary analysis of the primary textual evidence of Josh 24 does not, in any way, rely on the Samaritan sources. This would be problematic since, at this point, the earliest version of the Samaritan farewell speech of Joshua has only been preserved in very late manuscripts. Moreover, some features of the Samaritan farewell speech of Joshua overlap with literary and redaction criticism of the chapter, which is why I will also refer to SamJosh in the literary critical section 4.3.3.

3 Documented Evidence of Editing in Joshua 24

3.1 Introductory Remarks

The aim of this section is to evaluate the differences between the MT and OG versions of Josh 24. Ultimately, the analysis will result in a model of the latest diachronic development of the Hebrew text of Josh 24 as attested by textual evidence. The analysis of the text is divided into three sections (Josh 24:1–13, 14–27, 28–33) for the sake of clarity.[1] Each section has three parts. First, the MT and OG are presented in a table with translations. The most significant differences are marked already in the table.[2] Second, some key variants in the LXX manuscripts are introduced and analyzed to work with the best possible approximation of the OG.[3] Third, the variants between the OG and the MT are analyzed. This constitutes the longest part of the analysis.

Before moving on with the analysis, some observations need to be given on the second phase of the analysis, the evaluation of the variant Greek readings. The notes on the variant Greek readings are made up of three parts. First, a short listing of the most important variants is given in an apparatus format below the text. The apparatus is not complete, but records variants pertaining to the differences between the MT and the OG and the most notable secondary Greek revisions. The format of the apparatus is like that of the *Göttingen* editions.[4] To simplify the apparatus, I have utilized the manuscript groups discussed in section 2.3.1. The manuscript group siglum is used in the apparatus if the most important manuscripts, those printed in bold in the list below, have the reading. Accordingly, if some of the most important bolded manuscripts in that group do not contain the reading, this will be specified with a minus in the upper index. Second, the readings in the modern editions of Rahlfs and Margolis are discussed if they differ. These differences are analyzed building partly on the thorough

---

[1] The division also follows the basic literary distinctions within Josh 24. See section 4.
[2] The markings are as follows: plusses are boxed, different expressions are highlighted with a gray background, and a different order between the texts is marked with **bold**. Differences in the Greek created by a free and contextual translation technique are highlighted through a differing English translation.
[3] My approximation of the OG differs from the edition of Rahlfs in two instances (24:5, 27). There are also some additional cases where a different OG could be imagined. These possibilities will be discussed in the text-critical analysis of the OG.
[4] The readings in the LXX manuscripts have been consulted mostly from the Cambridge edition of Brooke-McLean and digital images. I also want to thank Christian Schäfer of the *Göttingen Academy of Sciences* for providing additional information concerning the Septuagint witnesses for Joshua.

study by Den Hertog.⁵ Third, the arguments for the most probable OG reading are given, and the possible reasons for the secondary readings are discussed.

In the apparatus, I utilize the manuscript groups of Margolis introduced in section 2.3.1. This is by far the best and most-used grouping of the Greek MSS material.⁶ The geographical connotations of the groups should not, however, be stressed too much. For this reason, I have used the more common sigla *L* and *O* instead of the sigla used by Margolis. Since the critical edition of Joshua is still currently underway for the series of the *Academy of Sciences in Göttingen*, the grouping used in this study is far from the final grouping of Joshua manuscripts. However, the division of the main witnesses to these groups is based on solid earlier research. The groups are presented in the list below. The most important representatives of each group are listed first and marked in bold.⁷

E	**B 120 129**
	707 946
	55 82 (mixed)
O	**G 19 108 376 426**
L	**54´ = 54 75**
	44´ = 44 106 134 314
	K 74 76 84 118 125 127 537 610
	Oxf. Bodl. Laud. gr. 36¹⁰
C	**A M V 29 55 59 82 121 407**
	W 68 71 122 318 488 527 669
M	**15 52 53 56 57 58 85 130 344 509**
	F 16 18 30 46 64 72 73 126 128 131 236 246 313 319 320 328 343 346 381 392 414 417 422 461 489 528 529 530 550 551 552 616 619 661 716 730 739 761
	(These MSS are not necessarily interdependent. Many of them rest on C but also include readings from other groups.)

---

5 Den Hertog 1996, 30–109. When differing from my main text, the readings of Rahlfs (Ra) and Margolis (Ma) are mentioned in the apparatus.
6 For an overview, discussion, and comparison with the groups of Pretzl, see Den Hertog 1996, 3–29. See also Tov 1999b, 26.
7 The identification of the bolded manuscripts as the most important is based on the work by Margolis and Den Hertog 1996, 5–6. The subgroupings of *O* by Margolis are not followed here, since they rely on the problematic Tetrapla assumption. See section 2.3.1. Since the focus is on the manuscripts printed with bold, the grouping given here is not complete. Indeed, it could not be, since research on the Greek Joshua manuscripts is still far from complete. La¹⁰⁰ is the only daughter version that is marked in the apparatus on a regular basis.

3.2 Joshua 24:1–13: Text and Apparatus

MT (*BHS*)	OG
¹ וַיֶּאֱסֹף יְהוֹשֻׁעַ אֶת־כָּל־שִׁבְטֵי יִשְׂרָאֵל שְׁכֶמָה וַיִּקְרָא לְזִקְנֵי יִשְׂרָאֵל וּלְרָאשָׁיו וּלְשֹׁפְטָיו וּלְשֹׁטְרָיו וַיִּתְיַצְּבוּ לִפְנֵי הָאֱלֹהִים	¹ Καὶ συνήγαγεν Ἰησοῦς πάσας φυλὰς Ἰσραὴλ εἰς Σηλὼ καὶ συνεκάλεσεν τοὺς πρεσβυτέρους αὐτῶν **καὶ τοὺς γραμματεῖς αὐτῶν** **καὶ τοὺς δικαστὰς αὐτῶν** καὶ ἔστησεν αὐτοὺς ἀπέναντι τοῦ θεοῦ.
And Joshua gathered all the tribes of Israel to Shechem, and summoned the elders of Israel, and their heads, **and their judges,** **and their scribes** and they set themselves before God.	And Iesous gathered all the tribes of Israel to Selo and summoned their elders **and their scribes** **and their judges** and set them before God.
² וַיֹּאמֶר יְהוֹשֻׁעַ אֶל־כָּל־הָעָם כֹּה־אָמַר יְהוָה אֱלֹהֵי יִשְׂרָאֵל בְּעֵבֶר הַנָּהָר יָשְׁבוּ אֲבוֹתֵיכֶם מֵעוֹלָם תֶּרַח אֲבִי אַבְרָהָם וַאֲבִי נָחוֹר וַיַּעַבְדוּ אֱלֹהִים אֲחֵרִים	² καὶ εἶπεν Ἰησοῦς πρὸς πάντα τὸν λαόν Τάδε λέγει κύριος ὁ θεὸς Ἰσραήλ Πέραν τοῦ ποταμοῦ κατῴκησαν οἱ πατέρες ὑμῶν τὸ ἀπ' ἀρχῆς, Θάρα ὁ πατὴρ Ἀβραὰμ καὶ ὁ πατὴρ Ναχώρ, καὶ ἐλάτρευσαν θεοῖς ἑτέροις.
And Joshua said to all the people: "Thus says YHWH, the God of Israel: 'Beyond the river lived your fathers in ancient times, Terah the father of Abraham and the father of Nahor and they served other gods.	And Iesous said to all the people: "Thus says Lord, the God of Israel: 'Beyond the river lived your fathers in ancient times, Thara the father of Abraam and the father of Nahor and they served other gods.

(Continued)

24:1 Σηλω] συχεμ $O^{-G\ 108}$ 15-85^{mg} | αυτων 1° E^{-120}-55 54´ La^{100}] pr και τους αρχοντας 15 Ma; + ιηλ (om 15-58-72) και τους αρχοντας αυτων (om 15 106) rel | ἔστησεν αὐτούς] εστησαν 19-426 314 $C^{-55\ 82}$ 56-344^{mg}-509 | om αυτών $L^{-44\ 314}$ 15

24:2 κατῴκησαν] παρωκησαν 44´$^{-44}$ C^{-82} 56-85-344^{mg}-509 | ἑτέροις] + και ελατρευσαν οις ουκ ειδησαν 55

MT (*BHS*)	OG
³ וָאֶקַּח אֶת־אֲבִיכֶם אֶת־אַבְרָהָם מֵעֵבֶר הַנָּהָר וָאוֹלֵךְ אוֹתוֹ בְּכָל־אֶרֶץ כְּנָעַן וָאַרְבֶּה אֶת־זַרְעוֹ וָאֶתֶּן־לוֹ אֶת־יִצְחָק	³ καὶ ἔλαβον τὸν πατέρα ὑμῶν τὸν Ἀβραὰμ ἐκ τοῦ πέραν τοῦ ποταμοῦ καὶ ὡδήγησα αὐτὸν ἐν πάσῃ τῇ γῇ καὶ ἐπλήθυνα αὐτοῦ σπέρμα καὶ ἔδωκα αὐτῷ τὸν Ἰσαάκ
And I took your father Abraham from beyond the river and led him in all the land of Canaan and made his offspring many. And I gave him Isaac	And I took your father Abraam from beyond the river and led him in all the land and made his offspring many. And I gave him Isaac
⁴ וָאֶתֵּן לְיִצְחָק אֶת־יַעֲקֹב וְאֶת־עֵשָׂו וָאֶתֵּן לְעֵשָׂו אֶת־הַר שֵׂעִיר לָרֶשֶׁת אוֹתוֹ וְיַעֲקֹב וּבָנָיו יָרְדוּ מִצְרָיִם	⁴ καὶ τῷ Ἰσαὰκ τὸν Ἰακὼβ καὶ τὸν Ἡσαύ· καὶ ἔδωκα τῷ Ἡσαῦ τὸ ὄρος τὸ Σηιρ κληρονομῆσαι αὐτῷ, καὶ Ἰακὼβ καὶ οἱ υἱοὶ αὐτοῦ κατέβησαν εἰς Αἴγυπτον καὶ ἐγένοντο ἐκεῖ εἰς ἔθνος μέγα καὶ πολὺ καὶ κραταιόν.
and to Isaac I gave Jacob and Esau. And I gave Esau the mountain of Seir to take into his possession. But Jacob and his sons went down to Egypt.	and to Isaac Jacob and Esau. And I gave Esau the mountain of Seir for him to inherit. But Jacob and his sons went down to Egypt and became there a great nation, populous and mighty,
⁵ וָאֶשְׁלַח אֶת־מֹשֶׁה וְאֶת־אַהֲרֹן וָאֶגֹּף אֶת־מִצְרַיִם כַּאֲשֶׁר עָשִׂיתִי בְּקִרְבּוֹ וְאַחַר הוֹצֵאתִי אֶתְכֶם	⁵ καὶ ἐκάκωσαν αὐτοὺς οἱ Αἰγύπτιοι, καὶ ἐπάταξεν κύριος τὴν Αἴγυπτον ἐν σημείοις οἷς ἐποίησεν ἐν αὐτοῖς, καὶ μετὰ ταῦτα ἐξήγαγεν ὑμᾶς and the Egyptians afflicted them.'

24:3 τῇ γῇ] γη χανααν 120; + χανααν O⁻ᴳ 108 44 82 52-56-57-58-72-85ᵐᵍ-344ᵐᵍ-509; + χαναν 53
24:4 καὶ 1°] + εδωκα O⁻ᴳ 108 54´ 52-53-130; εδωκεν 44´⁻³¹⁴ 85-344 | om καὶ τῷ Ισαακ 59 15 | αὐτῷ] αυτο 120 52 Ma; αυτου 426 72
24:5 Αἰγύπτιοι] και απεστειλα τον Μουσην MaConj | ἐπάταξεν] επαταξαν B*; επαταξα Bᵃᵇ 55 15 | om κύριος B 19-426 55 15 Ma | σημείοις] πασιν 55; + εν 376 15; > B 19-426 82 Ra Ma | ἐποίησεν] εποιησαν B 19 314 407; εποιησα 55 15; εποιει 106 | ἐν 2°] om E⁻¹²⁹ 44 82 509-72 Ra | σημείοις – αὐτοῖς] σιμεοις 75 | ὑμᾶς] om E⁻¹²⁰ Ma; ημας L⁻⁴⁴ 52-56 La¹⁰⁰

3.2 Joshua 24:1–13: Text and Apparatus

MT (*BHS*)	OG
Then I sent Moses and Aaron and I smote Egypt just as I did in its midst and afterwards I brought you out.	And the Lord smote Egypt with miracles that he did in their midst and afterwards he brought you out
6 וָאוֹצִיא אֶת־אֲבוֹתֵיכֶם מִמִּצְרַיִם וַתָּבֹאוּ הַיָּמָּה וַיִּרְדְּפוּ מִצְרַיִם אַחֲרֵי אֲבוֹתֵיכֶם בְּרֶכֶב וּבְפָרָשִׁים יַם־סוּף And I brought your fathers out of Egypt and you came to the sea. And the Egyptians pursued after your fathers with chariots and horses to the Sea of Reeds.	6 ἐξ Αἰγύπτου, καὶ εἰσήλθατε εἰς τὴν θάλασσαν τὴν ἐρυθράν. καὶ κατεδίωξαν οἱ Αἰγύπτιοι ὀπίσω τῶν πατέρων ὑμῶν ἐν ἅρμασιν καὶ ἐν ἵπποις εἰς τὴν θάλασσαν τὴν ἐρυθράν, of Egypt and you came to the Sea of Reeds. And the Egyptians pursued after your fathers with chariots and horses to the Sea of Reeds.
7 וַיִּצְעֲקוּ אֶל־יְהוָה וַיָּשֶׂם מַאֲפֵל בֵּינֵיכֶם וּבֵין הַמִּצְרִים וַיָּבֵא עָלָיו אֶת־הַיָּם וַיְכַסֵּהוּ וַתִּרְאֶינָה עֵינֵיכֶם אֵת אֲשֶׁר־עָשִׂיתִי בְּמִצְרָיִם וַתֵּשְׁבוּ בַמִּדְבָּר יָמִים רַבִּים	7 καὶ ἀνεβοήσαμεν πρὸς κύριον, καὶ ἔδωκεν νεφέλην καὶ γνόφον ἀνὰ μέσον ἡμῶν καὶ ἀνὰ μέσον τῶν Αἰγυπτίων καὶ ἐπήγαγεν ἐπ' αὐτοὺς τὴν θάλασσαν, καὶ ἐκάλυψεν αὐτούς, καὶ εἶδοσαν οἱ ὀφθαλμοὶ ὑμῶν ὅσα ἐποίησεν κύριος ἐν γῇ Αἰγύπτῳ. καὶ ἦτε ἐν τῇ ἐρήμῳ ἡμέρας πλείους.

(Continued)

24:6 ἐξ Αἰγύπτου $C^{-55\ 82}$ 58] pr και τους πατερας ημων 54-106-134 52-56-344; pr και τους πατερας υμων 44-75-314 53-57-72-130-85-509; pr και εξηγαγεν τους πατερας υμων 120 W-82; pr και εξηγαγον τους πατερας υμων O^{-G} 108; > 58; τους πατερας υμων 55 15 Ma; pr τους πατερας ημων rel | ὑμῶν] ημων $E\ O^{-G\ 376}\ L$ 59-82

24:7 ἀνεβοήσαμεν] ανεβοησαν 75-106-134; εβοησαμεν O^{-G} 108 15 | ἡμῶν] υμων 426* Ma | Αἰγύπτῳ] + και εν τη ερημω 44 52-53-57-85-130-344

MT (BHS)	OG
And they cried out to YHWH	And we cried out to the Lord
and he put darkness	and he put a cloud and darkness
between you and the Egyptians,	between us and the Egyptians,
and he brought the sea upon them	and he brought the sea upon them
and covered them.	and covered them.
And your eyes saw	And your eyes saw
what I did in Egypt.	what the Lord did in the land of Egypt.
Then you lived in the wilderness many days.	Then you were in the wilderness many days.

8 וָאָבִיא אֶתְכֶם אֶל־אֶרֶץ הָאֱמֹרִי	8 καὶ ἤγαγεν ὑμᾶς εἰς γῆν Ἀμορραίων
הַיּוֹשֵׁב בְּעֵבֶר הַיַּרְדֵּן	τῶν κατοικούντων πέραν τοῦ Ἰορδάνου,
וַיִּלָּחֲמוּ אִתְּכֶם	καὶ παρετάξαντο ὑμῖν,
וָאֶתֵּן אוֹתָם	καὶ παρέδωκεν αὐτοὺς κύριος
בְּיֶדְכֶם	εἰς τὰς χεῖρας ὑμῶν,
וַתִּירְשׁוּ אֶת־אַרְצָם	καὶ κατεκληρονομήσατε τὴν γῆν αὐτῶν
וָאַשְׁמִידֵם	καὶ ἐξωλεθρεύσατε αὐτοὺς
מִפְּנֵיכֶם	ἀπὸ προσώπου ὑμῶν.

MT	OG
And I brought you to the land of the Amorites	And he brought you to the land of the Amorites
who lived beyond Jordan.	who lived beyond Jordan.
And they fought against you	And they fought against you
and I handed them over into your hands.	and the Lord handed them over into your hands.
And you took possession of their land	And you took possession of their land
and I destroyed them before you.	and you destroyed them before you.

9 וַיָּקָם בָּלָק בֶּן־צִפּוֹר	9 καὶ ἀνέστη Βαλὰκ ὁ τοῦ Σεπφὼρ
מֶלֶךְ מוֹאָב	βασιλεὺς Μωὰβ
וַיִּלָּחֶם בְּיִשְׂרָאֵל	καὶ παρετάξατο τῷ Ἰσραήλ
וַיִּשְׁלַח וַיִּקְרָא	καὶ ἀποστείλας ἐκάλεσεν
לְבִלְעָם בֶּן־בְּעוֹר לְקַלֵּל אֶתְכֶם	τὸν Βαλαὰμ ἀράσασθαι ὑμῖν·

MT	OG
And rose Balak the son of Zippor,	And rose Balak the son of Zephor,
king of Moab, to fight against Israel.	king of Moab, to fight against Israel.
And he sent and invited	And he sent and invited
Balaam the son of Beor to curse you.	Balaam to curse you.

24:8 ὑμᾶς] ημας E^{-129} 19-108 $L^{-106\ 134}$ 52-57-85-509 | γῆν Ἀμορραίων] την γην των αμορραιων L^{-44} | καὶ παρετάξαντο ὑμῖν] και παρετάξαντο μωυσης 82 120; > E^{-120} 55 Ma | ὑμῶν 1°] ημων $E\ O^{-G}$ L 55-59 15-52-344 | ὑμῶν 2°] ημων 75

24:9 Βαλααμ] + υιον βεωρ 120 19 W-82 52-57-58; + υιων βεωρ 53; + υιων βαιωρ 376-426 85^{mg}-344^{mg}; + υιον βοωρ 509 | ὑμῖν] ημιν E 55-82; ημας 75 52-57-130; υμας 54-106-134 85; σε 509; > 58-72

3.2 Joshua 24:1–13: Text and Apparatus

MT (*BHS*)	OG
10 וְלֹא אָבִיתִי לִשְׁמֹעַ לְבִלְעָם	10 καὶ οὐκ ἠθέλησεν κύριος ὁ θεός σου ἀπολέσαι σε,
וַיְבָרֶךְ בָּרוֹךְ אֶתְכֶם	καὶ εὐλογίαν εὐλόγησεν ὑμᾶς,
וָאַצִּל אֶתְכֶם מִיָּדוֹ	καὶ ἐξείλατο ὑμᾶς ἐκ χειρῶν αὐτῶν
	καὶ παρέδωκεν αὐτούς.
But I would not listen to Balaam. And indeed, he blessed you (pl.) and I rescued you (pl.) out of his hand.	But the Lord your God would not destroy you (sg.). And indeed, he blessed you (pl.) and rescued you (pl.) out of their hands and handed them over.
11 וַתַּעַבְרוּ אֶת־הַיַּרְדֵּן	11 καὶ διέβητε τὸν Ἰορδάνην
וַתָּבֹאוּ אֶל־יְרִיחוֹ	καὶ παρεγενήθητε εἰς Ἰεριχώ·
וַיִּלָּחֲמוּ בָכֶם	καὶ ἐπολέμησαν πρὸς ὑμᾶς
בַּעֲלֵי־יְרִיחוֹ הָאֱמֹרִי	οἱ κατοικοῦντες Ἰεριχώ, ὁ Ἀμορραῖος
וְהַפְּרִזִּי וְהַכְּנַעֲנִי	καὶ ὁ Χαναναῖος καὶ ὁ Φερεζαῖος
	καὶ ὁ Εὑαῖος καὶ ὁ Ἰεβουσαῖος
וְהַחִתִּי וְהַגִּרְגָּשִׁי הַחִוִּי וְהַיְבוּסִי	καὶ ὁ Χετταῖος καὶ ὁ Γεργεσαῖος,
וָאֶתֵּן אוֹתָם בְּיֶדְכֶם	καὶ παρέδωκεν αὐτοὺς κύριος εἰς τὰς χεῖρας ὑμῶν.
You crossed over Jordan and came to Jericho and the citizens of Jericho fought against you; the Amorites, **the Perizzites, the Canaanites,** the Hittites, the Girgashites, **the Hivites, and the Jebusites;** and I handed them in your hands.	You crossed over Jordan and came to Jericho and the inhabitants of Jericho fought against you; the Amorites, **the Canaanites, the Perizzites the Hivites, the Jebusites,** the Hittites, and the Girgashites; and the Lord handed them in your hands.
12 וָאֶשְׁלַח לִפְנֵיכֶם	12 καὶ ἐξαπέστειλεν προτέραν ὑμῶν
אֶת־הַצִּרְעָה וַתְּגָרֶשׁ אוֹתָם	τὴν σφηκιάν, καὶ ἐξέβαλεν αὐτοὺς
מִפְּנֵיכֶם שְׁנֵי מַלְכֵי	ἀπὸ προσώπου ὑμῶν, δώδεκα βασιλεῖς
הָאֱמֹרִי לֹא בְחַרְבְּךָ	τῶν Ἀμορραίων, οὐκ ἐν τῇ ῥομφαίᾳ σου
וְלֹא בְקַשְׁתֶּךָ	οὐδὲ ἐν τῷ τόξῳ σου.

(Continued)

24:10 ὑμᾶς 1°] 108-426 44-54 C 15-53-56-57-58-72-130-344[txt] La[100]] ημας rel | ὑμᾶς 2°] 108-426 44-54 C[-55 59] 15-72-85-130-344-509 La[100]] ημας rel | αὐτῶν] εχθρων 44 52-57-85[txt]-130-344 | om καὶ παρέδωκεν αὐτούς L C[-55 82] 52-57-58-72-85[txt]-130-344 Ma | αὐτούς] + *in manus uestras* Arm Sah (*nostras*)

24:11 om κύριος 19-426 C[-55 82] | ὑμᾶς] ημας E 376 75 55-82 | ὑμῶν] ημων E 108 C[-59] 75 53-57-85-130-344-509

24:12 ἐξέβαλεν] εξαπεστειλεν B-129; εξαπεβαλεν 53 | ὑμῶν 1°] ημων E 190-108 C[-V] L[-54 44] 56-344-509 | ὑμῶν 2°] B 19-108 75 29 130-344[mg] | δώδεκα] δυο 19-426 15-58; εννεα και εικοσι 55 | βασιλεῖς] πολις A; πολεις 55-121

MT (*BHS*)	OG
I sent ahead of you the hornet and drove them from before you, the **two** kings of the Amorites; not by your sword or your bow.	He sent ahead of you the hornet and drove them from before you, the **twelve** kings of the Amorites; not by your sword or your bow.
¹³ וָאֶתֵּן לָכֶם אֶרֶץ אֲשֶׁר לֹא־יָגַעְתָּ בָּהּ וְעָרִים אֲשֶׁר לֹא־בְנִיתֶם וַתֵּשְׁבוּ בָּהֶם כְּרָמִים וְזֵיתִים אֲשֶׁר לֹא־נְטַעְתֶּם אַתֶּם אֹכְלִים	¹³ καὶ ἔδωκεν ὑμῖν γῆν, ἐφ' ἣν οὐκ ἐκοπιάσατε ἐπ' αὐτῆς, καὶ πόλεις, ἃς οὐκ ᾠκοδομήσατε, καὶ κατῳκίσθητε ἐν αὐταῖς· καὶ ἀμπελῶνας καὶ ἐλαιῶνας, οὓς οὐκ ἐφυτεύσατε, ὑμεῖς ἔδεσθε.
And **I gave** you a land which you did not labor, cities that you did not built, and you live in them; of vineyards and olive yards, that you did not plant, you will eat.'	And **he gave** you a land which you did not labor, cities that you did not build, and you were settled in them; of vineyards and olive yards, that you did not plant, you will eat.

24:13 ὑμῶν] B 56| ἐφ'] om 54´-314 | ἐπ' αὐτῆς] εν αυτη 54´-314

3.2.1 Text-Critical Analysis of the OG

24:1 The OG reading is σηλω as agreed by Rahlfs and Margolis. This is the reading supported not only by most Greek manuscripts, but also Old Latin and Ethiopic. Some Greek manuscripts secondarily correct towards the Hebrew with συχεμ, a reading also attested in the Syrohexapla.

The OG text of the list of leaders differs between the editions of Rahlfs and Margolis. Margolis includes the majority reading και τους αρχοντας αυτων "and their rulers" which is missing from some MSS in the *E* and *L* groups. The decision by Margolis has wide MSS support but one must agree with Den Hertog that this is probably a later revision towards the MT.[8] Here, it is best to follow the text of Rahlfs, which reads the shortest version of the list of leaders with only three groups of leaders. The other Greek readings are well explained as expansions of this shorter list towards some form of the Hebrew list of leaders.

Several MSS from all groups change the singular ἔστησεν αὐτούς "he set them" to the plural εστησαν "they appeared" changing the verb and omitting αὐτούς. This is probably an early correction towards Hebrew, and both Rahlfs and Margolis have the singular in the main text. The omission of αὐτούς in some *L* MSS is probably secondary and stylistic, since the object of the verb is already mentioned before.

---

8 Den Hertog 1996, 55–56.

24:2 The OG translator probably employs the common and better equivalent κατοικέω "to dwell" for the Hebrew ישׁב "to dwell" (see, for example, Gen 11:2; Exod 12:40; Josh 15:63, 19:48, 21:43, 22:33). The *C* group and some other MSS secondarily changes it to παροικέω "to live in as a stranger", highlighting that they did not belong in that land. However, one could also argue that the translator used this verb, and that it was secondarily changed to a verb closer to the Hebrew. Therefore, while it is possible that either verb goes back to the OG, it is probable that in any case the Hebrew *Vorlage* of the OG reflected ישׁב.

MS 55 contains an interesting isolated addition "they served those which they did not know" at the end of the verse. This secondary addition could be inspired by Deut 29:26.

24:3 The OG text does not have an equivalent for the Hebrew כְּנָעַן "Canaan" as agreed by Rahlfs and Margolis. An equivalent for Canaan is secondarily added in several MSS in different groups, in the Armenian and Ethiopic translations, and the Syrohexapla, to bring the text closer to the Hebrew. The addition χανααν is therefore probably Hexaplaric.

24:4 There is a minor difference between the editions of Rahlfs and Margolis. Rahlfs follows the majority of the MSS with κληρονομῆσαι αὐτῷ "for him to inherit". Margolis follows a small minority of MSS with the reading κληρονομῆσαι αυτό (substituting ω with ο). According to Thackeray, the distinction between long and short vowels disappeared in Egypt quite early sometime in the second century BCE, and is mostly confined to illiterate documents. There is some confusion between ω and ο between different MSS.[9] Den Hertog notes that for the Hebrew אותו the Greek dative αὐτῷ would not be a precise equivalent. The equivalence אותו – αυτό, on the other hand, is unproblematic. Den Hertog further adds that a scribal error from αυτό to αὐτῷ is easier to explain than the other way around. This is due to the τῷ Ησαυ "to Esau" that could have sparked the error.[10] It is difficult to reliably deduce which is the earlier vowel. The variant is relatively minor, and does not influence the text in any major way. Thus, in this study the majority of the manuscripts, and the manuscripts that usually reflect better readings (*E*), are followed with the reading αὐτῷ.

24:5–13 In the historical summary of vv. 5–13, there is variation in the verbal personal forms between the MT (first-person, YHWH as subject) and OG (third-person,

---

9 Thackeray 1909, 89.
10 Den Hertog 1996, 43.

Joshua as subject). The third-person formulations have strong MSS support and clearly belong to the OG. Also, Rahlfs and Margolis agree that the third-person formulation runs throughout the OG text of 5–13. There are only sporadic corrections to a first-person formulation in some MSS. These are presented in more detail in section 3.2.2.

24:5 Margolis omits κύριος "the Lord" after καὶ ἐπάταξεν "and he smote", a decision that is supported by B 19-426 55 15. It is probable that the omission of κύριος in these MSS is a secondary approximation towards the MT.[11] At this point, B is problematic. In addition to this omission, the verbal form is peculiar. The reading of B from the hand of the original scribe was the third-person plural επαταξαν "and they smote", and it has been later corrected towards the Hebrew first-person singular επαταξα "and I smote". B also reads the next verb ἐποίησεν "he did" in the third-person plural. The probable OG reading ἐπάταξεν κύριος "and the Lord smote" is attested in almost all the remaining MSS in all the groups.

The OG of Josh 24:5 read ἐν σημείοις οἷς ἐποίησεν ἐν αὐτοῖς "with the miracles that he did in their midst". The editions of Rahlfs or Margolis do not include the "miracles" in the OG. Contrary to their editions, ἐν σημείοις "with miracles" should be included in the OG. It is the reading furthest away from the MT and is supported by most MSS including Old Latin. The secondary omission of "miracles" can be explained as a later correction towards the proto-MT text. This earliest Greek reading should probably be seen as a translation of a different Hebrew *Vorlage* reading ויגף יהוה את מצרים באתות אשר עשה.[12] In addition, Rahlfs and Margolis disagree whether the second ἐν-preposition should be included in the OG. Margolis reads it in his OG, however Rahlfs omits it. Both the presence and omission of the second ἐν is attested in the *E* group. On top of that, excluding MSS 44 82 509-72, it is present in all the other Greek MSS and all the daughter translations. Its secondary omission is probably due do *parablepsis* (ἐν οἷς ἐποίησεν ἐν αὐτοῖς). In Josh 9:16, the OG translator translated בְּקִרְבּוֹ with ἐν αὐτοῖς. Here one should therefore follow the decision by Margolis and include it in the OG.[13]

---

[11] Den Hertog 1996, 51.
[12] Boling & Wright (1982, 530) agree, and propose that ἐν οἷς in the B-text probably reflects באשר, which became כאשר in the MT through a confusion between ב and כ in the copying process. An alternative explanation for the evidence would be that "miracles" was secondarily added as part of a Greek revision. However, a search of the variants in the Greek MSS reveals that there are no other similar additions in the whole book of Joshua. Furthermore, a reviser would not have had a plausible reason to make the addition, since the word is not attested in the Hebrew text and the text is understandable without the explicit mention of the miracles.
[13] Thus also Den Hertog 1996, 51.

At the beginning of the verse, Margolis gives a half-equivalent for the Hebrew reading: και απεστειλα τον Μωυσην "and I sent Moses". This reading is not attested in any MS, and is a conjectural emendation that should be forgotten.[14] The OG did not have an equivalent for וָאֶשְׁלַח אֶת־מֹשֶׁה וְאֶת־אַהֲרֹן "and I sent Moses and Aaron", as evidenced by all the Greek MSS.

24:6 The majority of the MSS begin the verse with τοὺς πατέρας ἡμῶν "our fathers", which probably does not belong to the OG text, as Rahlfs also concluded. Almost all the C MSS omit it. It is probably an early revision towards the MT וָאוֹצִיא אֶת־אֲבוֹתֵיכֶם missing from the OG.[15] It might have originated as a marginal correction. Some manuscripts even add an equivalent (και εξηγαγον) for the Hebrew וָאוֹצִיא, revising the text even further.

24:7 The L MSS 75-106-134 revise the first-person ἀνεβοήσαμεν "we cried" to the third-person plural ανεβοησαν "they cried", in line with the Hebrew וַיִּצְעֲקוּ "they cried" that probably refers to the fathers mentioned in the last verse. Margolis considers this reading to be OG. The more probable OG reading ἀνεβοήσαμεν retains a sudden change into the first-person in the verse 24:7a, which is smoothened out in the MT. This problem will be discussed in further detail in section 3.2.2.

24:8 In verse 8, the Hebrew text reads וַיִּלָּחֲמוּ אִתְּכֶם "and they fought against you". Rahlfs reads the equivalent καὶ παρετάξαντο ὑμῖν as OG while Margolis omits it. The decision of Margolis to omit the phrase is supported only by the three MSS B-129 55. The reading presented in Rahlfs, on the other hand, is witnessed by the majority of the Greek MSS from all groups and all the daughter translations. While one could argue that καὶ παρετάξαντο ὑμῖν was missing from the OG and later filled in as an approximation towards the Hebrew, its omission in the few MSS can simply be explained as a scribal error due to the repeating καὶ παρ- beginnings.

The matter is further complicated by the presence of the reading καὶ παρετάξατο μωυσης "and Moses fought" in some witnesses (120 82 Aeth Co). Den Hertog argues that this is the correct OG reading, which has been secondarily revised towards the Hebrew text creating the reading καὶ παρετάξαντο ὑμῖν. The omission of the phrase in some of the E witnesses would then be due to a *homoioarcton* (καὶ παρετάξαντο ὑμῖν/-μωυσης καὶ παρέδωκεν).[16] However, the reading

---

14 In addition to this, Margolis presents some conjectures in the OG which, according to Den Hertog (1996, 79), reveals his preconceived notion that the translator was working with a Hebrew *Vorlage* quite similar to the MT.
15 Also Den Hertog 1996, 51.
16 Den Hertog 1996, 67.

καὶ παρετάξατο μωυσης, with only minor MSS support, more likely represents a later modification that inserts Moses into the verse due to the influence of the plus וָאֶשְׁלַח אֶת-מֹשֶׁה "and I sent Moses" in MT Josh 24:5. An argument from content, namely the notion that Moses is not mentioned anywhere else in the OG text of Josh 24, further corroborates the lateness of this reading and weakens the argument by Den Hertog. He is, however, probably right in assuming a *homoioarcton*, which was the reason that manuscripts B-129 55 are missing the phrase altogether.

Thus, the phrase καὶ παρετάξαντο ὑμῖν should probably be included in the OG. This decision is supported by the majority of the Greek MSS. However, this is not the only option, since it is also possible that B-129 55 preserve an original minus which was later secondarily filled out towards the MT. Due to the sparse manuscript support and the clear possibility of *homioarcton*, I find this solution less likely.[17]

24:9–10 In the Balaam episode several MSS from groups *L*, *C*, and *M* read the first-person plural pronoun (ἡμᾶς) instead of the second-person plural pronoun (ὑμᾶς) in all three occurrences: "– and he (Balak) sent and invited Balaam to curse us – and indeed he (Balaam) blessed us and (the Lord) rescued us out of their hands". Greenspoon has argued that in the phrase εὐλογίαν εὐλόγησεν ὑμᾶς "and indeed he blessed you" the second-person pronoun is a *Kaige* feature, since it is the reading closer to the MT and it is probably the reading of Theodotion as attested by MS 344. The OG, according to him, thus read εὐλογίαν εὐλόγησεν ἡμᾶς "and indeed he blessed us".[18] While this is a possible solution, the matter is much more complicated. Greenspoon does not note that variation between ὑμεῖς and ἡμεῖς is a much wider phenomenon in 24:6–14, as can be seen in my apparatus. In these verses, the pronoun is used 16 times. The B-text is most consistent in giving ἡμεῖς (13), however it also reads ὑμεῖς 3 times. The majority reading is always ὑμεῖς – but ἡμεῖς is also used once in 24:7. Different manuscripts have different combinations of these pronouns. I suspect that either the secondary addition τους πατερας ημων at the beginning of 24:6, or the surprising first-person plural verb at the beginning of 24:7 (ἀνεβοήσαμεν), may have motivated later changes from ὑμεῖς to ἡμεῖς. Therefore, Rahlfs was probably right to recognize the secondary ἡμεῖς readings in his edition, which are preserved in varying amounts of manuscripts in different instances. Nevertheless, Greenspoon presents compelling arguments for going against the majority reading in vv. 9–10, and there may have indeed been more variation between ὑμεῖς and ἡμεῖς in the OG. However,

---

[17] B and 129 belong to the *E*-group, which often preserves the OG. However, these witnesses are not free from scribal errors. MS 55 could either have derived the scribal error from these manuscripts or made it independently.

[18] Greenspoon 1983, 155–156.

since variation between these pronouns is such a common itacistic confusion in the transmission of Greek manuscripts, I would not dare to reconstruct a Hebrew *Vorlage* differing from the MT in the case of the pronouns. In any case, the variation between these pronouns will produce a major challenge for the editor of the *Göttingen* critical edition.

24:9 The OG did probably not have an equivalent for בֶּן־בְּעוֹר "the son of Beor" as agreed by most of the Greek MSS, Margolis, and Rahlfs. Several secondary equivalents, scattered among the different groups of MSS, are found in some MSS as a later revision towards the MT expression "the son of Beor".

24:10 MSS 44 52-57-85^txt-130-344 read that the Lord rescued you "from the hands of the enemies" (ἐκ χειρῶν ἐχθρῶν). This expression is also used in 1 Sam 10:1, 12:10–11. Due to the sparse manuscript support, it is likely a late secondary replacement aiming at making the Greek of the verse more diverse.

At the end of 24:10, the phrase καὶ παρέδωκεν αὐτούς, which is a plus in the OG missing from the MT, is problematic. If one assumes that it was already present in the *Vorlage* of the translator, the phrase would be odd in Hebrew. The hypothetical *Vorlage* ויתן אותם does not occur as such in the Hebrew Bible, but always in conjunction with a designation of where something is delivered. Usually something is delivered into someone's hands, as is the case in Josh 24:8 and 11. We are then most probably dealing with a Greek development.[19]

Rahlfs includes the phrase in the OG text. Margolis does not. The reading is attested in groups *E* and *O* while many Greek MSS together with La^100 omit it. One possible textual development is that the OG translator added the phrase to harmonize the defeating of the king of Moab with 24:8 and 11. These verses also end with YHWH delivering their enemies into the hands of the Israelites. Accordingly, Den Hertog would include the phrase in the OG arguing that the phrase is designed to unify the statements of YHWH delivering the various peoples into the hands of the Israelites.[20] If the phrase is OG, its omission in some MSS would be explained as a harmonization towards the Hebrew text. Another line would then be visible in the Armenian and Sahidic witnesses, which add "into your (our) hands" to make the phrase more explicit.

---

19 Koopmans (1990, 254–255) suggests carefully that it might be possible to assume a Hebrew Vorlage that read ואתן אותם בידכם which would indeed fit well into the context, which has the expression twice in 24:8 and 11. This reading is, however, not supported by any Greek MSS in full. Only the Armenian and Sahidic witnesses witness to the retroversion בידכם. Thus, we must state together with Koopmans that the "actual proof for a retroversion to a differing Hebrew Vorlage is tenuous here".
20 Den Hertog 1996, 38.

One should, however, be cautious in accepting this line of development. The decision by Margolis not to include the phrase in the OG is supported by indirect evidence. Den Hertog lists the other usages of the phrase παραδίδωμι in OG Joshua as follows.²¹

παραδίδωμι + acc + εἰς (τὰς) χεῖράς	9 occurrences (8:18; 10:8, 19, 30, 32; 21:44; 24:8, 11, 33)
παραδίδωμι + acc + attrib. ὑποχείριος	3 occurrences (6:2; 10:12; 11:8)
παραδίδωμι + acc + dat	3 occurrences (2:14; 6:16; 7:7)
παραδίδωμι + acc + ἐν χειρὶ	2 occurrences (2:24; 10:35)
παραδίδωμι + acc + attrib. + ἐναντίον	1 occurrence (11:6)

In the light of these occurrences, the usage of παραδίδωμι only with the accusative pronoun (αὐτούς) is unique in OG Joshua. Especially the prominent role of the usage παραδίδωμι + acc + εἰς (τὰς) χεῖράς in the near context (24:8, 11, 33) suggests against the conclusion that the reading goes back to the OG translator. When we appreciate the fidelity of the translator to his Hebrew *Vorlage* and his sensitivity in terms of producing good Greek, including the phrase καὶ παρέδωκεν αὐτούς in the OG seems improbable. If the OG indeed lacked the expression, its addition in some MSS can be explained as a secondary development aiming at aligning the verse closer with 24:8 and 11.

All things considered, we are dealing with two explanations whose probabilities fall in the 50/50 category. Therefore, the matter cannot be completely settled. In any case, there is probably not enough ground to postulate a differing Hebrew *Vorlage*. Whichever is the OG reading, the developments most probably took place in the Greek tradition.

24:11 κύριος "the Lord" is secondarily omitted in some Greek manuscripts including the main C witnesses and some O MSS as a correction towards the Hebrew text.

24:12 Manuscripts B-129 deviate from the majority reading ἐξέβαλεν, by giving εξαπεστειλεν. The verb ἐκβάλλω is the normal translation equivalent for גרש in the LXX, also in Josh 24:18. It is also here the most likely OG translation since εξαπεστειλεν can be explained as a secondary harmonization towards the first verb in the verse.

The most probable OG reading, differing from the Hebrew, is δώδεκα βασιλεῖς "twelve kings" as given by Rahlfs and Margolis. Manuscripts A 55 121 read δώδεκα

---

21 Den Hertog 1996, 38.

πολ(ε)ις "twelve cities", where "cities" is probably used as a euphemism for the inhabitants of the cities. The reading πολεις could be explained as secondarily deriving from the next verse, which also mentions "cities".[22] The reading δυο "two" in some MSS is a secondary revision towards the Hebrew text.

3.2.2 Evaluation between the OG and the MT

The concluding chapter of the book of Joshua describes the making of a covenant at a holy site (MT Shechem, OG Shiloh). The scene is narrated in the form of a dialogue between Joshua and the people, together with a description of ritual action related to the making of a covenant. The chapter has puzzled many scholars. There are notable differences between the OG and the MT in almost every verse, and they begin already in the first verse of the chapter. Contrary to many other studies focusing on Josh 24, a thorough evaluation of these differences should be the starting point for understanding the chapter.

Harmonization of the List of Leaders (v. 1)
Verse 24:1 begins with the notion that Joshua gathered all the tribes of Israel at the holy site. The list of the different groups of people that Joshua gathered varies between the OG and the MT. While the MT reads לְזִקְנֵי יִשְׂרָאֵל "the elders of Israel", the OG reads the third-person plural personal pronoun ("their elders") instead of יִשְׂרָאֵל "Israel", and the following וּלְרָאשָׁיו "and their heads" is missing. Whereas the MT has two groups of leaders at the beginning, the OG reads simply τοὺς πρεσβυτέρους αὐτῶν "their elders". Moreover, the next two groups of leaders are in a different order: while the OG reads "scribes" first and "judges" second, the MT reads "judges" first and "scribes" second. This is if τοὺς γραμματεῖς αὐτῶν is an equivalent for the וּלְשֹׁטְרָיו in the MT. Otherwise, there might be a different word (ספר) in the Hebrew *Vorlage*. In any case, the list in OG Joshua is shorter and in a different order.[23]

Although this textual variant is somewhat minor, it has an impact on one key literary and redaction critical issue, which is the relationship of Josh 24 and 23. Many have noted that verse 24:1 forms a link with verse 23:2, in which Joshua also gathers the Israelites and its ruling elite for a farewell speech. The dependence

---
22 Koopmans 1990, 256.
23 Many commentators note this difference, but leave the question of priority between the versions open. See, for example, Boling & Wright 1982, 530 and Soggin 1982, 220–223.

of these verses has been explained in both directions.²⁴ Accordingly, this link relates to the literary-critical question of how these different farewell speeches are to be situated and dated in relation to each other. Another important textual link present in Josh 24:1 is the relationship of this verse with Josh 8:33, in which the Israelites gather for another cultic ceremony and reading of the law. In this section I will, nevertheless, concentrate on the text-critical issues at hand, and deal with the literary and redaction critical questions more closely in section 4.

For text-critical purposes, it is necessary to present the similar lists of leaders in 8:33 and 23:2 in a table to see the differences and similarities between the versions. This will especially help in evaluating how the translator of OG Joshua handled the lists of leaders.

MT 8:33	OG 9:2d	MT 23:2	OG 23:2
וּזְקֵנָיו	πρεσβύτεροι αὐτῶν	לִזְקֵנָיו	καὶ τὴν γερουσίαν αὐτῶν
וְשֹׁטְרִים ╲╱	καὶ οἱ δικασταί	וּלְרָאשָׁיו	καὶ τοὺς ἄρχοντας αὐτῶν
וְשֹׁפְטָיו ╱╲	καὶ οἱ γραμματεῖς αὐτῶν	וּלְשֹׁפְטָיו ╲╱	καὶ τοὺς γραμματεῖς αὐτῶν
		וּלְשֹׁטְרָיו ╱╲	καὶ τοὺς δικαστάς

MT 24:1	OG 24:1
לְזִקְנֵי יִשְׂרָאֵל	τοὺς πρεσβυτέρους αὐτῶν
וּלְרָאשָׁיו	
וּלְשֹׁפְטָיו ╲╱	καὶ τοὺς γραμματεῖς αὐτῶν
וּלְשֹׁטְרָיו ╱╲	καὶ τοὺς δικαστὰς αὐτῶν

By comparing the lists of leaders, at least three important observations can be made. First, a striking similarity in the OG translations of the lists of leaders is that they all end with the same two groups of leaders, which are translated with the same Greek equivalents and transposed. These transpositions could be due to a different Hebrew *Vorlage* or, perhaps more likely, deliberate action on behalf of the Greek translator. Second, the comparison confirms that the translator deliberately translated the Hebrew שטר "official (or scribe, secretary)" with the Greek equivalent γραμματεύς "scribe". Thus, the *Vorlage* did not read סופר as one could speculate.²⁵ Third, and most strikingly, the OG Josh 24:1 would be an almost literal

---
24 See for example Rösel 2011, 364: "The editor who juxtaposed the two chapters introduced the leaders (elders, heads, judges, and officers) from 23:2 in 24:1; that way he showed that he was dealing with the same assembly."
25 In the OG of Deuteronomium, שטר is translated with the neologism γραμματοεισαγωγεύς "instructor" (cf. Deut. 1:15, 16:18, 29:9, 31:28). Otherwise, γραμματεύς is the stock rendering for שטר also in the Pentateuch (Auld 2005, 91).

3.2 Joshua 24:1–13: Text and Apparatus — 65

translation for MT Josh 8:33. This last point suggests that the translator of OG Josh 24:1 might have been working with a different *Vorlage* than the Hebrew text now present in MT Josh 24:1. If this shorter Hebrew *Vorlage* was the earlier form, the reading in MT Josh 24:1 could have emerged through editing in the proto-MT phase that sought to unify the list of leaders in Josh 24:1 with the list in 23:2. As one can observe, the lists of leaders in MT Josh 24:1 and 23:2 are strikingly similar.[26] Before exploring this solution further, however, I should review two other possibilities.

One could argue that the differences in the OG list of leaders were prompted by a scribal lapse. The only possible error here might he a *homoioarcton*. More specifically וּלְרָאשָׁיו "and their rulers" would have dropped out because of the similar word beginnings in the list (וּלְ). This explanation would then have to assume that "Israel" dropped out due to no visible reasons for a scribal mistake. A combination of two scribal lapses could then be regarded as one explanation for the difference. Such an explanation, however, is based on unlikely assumptions, since the mistakes would have been prompted only by minor features in the text.

The difference could also be explained as deliberate editing by the translator. According to Koopmans, in this case, there is not enough evidence to assume a different Hebrew *Vorlage* for OG Josh 24:1. He points out that the OG does not always give word-for-word equivalents for such lists of leaders, as is the case in Deut 29:9 and 31:28. Koopmans also points out the similar list in Josh 23:2 and its translation. There the translator seems to be flexible in translating the list, since he gives a free equivalent τὴν γερουσίαν αὐτῶν "and their council" for the Hebrew לְזִקְנָיו "and their elders". Here the order of the last two groups of people is also different, as in 24:1. He also mentions the similarities in Josh 8:33 (OG 9:2d) and implies that the translator could have wanted to keep the same order in every one of these lists.[27] Koopmans is right in taking into account the similar lists in Josh 23:2 and 8:33. It should be, however, noted that the fact that the translator uses γερουσία for elders is just a "further case of the translator exploiting Greek synonyms"[28] and does not necessarily corroborate the assumption that the translator would have otherwise modified the list. Furthermore, the translator does not seem to harmonize between the lists, since he is not consistent in the order of the lists. For example, the order of leaders in OG 23:2 and 24:1 is different than in OG 9:2d.

---

26 The only difference being that 24:1 has לְזִקְנֵי יִשְׂרָאֵל "the elders of Israel", while 23:2 has לְזְקֵנָיו "their elders".
27 Koopmans 1990, 251.
28 Auld 2005, 221.

One could also attribute the variants to stylistic reasons. Butler notes that "LXX avoids repetition by substituting 'their' for 'Israel'".²⁹ This is not a satisfactory explanation, since the same desire to avoid repetitions is not visible in the other translations (9:2d, 23:2). For the same reason, this stylistic explanation does not work even if attributed to a Hebrew editor. It is easier to explain that "Israel" in MT Josh 24:1 was added later, than it was secondarily omitted. Nielsen, for example, has argued that an editor might have wanted to specify that we are dealing with the elders of Israel and not the elders of Shechem.³⁰ This would also explain why a similar addition was not needed in Josh 23:2, where no place name is needed. This explanation is even stronger when one considers that very later editors have felt some uneasiness over the event taking place in Shechem.³¹

The best explanation for the textual variant explains how all the other variants came to be. If OG Josh 24:1 goes back to a different and earlier Hebrew *Vorlage* that read the concise list of leaders לזקניו ושטרים ושפריו together with Josh 8:33, the reading in MT Josh 24:1 can be explained as having secondarily emerged through harmonization with Josh 23:2. The addition of "Israel" was then made as a clarification due to the mention of Shechem. Therefore, the Hebrew *Vorlage* of the OG likely preserves an earlier link of Josh 24 with Josh 8:30–35 that is not as clear in the MT version. Moreover, the link of Josh 24 with Josh 23 is secondarily created, which is important since textual links between Josh 24 and Josh 23 are rare.³²

Finally, the concluding clause of the verse has an interesting variant at the end where the leaders in question are presented before God. In OG Josh, it is Joshua who sets the leaders in front of YHWH (καὶ ἔστησεν αὐτοὺς). In MT Joshua, the *hitpa'el* third-person masculine form of יצב makes it clear that the leaders set themselves, or appeared before YHWH (וַיִּתְיַצְּבוּ). Nielsen rightfully concludes that there is a different sense of hierarchy.³³ In the MT, the leaders themselves are active before the Lord, while in the OG Joshua has a more active role. One should not give too much meaning to this single variant, since it may have emerged from the hands of the translator. What makes this variant more interesting is, however, that in OG Josh 24:5–13 the events are narrated by Joshua while in the MT the Lord himself speaks. Taken together with this variant, one cannot escape the conclusion that in the OG text Joshua has a more active role. This aspect will be discussed further in this section.

---

29 Butler 1983, 263.
30 Nielsen 1955, 87.
31 See the next variant.
32 This observation is discussed further in section 4.2, focusing on the textual links of Josh 24 with other texts.
33 Nielsen 1955, 87.

Replacement of Shechem with Shiloh (vv. 1, 25)

The location of the covenant making is different between the OG and the MT. In OG Josh 24:1 and 25 the scene is situated in Shiloh (Σηλω), while in the MT the scene takes place at Shechem (שְׁכֶמָה). This seemingly small difference is not only text-critically important, but also a key component in many literary and redaction critical models, be it in those models which assume that the chapter echoes an ancient Shechemite covenant renewal tradition,[34] or those models that assume a continuation with a Pentateuchal E source to Josh 24,[35] or models that assume an early continuation from Josh 24 to 1 Sam 1.[36]

Most scholars who have written on this textual problem argue that Shechem is probably the earliest reading, and Shiloh is a later harmonization either in the OG translation or its Hebrew *Vorlage*.[37] An accidental change is not a plausible explanation, since the place name is different in two different verses. The possibility of a scribal mistake is also undermined by the presence of the plus ἐνώπιον τῆς σκηνῆς τοῦ θεοῦ Ἰσραήλ "before the tent of the God of Israel" at the end of OG 24:25, which is clearly connected with the location Shiloh (cf. Josh 18:1). Hence someone has intentionally changed the location either way.

The most obvious argument for the originality of Shechem is the connection with the oak tree mentioned in 24:26, which implies that the covenant making took place in Shechem rather than Shiloh, especially in the light of Gen 12:6, 35:4, and Judg 9:6 where the oak relates to Shechem. In addition, a late change from Shechem to Shiloh is easier to explain than the other way around. As Tov has rightly noted, Shechem fits poorly in the larger context and narrative of the book of Joshua, and it could have been seen as necessary to harmonize the name of the holy place. Shiloh plays an important role in crucial places in the book of Joshua (Josh 18:1; 21:2; 22:9, 12), which could have been a motive for such a harmonization.[38] Donald G. Schley voices the argument concisely, stating that this is a "scribal alteration, to bring Joshua 24 into conformity with the emphasis placed on Shiloh in Joshua 18–22".[39] The assumed secondary change from Shechem to Shiloh has also been characterized as a "Midrash-type exegesis", wanting to highlight that

---

34 Von Rad 1962, 16–17.
35 Wellhausen 1899, 133–134.
36 Knauf 2008, 17–22 and 2013, 120.
37 Even Holmes (1914, 8–9, 78), who otherwise prefers the OG in most of the variants. Also Nielsen 1955, 86–87; Auld 1979, 14; Greenspoon 1983, 80; Koopmans 1990, 259–261; Nelson 1997, 262; Tov 1999a, 161; Becker 2006, 143; Aurelius 2008, 107; Pakkala 2013, 197.
38 Tov 1999a, 161. Thus also Nelson 1997, 262.
39 Schley 1989, 225.

the location of the camp has not been changed since 18:1.⁴⁰ The argument from harmonization could, however, perhaps also be imagined the other way around. Namely, in 24:32 the bones of Joseph are buried at Shechem (according to all the textual witnesses) and, for example, a later addition of this burial notice to chapter 24 could have prompted a secondary harmonization of an earlier Shiloh to Shechem in a late stage of transmission of the text.⁴¹ The argument from harmonization is therefore not conclusive.

Since the argument from harmonization with the context is ambiguous, other arguments have also been introduced. Several scholars have proposed that the place name has been intentionally changed due to anti-Samaritan feelings.⁴² In the three first centuries BCE, the relationship with the Samaritans worsened, and it could have been important for a Hebrew editor to remove the idea that the holy center of the Samaritan community could have had such a prominent role in the history of Israel. Such a change would have more probably happened already in the Hebrew *Vorlage* than the Greek translation, since "the conflict with the Samaritans was more a Palestinian issue and would not have been crucial in Egypt where the Greek translation was made".⁴³ Two different lines of development could thus be discerned from the later textual material.⁴⁴ On the one hand, the Samaritan Joshua traditions futher highlight the role of Shechem by adding to verse 24:1 "at Mt. Gerizim" and to 24:25–26 "at the foot of Mt. Gerizim".⁴⁵ On the other hand, the *Vorlage* of OG replaces Shechem with Shiloh, and Josephus continues the animosity against the Samaritans by remaining silent about the cultic ceremonies attached to Josh 24, thus diminishing the Samaritans claim of importance.⁴⁶

It has also been argued that the change to Shiloh could have been made by the translator.⁴⁷ Koopmans has suggested that the change to Shiloh relates to a motive

---

40 Den Hertog 2011, 654. Thus also Becker 2006, 143.
41 Although the mention of Shechem here could also corroborate the originality of it in Josh 24, as noted by Pakkala 2013, 197.
42 Already Hollenberg 1876, 17. Also, for example, Nielsen 1955, 86; Knauf 2008, 195; Pakkala 2013, 197.
43 Pakkala 2013, 197.
44 As envisioned also by Hjelm 2008, 4–7.
45 Hjelm 2000, 241.
46 See Ant. 5.115–116. This interpretation by Hjelm (2008, 2–5) and others is corroborated by other instances in Josephus which downplay the importance of Shechem by omitting it from several passages: Ant. 1.157 / Gen 12:6–7; Ant. 2.200, 5.117–118 / Gen 50:25, Exod 13:19, Josh 24:29–33. See also Thornton 1998, 128: "The more the existence of a sanctuary in the Shechem area was ignored or forgotten, the easier it would be to dismiss Samaritan claims to its importance".
47 Holmes (1914, 8–9) notes that in this case the translator "made his only important deliberate alteration." Against the anti-Samaritan motive, Auld (2005, 221) notes that in Josh 21:20–21 Shechem is also mentioned as a city of priests in the OG. The mention is, however, in a list of cities,

of making verses 24:1, 25 more "innocuous" by clarifying some objectionable elements present in the MT. The translator would, first, be responsible for adding the plus ἐνώπιον τῆς σκηνῆς τοῦ θεοῦ Ἰσραήλ "before the tent of the God of Israel" at the end of verse 25. This addition would have brought the verse closer to verse 1 (καὶ ἔστησεν αὐτοὺς ἀπέναντι τοῦ θεοῦ "and set them before God"), and also resembles the next verse 26 (καὶ ἔστησεν αὐτὸν ... ἀπέναντι κυρίου "and set it ... before the Lord"). In this way, the setting of the gathering was transformed into a regular meeting before the tabernacle, and the more mysterious setting of the MT (Josh 24:26: בְּמִקְדַּשׁ יְהוָה "in the sanctuary of the Lord") was downplayed. The translator who wanted to transform the setting for more innocent reasons would then also be responsible for substituting Shechem with Shiloh. According to Koopmans, he took his information for this change from Josh 22:12, 29 where an altar of YHWH was situated in Shiloh before the sanctuary. There, the translator also employed the phrase ἐναντίον τῆς σκηνῆς αὐτοῦ "before his tent", which is close to the phrase in verse 25.[48] It is not clear why the change of the setting, postulated by Koopmans, should be attributed particularly to the OG translator and not to an editor behind the Hebrew *Vorlage*. The relationship with 22:12, 29 does not, specifically, give any more weight to the argument that the translator rather than a Hebrew editor would have been responsible for such a change. Since the translator of OG Joshua is generally faithful to the Hebrew *Vorlage* he is translating, the replacement of the location together with an addition is probably too much to expect from him.

Despite the majority opinion, it has also been argued that Shiloh was the earlier reading. Möhlenbrinck was one of the few early scholars to argue for the priority of Shiloh in his 1938 article. His argument is closely connected with his literary-critical model, in which it is assumed that in Josh 24 two different conquest traditions are intertwined. According to Möhlenbrinck, these two conquest traditions, that are revealed by the changes in person in Josh 24 – *Josuarezension* and *Jahwerezension* – were already connected in early times, before J and E were incorporated, when Shiloh was the more important holy sight. The description of Shiloh as the center for the Amphictyony (*Amphiktyoniemittelpunkt*) in Josh 22 is evidence for Shiloh's early provenance. Shiloh was changed to Shechem already at an early stage by the E source.[49] The overall argument of Möhlenbrinck lies on the assumption that one can discern various sources based only on changes in verbal person forms.[50] In addition, Möhlenbrinck assumes that a rather late textual variant

---

which does not have the same weight as identifying it as the site for the making of the covenant, which would explain why it was not changed.
48 Koopmans 1990, 259–260.
49 Möhlenbrinck 1938, 250–254.
50 For criticism against this see, for example, Koopmans 1990, 107–109 and Noort 1998, 208.

witnesses a change that happened quite early in the textual history, in a phase that we have no text-critical evidence for. While this is possible, the model gets quite complicated. For text-critical purposes one should, however, note that the relationship with Josh 22 can be used as an argument for both the priority of Shechem and Shiloh. On the one hand, the importance of Shiloh in Josh 22, as Möhlenbrinck argues, could be seen as evidence of its primacy also in Josh 24. On the other hand, Shiloh's importance in Josh 22 could have prompted a harmonization in Josh 24.

Lastly, the relationship with the Samaritans has also been used as an argument to evaluate Shiloh (OG) as the earlier reading. Knauf holds that Shiloh is the more inclusive reading and therefore earlier.[51] He argues that Shiloh was first chosen for Josh 24, since it is situated in a central location between Samaria and Judah. Therefore, the covenant ceremony was addressed to both the Judahite and the Samaritan people. A later change to Shechem, the capital of the Samaritans, should then be read as an anticipation of what will happen in 1 Kgs 12 where the sin of Jeroboam takes place at Shechem. The upcoming fall of Samaria and Israel is then in a subtle way inserted to Josh 24. Knauf dates this anti-Samaritan and pro-Hasmonean change of location to the late second century BCE conflicts.[52] The main textual argument of Knauf depends on the question of how Shechem was understood by the editor responsible for inserting it to Josh 24. Due to the several literary connections of Josh 24 with the Patriarchal stories,[53] it is more compelling to understand Shechem not only as a place name with negative connotations (1 Kgs 12), but also as a back-reference to the portrayal of Shechem as the first cult site in Genesis (Gen 33:20, 35:1–15). The connotations of Shechem are therefore ambiguous, and it is hard to say which connotations later editors emphasized. In addition, the argument relies on an assumed ancient geographical understanding that differed between Shechem and Shiloh; namely, that Shiloh was more understood as combining the Northern and Southern kingdoms than Shechem. Since we do not know how different writers understood the geographical aspects of these sites, it is probably better to look at the literary connotations of the place names. At the time of the change reflected in textual evidence in Josh 24:1, 25, Shechem most probably had a literary connotation of belonging to the Samaritans. However, one should keep in mind that different editors may have understood Shechem in diverse ways. This might have prompted various kinds

---

[51] Knauf put this hypothesis forth in his commentary (2008, 195), and reports it as a fact in several later instances. See, for example, Knauf 2013a, 120 and 2014, 146.
[52] Shiloh as the earlier location plays a prominent role in the compositional model of Knauf. Since Josh 24 and 1 Sam 1 both take place in Shiloh, this provides for Knauf evidence that they were originally connected, and that the book of Judges is a later insertion in between. See section 4.3.5.
[53] See section 4.2.

of editing in several stages. In any case, an anti-Samaritan change of Shechem to Shiloh is more probable than an anti-Samaritan change from Shiloh to Shechem.

Due to the ambiguity related to the place names of Shiloh and Shechem in the various traditions in the Hebrew Bible, it seems that one should be careful in suggesting a definite solution to the question of primacy between Shechem and Shiloh in Josh 24. Overall, the arguments seem to favor the solution that Shechem was the earlier reading, which has been changed to Shiloh due to harmonization with Josh 18–22 and anti-Samaritan motivations. This solution gains corroboration from the variant in Josh 24:26, which is discussed in section 3.3.2. Locating the covenant ceremony at Shechem can indeed likely be interpreted in the way that Blum does when he notes: "Concerning the key question: 'Who belongs to Israel?' Joshua 24 defends for its audience an inclusive position."[54] Such an inclusive position has later been transformed into a more exclusive one by reducing the importance of the Northern holy site in Shechem. Moreover, the assumed omission of the Samaritans from the chapter is a relatively good argument, since it can be corroborated by later lines of development in other texts (SamJosh and Josephus) and it gives an overall historical point of reference for such a change. Therefore, the small textual change is probably related to the tensions between the Samaritans and the Judeans in the last centuries before the Common Era.

In the light of this discussion, it is also more probable that the plus at the end of OG Josh 24:25 ἐνώπιον τῆς σκηνῆς τοῦ θεοῦ Ἰσραήλ "before the tent of the Lord of Israel" is a later addition in the Hebrew *Vorlage* of the OG.[55] The variant is closely connected with the place name Shiloh, where the tent of the Lord is initially erected (Josh 18:1ff.). The tent is also connected to Shiloh elsewhere in the Hebrew Bible (i.e. Ps 78:60). Thus, the addition was likely made when the location of the scene was changed.

The uncertainty related to the holy site in Josh 24 has implications for literary and redaction critical models. Namely, one should not use Shechem or Shiloh as a deciding argument in literary and redaction criticism, since the textual material is already difficult to evaluate. Therefore, in this instance it is clear that careful textual criticism should precede literary and redaction criticism.

Differences in the Exodus Remembrance (vv. 4–7)
Josh 24:2–13 presents a historical summary that recalls how YHWH has led his people all the way from the calling of Abraham to the Promised Land. The connections of this summary to other passages in the Hebrew Bible are

---

54 Blum 1997, 181–212.
55 See the text in section 3.3.

numerous. Especially Josh 24:6–7, in both versions, borrow central elements from Exod 14.[56] While the basic elements of the summary are similar both in the MT and the OG, there are several differences that occasionally relate to the meaning of the text and create connections with texts elsewhere in the Hebrew Bible. The most important of these differences will be dealt with in the rest of section 3.2.

When the differences between the MT and the OG related to the Exodus remembrance (Josh 24:4–7) are analyzed carefully, both textual traditions reveal connections with texts in the Hebrew Bible. These connections are gathered in the tables below.

MT readings in Josh 24:4–7	1 Sam 12
וָאֶשְׁלַח אֶת־מֹשֶׁה וְאֶת־אַהֲרֹן (v. 5, absent in OG)	וַיִּשְׁלַח יְהוָה אֶת־מֹשֶׁה וְאֶת־אַהֲרֹן (v. 8)
וָאוֹצִיא אֶת־אֲבוֹתֵיכֶם (v. 6, absent in OG)	וַיּוֹצִיאוּ אֶת־אֲבֹתֵיכֶם (v. 8)
וַיִּצְעֲקוּ אֶל־יְהוָה (v. 7, different verbal form in OG)	וַיִּזְעֲקוּ אֶל־יְהוָה (v. 10)
וַיֹּאמְרוּ עֵדִים (v. 22, absent in OG)	וַיֹּאמֶר עֵד (v. 5)

OG readings in Josh 24:4–7	MT Deut 26	OG Deut 26
καὶ ἐγένοντο ἐκεῖ εἰς ἔθνος μέγα καὶ πολὺ καὶ κραταιόν. καὶ ἐκάκωσαν αὐτοὺς οἱ Αἰγύπτιοι (v. 4–5, absent in MT)	וַיְהִי־שָׁם לְגוֹי גָּדוֹל עָצוּם וָרָב וַיָּרֵעוּ אֹתָנוּ הַמִּצְרִים (v. 5–6)	καὶ ἐγένετο ἐκεῖ εἰς ἔθνος μέγα καὶ πλῆθος πολὺ καὶ μέγα· καὶ ἐκάκωσαν ἡμᾶς οἱ Αἰγύπτιοι (v. 5–6)
καὶ ἀνεβοήσαμεν πρὸς κύριον (v. 7, different verbal form in the MT)	וַנִּצְעַק אֶל־יְהוָה	καὶ ἀνεβοήσαμεν πρὸς κύριον (v. 7)

It can hardly be a coincidence that four variant readings in the MT, within such a small verse range, correspond to elements in 1 Sam 12. Also, the long plus in the OG is probably dependent on Deut 26:5–6, since the wording is practically similar. Among these differences the first plusses are of great interest here. The first two plusses in the MT and the one long plus in the OG are both situated in points in the historical remembrance where the happenings in Egypt are explained. In terms of content, this might have been an attractive juncture for later

---

56 See section 4.2.2.

editing. I will next analyze these plusses separately, starting from the plusses in the MT and ending with the plus in the OG.

"And I sent Moses and Aaron" (MT)

The first plus in MT Josh 24:5 introduces Moses and Aaron to the historical summary, with the reading וָאֶשְׁלַח אֶת-מֹשֶׁה וְאֶת-אַהֲרֹן "I sent Moses and Aaron". They are not mentioned anywhere else in the whole chapter. The lack of the phrase in the OG would be hard to explain as an omission. To be more accurate, the motivations for a translator or a Hebrew editor behind the OG tradition to intentionally omit the mention of Moses and Aaron are difficult to imagine. An omission could, theoretically, be unintentional. Boling & Wright argue that an omission in the OG "reflects a haplography in a series of clauses, each beginning with the identical consonant cluster of the converted imperfect form."[57] This is a weak foundation for arguing a scribal mistake, since the similarities between the different words are rather minor.

Conversely, several reasons can be adduced for the addition of this phrase. Nielsen notes: "The reference to the role of Moses and Aaron is easily explained as the addition of a late traditionist; the omission would be far more difficult to account for, and the speech of Joshua contains no mention of the events of Sinai/Horeb or Kadesh, traditions with which Moses is (or has later become) closely connected."[58] An addition of Moses and Aaron could in this way relate to later concerns. Josh 24 deals with an important covenant, but Moses and Sinai are not mentioned. Thus, it could have been perceived as necessary to add Moses and Aaron to the chapter. Aurelius further notes that the phrase does not fit into the context of Josh 24:5, since the context implies that the Lord, not Moses or Aaron, himself acts as the savior.[59] Butler correctly notes that the phrase could represent a later phase in the tradition, when authority was more and more derived from Moses and Aaron.[60]

The intertextual connections with several late passages in the Hebrew Bible corroborate the secondary nature of the phrase in Josh 24:5. First, the connection with 1 Sam 12:8 seems clear in the light of the other connections already mentioned. Second, the same phrase is used, although in a much fuller form, in Mic 6:4 וָאֶשְׁלַח לְפָנֶיךָ אֶת-מֹשֶׁה אַהֲרֹן וּמִרְיָם "I sent before you Moses, Aaron, and Miriam"

---

[57] Boling & Wright 1982, 530.
[58] Nielsen 1955, 88.
[59] Aurelius 2008, 108.
[60] Butler 1983, 83. Also Carr (2011, 135–136) and Koopmans (1990, 246) regard the phrase as a secondary harmonization.

which might have also been in the mind of the proto-MT editor.⁶¹ Third, the late Psalm 105:26 reads שָׁלַח מֹשֶׁה עַבְדּוֹ אַהֲרֹן אֲשֶׁר בָּחַר-בּוֹ "he sent his servant Moses (and) Aaron whom he had chosen". There, however, we are probably dealing with a rather late text which seeks to derive authority from the figure of Moses.⁶²

The historical summary in 24:2–13 has been understood by many scholars as a confession of faith, *kerygma*, together with texts such as Deut 26:5–9 and 6:20–24.⁶³ Regardless of the speculations on the *Sitz im Leben* of such texts, one feature of a confession of faith is that it needs to meet the demands of the community proclaiming it. Accordingly, Nielsen notes that the addition of Moses and Aaron is an insertion that aims at doing just this. The addition was made in an age where the tradition of the heritage of the desert was stressed. The absence of Moses and Aaron in Josh 24 was felt especially strong in the theology of a community in which Exod 18–24 had a prominent place.⁶⁴ The addition of Moses and Aaron can be seen as aiming at aligning Josh 24 with the tradition in Exod 18–24. Such an alignment between Joshua and Exodus should probably be seen as a rather late editorial intrusion aiming at tightening the unity of several books in the Hebrew Bible.

"And I took your fathers" (MT)

The second addition in the MT at the beginning of 24:6 is וָאוֹצִיא אֶת-אֲבוֹתֵיכֶם "and I took your fathers". In the case of this addition, it has also been argued that it belongs to the earlier text. There are some feasible reasons for an editor behind the Hebrew *Vorlage* of OG to have removed it. Stylistically, it creates a somewhat disturbing repetition with the preceding phrase וְאַחַר הוֹצֵאתִי אֶתְכֶם "and afterwards I brought you out", which could have prompted an editor to omit it.⁶⁵

Rösel pursues this line of argumentation, and interprets the manuscript evidence of the LXX as further illuminating the smoothing out of redundancies. He points to the differing readings in the A and B text. B reads ἐξήγαγεν τοὺς πατέρας ἡμῶν ἐξ Αἰγύπτου "and he brought our fathers out of Egypt", omitting the reference ὑμᾶς "you". A-text reads ἐξήγαγεν ὑμᾶς ἐξ Αἰγύπτου "and he brought you out of Egypt", omitting the reference to the fathers. According to Rösel, this reveals that different editors behind these two different Greek readings deleted

---

61 Sperling (1987, 124) notes interestingly that in Deuteronomy nothing is said in this manner of Aaron's mission. He is only mentioned as the recipient of YHWH's anger (Deut 9:20), and then his death is reported (Deut 10:6; 32:50).
62 On Ps 105 and other Second Temple period "historical" psalms, see section 4.2.7.
63 This line of interpretation traces back to Von Rad 1938, 6ff.
64 Nielsen 1955, 93–94.
65 The repetitiousness is also discussed by Boling & Wright 1982, 263.

the redundancy of the earlier text in their own ways.⁶⁶ This, however, is not the whole explanation for the A and B readings. That "your fathers" was already lacking in the OG is the best solution, since it explains all the manuscript evidence as approximations towards the Hebrew.⁶⁷ The reading with "the fathers" in some *E* MSS is best explained as an early revision towards the Hebrew text. Other shorter revisions can also be found in other MSS. For example, some *O* manuscripts just add the verb και εξηγαγον "and I brought" whose equivalent is also found in the Hebrew text. Thus, while the LXX manuscript evidence might reveal that the later LXX revisers secondarily removed redundancies, it is likely that the OG was simply lacking the expression altogether.

The argument from repetitiousness can also be used in the other direction. The repetitiousness of the verse could also be a result of it being a secondary addition. Without the removal of the fathers, the text flows smoothly: "and afterwards I brought you out (6.) of Egypt". When the addition was made, the verb יצא was repeated to tie it together with the ending of the preceding verse. When arguing for the priority of the MT, Rösel noted that the redundancy is "the result of deliberate editing of this text".⁶⁸ I can agree with this statement, but against Rösel it seems that the OG has preserved a version in which this editing has not yet taken place. This is the simplest explanation and best explains all the manuscript evidence.

"And became there a great and populous and mighty nation" (OG)

As already mentioned, the plus OG Josh 24:4–5, missing from the MT, finds an almost word-for-word counterpart in Deut 26:5–6. It is likely that the plus was already present in the Hebrew *Vorlage* of the translator, since such large additions do not fit the translation profile of the OG Joshua translator.⁶⁹ If the translator of OG Josh 24 would have made the addition based on OG Deut 26:5–6, one would have to also explain the subtle differences in relation to OG Deut 26:5–6 which the context does not need.

There are two possibilities for the absence of the plus in the MT: either the reference to Deut 25:5–6 was secondarily added to the Hebrew *Vorlage* of the OG, or it was secondarily omitted from the proto-MT. As I will demonstrate below, the latter seems to be more probable, and the plus as preserved by the OG is probably original.

---

66 Rösel 2011, 367.
67 See section 3.2.1.
68 Rösel 2011, 367.
69 See section 2.3.2.

OG Josh 24:4	MT Deut 26:5	OG Deut 26:5
καὶ <u>ἐγένοντο</u> ἐκεῖ εἰς ἔθνος μέγα καὶ πολὺ καὶ <u>κραταιόν</u>	וַיְהִי־שָׁם לְגוֹי גָּדוֹל עָצוּם וָרָב	καὶ <u>ἐγένετο</u> ἐκεῖ εἰς ἔθνος μέγα καὶ πλῆθος πολὺ καὶ <u>μέγα</u>
and <u>*they* became</u> there a great nation mighty and populous.	and <u>he became</u> there a great nation mighty and populous.	and there <u>he became</u> a great nation, numerous, mighty and great.
OG Josh 24:5	**MT Deut 26:6**	**OG Deut 26:6**
καὶ ἐκάκωσαν <u>αὐτοὺς</u> οἱ Αἰγύπτιοι	וַיָּרֵעוּ <u>אֹתָנוּ</u> הַמִּצְרִים	καὶ ἐκάκωσαν <u>ἡμᾶς</u> οἱ Αἰγύπτιοι
and the Egyptians afflicted <u>them</u>	and the Egyptians afflicted <u>us</u>	and the Egyptians afflicted <u>us</u>

It could be argued that the plus is a secondary addition in the Hebrew *Vorlage* of the OG. The addition could be motivated by the desire to bring the Exodus remembrance in Josh 24 nearer to that in Deut 26. Tov has proposed that either the translator of OG Joshua or his *Vorlage* could have been influenced by the tradition of the Passover *Haggadah* in which Deut 26:5–8 and its exposition takes a central place.[70] As additional evidence, Tov points out to OG Josh 4:6, where the Hebrew plural בְּנֵיכֶם "your sons" is replaced with the singular ὁ υἱός σου "your son", which would also be an influence of the *Haggadah*.[71] Without having to make any judgments on the early history of the Passover *Haggadah*, it could be argued that Deut 26:5–9 could have been an important text for a Hebrew editor, and thus have motivated a secondary addition. However, this explanation is undermined by the fact that one would have to assume an earlier form of the text without the plus. Such a text would have first reported that Jacob and his sons went down to Egypt, and immediately after this that YHWH smote Egypt. The following text would then keep coming back to the Egyptians who were after the Israelites, without ever having mentioned the repression in Egypt. Hence, there would be a remarkable gap in the historical summary, which would be hard to maintain as the work of an author or redactor who knew Exodus traditions.[72]

---

[70] Tov 1999a, 162.

[71] Tov 1999a, 158. "When your children ask..." (MT Josh. 24:6) / "...when your son asks..." (OG Josh 24:6).

[72] One could argue that the presence of the gap was the reason for making the secondary addition in the Hebrew *Vorlage* of the OG in the first place. However, I find this unlikely, since we would have to assume an earlier author or redactor who knew Deut 26:5–9 and other Exodus traditions in the Hebrew Bible and still intentionally left a remarkable gap in the historical summary.

If the plus is considered original, it is hard to argue that the proto-MT editor would have intentionally omitted it. There is nothing polemic in the content of the plus. However, the omission of the plus could have well happened unintentionally. This was argued already by two early commentators Hollenberg and Holmes.[73] They argued convincingly that the translator of LXX Joshua read in his Hebrew *Vorlage* ויהי שם לעם גדול ורב וחזק וירעו אתם המצרים "and became there a great, populous, and mighty nation and the Egyptians afflicted them". The omission of this sentence either in the copying of the proto-MT or the translation process was, according to Holmes, due to *homoioteleuton* caused by repetition of Egypt in the Hebrew text.

וְיַעֲקֹב וּבָנָיו יָרְדוּ מִצְרָיִם
ויהי שם לעם גדול ורב וחזק וירעו אתם המצרים
וָאֶגֹּף אֶת־מִצְרַיִם

Indeed, it is likely that the sentence goes back to an earlier Hebrew text, since the historical summary presented in Josh 24:2–13 is also otherwise closely related with the historical summary in Deut 26:5–9. They belong to a similar literary level.[74] This is even more probable when one considers the variant analyzed next, which also witnesses to an original link between Josh 24 and Deut 26. Therefore, it is likely that the OG preserves here an original link with Deut 26:5–6 which was accidentally lost in the MT text.

Lastly, this plus is even more interesting since, in the OG, the verbal person of the speech is third-person singular, while the MT continues the speech as YHWH's first-person speech. This change in verbal person, however, is not as such connected to the additions in the MT and the OG. The additions are already made in the style of each textual tradition: the addition in the MT is in first-person and the addition in the OG in third-person. Thus, I will return to the change in person lastly in this section.

Smoothing Out Later Additions (vv. 4, 7)

In Josh 24:7, there is also another connection with Deut 26. This textual link is especially interesting, since it is apparent in the OG text but blurred out or almost completely absent in the MT. This second connection is revealed by a slight difference in the personal form of a verb, and could thus be easily overlooked. Whereas the OG version of 24:7 reads καὶ ἀνεβοήσαμεν ... μέσον ἡμῶν "and we cried ... between us", that is the first-person plural form and a first-person plural genitive pronoun, the MT has a reading with the third-person masculine plural and the

---

[73] Hollenberg 1876, 16; Holmes 1914, 78.
[74] For a closer analysis see section 4.2.7.

second-person masculine suffix בֵּינֵיכֶם ... וַיִּצְעֲקוּ "when they cried out ... between you".[75] Is this variation due to a different Hebrew *Vorlage*, or is it the work of the translator? If the OG reflects a different Hebrew *Vorlage*, it would have read ונצעק "and we cried out" as in Deut 26:7 and Num 20:16. In the Greek translation of the Pentateuch, in both Deut 26:7 and Num 20:16, the Hebrew first plural is translated faithfully with καὶ ἀνεβοήσαμεν "and we cried out". This strengthens the assumption that the translator of OG Joshua might have also be working with a different Hebrew *Vorlage*.

The originality of the verbal form in the OG is supported by the earlier observation that the MT version of the historical summary has been secondarily aligned with 1 Sam 12. The MT verbal form וַיִּצְעֲקוּ is similar to the verbal form in 1 Sam 12:8 וַיִּזְעֲקוּ. Thus, a secondary change of this verbal form in the proto-MT phase could be connected to the other secondary additions made on the basis of 1 Sam 12.

In addition, there are not many possible convincing motives for such a change in the Hebrew tradition behind the OG. Koopmans has argued that the change might be due to a desire to "avoid any possible misunderstanding that it was the Egyptians who cried out to Yahweh".[76] The continuation of the verse, however, makes it rather clear that the crying out to the Lord led to fatal consequences for the Egyptians ("...and he brought the sea upon them and covered them"). This makes it improbable that the translator or a Hebrew editor would have assumed that such a misunderstanding is possible. Moreover, if the translator or a Hebrew editor would have intentionally wanted to avoid confusion with the Egyptians, he could have also employed the expression οἱ πατέρες ὑμῶν "your fathers", which is used directly before in verse 24:6. This would have also avoided a stylistic problem, namely that the first-person plural verb form does not fit to the overall context. It launches a sudden flashback scene that lasts for just one sentence, in a passage in which the first-person plural form is not otherwise used.

It is this abrupt style exactly, created by the first-person verb form which is not connected with the overall use of verb forms in 24:5–13, that is the main reason it is probable that this connection with Deut 26 is primary. Thus, the OG should be preferred here as the earlier text, preserving the roughness created by earlier redaction that connected Josh 24 with an important ceremonial text in

---

[75] There are also other minor differences between these verses in the MT and the OG. While the MT has only "darkness" (מַאֲפֵל, *hapax legomenon*) between the Israelites and the Egyptians, the OG has "a cloud and darkness" (νεφέλην καὶ γνόφον). According to Tov (1999a, 157) the translator was not working with a different Vorlage (העון והחשך), but was influenced by Exod 14:20 (σκότος καὶ γνόφος). The double translation based on Exod 14:20 could, in fact, be an attempt to elaborate the hard *hapax legomenon* to the Greek readers who knew the Pentateuch.
[76] Koopmans 1990, 252.

Deut 26. The earlier OG text relates more closely to the stream of tradition preserved in Deut 26 and Num 20:15–16, whose characteristic is the phrase "and we cried to the Lord". The verb form utilized in MT Joshua can be explained as an intentional editorial intrusion to smoothen out the roughness created by the first-person verb form. The editor responsible for such smoothening could have taken his cue from Exod 14:10, which utilizes the same third-person plural verb (וַיִּצְעֲקוּ בְנֵי־יִשְׂרָאֵל אֶל־יְהוָה) "the Israelites cried out for YHWH").

In fact, here the textual problem might relate to further redactional issues. The scene with the fathers at the Sea of Reeds might altogether be a later addition to the historical summary and OG Josh might preserve this addition in a rougher form, as seen from the contextually surprising and unique verb form in the first-person plural: "And the Egyptians pursued after your fathers with chariots and horses to the Sea of Reeds. And **we cried** out to the Lord, and he gave a cloud and a darkness between us and the Egyptians, and he brought the sea upon them and covered them". The nature of this scene as a later insertion is corroborated by the context. It is not really connected to what follows: "...and your eyes saw what the Lord did in the land of Egypt." While the crying out to the Lord and the perishing of the Egyptians takes place at the Sea of Reeds, the following sentence refers to what the Lord did in Egypt, probably reminiscing the plagues and wonders that the Lord performed before the Pharaoh. This interpretation is strengthened by Deut 29:2–3, which has the same exact phrase ὅσα ἐποίησεν κύριος ἐν γῇ Αἰγύπτῳ "what the Lord did in the land of Egypt" connected with the plagues. Additional evidence for the loose connection between the gloss and the following sentence can be seen in some LXX manuscripts (44 52-53-57-85-130-344) that have a reading that can be explained as a later addition attempting to strengthen the loose connection. This reading bridges the gap between the two sentences by adding και εν τη ερημω "and in the wilderness".[77]

Thus, it seems more probable that the connection of OG Josh 24:7 with Deut 26:7, created by earlier redaction, should be evaluated as text-critically earlier.[78] This correlates with the original plus in OG Josh 24:4–5, dropped due to a scribal mistake in the MT, which is also dependent upon Deut 26. The stylistic problems created by this redaction have been secondarily removed in the proto-MT phase and some later LXX manuscripts as corrections towards the Hebrew text. Therefore, OG Joshua reveals such redactional influence of the book of Deuteronomy on the book of Joshua that could not be recognized if we only had the MT. It is a good example of how all the preserved textual evidence should be considered

---

[77] For a more thorough literary-critical argumentation see sections 4.3.3 and 5.3.3.
[78] Thus also Nielsen 1955, 88.

before building any models on the redaction history of a biblical book. In section 4, I will return to the repercussions of this and other similar textual cases for the redaction history of Josh 24.

Change of Speaker and Related Variants (vv. 5–13)

A larger group of variants in the historical summary of Josh 24:2–13 are the variant verbal forms. The MT and OG versions begin with the same verbal forms. Verse 24:2 has, in both versions, a double introduction: first, the speech of Joshua is introduced by stating that Joshua "said to all the people". Second, the speech of YHWH is introduced with the formula: "thus says the LORD, the God of Israel". Both the OG and the MT then continue with YHWH as the speaker (vv. 2–4), who recalls the events beginning with the calling of Abraham from beyond the river and ending with the captivity in Egypt. In vv. 5–13, however, the MT and OG start to differ. In the OG, the speaker is Joshua, who refers to YHWH with third-person singular verb forms. In the MT, divergently, YHWH continues as speaker, and refers to himself with first-person singular verb forms.

The differences concerning the verb person should probably not be evaluated individually, since these changes form a somewhat coherent pattern.[79] All the variant verbal forms are presented in the table below. At the beginning of verse 7, there are two exceptions to the variation, marked with an asterisk. As for the textual criticism of LXX, it has already been argued in the text-critical notes that the third-person verbal forms reflect the OG text differing from the MT first-person forms.[80] To illustrate how later LXX revisers sporadically changed the verbal form towards the Hebrew first-person form, the revisional readings in the Greek MSS are cited in the last column of the table.[81]

Verse	MT	OG	LXX MSS
24:5	וָאֶשְׁלַח	-	-
24:5	וָאֶגֹּף	καὶ ἐπάταξεν	επαταξα B[ab] 55 15
24:5	עָשִׂיתִי	ἐποίησεν	εποιησα 55 15

---

[79] Thus also Koopmans (1990, 252): "The differences in vss.5–13 with respect to grammatical person cannot be solved individually. It is therefore necessary to list all the differences in the hope that a pattern or trend will become visible."

[80] However, in Josh 24:8 the OG gives the second-person plural form (ἐξωλεθρεύσατε), while the MT is consistent in reading the first-person singular.

[81] In addition to the Greek MSS listed in the table, some of these revisional features are found in Ethiopic and in the Syrohexapla.

Verse	MT	OG	LXX MSS
24:5	הוֹצֵאתִי	ἐξήγαγεν	εξηγαγον 376-426 55 15
24:6	וָאוֹצִיא	-	και εξηγαγον 19-376-426
			και εξηγαγεν 120 W-82
			(cf. *eduxit* OL)
24:7*	וַיָּשֶׂם	καὶ ἔδωκεν	
24:7*	וַיָּבֵא	καὶ ἐπήγαγεν	
24:7	עָשִׂיתִי	ἐποίησεν	-
24:8	וָאָבִאָה	καὶ ἤγαγεν	ηγαγον 426 15
24:8	וָאֶתֵּן	καὶ παρέδωκεν	-
24:8	וָאַשְׁמִידֵם	ἐξωλεθρεύσατε	-
24:10	וְלֹא אָבִיתִי	καὶ οὐκ ἠθέλησεν	-
24:10	וָאַצֵּל	καὶ ἐξείλατο	-
24:11	וָאֶתֵּן	καὶ παρέδωκεν	-
24:12	וָאֶשְׁלַח	καὶ ἐξαπέστειλεν	-
24:13	וָאֶתֵּן	καὶ ἔδωκεν	-

Changes in the personal forms of verbs are sometimes used in literary criticism as one criterion for recognizing various sources behind texts. Numerous examples could be given. When Noth wanted to show that Josh 24 could not be unequivocally attributed to the E source but also included material from the J source, he invoked, among many other arguments, the sudden change of YHWH to third-person in verses 7 and 14.[82] In Perlitt's model of Joshua 24 as an early Deuteronomistic text, YHWH as speaker is central, as is seen in the term *Jahwerede* (vv. 2–13) he employs.[83] Möhlenbrinck used the changes in person as the most important argument for his source distinction.[84] The sudden change from the first-person speech of God to the third-person speech of Joshua has posed a problem for even recent literary critical models.[85] While the reliance on these kinds of arguments in literary criticism has been criticized altogether,[86] in this case one can observe textual evidence clearly showing that someone has intentionally changed the

---

[82] Noth 1930, 134; 1953, 140.
[83] Perlitt 1969, 241–243.
[84] Möhlenbrinck 1938, 250–254.
[85] Müller 2004, 219.
[86] Nielsen (1955, 90), for example, calls this "the weakest foundation imaginable" for literary criticism. See also Noort 1998, 208: "...die Personwechsel in der Rede, reicht für eine literarkritische Zweiteilung nicht aus."

verb persons. It is thus important to text-critically evaluate the two differing versions. Only after such an evaluation can the repercussions of the verbal person changes for literary and redaction criticism be further discussed.

The MT is almost completely consistent in giving the speech as *Jahwerede*, which means that YHWH is always the speaker and the active agent (excluding the minor exceptions at the beginning of verse 7). The OG alternates more between the personal forms: while OG Josh 24:2–4 contains a first-person speech by YHWH, in OG 24:5–13 YHWH is mostly referred to in the third-person; however, in the latter two exceptions are found in a second-person plural form of OG 24:8 and a first-person plural form at the beginning of OG 24:7. I will argue that this more alternating text in Josh 24:2–13, referring to YHWH both in the first and third-person, preserved by the OG, is earlier. The change to the first-person speech by YHWH in MT 24:5–13 is a later harmonization and unification of the text made in the proto-MT editing. Thus, the more complicated form of the OG is more original.

It is not probable that the OG translator would have made the change from first-person to third-person verb, from *Jahwerede* to *Josuarede*. Some scholars have tried to argue for this. Holmes argues that the translator may have changed the speaker out of a spirit of reverence.[87] This reason is not probable, since in the case of the only other *Jahwerede* in the book of Joshua, namely in the beginning of the book (Josh 1:2–9), the translator does not change the speaker. Both the MT and the OG read the speech as YHWH's speech in the first-person. Butler, furthermore, proposes that the OG tradition[88] made the change due to the abrupt change of person in the MT between verses 13 and 14. Basically, the OG tradition then transferred this abrupt change to verse 5.[89] This, in my opinion, is not really an argument for the priority of the MT, but more a relocation of the problem. It is likewise possible that an editor behind the MT was disturbed by the abrupt change of speaker in verse 5 (attested by the OG), smoothed it out, and transferred the change of speaker to verses 13 and 14. Overall, that the translator or an editor behind the Hebrew *Vorlage* of Josh 1:2–9 does not change the person of the speaker is an indication that there was no motivation to change a *Jahwerede* to a *Josuarede*. Conversely, that Joshua's speech at the end of the book, referring to the deity in the third-person, was later changed to a first-person YHWH-speech could be motivated by the fact that there already was a first-person speech at the beginning of the book. This would be a harmonization that brought the book into closer stylistic unity. Hence, when looked at as a whole, the arguments for a

---

[87] Holmes 1914, 78.
[88] Butler (1983, 263) does not specify whether it was the translator or an editor behind the Hebrew Vorlage.
[89] Butler 1983, 263.

change of person in the OG tradition are not as convincing as the arguments for a change in the proto-MT tradition.

An important analogy should also be drawn for the verbal personal form change with a similar change in Decalogue, as found in Exod 20. The Decalogue begins with direct first-person speech of YHWH (Exod 20:1–6), but shifts then to referring to YHWH in the third-person (Exod 20:7–17). The form of the text – beginning with a direct proclamation by YHWH and changing to a third-person reference – is thus same as preserved in the OG of Josh 24:2–13. This analogy is important, since one of the themes of both texts is the fidelity to the YHWH only. This analogy strengthens the claim that such a style could be original in Josh 24:3–15, and has been secondarily harmonized to the thoroughly first-person style.

The form of the speaker has some implications for the meaning and structure in some verses of the historical summary. Three such related variants are discussed next. They corroborate the overall argument that the OG preserves the earliest form of the verbs.

First, in verse 24:7 (marked with an asterisk in the table), both versions refer to YHWH in the third-person when the text reports that YHWH put a darkness between the Israelites and the Egyptians and made the sea come upon them. In the OG, this third person grammatical form does not stand out in the context of 24:5–13, since there YHWH is normally referred to in the third-person. It fits well with the overall style. In the MT, however, this is the only instance where YHWH is referred to in the third-person. If a late editor was responsible for editing 24:5–13 from the third-person use of verb forms in the OG to the consistent first-person formulations in the MT, this instance could be explained as a lapse. The beginning of verse 7 is difficult, and there is other editing going on as well, which could explain such a mistake in the editorial intrusion aiming at unifying the verbal forms.[90] Alternatively, the obvious connection of Josh 24:7 with Deut 26:7 may have been a reason to intentionally preserve the established third-person reference to YHWH. However, if the first-person references to YHWH in the MT were argued to be earlier, the discrepancies in the verse would be hard to explain: first, YHWH is mentioned in the third-person ("he put darkness") and suddenly, right after that, YHWH himself is the speaker ("and your eyes saw what I did to Egypt").[91]

---

[90] For the analysis of 24:7 see the last section.
[91] The discrepancy has been noted by many commentators and explained in different ways. Noth (1930, 134) used the sudden third-person to differentiate between J and E sources. The source distinction is problematic when based on such a vague argument. Boling & Wright (1982, 535) attributes a rhetoric function to the change in style: "To focus attention on the nub of the matter,

Second, at the end of verse 8 there is a difference in who destroys the Amorites. In the OG, the second-person plural form ἐξωλεθρεύσατε "you completely destroyed" is used giving the impression that it was the Israelites themselves who were successful in battle. In the MT, in line with the overall tendency of giving the speech as a *Jahwerede*, the first-person form וָאַשְׁמִידֵם "and I destroyed them" is used making it clear that it was YHWH himself who destroyed the Amorites. The question is, then, who was the earlier subject for the verb שמד "to destroy, exterminate": the people or YHWH?

The question relates to the concept of holy war and the ban (חרם). When the people are introduced as the subject of the ban, we are dealing more closely with the original concept of the cultic ban (Num 33:52; Deut 2:12, 23; 7:24; 33:27; Josh 9:24; 11:14, 20; 2 Sam 22:38; Ps 106:34). In the context of Joshua, this concept, namely the ban as a duty of the people, is voiced clearly in Josh 7:12: "I will be with you no more, unless you destroy (תַשְׁמִידוּ) the devoted things (הַחֵרֶם) from among you." In a later stage, the concept of the ban has been altered according to a tendency to attribute all the war activity to YHWH (Deut 2:21, 9:3, 31:3; 2 Kgs 21:9).[92] In the context of Joshua, the active role of YHWH in the ban is noteworthy in chapter 23 (vv. 9, 13, 16). In the case of verse 24:8, the textual evidence might then point to two distinct phases in the development of the concept of the ban. The OG would preserve the earlier version, since it understands the ban more traditionally as a duty of the people. In the proto-MT editing, the active role in the ban was changed to YHWH, a decision which might be influenced by a harmonization with the concept of the ban in Josh 23.

It should also be noted that in every other case in the historical summary of Josh 24:2–13 it is emphasized that the Lord is the active agent in leading the Israelites in the promised land. For example, in 24:12 the Lord drives the Amorites

---

the divine communique itself resorts to third-person description." This explanation could reveal how the editor (and reader) of the MT could have made sense of the sudden change, but does not help in evaluating the reading against the LXX.

One could also argue that the beginning of Josh 24:7 ("And they cried out to YHWH and he put darkness between you and the Egyptians, and he brought the sea upon them and covered them") is a secondary addition to a thoroughly first-person *Jahwerede* (MT). The roughness created by this addition would have then resulted in a harmonization to the third-person forms in the OG. However, this model seems inadequate, since OG Josh 24:2–4 is not presented in third-person forms. One would also assume that a harmonizing editor would change "they cried out" to "you cried out", since this is the standard form in the speech. However, the OG rewrites the beginning to "we cried out", which preserves the roughness of the text. To be sure, it is still possible that the beginning of 24:7 is a later addition to the text. Nevertheless, for some reason later editors do not seem to have sought to better integrate the addition into its present context.

92 Vetter 1976, 963–965.

before the Israelites, and it is emphasized that this did not happen "by your sword or by your bow". Therefore, it is not likely that a scribe or the translator would have secondarily changed the ending of Josh 24:8 so that the Israelites took on a more active role. It is more likely that later proto-MT scribes would have harmonized the verb to make it better fit the context.

Third, the case of Balaam has a distinctive character in the MT and the OG due to the different beginnings of Josh 24:10. In verse 9, in both the MT and the OG, the narration recalls how Balaam was summoned by the king of Moab to come down and launch an attack against Israel. In MT Josh 24:10, keeping in line with the overall style, YHWH himself states that he was not willing to listen to Balaam (וְלֹא אָבִיתִי לִשְׁמֹעַ לְבִלְעָם). Because of that, Balaam blesses the Israelites (וַיְבָרֶךְ בָּרוֹךְ אֶתְכֶם) and YHWH himself delivers the Israelites from the hands of Balaam (וָאַצִּל אֶתְכֶם מִיָּדוֹ). The beginning of 24:10 in the OG is quite different and, in addition to using the third-person form of YHWH, it does not mention Balaam at all (καὶ οὐκ ἠθέλησεν κύριος ὁ θεός σου ἀπολέσαι σε "and the Lord your God would not destroy you"). Therefore, it is the Lord who blesses the Israelites (καὶ εὐλογίαν εὐλόγησεν ὑμᾶς). Later, the OG is again consistent in using the third-person form of the Lord (ἐξείλατο ὑμᾶς ἐκ χειρῶν αὐτῶν "he rescued you out of their hands"), and it gives a plus (καὶ παρέδωκεν αὐτούς "and delivered them") at the end of the verse. The main difference in content is who carries out the blessing: Balaam (MT) or YHWH (OG).

The OG reading has been explained as resulting from a scribal error. The translator could have had a corrupted reading of לְבִלְעָם in his Hebrew *Vorlage*, and he could have interpreted it as an infinitive of בלע "to destroy". The infinitive לִשְׁמֹעַ "listened" would then have been omitted as useless.[93] This does not explain how a pronoun suffix would have been included in the reading and it does not, more importantly, explain the verse's whole variant reading, which is much more extensive than a mere misreading of Balaam. Greenspoon, for one, correctly notes: "This suggestion does not seem to explain adequately all of the features of the Greek here. For example, would we not expect the third-person plural noun rather than the second singular after the infinitive?"[94]

When evaluating the readings, it is important to note the connection with Deut 23:6. As seen in the table below, the connection cannot be explained by any simple means.

---

[93] This explanation originates from Hollenberg (1876, 19) and it is later adapted by Holmes (1914, 79) and Boling & Wright (1982, 531).
[94] Greenspoon 1983, 157.

MT Deut 23:6	OG Deut 23:6	MT Josh 24:10	OG Josh 24:10
וְלֹא־אָבָה יְהוָה אֱלֹהֶיךָ לִשְׁמֹעַ אֶל־בִּלְעָם	καὶ οὐκ ἠθέλησεν κύριος ὁ θεός σου εἰσακοῦσαι τοῦ Βαλααμ	וְלֹא אָבִיתִי לִשְׁמֹעַ לְבִלְעָם	καὶ οὐκ ἠθέλησεν κύριος ὁ θεός σου ἀπολέσαι σε
And refused the Lord your God to listen to Balaam	And refused the Lord your God to listen to Balaam	And I refused to listen to Balaam	And refused the Lord your God to destroy you

Overall, it is probably safe to assume that the reading in OG Josh 24:10 reflects a different *Vorlage* from the MT.[95] It has been, conversely, suggested that the translator would have had theological reasons to avoid translating לִשְׁמֹעַ לְבִלְעָם "to listen to Balaam" literally, since the phrase implies that the Lord could be manipulated by the voice of man.[96] One could also argue that a Hebrew editor was concerned with this, and was responsible with this change. In any case, this is a hard argument to pursue when one considers both the observation that this would be an isolated case in the book of Joshua and that the OG translator of Deuteronomy had no problem with the notion that Balaam tried to manipulate the Lord. In the book of Joshua, it is merely an attempt to manipulate the Lord, and the text specifically states that it failed. Thus, a theologically motivated translator or even a Hebrew editor is not probable here.

The beginning of the verse in OG Josh 24:10 is like the beginning in Deut 23:6. This similarity raises the possibility that the OG text preserves an earlier link with Deut 23:6 which was lost in the MT when the personal form of the speech was harmonized to first-person. The presence of ἀπολέσαι "to destroy", which probably goes back to the Hebrew verb שמד "to destroy" (as in Josh 11:14), indicates that there might have originally been parallelism with verse 24:8 here. This idea of parallelism is strengthened by the presence of καὶ παρέδωκεν αὐτούς "and he delivered them" in both verses. Such parallelism preserved by the Greek text could then corroborate the assumption that the OG text is earlier in Josh 24:10.[97]

---

[95] Thus also Auld 2005, 223.
[96] Butler 1983, 264.
[97] This earlier parallelism preserved in the OG text was noted by Koopmans 1990, 254–255. He even speculates that the Greek ἐκ χειρῶν αὐτῶν καὶ παρέδωκεν αὐτούς "out of their hands and delivered them" in verse 24:10 might be a free rendition of the Hebrew וָאֶתֵּן אוֹתָם בְּיֶדְכֶם "handed them over into your hands", a doublet of the same phrase found in verse 24:8. Another explanation could be, as given by Nielsen (1955, 89), that the ἀπολέσαι reflects a misreading of לשמע with לשמד. In this case, it would be a remarkable coincidence that the misreading creates parallelism with the preceding context. In any case, Nielsen also contends that the change of person is here more easily explained from third-person singular to first-person singular.

The argument that the reading in MT is secondary is further strengthened by the usage of the ל-participle after the infinitive construct לִשְׁמֹעַ to indicate the object. This is an unusual grammatical form attested elsewhere only in Lev 26:21, Judg 19:25, and 2 Sam 13:16, and in all of those cases the object is a personal pronoun. That אֶל indicates the object, as is the case in Deut 23:6, with לִשְׁמֹעַ is certainly more common (1 Kings 8:28, 29; Jer 35:13; Ezek 3:7; 20:8; Neh 1:6; 2Chr 6:19). The unusual form לִשְׁמֹעַ לְבִלְעָם could be easily explained as secondarily grown out of the near context in which לְבִלְעָם is used (Josh 24:9). Therefore, it is most likely that in Josh 24:10 the OG also preserves the earliest reading, which was changed due to the overarching change of verbs to first-person in the proto-MT editing.

Finally, a recurring variant should also be mentioned here: as is fitting to the third-person formulation, the OG has κύριος "the Lord" as a plus in four verses (5, 7, 8, 11). If one were to evaluate this variant apart from the overall tendency of changing the personal form, one could judge it either as primary or secondary. The OG text could have made this addition in four places to support the change from the first-person to the third-person. Conversely, the four mentions of κύριος, translated from יְהוָה in an earlier Hebrew text, could have been removed in the proto-MT editing when the personal form was changed from the third to the first person. Thus, the evaluation of these plusses is dependent upon the evaluation of the larger variant of changing the personal form. In the light of the preceding analysis, it seems most probable that these plusses were present in the earlier Hebrew text, and were omitted when the personal form was changed in the proto-MT editing.

To conclude, that the earlier verbal form used in 24:5–13 was the third-person singular masculine (OG) and not the first-person singular masculine (MT) is corroborated by several arguments. In the historical summary of Josh 24:2–13, the OG preserves the earlier version with more complicated variation between different verbal forms. These changes were smoothened out in the proto-MT editing.

Thus, it is more plausible that the speech was secondarily changed to be a thorough *Jahwerede*. This notion is closely related to the changing genre of the text. In the earlier textual form, preserved in the OG, the historical summary was modeled as a confession of faith – a *credo*.[98] Speaking of the deeds of YHWH in a third-person formulation was in line with other confessions of faith such as Deut 26:5–10 and 6:20–24, with which Josh 24:5–13 has close affinities in the earlier textual form. When the earlier text is labeled as a confession of faith, however, one does not have to agree with the form-critical historical presuppositions, or a supposed *Sitz im Leben* of such textual forms. We are merely dealing with a

---

98 The nature of the text as a confession of faith was first formulated by Von Rad (1938). The idea has been further developed by Nielsen (1955, 92–98).

literary phenomenon, which can be illuminated in terms of textual connections between different texts in the Hebrew Bible. In the later proto-MT form of the text, the genre of a confession of faith was transformed into prophetic speech in which Joshua is the medium through which YHWH himself speaks. In this way, the text was made stylistically more coherent, but the earlier textual genre was lost.

The conclusion that the proto-MT editor changed the speech from a third-person formulation to a direct first-person address is important, since we know of a similar phenomenon from the Temple Scroll. In many instances the Temple Scroll quotes passages from the Pentateuch, but changes the form of the speech to a direct *Jahwerede*. The change even goes hand in hand with the omission of the name of YHWH, as was the case in Josh 24:5–13.[99] Therefore, there is evidence for this scribal technique of rewriting both in the biblical and non-biblical sources, highlighting that the editorial techniques utilized by Second Temple scribes do not conform to an anachronistic canonical classification of texts. I will resume discussing aspects of this editorial technique in section 5.5.

Rearrangement of the List of Defeated Nations (v. 11)

In verse 11, the list of the various nations that Joshua defeated west of Jordan differs between the MT and the OG.[100] This is the case in all such lists in the book of Joshua (Josh 3:10, 9:1, 11:3, 12:8). The nations given in both lists are the same, but their order is different. Both versions give the Amorites first. This is understandable since they are dealt with before and after the list. The next two people (Perizzites and Canaanites) are given in a transposed order. The key difference between the lists seems to reflect a transposition: the OG gives Hivites and Jebusites fourth and fifth while the MT situates them last. The differences are illustrated in the table below.

---

[99] See, for example, VanderKam 2010, 193–194, who presents as an illustrating example. Deut 17:14–15a reads: "When you have come into the land that the Lord your God is giving you, and have taken possession of it and settled in it, and you say, 'I will set a king over me, like all the nations that are around me,' you may indeed set over you a king whom the Lord your God will choose." (NRSV) This is rendered as first-person divine speech in 11QTa 56.12–14: "When you enter the land which I give you, take possession of it, dwell in it and say, 'I will appoint a king over me as do all the nations around me!', you may surely appoint over you the king whom I will choose."

[100] There is also a semantic difference between the Hebrew בַּעֲלֵי־יְרִיחוֹ "the lord of Jericho" and the Greek οἱ κατοικοῦντες Ιεριχω "the inhabitants of Jericho". As Butler (1983, 264) and Koopmans (1990, 255) note, the Greek rendering might reflect an avoidance of using the word "Baal". If this is the case, the difference might go back to a different Hebrew *Vorlage*. However, this difference might also simply be caused by a free translational choice.

3.2 Joshua 24:1–13: Text and Apparatus

MT Josh 24:11	OG Josh 24:11
הָאֱמֹרִי	ὁ Ἀμορραῖος
וְהַפְּרִזִּי	καὶ ὁ Χαναναῖος
וְהַכְּנַעֲנִי	καὶ ὁ Φερεζαῖος
	καὶ ὁ Εὐαῖος
	καὶ ὁ Ἰεβουσαῖος
וְהַחִתִּי	καὶ ὁ Χετταῖος
וְהַגִּרְגָּשִׁי	καὶ ὁ Γεργεσαῖος,
הַחִוִּי	
וְהַיְבוּסִי	

It is difficult to reliably evaluate which version preserves the earliest reading of the list of the seven nations in the context of Josh 24:11. Some scholars mention the differences between the lists but leave the question of text-critical priority open.[101] When one compares all of the similar lists of nations in the book of Joshua and elsewhere (e.g. Gen 15:19–21, Exod 23:23, Deut 7:1, Judg 3:5), no thoroughgoing patterns arise.[102] However, one interesting observation is that Hivites and Jebusites are often mentioned last in such lists. This is true also for the most important parallel of Josh 24:11–12 in Exod 23:23.[103] Based on this observation, I would cautiously suggest that the list of the seven leaders in MT Josh 24:11 is harmonized towards the more usual form of the list, which mentions the Hivites and Jebusites last. In the light of many other harmonizations in Josh 24 towards the Pentateuch, this explanation is plausible. It is then possible that the OG preserves the earlier version, which was made to conform more closely to its parallels through a transposition of Hivites and Jebusites.

Other Minor Variants

In Josh 24:3, the MT reads as a plus כְּנָעַן "Canaan", which is either an omission in the OG tradition or an addition in the proto-MT editing. It is possible that it is

---

[101] Koopmans 1990, 255: "The reason for the different order is a mystery - -." Also, Nielsen 1955, 89 and Butler 1983, 264.
[102] "the land of the Kenites, the Kenizzites, the Kadmonites, the Hittites, the Perizzites, the Rephaim, the Amorites, the Canaanites, the Girgashites, and the Jebusites" (Gen 15:19–21 [NRSV]); "When my angel goes in front of you, and brings you to the Amorites, the Hittites, the Perizzites, the Canaanites, the Hivites, and the Jebusites, and I blot them out" (Exod 23:23 [NRSV]); "When the Lord your God brings you into the land that you are about to enter and occupy, and he clears away many nations before you—the Hittites, the Girgashites, the Amorites, the Canaanites, the Perizzites, the Hivites, and the Jebusites, seven nations mightier and more numerous than you" (Deut 7:1 [NRSV]); "So the Israelites lived among the Canaanites, the Hittites, the Amorites, the Perizzites, the Hivites, and the Jebusites" (Judg 3:5 [NRSV]).
[103] It is the most important parallel, since they also share other material, most prominently the "hornets". See the discussion below.

simply an unintentional omission made in the Hebrew *Vorlage* of the OG, or during the translation process. The omission could be explained as a *homoioteleuton* between the similar looking words אֶרֶץ and וָאֶרֶב. This explanation is weakened by the presence of a ו in the latter word. It is true, as Auld notes, that the lack of Canaan in the OG does affect the meaning of the verse. The absence of Canaan could be explained as an amplification, showing that the divine protection of Abraham extended further than just the land of Canaan, from Mesopotamia to Egypt.[104] On the other hand, the addition of Canaan in the MT could be explained as a later addition making the historical summary more accurate. Some scholars, accordingly, have explained the addition as a late interpretation using familiar idiomatic language.[105] This simple explanation is more probable than an intentional omission in the OG, since it would entail more elaborate assumptions. The phrase אֶרֶץ כְּנַעַן "the Land of Canaan" is well attested elsewhere in the book of Joshua (Josh 5:12; 14:1; 21:2; 22:9–11, 32), and could well be a harmonization towards this idiomatic phrase.[106] Text-critical preference should thus be given to the OG.

The omission of וָאֶתֵּן "and I gave" in OG Josh 24:4 is probably stylistic in nature, as has been concluded by several scholars.[107] The phrase may have been lost in the translation. Its originality is corroborated by the notion that it creates parallelism in the verse together with the other וָאֶתֵּן.[108]

In Josh 24:6, the OG reads εἰς τὴν θάλασσαν τὴν ἐρυθράν "to the Red Sea", while the MT does not have the name of the specific sea but only reads הַיָּמָּה "the sea". It is clear in both versions which sea is meant. It is likely that a Hebrew scribe, or perhaps the OG translator, wanted to make the reference explicit and secondarily added "Red" (or "Reeds", if in Hebrew) to the text. This addition was motivated by the explicit mention of the Sea of Reeds at the end of the verse. Thus, the MT is the earlier text in this instance.

In Josh 24:9, the MT has as a plus the specification "son of Beor" בֶּן־בְּעוֹר to the name Balaam. MT has two similar plusses in 22:31–32, where it adds the title "son of Eleazar" בֶּן־אֶלְעָזָר to the name Phinehas. These represent secondary complementation of well-known names and titles.[109] There is no basis to argue for a scribal error or intentional omission.

---

[104] Auld 2005, 222. Thus also Nielsen 1955, 87: "...the omission in LXX ... leaves the impression that God conducted Abraham over the whole earth."
[105] Butler 1983, 263. Nelson (1997, 262) does not evaluate the reading, but considers it to be secondary and prints it in parenthesis.
[106] Holmes (1914, 78) notes that the phrase "land of Canaan" is priestly.
[107] Holmes 1914, 78; Nielsen 1955, 87; Butler 1983, 263.
[108] Koopmans 1990, 251.
[109] Thus also Butler 1983, 264.

3.2 Joshua 24:1–13: Text and Apparatus — 91

Verse 24:12 recalls how the הַצִּרְעָה "hornets, terror"[110] sent by the Lord drove the Amorite kings before the Israelites. The MT text apparently refers to the Sihon and Og tradition by reading the two kings of Amorites (שְׁנֵי מַלְכֵי הָאֱמֹרִי). The basic problem, noted by several scholars, is that this reference to Sihon and Og does not chronologically fit the context.[111] The territories of Sihon and Og were Transjordanian. Conversely, in Josh 24 the reference is located after the Israelites have already crossed the Jordan and defeated the Cisjordanian tribes. The OG has a variant δώδεκα βασιλεῖς τῶν Αμορραίων "the twelve kings of the Amorites" which is a novelty not attested anywhere else in the Hebrew Bible.[112] Even though "twelve" does not accord with any of the amounts of the defeated kings of cities in the earlier chapter in Joshua, the OG reading can be explained as an attempt to make sense of the chronologically incorrect reference to two Amorite kings. A scribe transmitting the Hebrew *Vorlage* of the OG could have noticed that number two does not make sense in a Cisjordanian context, and have added a "tens" digit to the text. It is also possible that the OG translator decided to use the number twelve in a metaphorical sense to specify that we are dealing with the numerous Cisjordanian tribes, and not Sihon and Og.[113] In any case, the OG reading is probably secondary, and can be explained as a later correction trying to make sense of the peculiar reference to Sihon and Og.[114] This explanation is further corroborated by the presence of the reading εννεα και εικοσι πολεις "twenty nine cities" in manuscript 55, which can also be seen as an attempt to modify the Transjordanian reference to a Cisjordanian one.[115]

---

[110] The meaning of צִרְעָה is unclear. In the OG, it is rendered as hornet (σφηκία) in all its three occurrences (Exod 23:28, Deut 7:20, Josh 24:12).

[111] Edelman 1991, 281 and Rösel 2011, 368–369. It is not necessary to assume with Soggin (1972, 171) that the two kings refer to an otherwise unknown incident involving two Cisjordanian Amorite kings.

[112] Auld 2005, 223.

[113] Edelman 1991, 281–282.

[114] Noth (1953, 135) explains the variant quite similarly. He perceives verse 12a, with the reference to the two Amorite kings, as secondary. Since the reference does not fit the context, the LXX tradition transformed the reference to a very open reference to the narratives in chapters 1–12.

[115] Edelmann (1991, 279–286) suggests a conjectural reading to explain the odd reference to the Amorite kings in the MT. She proposes that the Hebrew text originally read: "the kings of the Amorites are swept away, but not by your sword and not by your bow". The original Hebrew word, instead of שְׁנֵי, was נשאים that is the masculine plural participle form of the verb נשא. The number two in the MT text came about through a rather multiphase corruption: the final root consonant א was lost, the two remaining root consonants were transposed, and the final ם was dropped out. Edelmann's proposal is intriguing but unnecessarily complicated. Edelmann also proposes other candidates for the original verb, which reveals the subjectivity of proposing a conjectural reading to remove the obscure reference to Sihon and Og.

3.3 Joshua 24:14–27: Text and Apparatus

MT (*BHS*)	OG
¹⁴ וְעַתָּה יְראוּ אֶת־יְהוָה	¹⁴ καὶ νῦν φοβήθητε κύριον
וְעִבְדוּ אֹתוֹ בְּתָמִים	καὶ λατρεύσατε αὐτῷ ἐν εὐθύτητι
וּבֶאֱמֶת	καὶ ἐν δικαιοσύνῃ
וְהָסִירוּ אֶת־אֱלֹהִים	καὶ περιέλεσθε τοὺς θεοὺς ⟨τοὺς ἀλλοτρίους,⟩
אֲשֶׁר עָבְדוּ אֲבוֹתֵיכֶם	οἷς ἐλάτρευσαν οἱ πατέρες ὑμῶν
בְּעֵבֶר הַנָּהָר	ἐν τῷ πέραν τοῦ ποταμοῦ
וּבְמִצְרַיִם	καὶ ἐν Αἰγύπτῳ,
וְעִבְדוּ אֶת־יְהוָה	καὶ λατρεύετε κυρίῳ.

"And now fear YHWH	"And now fear the Lord
and serve him in sincerity	and serve him in straightness
and in faithfulness.	and in righteousness.
And put away the gods	And put away the ⟨foreign⟩ gods
that your fathers served	that your fathers served
beyond the river	beyond the river
and in Egypt,	and in Egypt,
and serve YHWH.	and serve the Lord.

MT	OG
¹⁵ וְאִם רַע בְּעֵינֵיכֶם לַעֲבֹד אֶת־יְהוָה	¹⁵ εἰ δὲ μὴ ἀρέσκει ὑμῖν λατρεύειν κυρίῳ,
בַּחֲרוּ לָכֶם הַיּוֹם	ἔλεσθε ὑμῖν ἑαυτοῖς σήμερον,
אֶת־מִי תַעֲבֹדוּן	τίνι λατρεύσητε,
אִם אֶת־אֱלֹהִים אֲשֶׁר־עָבְדוּ אֲבוֹתֵיכֶם	εἴτε τοῖς θεοῖς τῶν πατέρων ὑμῶν
אֲשֶׁר בְּעֵבֶר הַנָּהָר	τοῖς ἐν τῷ πέραν τοῦ ποταμοῦ,
וְאִם אֶת־אֱלֹהֵי הָאֱמֹרִי	εἴτε τοῖς θεοῖς τῶν Ἀμορραίων,
אֲשֶׁר אַתֶּם יֹשְׁבִים בְּאַרְצָם	ἐν οἷς ὑμεῖς κατοικεῖτε ἐπὶ τῆς γῆς αὐτῶν·
וְאָנֹכִי וּבֵיתִי	ἐγὼ δὲ καὶ ἡ οἰκία μου
נַעֲבֹד אֶת־יְהוָה	λατρεύσομεν κυρίῳ ⟨ὅτι ἅγιός ἐστιν.⟩

If it is bad in your eyes to serve YHWH	Now if it does not please you to serve the Lord
choose for yourselves today	choose for yourselves today
whom you will serve,	whom you will serve,
whether the gods that your fathers served	whether the gods of your fathers
that were beyond the river	those beyond the river
or the gods of the Amorites	or the gods of the Amorites
in whose land you are living.	among who you live in their land.
But I and my household	But I and my household
will serve YHWH."	will serve the Lord ⟨because he is holy."⟩

24:14 τοὺς ἀλλοτρίους] om 54´ La¹⁰⁰ | ὑμῶν] ημων B 56 | τῷ – Αἰγύπτῳ] αιγυπτω και εν τω περαν του ποταμου 54´ La¹⁰⁰; τω περαν του ιορδανου και εν αιγυπτω 44 52-57; τω περαν του ιορδανου και εν τω περαν του ποταμου και εν αιγυπτω 376

24:15 ἔλεσθε O⁻ᴳ ¹⁰⁸ C⁻ᴹ ⁸² ¹²¹ 15-56-58ᵗˣᵗ-85ᵐᵍ-509] εδεσθε M; εκλεξασθε rel Ma | ἐπὶ τῆς γῆς] εν τη γη 54´-314 55 509 La¹⁰⁰ | om ὅτι ἅγιός ἐστιν 58

3.3 Joshua 24:14–27: Text and Apparatus

MT (*BHS*)	OG
16 וַיַּעַן הָעָם וַיֹּאמֶר חָלִילָה לָּנוּ מֵעֲזֹב אֶת־יְהוָה לַעֲבֹד אֱלֹהִים אֲחֵרִים And the people answered and said: "Far be it from us that we forsake YHWH to serve other gods.	16 Καὶ ἀποκριθεὶς ὁ λαὸς εἶπεν Μὴ γένοιτο ἡμῖν καταλιπεῖν κύριον ὥστε λατρεύειν θεοῖς ἑτέροις. And the people answered and said: "May it not be that we forsake the Lord to serve other gods.
17 ‎כִּי ‏יְהוָה אֱלֹהֵינוּ הוּא הַמַּעֲלֶה אֹתָנוּ וְאֶת־אֲבוֹתֵינוּ מֵאֶרֶץ מִצְרַיִם מִבֵּית עֲבָדִים וַאֲשֶׁר עָשָׂה לְעֵינֵינוּ אֶת־הָאֹתוֹת הַגְּדֹלוֹת הָאֵלֶּה וַיִּשְׁמְרֵנוּ בְּכָל־הַדֶּרֶךְ אֲשֶׁר הָלַכְנוּ בָהּ וּבְכֹל הָעַמִּים אֲשֶׁר עָבַרְנוּ בְּקִרְבָּם For YHWH is our God he brought us and our fathers out from the land of Egypt, from the house of slavery and performed those great miracles before our own eyes. And he protected us along all the way that we went and among all the people through whom we passed.	17 κύριος ὁ θεὸς ἡμῶν, αὐτὸς θεός ἐστιν· αὐτὸς ἀνήγαγεν ἡμᾶς καὶ τοὺς πατέρας ἡμῶν ἐξ Αἰγύπτου καὶ διεφύλαξεν ἡμᾶς ἐν πάσῃ τῇ ὁδῷ, ᾗ ἐπορεύθημεν ἐν αὐτῇ, καὶ ἐν πᾶσιν τοῖς ἔθνεσιν, οὓς παρήλθομεν δι᾽ αὐτῶν· The Lord is our God, he is God he brought us and our fathers out from Egypt. And he protected us along all the way that we went and among all the people through whom we passed.
18 וַיְגָרֶשׁ יְהוָה אֶת־כָּל־הָעַמִּים וְאֶת־הָאֱמֹרִי יֹשֵׁב הָאָרֶץ מִפָּנֵינוּ גַּם־אֲנַחְנוּ נַעֲבֹד אֶת־יְהוָה כִּי־הוּא אֱלֹהֵינוּ	18 καὶ ἐξέβαλεν κύριος τὸν Ἀμορραῖον καὶ πάντα τὰ ἔθνη τὰ κατοικοῦντα τὴν γῆν ἀπὸ προσώπου ἡμῶν. ἀλλὰ καὶ ἡμεῖς λατρεύσομεν κυρίῳ· οὗτος γὰρ θεὸς ἡμῶν ἐστιν.

(Continued)

24:17 κύριος – ἐστιν] κυριος γαρ εστιν ο θεος ημων 54´-314 | αὐτὸς 2°] ουτος ος 54´; ος MaConj | και 1° – ημων 2°] om 44 52 | ἐξ] εκ γης $O^{-G\ 108}$ 44´-44 C^{-82} 15-58-509 | Αἰγύπτου] + εξ οικου δουλειας και οσα εποιησεν ημιν τα σημεια τα μεγαλα ταυτα 120 $O^{-G\ 108}$ 44 82 52-57-72-85^{mg}-344^{mg} | οὓς] εν οις L^{-44}

24:18 τον – τα 2°] παντα (συμπαντα 19) τα εθνη και τον αμορραιον τον $O^{-G\ 108}$ 15 | κυρίῳ] pr τω $O^{-G\ 108}$ L^{-44} 121 58

MT (BHS)	OG
And YHWH drove out **all the people and the Amorites** who inhabit the land before us. Also we will serve YHWH for he is our God."	And the Lord drove out **the Amorites and all the people** who inhabit the land before us. But we will serve the Lord for he is our God."
‎19 וַיֹּאמֶר יְהוֹשֻׁעַ אֶל־הָעָם לֹא תוּכְלוּ לַעֲבֹד אֶת־יְהוָה כִּי־אֱלֹהִים קְדֹשִׁים הוּא אֵל־קַנּוֹא הוּא לֹא־יִשָּׂא לְפִשְׁעֲכֶם וּלְחַטֹּאותֵיכֶם	‎19 καὶ εἶπεν Ἰησοῦς πρὸς τὸν λαόν Οὐ μὴ δύνησθε λατρεύειν κυρίῳ, ὅτι θεὸς ἅγιός ἐστιν, καὶ ζηλώσας οὗτος οὐκ ἀνήσει ὑμῶν τὰ ἁμαρτήματα καὶ τὰ ἀνομήματα ὑμῶν·
But Joshua said to the people: "You cannot serve YHWH for he is a holy God. He is a jealous God, he will not forgive **your transgressions and your sins.**	But Iesous said to the people: "You cannot serve the Lord for he is a holy and jealous God, he will not forgive **your sins and your transgressions.**
‎20 כִּי תַעַזְבוּ אֶת־יְהוָה וַעֲבַדְתֶּם אֱלֹהֵי נֵכָר וְשָׁב וְהֵרַע לָכֶם וְכִלָּה אֶתְכֶם אַחֲרֵי אֲשֶׁר־הֵיטִיב לָכֶם	‎20 ἡνίκα ἐὰν ἐγκαταλίπητε κύριον καὶ λατρεύσητε θεοῖς ἑτέροις, καὶ ἐπελθὼν κακώσει ὑμᾶς καὶ ἐξαναλώσει ὑμᾶς ἀνθ' ὧν εὖ ἐποίησεν ὑμᾶς.
When you forsake YHWH and serve foreign gods, then he will turn and do you harm and consume you, after having done you good."	When you forsake the Lord and serve other gods, then he will turn and do you harm and consume you, instead of having done you good."
‎21 וַיֹּאמֶר הָעָם אֶל־יְהוֹשֻׁעַ לֹא כִּי אֶת־יְהוָה נַעֲבֹד	‎21 καὶ εἶπεν ὁ λαὸς πρὸς Ἰησοῦν Οὐχί, ἀλλὰ κυρίῳ λατρεύσομεν.
And the people said to Joshua: "No, for we will serve YHWH!"	And the people said to Iesous: "No, for we will serve the Lord."

24:19 ζηλώσας] θ͞ς ζηλωτής (-τος 376) εστιν O⁻ᴳ 108 58 | ὑμῶν 1° – ἀνομήματα] τα ανομηματα υμων και τα αμαρτηματα O⁻ᴳ 108 15; υμων τα ανομηματα και τα αμαρτηματα 54´-314 52-53-57-85-130-344

24:20 ἑτέροις] αλλοτριοις O⁻ᴳ 108 L⁻⁴⁴ ³¹⁴ C⁻⁵⁵ ⁵⁹ ⁸² 15-52-53-57-58-85-130-344

3.3 Joshua 24:14–27: Text and Apparatus

MT (*BHS*)	OG
²² וַיֹּאמֶר יְהוֹשֻׁעַ אֶל־הָעָם עֵדִים אַתֶּם בָּכֶם כִּי־אַתֶּם בְּחַרְתֶּם לָכֶם אֶת־יְהוָה לַעֲבֹד אוֹתוֹ וַיֹּאמְרוּ עֵדִים	²² καὶ εἶπεν Ἰησοῦς πρὸς τὸν λαόν Μάρτυρες ὑμεῖς καθ' ὑμῶν, ὅτι ὑμεῖς ἐξελέξασθε κύριον λατρεύειν αὐτῷ·
Then Joshua said to the people: "You are witnesses against yourselves that you have chosen YHWH, to serve him." And they said: "(we are) witnesses."	Then Iesous said to the people: "You are witnesses against yourselves that you have chosen the Lord, to serve him."
²³ וְעַתָּה הָסִירוּ אֶת־אֱלֹהֵי הַנֵּכָר אֲשֶׁר בְּקִרְבְּכֶם וְהַטּוּ אֶת־לְבַבְכֶם אֶל־יְהוָה אֱלֹהֵי יִשְׂרָאֵל	²³ καὶ νῦν περιέλεσθε τοὺς θεοὺς τοὺς ἀλλοτρίους τοὺς ἐν ὑμῖν καὶ εὐθύνατε τὴν καρδίαν ὑμῶν πρὸς κύριον θεὸν Ισραήλ.
"And now put away the foreign gods that are among you, and direct your heart to YHWH, the God of Israel."	And now put away the strange gods that are among you, and direct your heart to the Lord, the God of Israel."
²⁴ וַיֹּאמְרוּ הָעָם אֶל־יְהוֹשֻׁעַ אֶת־יְהוָה אֱלֹהֵינוּ נַעֲבֹד וּבְקוֹלוֹ נִשְׁמָע	²⁴ καὶ εἶπεν ὁ λαὸς πρὸς Ἰησοῦν Κυρίῳ λατρεύσομεν καὶ τῆς φωνῆς αὐτοῦ ἀκουσόμεθα.
And the people said to Joshua: "YHWH our God we will serve and his voice we will obey."	And the people said to Iesous: "The Lord we will serve and his voice we will obey."
²⁵ וַיִּכְרֹת יְהוֹשֻׁעַ בְּרִית לָעָם בַּיּוֹם הַהוּא וַיָּשֶׂם לוֹ חֹק וּמִשְׁפָּט בִּשְׁכֶם	²⁵ Καὶ διέθετο Ἰησοῦς διαθήκην πρὸς τὸν λαὸν ἐν τῇ ἡμέρᾳ ἐκείνῃ καὶ ἔδωκεν αὐτῷ νόμον καὶ κρίσιν ἐν Σηλὼ ἐνώπιον τῆς σκηνῆς τοῦ θεοῦ Ἰσραήλ.

(Continued)

24:22 κύριον E^{-B} 376 314 55-82 54-56-72] κυριω B 75; pr τον rel | αὐτῷ] + καὶ ειπαν (-πον 376) μαρτυρες 120 O^{-G} 108 106-134 55-82-85^{mg}-344^{mg}

24:23 τους αλλοτριους τους] των αλλοφυλων των $L^{-106\ 134}$ 52-53-57-85^{txt}-130-344 La^{100}

24:24 Κυρίῳ] θῶ ημων 58; τω κῶ θῶ ημων $O^{-G\ 19}$; + τω θῶ ημων 120 19 82 85^{mg}-130-344^{mg}-509 | λατρεύσομεν] + τω θῶ ημων W | OG reading καὶ εἶπεν (= ויאמר) witnessed also by several Kennicott (1785, 109) MSS

24:25 Σηλώ] συχεμ $O^{-G\ 19}$ 15-85^{mg}-509 | om ενωπιον – ισραηλ 58 | om της σκηνης 120 | σκηνής] + κῦ L^{-106} 52-53-57-85-130-344 La^{100}

MT (*BHS*)	OG
So, Joshua made a covenant with the people that day and gave them statutes and ordinances at Shechem.	So, Iesous made a covenant with the people that day and gave them statutes and ordinances at Selo before the tent of the God of Israel.

²⁶ וַיִּכְתֹּב יְהוֹשֻׁעַ אֶת־הַדְּבָרִים הָאֵלֶּה בְּסֵפֶר תּוֹרַת אֱלֹהִים וַיִּקַּח אֶבֶן גְּדוֹלָה וַיְקִימֶהָ שָּׁם תַּחַת הָאַלָּה אֲשֶׁר בְּמִקְדַּשׁ יְהוָה	²⁶ καὶ ἔγραψεν τὰ ῥήματα ταῦτα εἰς βιβλίον νόμου τοῦ θεοῦ· καὶ ἔλαβεν λίθον μέγαν καὶ ἔστησεν αὐτὸν Ἰησοῦς ὑπὸ τὴν τερέμινθον ἀπέναντι κυρίου.
And Joshua wrote these words in the book of the law of God and he took a large stone, and set it there under the oak which is in the sanctuary of YHWH.	And he wrote these words in the book as the law of God and he took a large stone and Joshua set it under the oak before the Lord.

²⁷ וַיֹּאמֶר יְהוֹשֻׁעַ אֶל־כָּל־הָעָם הִנֵּה הָאֶבֶן הַזֹּאת תִּהְיֶה־בָּנוּ לְעֵדָה כִּי־הִיא שָׁמְעָה אֵת כָּל־אִמְרֵי יְהוָה אֲשֶׁר דִּבֶּר עִמָּנוּ וְהָיְתָה בָכֶם לְעֵדָה פֶּן־תְּכַחֲשׁוּן בֵּאלֹהֵיכֶם	²⁷ καὶ εἶπεν Ἰησοῦς πρὸς τὸν λαόν Ἰδοὺ ὁ λίθος οὗτος ἔσται ἐν ὑμῖν εἰς μαρτύριον, ὅτι αὐτὸς ἀκήκοεν πάντα τὰ λεχθέντα αὐτῷ ὑπὸ κυρίου, ὅ τι ἐλάλησεν πρὸς ἡμᾶς σήμερον· καὶ ἔσται οὗτος ἐν ὑμῖν εἰς μαρτύριον ἐπ' ἐσχάτων τῶν ἡμερῶν, ἡνίκα ἐὰν ἀποστῆτε ἀπὸ κυρίου τοῦ θεοῦ μου.
And Joshua said to all the people: "Look, this stone shall a witness against us for it has heard all the words of YHWH	And Iesous said to the people: "Look, this stone shall be in your midst a witness for it has heard all that was spoken to it by the Lord,

24:26 εγραψεν] + ιϛ 120 *O*⁻ᴳ ¹⁰⁸ 82 58 | νόμον] νομου 120 376 M-V-29 Ma | Ἰησοῦς] pr εχει 376 106-134; εχει 426 54´ 85ᵐᵍ; + εχει 19 44-314 15-52-53-57-509; > 121 La¹⁰⁰

24:27 τὸν] pr παντα 120 *O*⁻ᴳ ¹⁰⁸ 82 58 | ὑμῖν 1°] ημιν MaConj | αὐτῷ *E*⁻¹²⁰ 56] om rel | ὅ τι *E* 82 56] θς 407; οσα rel La¹⁰⁰ | σήμερον] κϛ 120 | οὗτος ἐν ὑμῖν] εν υμιν ουτος 54´-314 | om ἐπ' – ἡμερῶν 426 58 | ἀπόστητε ἀπό (+ προσωπου 75) κυρίου τοῦ θεοῦ *L*⁻⁴⁴ La¹⁰⁰] ψεύσησθε κυρίῳ τῷ θεῷ rel Ra Ma | μου *E*⁻¹²⁹ 82] ημων 129 19´-376 *L*⁻⁴⁴ ¹³⁴ A-59 56-85-130-344ᵗˣᵗ; υμων και αποστητε απ αυτου 58; υμων rel

MT (*BHS*)	OG
that he spoke to us	that he spoke to us today
and it shall be a witness against you	and it shall be in your midst a witness at the last days
lest you deal falsely with your God."	whenever you rebel against the Lord my God."

3.3.1 Text-Critical Analysis of the OG

24:14 There are four possible readings for the phrase which urges the Israelites to put away the gods that they served "beyond the river and in Egypt". It is likely that B and the majority contains the OG reading.[116]

ἐν τῷ πέραν τοῦ ποταμοῦ καὶ ἐν Αἰγύπτῳ (B Maj)
ἐν Αἰγύπτῳ καὶ ἐν τῷ πέραν τοῦ ποταμοῦ (54´ La[100])
ἐν τῷ πέραν τοῦ ιορδανου καὶ ἐν Αἰγύπτῳ (44 52-57)
ἐν τῷ πέραν τοῦ ιορδανου καὶ ἐν τῷ πέραν τοῦ ποταμοῦ καὶ ἐν Αἰγύπτῳ (376)

In the context of Josh 24, ἐν τῷ πέραν τοῦ ποταμοῦ "beyond the river" is used to refer to Mesopotamia where Abraham lived (24:2–3, 15). In 24:14, however, the mention of Egypt together with "beyond the river" has led later revisers to understand the river as Jordan. Accordingly, *L* secondarily transposes the sentence, probably understanding the phrase so that first the Israelites left Egypt and only then crossed Jordan. The substitution of ποταμοῦ with ιορδανου is another attempt to specify that here Jordan is the correct river. The reading in MS 376 is a conflation of the majority reading with this substitution.

24:15 Margolis reads εκλεξασθε "choose" in his OG. This is the reading found in groups *E* and *L*. Rahlfs, however, substitutes it with ἕλεσθε "choose" with several MSS from groups *C* and *O*. The former (ἐκλέγομαι) is the more common equivalent for בחר and it is almost consistently used by Aquila.[117] The rare αἱρέω is used in the LXX as an equivalent for בחר only in 2 Sam 15:15 and Jer 8:3. In OG Josh 24:15, ἕλεσθε should therefore be preferred as the rarer original equivalent. As illustrated by Greenspoon, εκλεξασθε is a *Kaige* reading substituting the rare verb with

---

116 The originality of the *L* and Old Latin reading could be argued on the basis that it is the reading further away from the MT. The majority reading would then reflect an early correction towards the proto-MT text. However, since there are stylistic reasons for a secondary transposition in *L*, it is perhaps more likely that the transposition is a secondary development.
117 Den Hertog 1996, 32.

a more common one. Accordingly, he notes that this is an example of an instance where a *Kaige* reading entered the B-text, and serves as a reminder to be careful not to mechanically equate B with OG.[118]

MSS 54´-314 55 509, the Armenian, Ethiopic, and Old Latin translations, secondarily change the more idiomatic Greek ἐπὶ τῆς γῆς αὐτῶν "in their land" closer to the Hebrew בְּאַרְצָם "in their land" by substituting ἐπὶ with εν.

MS 58 secondarily omits ὅτι ἅγιός ἐστιν "because he is holy" following the Hebrew text, which lacks an equivalent for this expression.

24:17 The replacement of ἐξ with εκ γης is a secondary correction towards the Hebrew text. It is likely Hexaplaric. Several MSS from various groups have an equivalent for the Hebrew plus מִבֵּית עֲבָדִים וַאֲשֶׁר עָשָׂה לְעֵינֵינוּ אֶת-הָאֹתוֹת הַגְּדֹלוֹת הָאֵלֶּה "from the house of slavery and did those great signs in our sight". They read εξ οικου δουλειας και οσα εποιησεν ημιν τα σημεια τα μεγαλα ταυτα "from the house of slavery and did us those great miracles". The Armenian and Ethiopic translations, as well as the Syrohexapla, also have it. This should not be included in the OG, since it has probably emerged as a later revision towards the Hebrew, as Margolis and Rahlfs also agree.

24:18 Manuscripts O^{-G} [108] 15 transpose the order τὸν Αμορραῖον καὶ πάντα τὰ ἔθνη "the Amorites and all the nations" to correspond with the Hebrew order -אֶת-כָּל הָעַמִּים וְאֶת-הָאֱמֹרִי "all the nations and the Amorites". Pretzl identifies this as a Hexaplaric correction.[119] In addition, MSS 19 secondarily replaces παντα with σύμπαντα.

24:22 The majority reading is the accusative κύριον: the Lord is understood as an object of ἐξελέξασθε. The dative form κυριω is given in manuscript B 75, probably because the Lord is coupled with λατρεύειν (as is the case in OG 24:14–16, 18–21). Since the translator was translating בְּחַרְתֶּם לָכֶם אֶת-יְהוָה, in which YHWH is the object, the majority reading is the most likely OG reading. The dative can be explained as inner-Greek harmonization within 24:18–22, where the Lord and gods are in dative when they are in conjunction with λατρεύω.

The equivalent for the Hebrew וַיֹּאמְרוּ עֵדִים "and they said: '(we are) witnesses'" in some Greek MSS emerged as a Hexaplaric addition. It is marked with an obelus in MS 344.

24:23 One could argue that the *L* reading τῶν αλλοφύλων, supported by the Old Latin *alienigenarum*, is earlier than the majority reading τοὺς ἀλλοτρίους – which

---

118 Greenspoon 1983, 111.
119 Pretzl 1928, 399.

could be explained as a harmonization towards a more usual form. In the case of הַנֵּכָר, the translation equivalent in the LXX is usually ἀλλότριος (e.g. Gen 35:2, 4; Judg 10:16; 1 Sam 7:3). When one observes how the Joshua translator dealt with the attributes of foreign or other gods, it becomes clear that he was not systematic, but gave varied translation equivalents. For example, ἕτερος was normally used to translate אַחֵר as in 24:2 and 16, but sometimes it is also the equivalent for נֵכָר as in 24:23. However, one should also note that αλλοφύλων usually referred to the Philistenes, and it is not used anywhere else in the book of Joshua.[120] It is possible that a later reviser was familiar with the term from the book of Judges and secondarily imported it in this context. Therefore, it is probably safest to follow Rahlfs and Margolis with the majority reading even though the *L* reading does have its merits.

24:24 The OG did not have an equivalent for אֱלֹהֵינוּ "our God". Consequently, several MSS secondarily add an equivalent to harmonize the text towards the MT. The addition is done in notably different ways and two different places. It is a good example of a short addition that could have been made in the margins of manuscripts in different ways.

24:25 On σηλω, see the comments on verse 1. Only a few MSS omit the clause ἐνώπιον τῆς σκηνῆς τοῦ θεοῦ Ἰσραήλ "before the tent of the God of Israel" which does not have an equivalent in the MT. The omission is probably a later development influenced by it having been marked with an obelus in the Syrohexapla.

The OG may have read the tetragrammaton in the Hebrew *Vorlage* and translated it with κυρίου. It is attested by the *nomina sacra* in the *L* group and some *M* MSS. Also, La[100] reflects it with the reading *Domino*. It is possible that the abbreviation κυ accidentally dropped out from the chain of possessive forms at some point in the copying of the Greek text. Against this conclusion one might argue that the abbreviation was added as a later Greek revision reflecting formulaic language. The matter is hard to settle, since the whole phrase is missing from the MT. The question of the originality of the tetragrammaton in the Hebrew *Vorlage* does not need to be settled here.

24:26 The addition of ις is Hexaplaric. It is marked with an obelus in the Syrohexapla. The omission of the latter ιησους in 121 and La[100] is a secondary development due to the Hebrew text.

24:27 The addition of παντα is probably Hexaplaric. The OG plusses σήμερον "today" and ἐπ' ἐσχάτων τῶν ἡμερῶν "at the last days" are marked with an

---

[120] Van der Kooij 2006.

obelus in the Syrohexapla. However, they are well attested in the MS material, and only the latter is missing from some Greek MSS. The replacement of σήμερον with κϲ̄ is an idiosyncrasy of MS 120.

At the end of the verse, there are considerable variants and the OG reading is not clear. In my opinion, the OG text most probably read ἡνίκα ἐὰν ἀπόστητε ἀπὸ κυρίου τοῦ θεοῦ "whenever you rebel against the Lord", as attested by the *L* group and La[100], since it best explains how the other readings came into being. This reconstruction differs from both Rahlfs and Margolis.

The *L* group supported by Old Latin utilizes the verb ἀφίστημι "to reject", which differs from the majority ψεύδομαι "to lie". The *L* verb ἀφίστημι does not correspond with the MT verb כָּחַשׁ "to deceive". In Josh 22:18–19, ἀφίστημι is a translation of מָרַד "to rebel". In Josh 22, the rebelling is connected to the attempt by the eastern tribes to build a competing altar for YHWH, which was considered a fatal sin. Josh 22:19 uses the phrase καὶ μὴ ἀπόστητε ἀπὸ κυρίου "and do not rebel against the Lord" (וּבַיהוָה אַל־תִּמְרֹדוּ), which is close to the phrase in the *L* variant in 24:27. Therefore, it is possible that *L* preserves at the end of Josh 24:27 the OG reading, which has been translated from a variant Hebrew *Vorlage* which utilized the verb מרד "rebel". If this reading is assumed to be earlier, and goes back to an earlier Hebrew *Vorlage*, a later replacement in the proto-MT could be explained as a removal of the reference to Josh 22 by changing the verb מרד to כחש. This would be due to the context of Josh 24. After all, in Josh 24 the triple promise by the Israelites to serve only YHWH and the making of the covenant should not end with a reference to a fatal sin. Moreover, כחש could be understood as a secondary change towards a verb that better suits the context; namely, it is easier to understand how a stone of witness could prevent the Israelites from "deceiving" or "lying" to YHWH than it is to understand how a stone could prevent the Israelites from "rebelling". The majority Greek reading ψεύδομαι could then be explained as a later revision towards the secondarily replaced Hebrew כָּחַשׁ in the MT. Interestingly, MS 58 preserves both readings by first following the majority text and then giving και αποστητε απ αυτου as a plus.[121]

In terms of the personal pronoun, the probable OG reading θεοῦ μου "Lord my God" differs from the MT reading בֵּאלֹהֵיכֶם "with your God". The OG personal pronoun is supported by three *E* MSS (B 82 120), and it probably reflects יהוה אלהי "YHWH my God" in the Hebrew *Vorlage* of the translator (cf. Josh 9:23, 14:8). The

---

121 Against the priority of *L*, however, it could be argued that the OG translator faithfully translated ψεύδομαι from כָּחַשׁ and that ἀφίστημι is a later inner-Greek development towards another verb. In that case one would have to assume that the reviser of *L* secondarily created a problematic intertextual connection with Josh 22:18–19. This makes it slightly more probable that "rebel" is the earlier reading in Greek, which is based on a different Hebrew *Vorlage*.

other readings can be explained as deriving from this OG reading. The secondary reading θεῷ ἡμῶν "our God" is probably a later correction towards another form. This form, however, is also given by most *L* witnesses, and the development could be explained the other way around. The replacement of μου with υμων in several MSS is a revision towards the Hebrew text. The reading יהוה אלהי "YHWH my God" in the Hebrew *Vorlage* of the OG might well be earlier than בֵּאלֹהֵיכֶם "your God", since the latter could be explained as a harmonization towards the second-person plural masculine forms utilized in the preceding clauses.

All in all, verse 24:27 attests to several complex variants and diverse combinations of readings in the manuscript material. Thus, the reconstruction of the OG remains tentative. The plurality of the Greek readings seems to correlate with the several variants between the MT and the OG which will be analyzed in section 3.3.2 below. My text-critical suggestion here goes together with the arguments presented there. The verse has obviously been challenging for various scribes at several points in its textual history.

3.3.2 Evaluation between the OG and the MT

Minor Theological Cleansing (v. 15)

Sometimes even a minor textual variant might reveal ideological motivations behind scribal work. This might be the case with a variant in Josh 24:15 where Joshua, recognizing that the Israelites cannot serve YHWH, urges them to choose between the gods that their fathers served beyond the river or the gods of the Amorites. This verse ends in the well-known phrase uttered by Joshua: "But I and my household will serve the Lord."[122] The difference between the MT and the OG relates to the gods beyond the river: in the MT, Joshua refers to the foreign gods as אֶת־אֱלֹהִים אֲשֶׁר־עָבְדוּ אֲבוֹתֵיכֶם "the gods that your fathers served", while the OG utilizes a more intense possessive form τοῖς θεοῖς τῶν πατέρων ὑμῶν "the gods of your fathers". This change could merely be attributed to the translator. In that case, the variant in the OG would be "another example of non-literal translation for stylistic reasons".[123] Following this reasoning, Schmitt regards the variant a Greek stylistic simplification.[124] Butler interprets further that the OG represents a sermonic idiom that aims at making the call more personal by using the second-person formulation together with a possessive form.[125]

---

[122] The OG plus at the end of the verse will be dealt later in this section.
[123] Koopmans 1990, 256–257.
[124] Schmitt 1964, 9.
[125] Butler 1983, 264.

How probable is it that the change could be attributed to the translator? In theory, it is possible. The change could be well integrated into the overall profile of the translator. The explanation is, however, undermined by the translation of the previous verse. There also, the MT refers to אֶת־אֱלֹהִים אֲשֶׁר עָבְדוּ אֲבוֹתֵיכֶם "the gods that your fathers served", but the translation given is τοὺς θεοὺς τοὺς ἀλλοτρίους οἷς ἐλάτρευσαν οἱ πατέρες ὑμῶν "the other gods that your fathers served". So there the translator did not translate the relative clause with a possessive form. In addition, if the variant were secondary, it would imply that the translator or a Hebrew reviser secondarily created a theologically problematic reading. This possessive expression is, after all, normally used when referring to YHWH (e.g. Exod 3:13, 15, 16; Deut 1:11, 21; 4:1). One would then have to argue that stylistic motives override the theological problem created.

A suspicion towards the reading in the MT is raised when the following clause in verse 15 is considered:

אִם אֶת־אֱלֹהִים אֲשֶׁר־עָבְדוּ אֲבוֹתֵיכֶם אֲשֶׁר בְּעֵבֶר הַנָּהָר
וְאִם אֶת־אֱלֹהֵי הָאֱמֹרִי אֲשֶׁר אַתֶּם יֹשְׁבִים בְּאַרְצָם

The possessive form "the gods of the Amorites" would form a parallelism with the possessive form in the OG. The relative clause in the MT text is cumbersome when viewed from this perspective. If the Hebrew *Vorlage* of the OG read את אלהי אבותכם "the gods of your fathers" it could be parallelism originally intended here. The explanation first introduced by Holmes should thus be taken up.[126] A Hebrew reviser may have objected to referring to the foreign gods with the earlier formula את אלהי אבותכם. The main reason for the objection was ideological, since the possessive expression should only be used with YHWH. Hence, the proto-MT editor might have changed the possessive form to a similar relative clause that was already used in verse 14. Granted, the Hebrew reading behind the OG is unusual; however, it is not impossible, since a kindred reading occurs in Dan 11:37: אֲבֹתָיו אֱלֹהֵי "the gods of his fathers".

The ideological motive at play here could also been characterized as undermining the polytheism of the Israelite fathers. Such subtle editing also takes place elsewhere.[127] The Samaritan Joshua texts further continue this line of development by omitting all the references to the fathers serving foreign gods beyond the river. In the Samaritan version of the speech, the choice is between either YHWH or the gods of those peoples among which the Israelites are currently living.[128]

---

126 Holmes 1914, 79.
127 See, for example, Pakkala 2013, 185–191.
128 See section 3.6.

In my opinion, thus, the argument that there was an intentional theological cleansing behind the MT reading is more probable than assuming a stylistic change in the OG tradition. The explanation is even more probable when connected with the observation that many other parts of Josh 24 were ideologically edited in the proto-MT phase.

Variants in the Exodus Remembrance (v. 17)

The chapter continues with the response and commitment of the Israelites. In verse 16, there are no differences between the OG and the MT. In verse 17, the Israelites recall how YHWH brought them out of Egypt and protected them. The textual witnesses of verse 17 are particularly rich with variants. Three variants should be addressed: (1) the phrase αὐτὸς θεός ἐστιν "he is God", which is a plus in the OG, (2) the phrase וְאֶת־אֲבוֹתֵינוּ "and our fathers", missing in two Greek witnesses and the Peshitta, and (3) the substantial plus in the MT that amplifies the deeds of YHWH in Egypt.

Holmes explains the first variant, the plus "he is God" in the OG, as a case of misunderstanding by the translator.[129] According to him, the translator did not grasp the force of the Hebrew syntax that uses the pronoun as a copula in the nominal clause, highlighting what YHWH has done כִּי יְהוָה אֱלֹהֵינוּ הוּא הַמַּעֲלֶה "For YHWH is our God, he took us". A similar misunderstanding is, according to Holmes, seen in Josh 2:11 כִּי יְהוָה אֱלֹהֵיכֶם הוּא אֱלֹהִים בַּשָּׁמַיִם "For YHWH is your God, he is the God of heavens" where no equivalent is given in the OG for the third-person singular masculine pronoun.[130] In this manner, the plus in OG Josh 24:17 could be explained as a secondary explanatory addition emerging from a misunderstanding in the translation process. The addition could further be explained as having derived from the end of verse 18 נַעֲבֹד אֶת־יְהוָה כִּי־הוּא אֱלֹהֵינוּ "we will serve YHWH for he is our God".[131] Given the overall nature and competence of the translator, an argument assuming a misunderstanding in a relatively simple phrase seems somewhat unfounded.

Against the conclusion that the translator misunderstood the passage, I would argue that the OG reflects an earlier Hebrew *Vorlage*. This Hebrew text could have read כי יהוה אלהינו הוא האלהים "for YHWH our God, he is God". The closest parallel for such a formulation can be found in Deut 7:9 וְיָדַעְתָּ כִּי־יְהוָה אֱלֹהֶיךָ הוּא הָאֱלֹהִים "you will therefore know that YHWH your God, he is God". In light of the translation style of Joshua, this is more likely than to assume that the translator would have

---

129 Holmes 1914, 79. This solution is followed by Butler 1983, 264 and Koopmans 1990, 257.
130 Holmes 1914, 20. The OG text in this case, however, is not that simple. The text of B, for example, has an equivalent to the pronoun.
131 Den Hertog 2011, 655.

made such an addition. This Hebrew text was likely earlier than the MT, since "he is God" may have easily dropped out due to a scribal mistake. There is a clear possibility for a *homoioteleuton* in the assumed Hebrew *Vorlage* due to the close repetition of the pronouns הוּא הָאֱלֹהִים הוּא הַמַּעֲלֶה.[132]

The second notable variant is not clear from a comparison of the OG and the MT above. The phrase וְאֶת־אֲבוֹתֵינוּ "and our fathers" is missing from the Peshitta, which has led some scholars to omit it as secondary both from the MT and the OG.[133] If the argument was dependent only on Peshitta it would be tenuous. Peshitta tends to paraphrase in many instances, and this variant could be attributed to that tendency.[134] Moreover, the omission of the phrase in Peshitta could be explained as *homoioteleuton* caused by the similar endings (אֹתָנוּ וְאֶת־אֲבוֹתֵינוּ).

There are, however, other arguments to be considered. First, the variant beginning of verse 24:6 in the MT should be mentioned again, since it includes as a plus the same phrase וָאוֹצִיא אֶת־אֲבוֹתֵיכֶם "and I brought your fathers". I have already concluded that the plusses in the MT at the beginning of 24:5 and 6 are best explained as secondary developments. As concluded earlier, this sentence shows signs of later harmonization with 1 Sam 12.[135] Second, there are some Greek manuscripts (44 and 53) that omit καὶ τοὺς πατέρας ἡμῶν "your fathers" in verse 24:17. Since the Greek manuscript support for not omitting the phrase is solid, extending firmly to all MS groups, it is safest to assume that the phrase was present in the OG and their absence from some Greek manuscripts is a later development. Based on the support of Peshitta, these sporadic Greek manuscripts, and the variant reading in verse 24:6, however, one could formulate a cumulative argument that there was an earlier Hebrew version for 24:17 from which the phrase was missing. One could then argue that in Josh 24 there is a tendency to secondarily add the mention of the fathers in several places. This argument would accord with the literary-critical model, which assumes that the mentions of the fathers has been secondarily expanded to YHWH's speech.[136] Nonetheless, since the manuscript evidence for the omission is late and scarce, it is more likely that the convergence with literary-critical observations is in this case coincidental.

---

[132] The other possibility is that הוּא הָאֱלֹהִים was secondarily added to the Hebrew *Vorlage* of the OG. Such an addition could have been inspired by late monotheistic texts that wish to highlight the oneness of God (e.g. Deut 7:9, cf. Pakkala 2007, 159–178). However, since the grounds for a scribal mistake are clear here, OG Josh 24:17 should hold the text-critical priority. This is not to say that הוּא הָאֱלֹהִים could not be a monotheistic gloss in the earlier literary development of the text.
[133] Holmes 1914, 78–79 and Nielsen 1955, 99.
[134] Koopmans 1990, 257.
[135] Thus also Holmes 1914, 78. The addition forms a repetition in the MT text: "Then I brought you out. (6) And I brought your fathers out". See section 3.2.2.
[136] See section 4.3.3.

The third variant in verse 24:17, the long plus in the MT, expands the Exodus remembrance. The plus reads first "from the land of" before Egypt (מֵאֶרֶץ מִצְרַיִם), and then specifies that Egypt is "the house of slavery" (מִבֵּית עֲבָדִים). Finally, it states that YHWH "performed those great miracles before our own eyes" (וַאֲשֶׁר עָשָׂה לְעֵינֵינוּ אֶת־הָאֹתוֹת הַגְּדֹלוֹת הָאֵלֶּה). From this whole sentence, the OG has an equivalent for "Egypt" only. To explain this variant as a textual corruption in the OG tradition, one would have to assume a rather complicated error, since the plus is situated around the word "Egypt". In addition, it is hard to explain why the plus would have been intentionally omitted from the OG. There are no convincing theological or stylistic reasons for such an omission.[137] Nielsen, for one, suggested that the OG tradition might have found problematic the notion that the great miracles that happened in Egypt were seen not only by the fathers but also by the generation in question (לְעֵינֵינוּ "before our own eyes").[138] According to such an argument, the scribe deleted this part, since the generation in Josh 24 was not present in Egypt. However, the reference to "miracles" here does not necessarily have to do with Egypt, but could also refer to later miracles. Moreover, an omission motivated by a precision for the correct division between "us" and "the fathers" is not that plausible, since such a motivation is not at play in other significant instances. For example, in the historical remembrance in 24:2–13 the fathers and the generation that the speech is addressed to are used interchangeably, both in the MT and the OG.[139] This is seen, specifically, when in 24:2–5 the fathers are the objects of YHWH's activity but suddenly in 24:5, in both the MT and the OG, YHWH brings "you" out of Egypt.

We are then most probably dealing with a secondary addition in the proto-MT tradition. This is, in fact, a position held by several scholars.[140] The expansion in the MT consists of two parts: the specification of Egypt as the house of slavery, and the reminder of YHWH's great deeds performed before the eyes of the Israelites. The phrase מֵאֶרֶץ מִצְרַיִם מִבֵּית עֲבָדִים "from the land of Egypt, the house of slavery", in the first part of the addition, is formulaic language influenced by Deuteronomy (e.g. Deut 5:6, 6:12, 8:14, 13:11), also known from both versions of the Decalogue (Exod 20:2, Deut 5:6). The influence of Deuteronomy on the editing of Josh 24 has also been

---

[137] Thus also Koopmans 1990, 248.
[138] Nielsen 1955, 99.
[139] Boling & Wright (1982, 538) characterize the rhetorical function of this interchange as follows: "This compact unit employs the same technique that was noted in alternation between second and third person forms in the initial communique (vv. 2b–13), to elicit and signal identification with the experience of others."
[140] See, for example, Butler 1983, 264; Koopmans 1990, 248–250; Nelson 1997, 265; Den Hertog 2011, 655; Rösel 2011, 372.

noted earlier in this analysis.¹⁴¹ In addition, it is interesting to note that this is the second case where Josh 24 has, only in the MT, a connection with Mic 6:4. The earlier connection was in the case of the addition of Moses and Aaron in MT Josh 24:5. This points towards late editing harmonizing various texts closer to one another.

Mic 6:4	Josh 24
כִּי הֶעֱלִתִיךָ מֵאֶרֶץ מִצְרַיִם וּמִבֵּית עֲבָדִים פְּדִיתִיךָ וָאֶשְׁלַח לְפָנֶיךָ אֶת־מֹשֶׁה אַהֲרֹן וּמִרְיָם	מֵאֶרֶץ מִצְרַיִם מִבֵּית עֲבָדִים (v. 17) וָאֶשְׁלַח אֶת־מֹשֶׁה וְאֶת־אַהֲרֹן (v. 5)
I brought you up from the land of Egypt, (from) the house of slavery I delivered you. I sent Moses, Aaron, and Miriam to lead you.	from the land of Egypt, the house of slavery I sent Moses and Aaron

The second part of the expansion וַאֲשֶׁר עָשָׂה לְעֵינֵינוּ אֶת־הָאֹתוֹת הַגְּדֹלוֹת הָאֵלֶּה "and performed those great miracles before our own eyes" consists of common language (גָּדוֹל "great" together with אוֹת "miracle") and the common theme of YHWH performing great miracles used in Deuteronomy (e.g. Deut 4:34, 6:22, 7:19, 26:8, 29:2) and Jer 32:21. There is, however, one noteworthy difference. In Deuteronomy, the word אוֹת is never used alone, but always together with a synonym (מוֹפֵת "sign"). The combination of these two synonyms is also used outside Deuteronomy in Exod 7:3; Is 8:18, 20:3; Ps 78:43, 135:9; Neh 9:10; and Jer 32:20ff. Koopmans correctly notes: "In other words, an expansion in Josh 24:17 could have been influenced by traditional language from Deuteronomy, but the language and style stops short of the stereotyped collocation of nouns found in Deuteronomy."¹⁴² Thus, one has to be careful when making conclusions on the editing behind MT Josh 24:17 based on formulaic language. The addition does not bring anything ideologically new to the text. We are, therefore, probably not dealing with a Deuteronomistic redaction, but editing influenced by common language and themes found in Deuteronomy and elsewhere in the Hebrew Bible. This editing seems to attempt to tighten the connections of Joshua with the books preceding and following it. It is probably connected with the increasing authority of Deuteronomy in the late Second Temple period.¹⁴³

Lastly, it is significant that this is the only place in the book of Joshua where the miracles performed by YHWH in Egypt are explicitly mentioned. Taken together with the addition of Moses and Aaron in 24:5, one can probably conclude that the editor responsible for the additions behind the proto-MT text was

---

141 See also Tov 1999c, 394 on the influence of Deuteronomy on several additions in MT Josh overall.
142 Koopmans 1990, 249.
143 On the popularity of Deuteronomy in late Second Temple Judaism, see Crawford 2005.

motivated by a desire to fill in missing details from the Exodus narrative. The earlier allusions to the Exodus in the OG text were not that detailed, and the editor felt a need to bring them into closer conformity with the Exodus traditions that were already developed further in Deuteronomy and the Pentateuch. This evidence therefore strengthens the literary and redaction critical notion that references to the Exodus have been secondarily added and expanded in the diachronic development of the book of Joshua.[144]

Addition Relating to Earlier Redaction (v. 22)
In verse 22, Joshua states that the people themselves are witnesses to their own choice to serve YHWH. The MT has as a plus after Joshua's statement, an affirmation by the people וַיֹּאמְרוּ עֵדִים "and they said: 'we are witnesses!'". There are two instances in Josh 24 where a witness to the people's decision is highlighted. This verse likely represents a later abstract and theological conception of a witness, while the stone of witness in verse 27 is likely an older concept.[145] The importance of witnesses is central in the current form of Josh 24, as seen in the double appearance, since it highlights that the people themselves are fully responsible for any consequences ensuing from breaches of the contract. YHWH is not responsible for what happens when the covenant is broken. This important function of the double witnesses might, in fact, be the reason why there are significant textual variants in both passages referring to different witnesses. For this reason, later editors have wanted to continue to stress the importance of the witness.

In light of the function of this verse, the sentence וַיֹּאמְרוּ עֵדִים could be explained as a secondary addition behind the MT tradition, one that wishes to underline that the people themselves took all the responsibility for the covenant and the results of breaking it. It is a "basis for guilt of the people", as Butler puts it, when the covenant is eventually broken by serving other gods.[146] This argument is further supported by the notion that a late insertion of this sentence has created syntactical problems in the transition between 24:22 and 23. When 24:23 is read after וַיֹּאמְרוּ עֵדִים, Joshua is not introduced again as the speaker, and the reader could easily make the mistake of thinking that the speech of the people continues.[147]

---

[144] For example, the circumcision scene containing several references to the Exodus in Josh 5:4–8 is likely a quite late addition to the book of Joshua, which has further gone through complex editing. Bieberstein (1995, 408–412), for instance, attributes the scene to a late post-priestly editor. For the textual issues in Josh 5:4–8 see section 3.4.2.
[145] Rösel 2011, 373.
[146] Butler 1983, 265.
[147] Holmes (1914, 79) puts it bluntly: "It interrupts the speech." Also, Butler (1983, 265) notes that the "phrase does not fit the following syntax, where Joshua is not mentioned as subject

Verse 23 does not work after this plus, since it does not reintroduce the speaker and continues as a quotation. In all the other instances in Josh 24, when the people finish speaking Joshua is again introduced as the speaker. The OG, without the insertion, reads smoothly as a continuation of the speech of Joshua.

This observation, however, has also been used as an argument in the other direction. An omission of וַיֹּאמְרוּ עֵדִים in the OG could seek to simplify the problematic syntax created by an earlier redactor. Aurelius points out that various textual traditions try to deal with the problem of continuity between 24:22 and 23; while Peshitta adds an introduction stating that it is Joshua who speaks in 24:23, the OG deletes the answer of the people at the end of 24:22.[148] Nielsen correspondingly notes that the deletion of the phrase in the OG happened because verse 23 in connection with this phrase "might at first sight be interpreted as the words of the people."[149] Therefore, while the originality of the phrase וַיֹּאמְרוּ עֵדִים could be argued on the basis of it being the *lectio difficilior*, its secondary nature could be argued on the basis of it disturbing the earlier speech by Joshua.

Finally, the usage of the word עֵדִים "witness" as an affirmation of a second party to an agreement is similar to Ruth 4:10–12. There, the people at the gate declare that they are witnesses that Boaz has acquired all the property of Elimelech.[150] This usage may have influenced a secondary addition in Josh 24:22. On the other hand, Ruth 4:10–12, 1 Sam 12:5, and Josh 24:22 together might attest to a fixed legal formula, to which the confirmation of the people that they are witnesses belongs as an integral part.[151] This form-critical observation would then indicate that either the answer of the people was a part of the earliest textual form of Josh 24:22, or the form was harmonized towards a common legal formula.

Since the text-critical arguments are not decisive, in this case it is helpful to consider a literary-critical possibility. The key observation is that Josh 24:23 contains the idea that foreign gods are already among the Israelites in the Promised Land (אֶת־אֱלֹהֵי הַנֵּכָר אֲשֶׁר בְּקִרְבְּכֶם) and that they should be put away. This idea is different from the one presented earlier in Josh 24, where the choice between YHWH and a foreign god is theoretical and the foreign gods were just associated with the fathers.[152] Therefore, 24:23–24 altogether can be seen as a later addition in

---

again". This sudden interruption changing the speaker is used as a literary-critical argument by, for example, Becker 2006, 144.
148 Aurelius 2008, 101.
149 Nielsen 1955, 100.
150 In both cases "it is clear that the distinction between civil law and religious law is completely blurred" (Boling & Wright 1982, 539).
151 As argued by Müller 2004, 216.
152 Thus also, for example, Levin 1985, 114; Becker 2006, 144; Aurelius 2008, 101.

the literary growth of the chapter. If, then, one assumes that the response of the people "we are witnesses" was present in the text to which 24:23–24 was added, the addition would have been made poorly, since no introduction was given indicating that Joshua is the speaker. It is therefore more plausible that while 24:23–24 is an early addition, the phrase וַיֹּאמְרוּ עֵדִים is an even later addition attested by documented evidence. When such a short addition was made, it was understandable that the scribe did not notice the need for a new introductory speech formula. Perhaps the most likely development here is then a model of subsequent expansions, where every phase represents a plausible text and scribal development.

First phase	Second phase (OG Josh)	Third phase (MT Josh)
22. Then Joshua said to the people: "You are witnesses against yourselves that you have chosen YHWH, to serve him."	22. Then Joshua said to the people: "You are witnesses against yourselves that you have chosen YHWH, to serve him.	22. Then Joshua said to the people: "You are witnesses against yourselves that you have chosen YHWH, to serve him." **And they said: "(we are) witnesses."**
	23. And now put away the foreign gods that are among you, and direct your heart to YHWH, the God of Israel."	23. "And now put away the foreign gods that are among you, and direct your heart to YHWH, the God of Israel."
	24. And the people said to Joshua: "YHWH we will serve and his voice we will obey."	24. And the people said to Joshua: "YHWH **our God** we will serve and his voice we will obey."
25. So Joshua made a covenant with the people that day...	25. So Joshua made a covenant with the people that day...	25. So Joshua made a covenant with the people that day...

The literary-critical observations made here will be discussed further in section 4.3.3. It should be noted that even if one does not agree with the assumption of the first phase that is not attested by text-critical evidence, the two latest phases above are a likely explanation for the textual evidence. Text-critically speaking, וַיֹּאמְרוּ עֵדִים is probably a small addition utilizing formulaic language. The problem of continuity between 24:22 and 23 came into being only after this addition. It is noteworthy that in order to solve this variant, the whole textual and editorial history has to be taken into account. While text-critical evidence reinforces the problems of continuity related to the bridge between 24:22–23, a literary-critical observation is useful in setting the background for the text-critical evaluation.

Omission of the Sanctuary (v. 26)

In 24:26, the most notable variant is at the end of the verse.[153] The MT reads that the large stone bearing witness to the covenant (24:27) was put under the oak in the sanctuary of YHWH (בְּמִקְדַּשׁ יְהוָה). The OG text does not mention any shrine or sanctuary, but denotes that the stone was put under the oak which was directly before YHWH (ἀπέναντι κυρίου). This difference is another example of a minor variant which probably reflects theological motivations behind the scribal work.[154] Specifically, Pakkala has put forth an argument that the OG text preserves a theologically offensive idea "suggesting that YHWH was represented by a statue or other physical object." This idea was assumably already present in the Hebrew *Vorlage* of OG Josh 24:26, which read לפני יהוה "before YHWH". Such an idea is in contradiction with many important passages, most notably the Decalogue in Exod 20:4 and Deut 5:8. This is the reason why the editors behind the MT, according to Pakkala, omitted the physical presence of YHWH by inserting the sanctuary into the text. Pakkala's argument is further supported by the usage of the word "sanctuary" (מִקְדָּשׁ) in the MT. A sanctuary does not play a role in the current chapter, and the word is not mentioned elsewhere in the book of Joshua. Furthermore, Josh 24:1 seems to imply, according to Pakkala, that the statue or image of YHWH was standing in the open, and that the people could gather in front of it.[155]

The argument set forth by Pakkala is intriguing and possible. However, two weaknesses should be noted. First, as Pakkala himself acknowledges, the idea in MT Josh 24:26 is also theologically offensive. There are several passages in Deuteronomy and 1–2 Kings where holy trees and stones are condemned (e.g. Deut 12:2, 16:21, 2 Kgs 16:4). In contradiction to those passages, the MT conveys an idea that a stone and a tree was a legitimate part of the cult in YHWH's sanctuary. The text-critical argument thus relies on evaluating which theologically offensive idea is more offensive, and proposing a model of how this relative offensiveness was removed by the editor. Such reasoning should be explored, but inevitably remains speculative since other possible models can also be put forth. Butler, for one, builds an argument from theological offensiveness the other way around.

---

[153] Another minor variant in the verse is the different position of Joshua between the OG and the MT. While the MT reads וַיִּכְתֹּב יְהוֹשֻׁעַ "And Joshua wrote", the OG text reads καὶ ἔγραψεν "And he wrote". Later, the OG reads καὶ ἔστησεν αὐτὸν Ἰησοῦς "And Joshua set it" while the MT only gives the verb without mentioning Joshua וַיְקִימֶהָ שָּׁם "And he set it up there". This might be a stylistically motivated change in either one of the traditions. Butler (1983, 265) argues that it is a simplification in the Greek text. The variant does not have any major repercussions, and thus does not need to be settled here.

[154] For another case, see Josh 24:15 in section 3.3.2.

[155] Pakkala 2013, 198.

The reading ἀπέναντι κυρίου "before the Lord" is, according to him, a secondary attempt to specify that the tree was not within the sanctuary, since trees are specifically forbidden in Deuteronomy. In this way, the OG tradition diminishes the theological problems present in the MT.[156]

A second weakness is related to the assumed Hebrew reading לפני יהוה "before YHWH". It is, first of all, not clear whether this was the reading in the Hebrew *Vorlage*, since ἀπέναντι κυρίου is a rare phrase in the LXX. This is the only occurrence in Joshua. It is also questionable whether this reading would have necessarily brought to the mind of an ancient Hebrew editor a statue or image of YHWH. If this was the case, one would not expect to meet this exact expression 8 times in the book of Joshua (Josh 4:13; 6:8, 26; 7:23, 18:6, 8, 10; 19:51). On the contrary, the expression could simply be understood in a metaphorical sense, especially for editing of the biblical text that took place at later times. If the proto-MT editor, however, did understand the expression as referring to a physical image of YHWH, one would expect that such a diligent editor would have also removed the other theological problems in the same verse. This being said, it is also true that the editors do not show the same degree of consistency that a modern scholar would expect.

Whether or not one subscribes here to explanations relying on perceived theological problems, one cannot escape the notion that מִקְדָּשׁ "the sanctuary" is a foreign concept for Josh 24, and the whole book of Joshua for that matter.[157] Therefore, the expression "in the sanctuary of YHWH" can be regarded as a more problematic reading, and thus it might be earlier. The mention of a sanctuary could, in fact, be linked with the place name Shechem. There are some indications in the Pentateuch that Shechem was imagined at some point as having a sanctuary for YHWH (Gen 12:6–7, 33:20, 35:1–5).[158] Furthermore, a secondary removal of a sanctuary at Shechem could well be linked to an anti-Samaritan or anti-Northern ideology.[159] A Hebrew editor could have wanted to make sure that this important chapter was not used to legitimize the holy place of the Samaritans in Shechem. Such a removal would have most probably taken place already in the editing of the Hebrew *Vorlage* of OG Josh 24. This possible motivation for

---

156 Nelson (1997, 265) also notes that the change happened in the OG tradition "due to theological disquiet over the presence of a sacred tree". Den Hertog (2011, 655) connects the later specification "before the Lord" to a translator who wishes to remove a possible reference to heathen practices, since trees in a sanctuary are well-known in the Greek religious realm.
157 Holmes (1914, 80) notes that the expression is Priestly. The foreignness of a sanctuary in the context of Josh 24 is illustrated by the comment of Woudstra (1981, 357), which downplays the physical interpretation of מִקְדָּשׁ: "One should not think of this holy place as a formal structure but rather as a sacred precinct within which a tree could be found."
158 Knauf 2008, 199.
159 See also the variant in Josh 24:1, 25, regarding the place name, discussed in section 3.2.2.

an omission is strengthened by the reading present in SamJosh that the stone was put "in the place of the sanctuary of YHWH at the foot of Mt. Gerizim".[160] In this way, SamJosh illustrates that imagining a sanctuary at Shechem was indeed easily, through a minor addition, transformable into a Samaritan reading.

At this point, several variants should probably be explained together. The most plausible line of development is: the scene in Josh 24:25–26 was first depicted as taking place at Shechem, involving a sanctuary of YHWH and cultic elements that were elsewhere forbidden (MT). The scene was later rewritten as taking place in Shiloh, in front of the tent of YHWH (Hebrew *Vorlage* of OG), to harmonize it with earlier parts of the book of Joshua, to remove theological problems, and to diminish its importance for the Samaritans. Therefore, the MT probably preserves the earlier version in Josh 24:25–26, while the OG reflects later anti-Samaritan corrections probably already made to its Hebrew *Vorlage*.

Regardless of which tradition is deemed earlier, documented evidence points to the existence of two different settings for the covenant making in Josh 24. The setting was arguably earlier in one tradition and secondarily changed in the other; nevertheless, the two traditions might have lived concurrently in different communities. In late Second Temple Judaism, the important covenant scene could have legitimized the aims of various communities with simple textual variants. Thus, the possibility that the historical textual growth of Josh 24 may not be modeled as simply unilinear, but as having several trajectories in the evolution of the chapter, needs to be considered.

Variants Relating to the Stone of Witness (v. 27)

In verse 24:27, Joshua highlights that the stone mentioned in 24:26 acts as a stone of witness against the people when they deal falsely with YHWH. The text is presented in a much fuller form in the OG than in the MT. Also, the meaning can be interpreted differently.

The first variants affecting the meaning of the text are the two OG plusses that specify the timeframe of things happening in the verse: the witness stone in question has heard what YHWH has spoken "today" (σήμερον) and the stone shall be a witness when the people speak against YHWH "at the last days" (ἐπ' ἐσχάτων τῶν ἡμερῶν). The first plus might reflect the Hebrew היום "today" in the *Vorlage*.[161] The second plus, in turn, is especially interesting, since it gives the verse an eschatological flavor. The expression might reflect a different Hebrew *Vorlage*,

---

[160] See section 3.6.
[161] "Today" is restored to the main text, on the basis of the OG, already in the 1905 *Biblia Hebraica Kittel* by Samuel R. Driver. Thus also Boling & Wright 1982, 529. Koopmans (1990, 262) notes that "today" fits well with the poetic structure of the verse, creating a parallelism with the latter plus.

3.3 Joshua 24:14–27: Text and Apparatus — 113

since the phrase הַיָּמִים בְּאַחֲרִית "at the last days" is well-known elsewhere in the Hebrew Bible, especially in the prophetic literature (e.g. Gen 49:1, Hos 3:5, Mic 4:1, Ezek 38:16). The most important parallel to be mentioned here is Deut 31:29, in which the expression is used in a similar setting just before the death of Moses and after Joshua has been designated as the successor of Moses.

The pluses can be explained in two ways. They can be regarded either as additions in the OG or its Hebrew *Vorlage*, or as omissions in the proto-MT editing. Following the former solution, Butler proposes that "today" was added because of liturgical use.[162] Nielsen, on the other hand, regards it a simple harmonization with 24:15, which also contains the phrase הַיּוֹם "today".[163] That 24:27 was later made to refer to 24:15 is possible, since 24:27 refers to the things spoken by YHWH. A secondarily added connection between 24:27 and 24:15 would increase the coherence of the chapter, which would then corroborate that "today" is a secondary addition. The plus "at the last days", in turn, can be seen as a later addition attempting to "make the passage relevant to its own time" by utilizing prophetic language.[164] The scribe would have utilized the parallels already mentioned (most notably Deut 31:29). The addition would have given the verse an eschatological flavor. Conversely, one could also argue for the intentional omission of these plusses in the proto-MT editing. The phrase "at the last days", specifically, could have been omitted by a scribe who wanted to highlight the close connection between the stone of witness and the book of the law. It could have been perceived that the law should be held as a witness for all days, and not just for the last days. From this point of view, "today" could have also been regarded as unnecessary, since the law is older than that which was spoken "today".

As such, the arguments do not seem decisive regarding the priority of either tradition. Plausible motivations can be found to support both directions. However, when one looks at the changes at the end of Josh 24:27 discussed earlier in section 3.3.1 it seems that, in the case of the latter plus "at the last days", a difference in meaning favors the OG as preserving the earlier reading. The reading "and it shall be in your midst a witness at the last days whenever you rebel against the Lord my God" (OG) is more despairing, since it highlights the possibility of apostasy "at the last days", while the context of Josh 24 underlines the faithfulness of the Israelites. Thus, it is possible that the later editor who made the ending of the verse more diluted by changing "rebel" (OG) to "deal falsely" (MT) also omitted "at the last days" as part of his softening revision. The fuller and more hopeless reading preserved in the OG was likely originally created in light of Deut 31:29, whose tone is

---

[162] Butler 1983, 265.
[163] Nielsen 1955, 108.
[164] Butler 1983, 265.

similar, and which also contains the phrase בְּאַחֲרִית הַיָּמִים, as well as the rare Hebrew poetic noun "words" (אִמְרֵי) in its near context (Deut 32:1). This ending of the verse seems to better preserve an earlier connection to Deuteronomy, and has been made simpler in the proto-MT text. If this suggestion is correct, it is more probable, however, that "today" has come about as a later corrective addition to the OG. Considering the eschatological nature of the verse, a later scribe could have wanted to highlight that the things were spoken, and that the covenant was made "today".

Some minor variants remain in 24:27. While in the MT, Joshua speaks to אֶל־כָּל־הָעָם "all the people", OG only mentions πρὸς τὸν λαόν "the people". In the light of verse 24:2, which also reads "all the people", this reading should probably be preferred here, especially when the reading in the OG can be explained with an omission through *homoioteleuton* אֶל־כָּל־הָעָם.[165] At the end of the verse, the MT reads בֵּאלֹהֵיכֶם "your God" while the OG reads κυρίῳ τῷ θεῷ μου "the Lord my God". The reading in the OG highlights the authoritative role of Joshua, by attributing the divinity to him rather than to the people.[166] In Josh 14:8, Caleb uses the same expression when talking to Joshua. There, it is preserved both in the MT and the OG, and the Hebrew phrase יהוה אלהי "YHWH my God" could also be behind the Hebrew *Vorlage* of OG 24:27. An even more interesting parallel is present in Deut 26:3, where a similar variant is preserved between the MT and the OG. In the MT, the words of the priest begin with הִגַּדְתִּי הַיּוֹם לַיהוָה אֱלֹהֶיךָ "I declare today to YHWH your God" while the OG reads Ἀναγγέλλω σήμερον κυρίῳ τῷ θεῷ μου "I declare today to the Lord my God". Since the second-person "your God" is the more common phrase in such a context, it might be that, in both Deut 26:3 and Josh 24:27, the MT version reflects a secondary harmonization of an unusual form to a more common one. Lastly, a secondary omission of the tetragrammaton in the MT is likely related to the change of the verb towards a "softer" choice; the earlier reading "whenever you rebel against YHWH my God" (Hebrew *Vorlage* of the OG) is more blatant than the later "lest you deal falsely with your God" (MT).[167] Accordingly, it has been noted that in this instance there might be more reason to omit the name of God than to add it for reasons pertaining to theological sensitivity.[168]

To sum up, Josh 24:27 is a complicated verse with several textual variants. The OG – whose original wording remains tentative – contains two eschatological

---

[165] Thus also Boling & Wright 1982, 532. Koopmans (1990, 261) argues that the MT secondarily makes a deliberate inclusion with the beginning of the dialogue in 24:2. This reference to verse 24:2 might, however, also be earlier and might even be a literary technique (*Wiederaufnahme*) with which the verse was added to the chapter.
[166] Butler 1983, 265.
[167] The change of the verb has already been evaluated in section 3.3.1.
[168] Nielsen 1955, 108.

plusses which may or may not have belonged to the earlier text of the verse. The MT, in turn, is corrupted by a *homoioteleuton*, a secondary harmonization of a personal pronoun, a change of the verb to better suit the context, and an omission of the tetragrammaton. Therefore, while there is uncertainty relating to the two eschatological plusses, overall it is safe to follow the OG in Josh 24:27.

Other Minor Variants

In 24:14, Joshua urges the Israelites to put away the foreign gods that their ancestors served beyond the river. While the MT only mentions אֶת־אֱלֹהִים "the gods", the OG has a plus reading τοὺς θεοὺς τοὺς ἀλλοτρίους "the foreign gods". The reading in OG is related to verse 23, where the MT also reads "the foreign gods" (אֶת־אֱלֹהֵי הַנֵּכָר). This connection makes it more probable that the plus in the OG is a secondary harmonizing addition.[169] If the attribute "foreign" reflected a different *Vorlage* with the designation הַנֵּכָר, its secondary omission would be hard to explain. There are no grounds for a scribal mistake, nor would an intentional omission make sense, since the attribute is preserved in v. 23.

At the end of 24:15, the OG has as a plus ὅτι ἅγιός ἐστιν "because he is holy". The sentence is connected to verse 19, where both versions read it. There, Joshua proclaims that the Israelites will not be able to serve YHWH since he is a holy God (LXX ὅτι θεὸς ἅγιός ἐστιν / MT אֱלֹהִים קְדֹשִׁים הוּא כִּי). Koopmans notes that the sentence in verse 15 could be an earlier reading, since it makes a connection with verse 19 "thereby bracketing the answer of the people with a twofold assertion of Yahweh's holiness."[170] A literary-critical argument might also support its originality. According to several scholars, the motive of the people's inability to serve YHWH (vv. 19–21) is likely a secondary insertion in this chapter.[171] The editorial technique used in inserting these verses is resumptive repetition which picks up the phrase "we will serve YHWH" (נַעֲבֹד אֶת־יְהוָה) from verse 18. If כִּי־אֱלֹהִים קְדֹשִׁים הוּא was already present in the earlier Hebrew text of verse 15, as attested by the OG version, it would mean that the late insertion of 19–21 carries in it yet another repetition. Thus, it would not be the case that the OG "gives away the punchline of verse 19",[172] but that the punchline of verse 19 was secondarily taken from the

---

[169] Nielsen 1955, 99; Butler 1983, 264. Den Hertog 2011, 655: "Die Ergänzung τοὺς ἀλλοτρίους stellt eine Vorwegnahme der nachfolgenden Erwähnungen fremder Götter in 24,16.20.23 dar." Overall, in verse 24 both the designations נכר and אחר are used for other gods and they are translated in the OG as following: אֲחֵרִים with ἑτέροις (2, 16), נֵכָר with ἑτέροις (20), and הַנֵּכָר with τοὺς ἀλλοτρίους (23).
[170] Koopmans 1990, 257.
[171] Noth 1953, 136; Fritz 1994, 246–247; Müller 2004, 217; Aurelius 2008, 100; Rösel 2011, 372. See section 4.3.3 for further arguments.
[172] Butler 1983, 264.

earlier text of OG Josh 24:15. It would then, further, make sense that the phrase was removed in the proto-MT editing as an unnecessary doublet. Similar smoothening out of the traces of earlier redaction has already been noted elsewhere in the textual analysis of this chapter.

Conversely, one could argue that ὅτι θεὸς ἅγιός ἐστιν is simply a later addition to 24:15 taken from 24:19.[173] The problem of explaining the development this way is related to the content of verse 15. There, Joshua gives YHWH's holiness as a reason for him choosing to serve YHWH. If YHWH's holiness was originally introduced as a reason that he cannot be served (as in verse 19), it would not make much sense to add it to Joshua's pious proclamation in verse 15. If YHWH's holiness was, however, originally presented as the reason that Joshua chooses to serve him, the addition of YHWH's holiness secondarily in verse 19 would make more sense. It is a way of making a demarcation between the God's chosen, Joshua, and the constantly failing people.

In 24:18, it is remembered how YHWH drove out the inhabitants of the land before the Israelites. While the OG reads τὸν Ἀμορραῖον καὶ πάντα τὰ ἔθνη τὰ κατοικοῦντα τὴν γῆν "the Amorites and all the people who inhabit the land", the MT has a different order אֶת־כָּל־הָעַמִּים וְאֶת־הָאֱמֹרִי יֹשֵׁב הָאָרֶץ "all the people and the Amorites who inhabit the land". The phrase אֶת־כָּל־הָעַמִּים "all the people" is only loosely connected to the preceding verses, where the Amorites have been the people living in the land (v. 15). Accordingly, several scholars already in early times have seen the phrase as a later insertion. This is because it is not necessary to mention the Amorites separately, since all the people who inhabited the land are already mentioned.[174] This conclusion is corroborated by the observation that the participle יֹשֵׁב is singular without an article, and can therefore only refer to the collective "Amorites". The insertion of "all the people" might have been made on the basis of the phrase וּבְכֹל הָעַמִּים "among all the people" in the preceding verse.[175] Holmes proposes that the different order between the MT and the OG shows that the phrase was added to the MT and later also added to the OG.[176] On the other hand, it is also imaginable that two different copyists found the phrase in the margin, and added it to different locations in the running text. In any case, the mobility of the phrase is connected to it being a later gloss.[177] If this is the case, the reading in the

---

[173] Nielsen 1955, 99.
[174] Already Dillmann (1886, 587): "…ohne Zweifel Zusatz". The opinion is also shared by Noth 1953, 140.
[175] Nielsen 1955, 99.
[176] Holmes 1914, 79.
[177] Koopmans (1990, 257–258) objects to the phrase being a gloss on the basis of an assumed alternating parallelism between vv. 17d and 18. According to him, the LXX does not recognize the

3.3 Joshua 24:14–27: Text and Apparatus — 117

OG is likely earlier, since it retains the earlier structure of the sentence καὶ ἐξέβαλεν κύριος τὸν Αμορραῖον "and the Lord drove out the Amorites" to which "and all the people" has been added. The MT represents either an independent insertion of the gloss in the running text or a stylistic refinement of the sentence in the OG.

In verse 24:19, Joshua gives reasons for why the people will not be able to worship YHWH. One of the reasons, according to the MT, is that "he is a jealous god" (הוּא אֵל־קַנּוֹא). The OG only reads καὶ ζηλώσας οὗτος "and he is jealous" without אֵל "God". An omission in the OG is probable. As Nielsen notes, the translation equivalent in Greek is a free rendering.[178] It might be that the translator chose a translation which removed the repetition of θεός "God". The translator usually translated both אֱלֹהִים and אֵל with θεός, and since both words occur here within a short word range, the translation choice might aim at a simpler sentence.[179] Against this popular explanation, it could be noted that in Exodus and Deuteronomy there are several passages where both אֱלֹהִים and אֵל־קַנּוֹא occur within a short range of words and the translator translates them both using θεός (Exod 20:5, 34:14, Deut 4:24, 5:9, 6:15). Based on this observation, one could argue that the OG reflects an earlier Hebrew *Vorlage* and אֵל has been secondarily added to the MT. However, this explanation is unlikely, because when קַנָּא is used for God in the Hebrew Bible it is always coupled with אֵל. When comparing Josh 24:19 with similar passages in Exodus and Deuteronomy, it should also be noted that Josh 24:19 is a unique passage for two reasons. First, Hebrew utilizes the word "jealous" in the form קַנּוֹא and not קַנָּא (only other occurrence in Nah 1:2). Second, the translator utilizes the participle form ζηλώσας and not the more common noun ζηλωτής.[180] This free rendering speaks for a syntactical simplification and an omission of the אֵל in the translation process.

In verse 24:24, the people proclaim one last time that they will serve YHWH. While the MT reads אֶת־יְהוָה אֱלֹהֵינוּ נַעֲבֹד "YHWH our God we will serve" the OG only reads Κυρίῳ λατρεύσομεν "YHWH we will serve". Several scholars follow the OG, partly based on the similar expressions used in 24:21–22.[181] Accordingly, the element אֱלֹהֵינוּ could be well explained as a secondary addition utilizing common

---

poetic form and inverts the order "for a syntactically and stylistically smoother reading". The argument that the LXX translator or editor of the Hebrew *Vorlage* not understanding the poetic structure is not compelling since elsewhere Koopmans (1990, 247–278) postulates that the LXX makes poetically motivated additions.

[178] Nielsen 1955, 99.
[179] Koopmans 1990, 258.
[180] MSS 19-376-426 58 secondarily correct the OG participle ζηλώσας to the more common noun ζηλωτής.
[181] Holmes 1914, 79; Nielsen 1955, 100; Boling & Wright 1982, 531; Butler 1983, 265.

language used in the Hebrew Bible. Knauf notes that verse 24:24 parallels with 1 Sam 12:14, in that they both employ the expressions "serve" and "hear" YHWH in the same order.[182] Therefore, it is interesting that in 1 Sam 12:14 the MT seems to also secondarily add אֱלֹהֵיכֶם after YHWH. This strengthens the idea that formulaic language might motivate such additions. Thus, the OG should probably be followed in Josh 24:24.

3.4 Joshua 24:28–33: Text and Apparatus

MT *(BHS)*	OG
²⁸ וַיְשַׁלַּח יְהוֹשֻׁעַ אֶת־הָעָם אִישׁ לְנַחֲלָתוֹ	²⁸ καὶ ἀπέστειλεν Ἰησοῦς τὸν λαόν, καὶ ἐπορεύθησαν ἕκαστος εἰς τὸν τόπον αὐτοῦ.
And Joshua sent the people away, each to his inheritance.	And Iesous sent the people away, and they went each to his place.
	²⁹ καὶ ἐλάτρευσεν Ἰσραὴλ τῷ κυρίῳ πάσας τὰς ἡμέρας Ἰησοῦ καὶ πάσας τὰς ἡμέρας τῶν πρεσβυτέρων, ὅσοι ἐφείλκυσαν τὸν χρόνον μετὰ Ἰησοῦ καὶ ὅσοι εἴδοσαν πάντα τὰ ἔργα κυρίου, ὅσα ἐποίησεν τῷ Ἰσραήλ. And Israel served the Lord all the days of Iesous and all the days of the elders who outlived Joshua and who had seen all the works of the Lord that he did for Israel.

24:28 ἀπέστειλεν] εξαπεστειλεν 44´ C⁻⁸² 52-53-57-58-72-85-130-509 | ἐπορεύθησαν] απηλθον 58 | τον τοπον] την πολιν 85^mg-344^mg; *domum* La¹⁰⁰
24:29 tr καὶ 1° – Ἰσραήλ 2° post 31a O⁻ᴳ ¹⁰⁸ | Ἰησοῦ 2°] ιεσουν 54-44-314 52-57-85 Ma

---

[182] Knauf 2008, 198.

3.4 Joshua 24:28–33: Text and Apparatus

MT (BHS)	OG
²⁹ וַיְהִי אַחֲרֵי הַדְּבָרִים הָאֵלֶּה וַיָּמָת יְהוֹשֻׁעַ בִּן־נוּן עֶבֶד יְהוָה בֶּן־מֵאָה וָעֶשֶׂר שָׁנִים	³⁰ Καὶ ἐγένετο μετ' ἐκεῖνα καὶ ἀπέθανεν Ἰησοῦς υἱὸς Ναυὴ δοῦλος κυρίου ἑκατὸν δέκα ἐτῶν.
And it happened after these things that died Joshua son of Nun, the servant of YHWH one hundred ten years old.	And it happened afterwards that died Iesous son of Naue, the servant of the Lord at one hundred ten years.
³⁰ וַיִּקְבְּרוּ אֹתוֹ בִּגְבוּל נַחֲלָתוֹ בְּתִמְנַת־סֶרַח אֲשֶׁר בְּהַר־אֶפְרָיִם מִצְּפוֹן לְהַר־גָּעַשׁ	³¹ καὶ ἔθαψαν αὐτὸν πρὸς τοῖς ὁρίοις τοῦ κλήρου αὐτοῦ ἐν Θαμναθασαχαρα ἐν τῷ ὄρει τῷ Ἐφράιμ ἀπὸ βορρᾶ τοῦ ὄρους Γαάς·
And they buried him at the borders in his inheritance in Timnath-serah, which is at Mount Ephraim, north of Mount Gaash.	And they buried him at the borders of his inheritance in Thamnathasachara, which is at Mount Ephraim, north of Mount Gaas.
	³¹ₐ ἐκεῖ ἔθηκαν μετ' αὐτοῦ εἰς τὸ μνῆμα, εἰς ὃ ἔθαψαν αὐτὸν ἐκεῖ, τὰς μαχαίρας τὰς πετρίνας, ἐν αἷς περιέτεμεν τοὺς υἱοὺς Ἰσραηλ ἐν Γαλγάλοις, ὅτε ἐξήγαγεν αὐτοὺς ἐξ Αἰγύπτου, καθὰ συνέταξεν αὐτοῖς κύριος, καὶ ἐκεῖ εἰσιν ἕως τῆς σήμερον ἡμέρας.
	There they put with him into the tomb in which they buried him, the flint knives with which he circumcised the sons of Israel in Galgala, when he led them out of Egypt, as the Lord instructed them, and there they are until this very day.

(Continued)

24:30 μετ' ἐκεῖνα] μετα τα πραγματα ταυτα 426 | εκατον δεκα] pr ων 106-314; pr υιος 19; post ετων 44 52-53-57-85-130-344; υς εκατον και δεκα 426; υιος δεκα και εκατον 376

24:31 τοῦ κλήρου] τῆς κληρονομίας O⁻ᴳ 108 15-58-85ᵐᵍ | Γαάς] του γαλααδ E⁻¹²⁰ 56 | OG reading om. אֲשֶׁר witnessed also by several Kennicott (1785, 109) mss.

24:31a om ἐκεῖ 2° 19 75 55 58-72 | ἐξ] ex γης L⁻⁴⁴; ex της 56

MT (BHS)	OG
³¹ וַיַּעֲבֹד יִשְׂרָאֵל אֶת־יְהוָה כֹּל יְמֵי יְהוֹשֻׁעַ וְכֹל יְמֵי הַזְּקֵנִים אֲשֶׁר הֶאֱרִיכוּ יָמִים אַחֲרֵי יְהוֹשֻׁעַ וַאֲשֶׁר יָדְעוּ אֵת כָּל־מַעֲשֵׂה יְהוָה אֲשֶׁר עָשָׂה לְיִשְׂרָאֵל	
And Israel served YHWH all the days of Joshua and all the days of the elders who outlived Joshua and who had known all the works of YHWH that he did for Israel.	
³² וְאֶת־עַצְמוֹת יוֹסֵף אֲשֶׁר־הֶעֱלוּ בְנֵי־יִשְׂרָאֵל מִמִּצְרַיִם קָבְרוּ בִשְׁכֶם בְּחֶלְקַת הַשָּׂדֶה אֲשֶׁר קָנָה יַעֲקֹב מֵאֵת בְּנֵי־חֲמוֹר אֲבִי־שְׁכֶם בְּמֵאָה קְשִׂיטָה וַיִּהְיוּ לִבְנֵי־יוֹסֵף לְנַחֲלָה	³² καὶ τὰ ὀστᾶ Ἰωσὴφ ἀνήγαγον οἱ υἱοὶ Ἰσραὴλ ἐξ Αἰγύπτου καὶ κατώρυξαν ἐν Σικίμοις ἐν τῇ μερίδι τοῦ ἀγροῦ, οὗ ἐκτήσατο Ἰακὼβ παρὰ τῶν Ἀμορραίων τῶν κατοικούντων ἐν Σικίμοις ἀμνάδων ἑκατὸν καὶ ἔδωκεν αὐτὴν Ἰωσὴφ ἐν μερίδι.
And the bones of Joseph, which the Israelites had brought up from Egypt, they buried at Shechem in the portion of the field that Jacob had bought from the children of Hamor, the father of Shechem, for one hundred pieces of money. It was an inheritance to the children of Joseph.	And the bones of Joseph, the Israelites brought up from Egypt, they buried at Sikima, in the portion of the field that Jacob had bought from the Amorites, living in Sikima, for one hundred lambs. And he gave it to Joseph as an inheritance.
³³ וְאֶלְעָזָר בֶּן־אַהֲרֹן מֵת וַיִּקְבְּרוּ אֹתוֹ בְּגִבְעַת פִּינְחָס בְּנוֹ	³³ Καὶ ἐγένετο μετὰ ταῦτα καὶ Ἐλεαζὰρ υἱὸς Ἀαρὼν ὁ ἀρχιερεὺς ἐτελεύτησεν καὶ ἐτάφη ἐν Γαβααθ Φινεὲς τοῦ υἱοῦ αὐτοῦ,

24:32 ἀνήγαγον] pr α Ma | ἐξ] εκ γης 54´
24:33 ἀρχιερεὺς] ιερευς 44´⁻³¹⁴ C⁻⁵⁹ 52-53-57-72-85-130-344

3.4 Joshua 24:28–33: Text and Apparatus

MT *(BHS)*	OG
אֲשֶׁר נָתַן־לוֹ בְּהַר אֶפְרָיִם	ἣν ἔδωκεν αὐτῷ ἐν τῷ ὄρει τῷ Ἐφράιμ.
And Eleazar son of Aaron died and they buried him at Gibeah, of Phinehas his son, which had been given him in Mount Ephraim.	And it happened after these things that Eleazar son of Aaron, the high priest, died and was buried in Gabaath, of Phinees his son, which he gave him in Mount Ephraim.
	³³ᵃ ἐν ἐκείνῃ τῇ ἡμέρᾳ λαβόντες οἱ υἱοὶ Ἰσραὴλ τὴν κιβωτὸν τοῦ θεοῦ περιεφέροσαν ἐν ἑαυτοῖς, καὶ Φινεὲς ἱεράτευσεν ἀντὶ Ἐλεαζὰρ τοῦ πατρὸς αὐτοῦ, ἕως ἀπέθανεν καὶ κατωρύγη ἐν Γαβαὰθ τῇ ἑαυτοῦ.
	On that day the Israelites took the ark of God and carried it in their midst. And Phinees served as priest instead of Eleazar his father until he died and was buried in Gabaath which was his own.
	³³ᵇ οἱ δὲ υἱοὶ Ἰσραὴλ ἀπήλθοσαν ἕκαστος εἰς τὸν τόπον αὐτῶν καὶ εἰς τὴν ἑαυτῶν πόλιν. καὶ ἐσέβοντο οἱ υἱοὶ Ἰσραὴλ τὴν Ἀστάρτην καὶ Ἀσταρὼθ καὶ τοὺς θεοὺς τῶν ἐθνῶν.

24:33a κιβωτὸν] + της (om 121) διαθηκης 44´ *C M*⁻¹⁵ ⁵⁶ | ἑαυτοῖς] pr τω ιηλ 120; τω ιηλ 19 44 15-52-57-85ᵗˣᵗ-130-344ᵗˣᵗ; αυτοις εν τω ιηλ 376; τοις υιοις ιηλ *L*⁻⁴⁴ ³¹⁴ | ἑαυτοῦ 120 A-121 15] εαυτων B 376; αυτων *L*⁻⁴⁴; αυτου rel Ma
24:33b Ασταρωθ *E*⁻¹²⁰ 376 106 56] pr τὴν rel Ma

MT *(BHS)*	OG
	τῶν κύκλῳ αὐτῶν·
	καὶ παρέδωκεν αὐτοὺς κύριος
	εἰς χεῖρας Ἐγλὼμ τῷ βασιλεῖ Μωάβ,
	καὶ ἐκυρίευσεν αὐτῶν ἔτη δέκα ὀκτώ.
	And the Israelites departed
	each to their places
	and to their cities.
	And the Israelites started to worship
	Astarte and Astaroth
	and the gods of the nations
	that surrounded them.
	And the Lord gave them
	into the hands of Eglom, the king of Moab,
	and he dominated them for eighteen years.

3.4.1 Text-Critical Analysis of the OG

24:28 The replacement of ἀπέστειλεν with εξαπεστειλεν in some MSS is probably a secondary development due to the parallel verse in Judg 2:6 or the similar verse in Josh 22:6. The usual equivalent for sending people away in Joshua is ἀποστέλλω without the prefix (e.g. Josh 7:2, 22; 8:3, 9). A similar replacement has taken place in MS 58, in which the common verb reflected also in Judg 2:6 has motivated a change from ἐπορεύθησαν to απηλθον. Both 85 and 344 contain πόλις instead of τόπος as a marginal reading. The Old Latin reading might reflect a different Greek text, and will be discussed in section 3.4.2.

24:29 In the OG, verse 29 is situated in a different location than in the MT (24:31). $O^{-G\ 108}$ secondarily follows the order of the MT.

24:30 The readings preserved in MSS 19 376 426 are once again best explained as secondary developments bringing the text closer to the Hebrew text.

24:31 The Greek τῆς κληρονομίας in $O^{-G\ 108}$ 15-58-85^{mg} might be a secondary harmonization with the parallel verse in Judg 2:9.

B, together with 129 and 56, deviate from the reading "mount Gaash" in the majority text, by reading that it was the mountain of γαλααδ "Gilead". One could argue that the OG read "mount Gilead" and that this reading was later corrected towards the MT. While this is the only mention of Gaash in Joshua, Gilead is a very common place name (e.g. Josh 22). However, since this is the only mention of Gaash in Joshua, while Gilead, on the other hand, is a very common place name (e.g. Josh 22), it is more likely that Gilead is a later harmonizing replacement of Gaash with a more common place name.

24:31a Most of the Greek MSS read ἐξ Αἰγύπτου "from Egypt", while the majority of the Antiochene witnesses read ἐκ γῆς Αἰγύπτου "from the land of Egypt". This is a hard reading to evaluate, since the verse has no counterpart in the MT. Normally, ἐξ Αἰγύπτου is used as a translation equivalent for the Hebrew מִמִּצְרַיִם while ἐκ γῆς Αἰγύπτου reflects מֵאֶרֶץ מִצְרַיִם. Earlier in Josh 24, there are three occurrences of these phrases.

Josh 24:6	MT מִמִּצְרַיִם	OG ἐξ Αἰγύπτου
Josh 24:17	MT מֵאֶרֶץ מִצְרַיִם	OG ἐξ Αἰγύπτου[183]
Josh 24:32	MT מִמִּצְרַיִם	OG ἐξ Αἰγύπτου[184]

The closest parallel to the reading in verse 24:31a is found in Deut 29:24 ὅτε ἐξήγαγεν αὐτοὺς ἐκ γῆς Αἰγύπτου "when he brought them out of the land of Egypt", where it is a translation of בְּהוֹצִיאוֹ אֹתָם מֵאֶרֶץ מִצְרַיִם. Thus, it is possible that the translator of OG Josh 24:31a had a similar reading in his *Vorlage* and he translated it with ἐκ γῆς Αἰγύπτου, which is preserved in *L*. The majority reading ἐξ Αἰγύπτου could be explained as a harmonization in the light of the three other occurrences in Josh 24. Hence it is possible that *L* preserves the earliest reading here. Based on the next verse, however, it could be argued that *L* text has a stylistic tendency to secondarily add the element γῆς. Since this is a relatively minor variation which could easily happen at any point of copying of the text, the question remains open.

24:32 Here again, two *L* MSS give the reading ἐκ γῆς Αἰγύπτου instead of the majority reading ἐξ Αἰγύπτου. See the notes of the preceding verse.

Margolis adds the relative pronoun, creating the reading ἃ ἀνήγαγον "which was brought", attested only by the Ethiopic translation and the Syrohexapla. However, the pronoun should probably rather be explained as a later revision

---

[183] There several MSS, most prominently from *C* and *O* groups, that give ἐκ γῆς in 24:17. There, however, it is clearly a correction towards the Hebrew text.
[184] However, two Antiochene MSS also give there the reading ἐκ γῆς Αἰγύπτου.

towards the Hebrew אֲשֶׁר־הֶעֱלוּ "which they brought". It should not be included in the OG, as is the case in the edition by Rahlfs.

The OG translates the rare and uncertain קְשִׂיטָה "weight used as money" with ἀμνάδων "lambs", as is also the case in Gen 33:19 and Job 42:11. One cannot completely rule out the possibility of a different Hebrew *Vorlage* (כבשים "lambs"). Römer notes that if קְשִׂיטָה refers to coins, its usage indicates that "Joshua 24 could hardly be older than the 5th century, since it was only at this time that people started to use coins in Palestine."[185] However, the case is not that simple. Since the OG could reflect a different Hebrew *Vorlage*, one could argue that קְשִׂיטָה was a late change from the earlier "lambs" to the current form of currency. Nevertheless, a different *Vorlage* is not certain, since the OG equivalent could also be dependent on Gen 33:19 from where the translator sought help to translate an obscure Hebrew word.

24:33 The substitution of ἀρχιερεύς with ἱερεύς in the *L* group and some other MSS is probably a correction towards the more common title ἱερεύς "priest" of Aaron. The title is missing altogether from the MT. However, in MT Josh 22:13 the title of Eleazar is הַכֹּהֵן which the OG translated with the rare ἀρχιερεύς. In 22:13, there is a widespread secondary correction toward the more common ἱερεύς attested in MSS 120 *O*$^{-G108}$ 54´-314 55-82-121 *M*$^{-56\ 58}$. Therefore, the secondary change towards ἱερεύς in 24:33 might also be related to this reading. The originality of ἀρχιερεύς is corroborated by the notion that it is a rare translation equivalent. Everywhere else in the LXX the title of Eleazar or Aaron is ἱερεύς.

24:33a The secondary addition of τῆς διαθηκης is based on idiomatic language, and must be relatively early since it is widely attested in the MS groups. Some MS specify that the ark was carried among the Israelites. Four *L* MSS repeat the expression "sons of Israel" at this point.

24:33b Rahlfs follows the MSS that omit the second article τὴν Ἀστάρτην καὶ Ασταρωθ "(the) Astarte and Astaroth". Most of the manuscripts, and the edition by Margolis, however, read also the second article (τὴν Ἀστάρτην καὶ τὴν Ασταρωθ "[the] Astarte and [the] Astaroth"). Den Hertog notes that a congruence with the following expression speaks for the originality of the second article (τὴν Ἀστάρτην καὶ τὴν Ασταρωθ … τοὺς θεοὺς τῶν ἐθνῶν).[186] However, it is more likely that the OG did not have the second article, since its addition can be explained as an attempt to make the Greek text better. The congruence is more likely a secondary development.

---

[185] Römer 2017, 206.
[186] Den Hertog 1996, 106.

3.4.2 Evaluation between the OG and the MT

Relationship with Judg 2:6–9

In the text-critical analysis of the last verses in Josh 24, the existing parallel version in Judg 2:6–9 should also be considered, since it offers additional documented evidence for the textual growth of this pericope. The complex relationship between these accounts is illustrated in the table below.

MT Josh 24:28–31	OG Josh 24:28–31	MT Judg 2:6–9	OG Judg 2:6–9[1]
²⁸ וַיְשַׁלַּח יְהוֹשֻׁעַ אֶת־הָעָם	²⁸ καὶ ἀπέστειλεν Ἰησοῦς τὸν λαόν	⁶ וַיְשַׁלַּח יְהוֹשֻׁעַ אֶת־הָעָם	⁶ Καὶ ἐξαπέστειλεν Ἰησοῦς τὸν λαόν
	καὶ ἐπορεύθησαν	וַיֵּלְכוּ בְנֵי־יִשְׂרָאֵל	καὶ ἀπῆλθαν οἱ υἱοὶ Ἰσραήλ
אִישׁ	ἕκαστος	אִישׁ	ἕκαστος[2]
			εἰς τὸν οἶκον αὐτοῦ καὶ[3]
לְנַחֲלָתוֹ	εἰς τὸν τόπον αὐτοῦ.	לְנַחֲלָתוֹ	εἰς τὴν κληρονομίαν αὐτοῦ
		לָרֶשֶׁת	τοῦ κατακληρονομῆσαι
		אֶת־הָאָרֶץ	τὴν γῆν.
(situated at the end)	²⁹ καὶ ἐλάτρευσεν Ἰσραὴλ τῷ κυρίῳ πάσας τὰς ἡμέρας Ἰησοῦ καὶ πάσας τὰς ἡμέρας τῶν πρεσβυτέρων, ὅσοι ἐφείλκυσαν τὸν χρόνον μετὰ Ἰησοῦ καὶ ὅσοι εἴδοσαν πάντα τὰ ἔργα κυρίου ὅσα ἐποίησεν τῷ Ἰσραήλ	⁷ וַיַּעַבְדוּ הָעָם אֶת־יְהוָה כֹּל יְמֵי יְהוֹשֻׁעַ וְכֹל יְמֵי הַזְּקֵנִים אֲשֶׁר הֶאֱרִיכוּ יָמִים אַחֲרֵי יְהוֹשֻׁעַ אֲשֶׁר רָאוּ אֵת כָּל־מַעֲשֵׂה יְהוָה הַגָּדוֹל אֲשֶׁר עָשָׂה לְיִשְׂרָאֵל	⁷ καὶ ἐδούλευσεν ὁ λαὸς τῷ κυρίῳ πάσας τὰς ἡμέρας Ἰησοῦ καὶ πάσας τὰς ἡμέρας τῶν πρεσβυτέρων, ὅσοι ἐμακροημέρευσαν μετὰ Ἰησοῦν, ὅσοι ἔγνωσαν πᾶν τὸ ἔργον κυρίου τὸ μέγα ὃ ἐποίησεν τῷ Ἰσραήλ.
²⁹ וַיְהִי אַחֲרֵי הַדְּבָרִים הָאֵלֶּה וַיָּמָת יְהוֹשֻׁעַ בִּן־נוּן עֶבֶד יְהוָה בֶּן־מֵאָה וָעֶשֶׂר שָׁנִים	³⁰ Καὶ ἐγένετο μετ' ἐκεῖνα καὶ ἀπέθανεν Ἰησοῦς υἱὸς Ναυή δοῦλος κυρίου ἑκατὸν δέκα ἐτῶν.	⁸ וַיָּמָת יְהוֹשֻׁעַ בִּן־נוּן עֶבֶד יְהוָה בֶּן־מֵאָה וָעֶשֶׂר שָׁנִים	⁸ καὶ ἐτελεύτησεν Ἰησοῦς υἱὸς Ναυή δοῦλος κυρίου υἱὸς ἑκατὸν δέκα ἐτῶν.
³⁰ וַיִּקְבְּרוּ אֹתוֹ בִּגְבוּל	³¹ αἱ ἔθαψαν αὐτὸν πρὸς τοῖς ὁρίοις[4]	⁹ וַיִּקְבְּרוּ אוֹתוֹ בִּגְבוּל	⁹ καὶ ἔθαψαν αὐτὸν ἐν ὁρίῳ

(Continued)

MT Josh 24:28–31	OG Josh 24:28–31	MT Judg 2:6–9	OG Judg 2:6–9[1]
נַחֲלָתוֹ	τοῦ κλήρου αὐτοῦ	נַחֲלָתוֹ	τῆς κληρονομίας αὐτοῦ
בְּתִמְנַת־סֶרַח <u>אֲשֶׁר</u>	ἐν Θαμναθασαχαρὰ	בְּתִמְנַת־חֶרֶס	ἐν Θαμναθάρες
בְּהַר־אֶפְרָיִם	ἐν τῷ ὄρει τῷ Ἐφράιμ	בְּהַר אֶפְרָיִם	ἐν ὄρει Ἐφράιμ
מִצְּפוֹן	ἀπὸ βορρᾶ	מִצְּפוֹן	ἀπὸ βορρᾶ
לְהַר־גָּעַשׁ	τοῦ ὄρους Γάας·	לְהַר־גָּעַשׁ	τοῦ ὄρους Γάας.
³¹ וַיַּעֲבֹד יִשְׂרָאֵל אֶת־יְהוָה כֹּל יְמֵי יְהוֹשֻׁעַ וְכֹל יְמֵי הַזְּקֵנִים אֲשֶׁר הֶאֱרִיכוּ יָמִים אַחֲרֵי יְהוֹשֻׁעַ וַאֲשֶׁר יָדְעוּ אֵת כָּל־מַעֲשֵׂה יְהוָה אֲשֶׁר עָשָׂה לְיִשְׂרָאֵל			
	³¹ᵃ ἐκεῖ ἔθηκαν μετ᾿ αὐτοῦ εἰς τὸ μνῆμα, εἰς ὃ ἔθαψαν αὐτὸν ἐκεῖ, τὰς μαχαίρας τὰς πετρίνας, ἐν αἷς περιέτεμεν τοὺς υἱοὺς Ἰσραὴλ ἐν Γαλγάλοις, ὅτε ἐξήγαγεν αὐτοὺς ἐξ Αἰγύπτου, καθὰ συνέταξεν αὐτοῖς κύριος, καὶ ἐκεῖ εἰσιν ἕως τῆς σήμερον ἡμέρας.		

Notes

[1] The textual history of LXX Judges is complex. The B and A texts, printed in parallel columns in the edition of Rahlfs, differ considerably. The majority of scholars now hold that there was an OG which all the manuscript evidence derives from. The B-text contains a strong *Kaige* revision, and the A-text and the Antiochene manuscripts are often seen as the best representatives of the OG. In any case, all

readings have to be assessed individually. The *Göttingen* edition is still under preparation in Madrid by José Manuel Cañas Reíllo. For helpful resources on LXX Judges see, for example, Schreiner 1957, Bodine 1980, and Dogniez 2016. In the text cited above, only Judg 2:6 contains significant variants.

[2] Here I follow the A and majority reading. B reads καὶ ἦλθεν ἀνήρ. ἀνήρ is a typical *Kaige*-feature for איש. It is likely that the singular ἦλθεν has come about secondarily influenced by the *Kaige* reading. Some manuscripts read ἐπορεύθησαν, probably harmonizing towards the reading in Josh 24:28.

[3] The doublette εἰς τὸν οἶκον αὐτοῦ καὶ is marked with an obelos in the Syrohexapla. However, it is found in majority of the manuscripts and its omission is attested only by manuscripts A 58 426. Since the phrase is more likely a Greek doublette and does not witness to a differing Hebrew *Vorlage*, I do not need to settle the question whether it was already in the OG or not.

[4] This plural from should probably be credited to the translator and not to a different Hebrew Vorlage.

Transposition in the MT (OG 24:29, MT 24:31)

The first striking difference between the four versions is the different sequence in MT Josh. The last verse in MT Josh (24:31) is situated after Joshua's death and burial. As a contrast, in all the other witnesses it is placed before as the second verse. In terms of content, this verse highlights people's fidelity to YHWH during not only Joshua's lifetime but also during the lifetime of the elders that outlived Joshua and knew of YHWH's deeds.

Overall, this verse seems to be better suited in the context of Joshua than Judges, and it probably originated there. The main structure of Josh 24 is a dialogue between Joshua and the people, in which the question of loyalty to YHWH is central. This dialogue ends with a triple promise by the people to serve only YHWH (24:18–20, 21, and 24). In this verse, the realization of this promise is narrated. The vocabulary used in the verse is drawn from earlier verses in Josh 24, which corroborates the argument that the verse was originally created for chapter 24: the verb עבד "to serve" is central to the earlier narrative (24:2, 14, 20), הַזְּקֵנִים "the elders" are mentioned again (24:1), the people are referred to as יִשְׂרָאֵל "Israel" (24:1) and not עָם "the people" as in Judg 2:6, and the theme of YHWH doing deeds for the people is repeated at the end of the verse (24:5, 7, 17). In the context of Judges, conversely, this verse is in contradiction with the context and especially the preceding verses, e.g. Judg 2:2, which recalls the infidelity of the Israelites. Moreover, in Judg 2:1–5 an angel of the Lord is the speaker, while in verse 2:6 Joshua is abruptly introduced as the subject.

A more complicated question is whether the more original location for this verse was before (OG) or after (MT) Joshua's death has been narrated. The main narrative of Joshua's speech and his dialogue with the people is in verses 24:1–28, while verses 29–33 deal with the burials of four key figures (Joshua, Joseph, Eleazar, and Phinehas in the OG). OG Josh 24:29, emphasizing the realization of the people's fidelity to YHWH, is more connected with the former entity. Therefore, OG Josh 24:29 can be seen as a realization and conclusion to the dialogue in 24:1–28 created by the original author or a redactor.¹⁸⁷ In OG Josh 24 this function is preserved, since the verse directly follows the dialogue. The order preserved in OG Josh and both versions of Judges is then probably earlier, and the sequence in MT Josh is secondary.¹⁸⁸ The argument for the secondary of the MT sequence is strengthened by a comparison with the sequence of events in Deut 34, where the death of Moses is narrated. The sequence of events is similar to that of MT Josh 24. First, Moses dies and is buried (Deut 34:5–6, Josh 24:29–30), and then the fidelity of the Israelites after the death of Moses is narrated (Deut 34:9, MT Josh 24:31). Thus, it seems that the order in MT Joshua reflects harmonization with the account of Moses' death. The sequence may have been adjusted to make the ending of Josh 24 correspond more closely with Deut 34. This could be seen as an attempt to derive more authority from the figure of Moses.¹⁸⁹

Contrary to this suggestion, Nelson defended in his commentary the order of the MT as the earlier one. According to him, the verse was originally given after Joshua's death and burial as a summary of his accomplishments for the Israelites. The argument relies on two clues. First, the introduction to Joshua's death in OG 24:30 Καὶ ἐγένετο μετ' ἐκεῖνα "and it happened after this", according to Nelson, makes no sense in the OG since he regards it as a reference to Josh 24:28. However, this is not clear, and the phrase could be seen rather as a reference to the preceding section as a whole. This is seen especially in the MT, and the probable Hebrew *Vorlage* of the OG, which repeats the phrase הַדְּבָרִים הָאֵלֶּה from Josh 24:26. Second, according to Nelson, the two different orders fit well into their respective contexts. In Judges, the key issue is the question of loyalty and apostasy, which is the reason that the topic is raised immediately after the people has been dismissed and before Joshua has died. Nelson argues that OG Josh secondarily followed Judges, and chose this order because it better fits the larger canonical story and is more chronological.¹⁹⁰ In the light of the nature of the OG translation

---

187 The nature of the verse as a positive conclusion to the dialogue is also reflected in the comments of Woudstra 1981, 360.
188 Thus also Boling & Wright 1982, 541; Rofé 1982, 22; Auld 1998, 81. Contra, for example, O'Brien (1990, 81) who argues that LXX Josh 24 secondarily changes the sequence due to the sequence in Judg 2:6–7. His argument relies on the literary-critical assumption that in the original text of the DtrH there was no assembly or dismissal, but only verses MT Josh 24:29–31. This does not seem probable, since MT Josh 24:31 probably owes its content to Josh 24:1–28. Jericke (1996, 353) agrees that the order in Judges is original since it is, according to him, historically more plausible. He argues, however, that OG Joshua secondarily mimics the order in Judges.
189 For the depiction of Joshua as a second Moses in Josh 24, see Römer 2010, 97. Rofé (1982, 23) argues that the MT relocation was made because a scribe perceived that the verse dealt primarily with the times of the elders after the death of Joshua. The sequence was thus made more logical.
190 Nelson 1997, 278–284.

of Joshua, this explanation is harder to accept. The translator would probably not override the order of his Hebrew *Vorlage* in the light of the text of Judges. Moreover, the chronological and canonical benefits of relocating the verse do not seem so obvious that an editor of the Hebrew *Vorlage* would have done it.

In any case, the documented evidence reveals that MT Josh 24:31 is a loose and flexible verse. It can be located in various places in different contexts. Whether one deems the order in the MT or the OG of Joshua to be the more original, the verse has been freely transposed in several stages of editing the text. This hints towards the secondary nature of the verse. Thus, in literary and redaction criticism the verse should probably be evaluated as belonging to the later developmental stages of the text. I will return to this issue in the discussion of the book transition from Joshua to Judges.[191]

The order of the verses and the relocation of the faithfulness verse is also connected to the different beginnings of the next verse, which reports the death of Joshua (MT Josh 24:29, OG Josh 24:30, and Judg 2:8). Here MT and OG Josh have introductory words before the actual death is narrated.[192] One could argue that the earliest reading is attested in Judges, since there the introductory formula is missing altogether. The introductory formula would then have been secondarily added when the death of Joshua was secondarily reported in the context of Josh 24. However, since the passage in Judges seems to be a secondary adaption of the death and burial of Joshua, it is perhaps more likely that the introductory formula in OG and MT Josh represents the earliest reading, through which the death account was originally linked with the rest of Josh 24. As mentioned above, the link was made by repeating the phrase הַדְּבָרִים הָאֵלֶּה from Josh 24:26 in the introductory formula. The absence of the introductory formula in Judges can further be explained as an intentional omission due to the new context: in the context of Joshua, the introduction was needed to link the dialogue part (OG 24:1–29) with the death and burial notices (OG 24:30ff.). In Judges, this link was no longer needed.[193]

---

191 See section 4.3.5.
192 According to Rofé (1982, 23) the words Καὶ ἐγένετο μετ' ἐκεῖνα "and it happened after this" in OG Josh cannot be a translation of the Hebrew וַיְהִי אַחֲרֵי הַדְּבָרִים הָאֵלֶּה "and it happened after these things" in MT Josh. In the LXX, this expression can only be found in Gen 6:4 (καὶ μετ' ἐκεῖνο) where it is translated from the Hebrew אַחֲרֵי־כֵן. The *Vorlage* of OG Josh then, according to Rofé, read ויהי אחרי כן. However, this is not clear, since the OG translator may have read the introductory formula in the MT and shortened the expression. This would be in line with the other freedoms taken by the Joshua translator.
193 Noort (1993, 114) argues that the introductory formula was omitted in Judges because of the different function of the verse. In Joshua, the death notice was given as a conclusion, and this is why an introduction was originally needed. In Judges, the previous verse 2:6 has a new

To sum up, the most plausible development here is as follows. The text-critically earliest ending for the covenant scene is preserved in OG Josh 24:28–29. At some point in the development of the text, the death and burial notice of Joshua (OG Josh 24:30–31) was linked with the covenant scene. A sign of this linkage is preserved in the introductory formula in the OG and MT Josh ("and it happened after these things").[194] Judg 2:6–9 secondarily adapted the Hebrew *Vorlage* of OG Josh 24:28–31 into a new context, in which the verse reporting the fidelity of the people was contrasted with the infidelity of the new generations (Judg 2:10).[195] Due to this dependence, both OG Josh 24:28–31 and Judg 2:6–9 preserve the earliest sequence of the pericope. Furthermore, MT Josh 24:28–31 reflects a secondary reworking of the sequence of events. This reworking might have been prompted by an editorial motive to better integrate the death and burial notice(s) with the verse reporting the fidelity of the Israelites after the "days of Joshua". It might have also been influenced by a harmonization with the death and burial account of Moses. This is an intriguing option since, in the textual evidence, there are also other editorial developments behind MT Josh 24 that aim at emphasizing the role of Moses.

Nomistic Editing Related to the Circumcision (vv. 31a, 21:42d, 5:2–9)
The most notable variant in these verses is the long plus OG Josh 24:31a, which is not present in the MT. Many scholars have noted that this plus needs to be explained together with two other passages; namely, the similar plus in Josh 21:42d ("And Iesous took the flint knives with which he circumcised the sons of Israel born on the way in the wilderness, and he put them in Thamnasarach." [NETS]) and with the complicated circumcision account in Josh 5:2–9.[196] The circumcision of the Israelites by Joshua at Gilgal and the flint knives used for this circumcision are the central themes in these passages. Since there are two similar plusses in the OG (24:31a, 21:42d) that are closely related to the rewriting in 5:4–6, these differences should not be explained as merely unintentional scribal errors.[197] Someone has intentionally changed things.

---

programmatic meaning compared to 24:28, preparing the people for the conquest of the land, and the introductory formula was thus not needed.
194 The death and burial account of Joshua may have originally been a part of some other literary whole, but when the covenant scene in Josh 24 was developed, the death of Joshua was linked at the end of this scene. See 4.3.
195 That Judg 2:6–9 is a later adaptation is also seen in several secondary textual developments that are analyzed below.
196 See, for example, Holmes 1914, 72 and Greenspoon 2005, 239–240.
197 Thus also Boling & Wright 1982, 189.

Earlier I have concluded that the translator of the OG should not be credited with radical editorial intrusions. Here, however, many scholars have suggested such activity, and it should therefore be considered as a theoretical solution for the text-critical problems. Thus, there are three possible explanations for what may have happened to the texts: (1) the MT is mostly original, and the translator of OG has rewritten 5:4–6 and made two additions to Josh 21 and 24, (2) the MT is mostly original, and the rewriting and the additions reflected in the OG took place already in the Hebrew *Vorlage*, or (3) the OG is mostly original, and an editor rewrote 5:4–6 and omitted the plusses in Josh 21 and 24 in the proto-MT phase. The third option is most probable, as is revealed by a closer analysis of the relevant textual differences.[198]

It is helpful to begin the analysis with a closer look at Josh 5:2–9, and especially the rewriting in 5:4–5, then briefly turn to verse 21:42d, and finally consider the plus in OG Josh 24:31a in the light of these earlier variants.

MT (Josh 5:2–9)	OG (Josh 5:2–9)
בָּעֵת הַהִיא	² Ὑπὸ δὲ τοῦτον τὸν καιρὸν
אָמַר יְהוָה אֶל־יְהוֹשֻׁעַ	εἶπεν κύριος τῷ Ἰησοῖ
עֲשֵׂה לְךָ חַרְבוֹת	Ποίησον σεαυτῷ μαχαίρας
צֻרִים	ἐκ πέτρας ἀκροτόμου ¹
וְשׁוּב מֹל	καὶ καθίσας περίτεμε
אֶת־בְּנֵי־יִשְׂרָאֵל	τοὺς υἱοὺς Ἰσραήλ.
שֵׁנִית	²
At that time, YHWH said to Joshua: "Make flint knives and circumcise again the Israelites a second time."	At that time, the Lord said to Iesous: "Make flint knives out of sharp rock and sit down to circumcise the Israelites."
³ וַיַּעַשׂ ־לוֹ יְהוֹשֻׁעַ	³ καὶ ἐποίησεν Ἰησοῦς
חַרְבוֹת צֻרִים	μαχαίρας πετρίνας ἀκροτόμους
וַיָּמָל אֶת־בְּנֵי יִשְׂרָאֵל	καὶ περιέτεμεν τοὺς υἱοὺς Ἰσραήλ
	ἐπὶ τοῦ καλουμένου τόπου ³
אֶל־גִּבְעַת הָעֲרָלוֹת	Βουνὸς τῶν ἀκροβυστιῶν
	(καὶ ἔθηκεν θιμωνιὰς ἀκροβυστιῶν)⁴

(Continued)

---

[198] Steuernagel (1900, 167–168) already argued that the LXX preserves earlier readings in Josh 5. Scholars arguing for the general priority of OG in these verses are, for example, Holmes 1914, 9–10; Boling & Wright 1982, 193; Mazor 1994, 36; and Nelson 1997, 71–82.

MT (Josh 5:2–9)	OG (Josh 5:2–9)
And Joshua made flint knives and circumcised the Israelites at the hill of foreskins.	And Iesous made sharp flint knives and circumcised the Israelites in the place called the hill of foreskins. (And he formed heaps of foreskin.)
⁴ וְזֶה הַדָּבָר אֲשֶׁר־מָל יְהוֹשֻׁעַ כָּל־הָעָם הַיֹּצֵא מִמִּצְרַיִם הַזְּכָרִים כֹּל אַנְשֵׁי הַמִּלְחָמָה מֵתוּ בַמִּדְבָּר בַּדֶּרֶךְ בְּצֵאתָם מִמִּצְרָיִם	⁴ ὃν δὲ τρόπον περιεκάθαρεν Ἰησοῦς τοὺς υἱοὺς Ἰσραήλ, ὅσοι ποτὲ **ἐγένοντο ἐν τῇ ὁδῷ** καὶ ὅσοι ποτὲ ἀπερίτμητοι ἦσαν τῶν ἐξεληλυθότων ἐξ Αἰγύπτου
Therefore, **Joshua circumcised** them: of all the people who had left Egypt all the males and all the warriors had died on the way through the wilderness, when they came out of Egypt.	How Iesous purified the Israelites as many as were **born on the way** and as many as were uncircumcised of those that came out of Egypt,
⁵ כִּי־מֻלִים הָיוּ כָּל־הָעָם הַיֹּצְאִים וְכָל־הָעָם הַיִּלֹּדִים בַּמִּדְבָּר בַּדֶּרֶךְ בְּצֵאתָם מִמִּצְרַיִם לֹא־מָלוּ	⁵ πάντας τούτους **περιέτεμεν Ἰησοῦς**·
For all people who came out had been circumcised, but all **born on the way** in the wilderness, when they came out of Egypt, had not been circumcised.	all these **Iesous circumcised**.
⁶ כִּי אַרְבָּעִים שָׁנָה הָלְכוּ בְנֵי־יִשְׂרָאֵל בַּמִּדְבָּר עַד־תֹּם כָּל־הַגּוֹי אַנְשֵׁי הַמִּלְחָמָה הַיֹּצְאִים מִמִּצְרַיִם אֲשֶׁר לֹא־שָׁמְעוּ בְּקוֹל יְהוָה אֲשֶׁר נִשְׁבַּע יְהוָה לָהֶם לְבִלְתִּי הַרְאוֹתָם אֶת־הָאָרֶץ אֲשֶׁר נִשְׁבַּע יְהוָה לַאֲבוֹתָם לָתֶת לָנוּ אֶרֶץ זָבַת חָלָב וּדְבָשׁ	⁶ τεσσαράκοντα γὰρ καὶ δύο ἔτη ἀνέστραπται Ἰσραὴλ ἐν τῇ ἐρήμῳ τῇ Μαδβαρείτιδι⁵ διὸ ἀπερίτμητοι ἦσαν οἱ πλεῖστοι αὐτῶν τῶν μαχίμων τῶν ἐξεληλυθότων ἐκ γῆς Αἰγύπτου οἱ ἀπειθήσαντες τῶν ἐντολῶν τοῦ θεοῦ οἷς καὶ διώρισεν μὴ ἰδεῖν αὐτοὺς τὴν γῆν ἣν ὤμοσεν κύριος τοῖς πατράσιν αὐτῶν δοῦναι ἡμῖν, γῆν ῥέουσαν γάλα καὶ μέλι.
For **forty years**, the Israelites had walked in the desert	For **forty-two years**, the Israelites had walked in the desert of Madbaritis,

3.4 Joshua 24:28–33: Text and Apparatus

MT (Josh 5:2–9)	OG (Josh 5:2–9)
until had perished all the people the warriors that came out of Egypt. They had not listened to the voice of YHWH. To them YHWH swore that he would not let them see the land that YHWH had sworn to their fathers to give us, the land flowing milk and honey.	therefore were uncircumcised most of the warriors that came out of the land of Egypt who had disobeyed the commandments of the Lord, to whom he also declared that he would not let them see the land that the Lord had sworn to their fathers to give us, the land flowing milk and honey.
⁷ וְאֶת־בְּנֵיהֶם הֵקִים תַּחְתָּם אֹתָם מָל יְהוֹשֻׁעַ כִּי־עֲרֵלִים הָיוּ כִּי לֹא־מָלוּ אוֹתָם בַּדָּרֶךְ	⁷ ἀντὶ δὲ τούτων ἀντικατέστησεν τοὺς υἱοὺς αὐτῶν οὓς Ἰησοῦς περιέτεμεν διὰ τὸ αὐτοὺς γεγενῆσθαι κατὰ τὴν ὁδὸν ἀπεριτμήτους.
And their sons he raised in their place, them Joshua circumcised. For they were uncircumcised on the way, they had not been circumcised	And in their place he raised their sons, whom Iesous circumcised for they had remained on the way uncircumcised.
⁸ וַיְהִי כַּאֲשֶׁר־תַּמּוּ כָל־הַגּוֹי לְהִמּוֹל וַיֵּשְׁבוּ תַחְתָּם בַּמַּחֲנֶה עַד חֲיוֹתָם	⁸ περιτμηθέντες δὲ ἡσυχίαν εἶχον αὐτόθι καθήμενοι ἐν τῇ παρεμβολῇ ἕως ὑγιάσθησαν.
When all the nation had been circumcised, they remained in their camp until they were healed.	When they had been circumcised they remained quiet in their camp sitting until they were healed.
⁹ וַיֹּאמֶר יְהוָה אֶל־יְהוֹשֻׁעַ הַיּוֹם גַּלּוֹתִי אֶת־חֶרְפַּת מִצְרַיִם מֵעֲלֵיכֶם וַיִּקְרָא שֵׁם הַמָּקוֹם הַהוּא גִּלְגָּל עַד הַיּוֹם הַזֶּה	⁹ καὶ εἶπεν κύριος τῷ Ἰησοῖ υἱῷ Ναυή τῇ σήμερον ἡμέρᾳ ἀφεῖλον τὸν ὀνειδισμὸν Αἰγύπτου ἀφ' ὑμῶν. καὶ ἐκάλεσεν τὸ ὄνομα τοῦ τόπου ἐκείνου Γάλγαλα.
And YHWH said to Joshua: "Today I have rolled away the disgrace of Egypt from upon you." So, he called the name of that place Gilgal until this day.	And the Lord said to Iesous son of Naue "Today I have remove the disgrace of Egypt from upon you." So, he called the name of that place Galgala.

Notes

¹ B reads μαχαίρας πετρίνας ἐκ πέτρας ἀκροτόμου. The more literal πετρίνας is probably a secondary interpolation from the next verse, where it is used for the same Hebrew חֲרָבוֹת, as Margolis argued in his critical edition. Greenspoon (1983, 62–63) and Tov (1999e, 53) also agree. The OG reading without the πετρίνας is found in the A-text and MSS 19-426 29-82-121.

Two MSS (44 72) omit ἐκ πέτρας which is a later development bringing the text closer to the MT.

² The OG reading, which does not have an equivalent for שֵׁנִית is preserved in MSS B 19 407 and Old Latin. Most of the Greek witnesses in all MS groups add ἐκ δευτέρου, but this is probably a development towards the שֵׁנִית in MT. The OG did not have this element, and it may well be a later explanatory gloss from the hands of a Hebrew editor. The secondarity of this element is corroborated by the notion that it was also probably missing from 4QJoshᵃ, whose reconstruction does not leave room for the word (Ulrich 1995, 147). It may have come about in the proto-MT editing. The verb שׁוב in וְשׁוּב מֹל אֶת-בְּנֵי-יִשְׂרָאֵל is ambivalent, and a later editor could have wanted to secure its usage by adding an explanatory שֵׁנִית at the end. This interpretative addition ("the second time") stressed the importance of the circumcision being performed right before entering the Promised Land. This ambivalence is also evident by the Greek translator's translation equivalent καθίσας "sit down". This probably reflects the translator's context; it was an Egyptian practice to perform circumcisions in a sitting position. This practice is evidenced by e.g. a relief from Sakkarah (Pritchard 1954, no. 629). As a reservation regarding this piece of evidence, it should be noted that this relief, coming from the 23rd century BCE, is temporally far away from the translator's time. This, however, does not downplay the argument of שֵׁנִית being a later gloss in a Hebrew phase.

³ Targum Jonathan (5:3) has a striking similarity with this plus. It is possible that the plus in the OG goes back to a different Vorlage which was known to the writer of Targum Jonathan. Van der Meer (2004, 342), however, argues that the Greek and Aramaic translators made a similar interpretive addition independently.

⁴ This reading ("and he formed heaps of foreskin") is preserved in some L sources (314 OL), Sahidic manuscripts, and in a citation from Justin Martyr. According to Tov (1999a, 156) this plus might belong to the OG, since many unique Antiochene elements in the books of Reigns are also original. Tov classifies this as a midrashic interpretation made by the translator. Tov's argument has its appeal but, in my opinion, this sentence should not be included in the OG without reservations. The weak manuscript support in itself is not a problem, but the nature of this clause resembles a later interpretation that could have been easily added later to clarify a problematic place name. A similar midrashic explanation is found in several rabbinic sources, for example Shir Hashirim Rabba.

⁵ The curious transcription τῇ Μαδβαρείτιδι in the doublette is probably earlier, and the correct translation ἐν τῇ ἐρήμῳ may have originally come about as a correction in the marginals. Boling & Wright 1982, 193 conversely argue that τῇ Μαδβαρείτιδι is a later misreading of בַּמִּדְבָּר "in the desert". This is not likely, since it is not probable that later scribes would have inserted such a curious form into a completely understandable text. In any case, the MT likely has the earlier reading, and the doublette is a secondary Greek development. The Sahidic and Old Latin texts are also missing this plus.

There are several minor differences between these accounts, but the locus of the rewriting is in verses 4–6.[199] OG Josh claims that many of the Israelites coming out of Egypt were uncircumcised. MT Josh, however, specifies extensively that

---

199 For the evaluation of some of the minor differences, see the footnotes of the preceding table. Although I disagree with Van der Meer (2004, 249–416) regarding the text-critical evaluation of 5:4–6, his study on 5:2–12 is an excellent treatise on the manifold textual problems involved. For the Old Latin version, dealing with the textual problems in its own way, see Sipilä 2014, 257–272.

everyone coming out of Egypt were circumcised and Joshua only had to circumcise those who were born in the wilderness. When comparing the heavily rewritten section in verses 5:4–5, only some phrases in the Hebrew have counterparts in the Greek.

There are two main thematical differences that are achieved through the rewriting. First, OG suggests that the Israelites did not universally practice circumcision in Egypt. Conversely, in the MT everyone coming out of Egypt were circumcised and were thus ritually pure. Second, OG allows for a greater continuity between those coming out from Egypt and those who eventually conquered the land of Canaan, since the older generation does not die out. MT, however, makes it clear that the generation that came out of Egypt died out before the actual conquest (עַד־תֹּם כָּל־הַגּוֹי אַנְשֵׁי הַמִּלְחָמָה).[200] In this way, the MT has a stricter separation between the old Exodus generation and the new generation that conquered the Promised Land.[201] These two key differences in meaning might also be reflected in a smaller detail. The Greek text seems to place much more emphasis on the knives used in the circumcision, adding in verses 2–3 that the flint knives were sharp (ἀκροτόμους). The emphasis put on the knives is therefore either diminished (MT) or increased (OG).

The best explanation for these differences is an expansive rewriting in the proto-MT editing of 5:4–6. The section in the MT has many signs of being a result of later editing. This editing is best described as nomistic. In other words, it seeks to align the circumcision account more closely with some key passages in the Pentateuch. It was important for the nomistic editor(s) to show that Joshua and the Israelites were faithful to the law before the successful conquest of the Promised Land.[202] To be more accurate, there are three legal issues that guided the rewriting.

---

[200] The second point is aptly formulated by Mazor 1994, 36.
[201] Note that the idea of a new generation replacing the older generation is present in both traditions, since they both read in Josh 5:7 that "their sons he raised in their place." The MT merely makes the idea of a new generation more consistent and strict, by insisting in MT Josh 5:6 that the older generation died out altogether from among the people.
[202] Josh 5 is a juncture in the book of Joshua which was the focus of editing in several stages and contexts. Dozeman (2015, 296) writes: "The circumcision of the Israelite males in Josh 5:2–9 is the most edited episode in the story of the crossing of the Jordan in Josh 3:1–5:12. The reason is likely the growing importance of circumcision in postexilic Judaism and the continuing debate over its meaning well into the Hellenistic period." In 4QJosh[a] Josh 5 also exhibits late nomistic editing. It contains a reading which was achieved by transposing the reading of the law from Josh 8:34–35 to the beginning of Josh 5. This transposition was probably sparked by Josh 4:10 (Feldman 2013, 116–118). In this way, the reading and observance of the law was actualized before the conquests.

First, the rewriting could have been triggered by the worrying notion in the earlier text, preserved in the OG, that there were uncircumcised people among the Israelites coming out of Egypt. An editor wanted to omit this and "correct" the reasons for the circumcision performed by Joshua. Since YHWH had so greatly helped the Israelites in getting out of Egypt, surely they would have all had to have been loyal in circumcision. Thus, only those born in the wilderness needed to be circumcised. This idea was already present in the earlier Hebrew version, as witnessed by the OG, but in a different location in Josh 21:42d (τοὺς γενομένους ἐν τῇ ὁδῷ ἐν τῇ ἐρήμῳ "born on the way in the wilderness"). Thus, it is likely that the proto-MT editor took the phrase from this later verse, which he also omitted (see below). In both textual traditions, the circumcision performed by Joshua is said to have removed the "disgrace of Egypt" (Josh 5:9, אֶת-חֶרְפַּת מִצְרַיִם). This disgrace refers to the state of some Israelite warriors being uncircumcised (cf. Gen. 34:14), which makes sense in the OG. In the MT, conversely, there is no disgrace left, since everyone in Egypt were circumcised.[203] In this way, the rewriting of MT verses 4–6 left verse 9 in contradiction with the new meaning.[204]

Two passages in the Pentateuch are echoed in the background of this editorial motivation. In Gen 17, circumcision is an integral part of the covenant that the Lord makes with Abraham. It was important for an editor to show that the Israelites of the Exodus had not broken this covenant. Second, the circumcision performed by Zipporah in Exod 4:24–26 might have had an influence on MT Josh 5. In this peculiar text, faithfulness to circumcision plays a significant role right at the beginning of the Exodus from Egypt. Moses almost died for having neglected the circumcision. In the eyes of some late editors, therefore, circumcision seems to have been a pre-requisite for the success of the Exodus. This view was strengthened in the proto-MT editing of Josh 5.

Second, the proto-MT rewriting makes a greater discontinuity between the warriors coming out of Egypt and the men taking over Canaan. This is seen in two features in the MT, missing from the OG: Josh 5:4: "all the people who had

---

[203] Other interpretations for the expression "disgrace of Egypt" have also been suggested. Van der Meer (2004, 311–315) argues that the clause "today I have rolled away the disgrace of Egypt" is a later addition after 5:2–8, and that its meaning should not be sought in this context. It marks the ending of slavery and wandering in the desert, and is connected with the erection of the twelve stones (Josh 4:20). It may well include those connotations, but the clause is so closely connected (including הַיּוֹם) with the immediate context (vv. 2–8) reporting the circumcision that it would be futile to try to explain this connection away. Hollenberg (1874, 462–507) already linked the expression with the notion that none of the Israelites were circumcised in Egypt. For the meaning of the phrase see also Dozeman 2015, 298.

[204] This contradiction in the MT would have made scholars notice that something has been edited, even if the earlier reading in the OG had not survived.

left Egypt all the males and all the warriors had died on the way through the wilderness after they came out of Egypt", and 5:6: "until had perished all the people the warriors that came out of Egypt."[205] This seems to be an attempt to harmonize the passage with notions in Deuteronomy that all the warriors died out before attacking Canaan (Deut 1:34–46, 2:16). It also makes the text more coherent, since already the earlier text in OG Josh 5:7 noted that a new generation was raised in the place of the old generation. The change in emphasis would not make sense the other way around; a later editor would probably not delete the notions of the earlier generation dying, since it is in conformity with Deuteronomy.

Third, the upcoming Passover celebration in Josh 5:10–12 probably affected the rewriting. The desire of the proto-MT editor to emphasize that all the Israelites were circumcised probably relates to ritual purity related to the Passover.[206] Although the text does not explicitly advance this motive, a late editor might easily have been motivated by Pentateuchal decrees relating to the Passover. Especially Exod 12:43–48 might have influenced the editor. Exod 12:43–48 highlights that circumcision is a central requirement for everyone – even non-native Israelites – who want to take part in the Passover celebration. This argument is strengthened by the addition כָּל־הַגּוֹי "whole nation" in MT Josh 5:8, which highlights that it was the entire nation that was circumcised and thus ritually pure for the Passover. So, while the Passover ritual might have been one of the "Priestly" motives for introducing the circumcision in chapter 5 in the first place, the proximity of the Passover celebration seems to have affected the editing of the circumcision account in several stages. The proto-MT editing presents the last one of these editorial stages.

At this point, it should be highlighted that these three legal issues are quite decisive as text-critical arguments. It is hard to imagine a rewriting in the other direction. While it is plausible that later editors would rewrite texts to harmonize them with Pentateuchal commandments, it is hard to imagine why later editors would rewrite texts that are in conformity with the Pentateuch in a direction that makes them more in contradiction with the Pentateuch. The OG implies that the Israelites did not practice circumcision universally in Egypt and were, therefore, disobedient to the law. Why a later writer would have wanted to create such a state of affairs is hard to explain in the light of the following successful Exodus.[207]

---

[205] Nelson (1997, 71–80) notes that here the MT utilizes a word play with the Hebrew תמם "to finish" between verses 4 and 6, which reveals purposeful secondary editing.
[206] Thus also Dozeman 2015, 268 and Nelson 1997, 71–80.
[207] As also noted by Holmes (1914, 9): "The LXX translator could not possibly have gone out of his way to make a statement which implied that the Israelites did not universally practise cir-

The variants between the MT and the OG probably emerged during times when the Pentateuch had already gained significant authority. Therefore, it would be hard to argue that the MT would be earlier, in this instance, and that the OG would be a result of later rewriting. Some scholars have tried to do this by insisting that the rewriting took place in Alexandria by the translator. A closer look at these arguments, however, reveals that it is not a more likely explanation.

A deliberate reworking by the OG translator is thoroughly argued by Bieberstein and Van der Meer.[208] Bieberstein argues that the MT is earlier in almost every aspect, and that the OG has come about through scribal activity and interpretation of the Hebrew text by the translator.[209] Bieberstein turns the arguments supporting the priority of OG upside down. He argues that it was the Greek translator who aimed at harmonizing the verses with the Pentateuch. The addition of the notion that Joshua had to circumcise some of the men who came out of Egypt is done because in the Pentateuch there were non-Israelites, עֶרֶב or ἐπίμικτος, among these people (Exod 12:38; Num 11:4). In addition, there were those who were under twenty years old when the sentence of the wandering in the desert was pronounced (Num 14:29).[210] The addition of the circumcision of this group by the translator also resulted in other minor adjustments, such as the omission of כָּל־הַגּוֹי. Thus, Bieberstein argues that the modifications in the translation are based on learned activity and aim at balancing the passage with the Pentateuch, especially in terms of chronology.[211] The OG text would thus be a "product of scholarly research".[212] If one does not accept the claim that this "scholarly research" was performed by the translator, the arguments proposed by Bieberstein might still be used in defending a rewriting behind the Hebrew *Vorlage* of the OG.

However, the arguments are not without problems. The assumed references to the Pentateuch are rather obscure. In the Greek text, Joshua circumcises τοὺς υἱοὺς Ἰσραήλ "sons of Israel" (OG Josh 5:4), and most of the warriors coming out of Egypt are uncircumcised (διὸ ἀπερίτμητοι ἦσαν οἱ πλεῖστοι αὐτῶν, OG Josh 5:6). To argue that these phrases refer to ἐπίμικτος "mixed (non-Israelite) people", would mean understanding the Greek text as making connections that

---

cumcision while in Egypt. If probability is to be any guide it must be admitted that LXX here had a very different text from ours and one that was earlier in point of view."
208 Bieberstein 1995, 203–206 and Van der Meer 2004, 249–415. Also Gooding 1974, 149–164 and Krause 2014, 300–302.
209 Bieberstein 1995, 198–206.
210 Bieberstein 1995, 200–201.
211 "G hingegen bassiert auf schriftgelehrten Recherchen und chronologischen Ausgleichversuchen mit Ex 12,38 und Num 10,11; 11,4; 14,29.33-34 - -" Bieberstein 1995, 206.
212 As summarized by Van der Meer 2004, 281.

are not that clear. Including the Israelites under twenty years of age in these categories somewhat balances the argument. Nevertheless, it does not sit well with the reference to Israelite warriors. An editor aiming at a careful "scholarly" interpretation would have likely used a more exact phrase, such as ἐπίμικτος. The evaluation of the translator or a Hebrew editor as a careful scholar is also problematic in relation to the above-mentioned passages in Deut 1:34–46. Why would a careful scholar create such an obvious contradiction with Deuteronomy?[213]

Van der Meer, on the other hand, emphasizes the creativity and contextualizing efforts of the translator more than Bieberstein.[214] His analysis is careful, and includes many valid observations concerning the freedoms taken by the translator. Some concerns with the analysis, however, should be noted here. Van der Meer arrives at a too clear-cut conclusion concerning OG Josh 5:2–12. He states that it is "an interpretative version through and through".[215] The Greek version of the pericope is best understood, according to Van der Meer, as an answer to questions that arose to the translator when reading a text similar to the MT, which had developed through different redactional stages.

The first concern proposed by Van der Meer is that, when reading the MT, the translator felt that the idea of a collective circumcision encompassing all ages was problematic. This problem was strengthened by the stone knives that were perceived by the translator as an outdated means for performing the circumcision. The translator wanted to explain and even soften this peculiar scene for the Hellenistic Jews in Egypt. This led to several interpretive translation equivalents. The translator, for example, added the attribute ἀκροτόμους "sharp" to the stone knives, utilized the Greek verb περικαθαίρω "purify" (5:4) to describe the circumcision, and amplified the period of rest in the camp after the circumcision by adding that they kept quiet in the camp (ἡσυχίαν εἶχον in 5:8).[216] Overall it is true, as Van der Meer states, that the translation of 5:2–12 includes several free and interpretive translation equivalents and solutions. Translating circumcision as "purification" is one of those. The flexibility in choosing different and interpretative Greek equivalents for some Hebrew words does not, however, mean that the translator would freely change the meaning of the text by adding and omitting elements. These should be seen as two different phenomena; the former freedom is still anchored in a Hebrew text, while the latter entails interpretative actions without any source text. Adjusting these observations to the translation style as a

---

[213] Van der Meer (2004, 281–285) also points to some details in the text that make the suggestion of Bieberstein improbable.
[214] Van der Meer 2004, 334–415.
[215] Van der Meer 2004, 408.
[216] Van der Meer 2004, 408–409.

whole,²¹⁷ it seems that the translator may have taken liberties in choosing translation equivalents due to his context, but he would not have gone beyond the Hebrew source text in creating or deleting elements.

The second concern for the translator, according to Van der Meer, was a contradiction he found in the MT. Van der Meer assumes that when the Greek translator read his source text, which was similar to the MT, he falsely interpreted the disgrace of Egypt (5:9) as referring to the preceding context. The translator inferred from this expression that there must have been several Israelites who were not circumcised in Egypt. This led to the interpretive addition καὶ ὅσοι ποτὲ ἀπερίτμητοι ἦσαν τῶν ἐξεληλυθότων ἐξ Αἰγύπτου "and as many as were uncircumcised of those that came out of Egypt". In this way, the translator created an additional group of those that had not been circumcised in Egypt.²¹⁸ To support this argument, Van der Meer notes that ὅσοι ποτὲ "as many as" has no equivalent as such in biblical Hebrew. This would point towards an initiative on behalf of the translator. However, as Holmes already pointed out, the Hebrew *Vorlage* could have simply read כל ... וכל "all ... and all", and the translator could have exhibited the freedom he is known for; that is, not slavishly reproducing the units of Hebrew grammar in his rendering of Greek.²¹⁹ As Van der Meer himself also notes, the pronoun ὅσος occurs frequently in the Greek translation of Joshua and other books the Hebrew Bible.²²⁰ For example, Deut 1:46 reads וַתֵּשְׁבוּ בְקָדֵשׁ יָמִים רַבִּים כַּיָּמִים אֲשֶׁר יְשַׁבְתֶּם "and you had stayed at Kadesh as many days as you did" which is translated καὶ ἐνεκάθησθε ἐν Καδὴς ἡμέρας πολλάς, ὅσας ποτὲ ἡμέρας ἐνεκάθησθε "and you stayed at Kadesh for many days, as many days as you stayed". Here as well, the translator exhibits freedom in the Greek grammatical structure but retains the basic meaning of his Hebrew source text. Therefore, the freedom in using Greek grammatical units does not corroborate that the translator would have created an additional group to the pericope and altered the meaning. One would expect that a translator concerned with removing perceived inconsistencies in the text would be more active in other parts of the translation as well.

Lastly, the methodological steps taken by Van der Meer in his analysis of Josh 5:2–12 can be questioned. After critically reviewing other work done on the subject,²²¹ his treatment of Josh 5:2–12 begins with a redaction-critical analysis of

---

217 See section 2.3.2.
218 Van der Meer 2004, 350–355.
219 Holmes 1914, 29.
220 Exactly 29 times in the book of Joshua, according to a calculation based on the text of Rahlfs. The particle ποτὲ, on the other hand, occurs only 29 times in the LXX, and often reflects a free rendering of the Hebrew source text (Van der Meer 2004, 351).
221 Van der Meer 2004, 253–287.

the Hebrew text as preserved in the MT,²²² continues to evaluate Hebrew Qumran witnesses,²²³ and ends with an analysis of the Greek version "in its own right".²²⁴ Even though Van der Meer advocates for an initial separation of these methodological steps, the redaction-critical analysis of the MT impacts his interpretation of the OG. For example, Van der Meer concludes in his redaction-critical analysis that the expression אֶת־חֶרְפַּת מִצְרַיִם "disgrace of Egypt" should not be understood as referring to the circumcision in 5:2–8 since Josh 4:21–5:8 is a Deuteronomistic addition to a pre-Deuteromistic stratum. Thus, Josh 5:9 would not have originally related to Josh 5:2–9.²²⁵ This redaction-critical interpretation then influences Van der Meer's analysis of the Greek translation, and lets him conclude that when the translator read verse 5:9 together with 5:2–8 in his *Vorlage*, this was a false interpretation on behalf of the translator.²²⁶ Assuming that the interpretation by the translator is false requires that Van der Meer's redaction-critical conclusion be right. When Van der Meer, then, states in his conclusions that "it has proven helpful, necessary and illuminating to keep text-critical data and literary-critical observations separate",²²⁷ it is questionable whether he has really done that, or whether the literary-critical observations based on the MT have influenced the analysis of the Greek text. Furthermore, many of the redaction-critical arguments put forth by Van der Meer could be disputed, since several differing models of the redaction history of Josh 5:2–12 have been put forth.²²⁸ Therefore, I think it is more fruitful to begin the analysis of Josh 5:2–12 from all the relevant textual evidence, and only then consider literary and redaction critical aspects. If the OG in fact preserves an unrevised version of the pericope, as was argued above, this way of proceeding is the only way to gain accurate information on the textual history of this pericope.

To sum up the text-critical discussion, it is most probable that OG Josh 5:2–9 and especially vv. 4–6 were translated from a Hebrew *Vorlage* with a slightly different meaning than the MT. This Hebrew text is, at least in 5:4–6, earlier than the MT. It is the "unrevised" version of the circumcision account. A possible retroversion for this *Vorlage* in the most crucial verses 5:4–6 is given below. Note that the retroversion is only tentative, and often there is more than one option for the possible equivalent in Hebrew. In unclear cases, I will follow the MT if the difference in Greek is attributable to the freedom of the translator.

---

222 Van der Meer 2004, 289–327.
223 Van der Meer 2004, 328–333.
224 Van der Meer 2004, 334–412.
225 Van der Meer 2004, 311–315.
226 Van der Meer 2004, 351–352.
227 Van der Meer 2004, 414.
228 See, for example, the critical survey and comments by Dozeman 2015, 271–301.

Hebrew *Vorlage* Josh 5:4–6	OG Josh 5:4–6
⁴ וזה הדבר אשר מל יהושע את בני ישראל כל הילדים בדרך וכל הערלים בצאתם ממצרים	⁴ ὃν δὲ τρόπον περιεκάθαρεν Ἰησοῦς τοὺς υἱοὺς Ἰσραήλ, ὅσοι ποτὲ ἐγένοντο ἐν τῇ ὁδῷ καὶ ὅσοι ποτὲ ἀπερίτμητοι ἦσαν τῶν ἐξεληλυθότων ἐξ Αἰγύπτου
⁵ את כל אלה מל יהושע	⁵ πάντας τούτους περιέτεμεν Ἰησοῦς·
⁶ כי ארבעים ושתים שנה הלכו ישראל במדבר לכן ערלים היו רבים אנשי המלחמה היצאים מארץ מצרים אשר לא שמעו בקול אלוהים¹ ואשר נשבע להם לבלתי הראותם את הארץ אשר נשבע יהוה לאבותם לתת לנו ארץ זבת חלב ודבש	⁶ τεσσαράκοντα γὰρ καὶ δύο ἔτη ἀνέστραπται Ἰσραὴλ ἐν τῇ ἐρήμῳ τῇ Μαδβαρίτιδι, διὸ ἀπερίτμητοι ἦσαν οἱ πλεῖστοι (αὐτῶν) τῶν μαχίμων τῶν ἐξεληλυθότων ἐκ γῆς Αἰγύπτου οἱ ἀπειθήσαντες τῶν ἐντολῶν τοῦ θεοῦ, οἷς καὶ διώρισεν μὴ ἰδεῖν αὐτοὺς τὴν γῆν, ἣν ὤμοσεν κύριος τοῖς πατράσιν αὐτῶν δοῦναι ἡμῖν, γῆν ῥέουσαν γάλα καὶ μέλι.

Note

[1] Here also the verb מרה "disobey" is possible. The rare τῶν ἐντολῶν τοῦ θεοῦ could also possibly reflect מצות אלוהים.

The proto-MT editor(s) edited a Hebrew text like the *Vorlage,* guided by nomistic motivations. The existence of uncircumcised Israelites among the Exodus generation was removed, the passing of the generation that was disobedient to the Lord was underlined, and the purity of the people for the upcoming Passover celebration was ensured. In this way, the passage was brought into closer conformity with the key passages and ideas in the Pentateuch.

Since the circumcision and the flint knives were at the core of this revision, one can assume that this nomistic editing probably also influenced the later mentions of the flint knives in Josh 21:42d and Josh 24:31a. I will turn to these mentions next.

MT (Josh 21:42)	OG (Josh 21:42)
	42a Καὶ συνετέλεσεν Ἰησοῦς διαμερίσας τὴν γῆν ἐν τοῖς ὁρίοις αὐτῶν. 42b καὶ ἔδωκαν οἱ υἱοὶ Ἰσραὴλ μερίδα τῷ Ἰησοῖ κατὰ πρόσταγμα κυρίου· ἔδωκαν αὐτῷ τὴν πόλιν, ἣν ᾐτήσατο·

3.4 Joshua 24:28–33: Text and Apparatus — 143

MT (Josh 21:42)	OG (Josh 21:42)
	τὴν Θαμνασάραχ ἔδωκαν αὐτῷ
	ἐν τῷ ὄρει Ἐφράιμ.
	[42c] καὶ ᾠκοδόμησεν Ἰησοῦς
	τὴν πόλιν καὶ ᾤκησεν ἐν αὐτῇ.[1]
	[42d] καὶ ἔλαβεν Ἰησοῦς
	τὰς μαχαίρας τὰς πετρίνας,
	ἐν αἷς περιέτεμεν τοὺς υἱοὺς Ἰσραὴλ
	τοὺς γενομένους ἐν τῇ ὁδῷ ἐν τῇ ἐρήμῳ,
	καὶ ἔθηκεν αὐτὰς ἐν Θαμνασαράχ.
	[42a] So Iesous stopped dividing the land in their boundaries.
	[42b] And the Israelites gave a portion to Iesous according to the ordinance of the Lord. They gave him the city he asked: Thamnatsachar in Mt. Ehpraim.
	[42c] And Iesous built the city and lived in it.
	[42d] And Iesous took the flint knives with which he circumcised the Israelites born on the way in the wilderness and he put them in Thamnatsachar.

Note

[1] Verses 42a–c are a repetition from 19:49–50. Here one has to agree with Holmes (1914, 73–74) that such a repetition could not have been created by the translator of OG. A Hebrew reviser, however, would have had a motive to delete this as a redundant repetition, which is probably what happened. That this repetition is preserved in the OG is an important factor in redaction criticism, since this earlier repetition, probably created by redaction, is removed later in the proto-MT phase of editing and is not preserved by the textual witnesses relying on the MT.

In OG Josh 21:42, there are several plusses not present in the MT. The last plus (42d) mentions the flint knives used in the circumcision in Josh 5, and is probably dependent on that chapter.[229] This verse should be evaluated together with 24:31a, since in light of the proposed rewriting in the proto-MT phase of Josh 5:4–6 it seems that the same editor who wanted to delete the presence of uncircumcised Israelites coming out of Egypt would have wanted to remove these verses,

---

229 Holmes (1914, 74) already noted that this plus "stands or falls" with 24:31.

since they commemorate the flint knives with which the Israelites were "purified" (περιεκάθαρεν). The editor was disturbed by the notion that the Israelites did not universally practice circumcision in Egypt, and wanted to omit any recollections of that.[230] Thus, he omitted verses 21:42d and 24:31a.

Some scholars have suggested that verse 24:31a is a secondary addition made to the Hebrew *Vorlage* of the OG. While there is some appeal to this argument, it does not sufficiently explain the connection of 24:31a with the rewriting in chapter 5. Hartmut Rösel has noted that the beginning of the OG addition in 24:33b is similar to verse 28 (ἕκαστος εἰς τὸν τόπον αὐτῶν), which forms a resumptive repetition that corroborates the lateness of all the plusses between them.[231] This, according to Rösel, speaks for the secondary nature of 24:31a. The problem with this latter argument is, however, that it presumes that all the plusses in the OG version of verses 31–33 can be explained together. In my opinion, this *Wiederaufnahme* would support only the possible secondary nature of all or some of the plusses in verse 33. It would not corroborate the secondary nature of verse 31a.

If this were a secondary addition, what would be the motive for conjuring up this kind of an expansion? Not many convincing reasons have been put forth in research. Arnold Ehrlich suggested in his early commentary that this could be an addition made by a Hellenistic Jew who found the idea of Joshua circumcising the people embarrassing, and thus wanted to make sure that the "grotesque rite" was buried with Joshua.[232] This, in my opinion, is a highly conjectural statement. A more plausible motive would be the desire to indicate the final repository of the flint knives with which an important covenantal act was performed. In verse 32, the burial of Joseph's bones with him was reported, and that would have provided the spark for an editor to include the flint knives in Joshua's burial. Nelson has noted that the verse "represents just the sort of folkloristic, Midrashic detail typical of textual expansions" without allusions to other cases in support of this statement.[233] While these are theoretically possible explanations, the theological peculiarity and the connections of this verse to earlier material in OG Joshua could open a much more persuasive explanation.

---

[230] A similar suggestion was made by Holmes 1914, 9–10.
[231] Rösel 1980, 349.
[232] "Dieses Plus rührt im griechischen Texte von irgendeinem witzigen hellenistischen Juden her, den die Beschneidung genierte (vgl. zu Gen. 17:13) und der darum den grotesken Ritus gern mit Josua begraben wissen wollte." Ehrlich 1910, 66.
[233] Nelson 1997, 282. He also notes that "the expanded form of the text depends on 5:4" but does not explain how this would lead to verse 24:31a being a later addition. As we have seen earlier, the connection with Josh 5 could also speak for the priority of this verse.

The theological peculiarity of this material lies in two claims it makes: that the Israelites buried the same flint knives with Joshua with which he once circumcised them (Josh 5:2–9), and that it was Joshua, not Moses, who lead the Israelites out of Egypt.[234] The first point concerning the burying of the flint knives implies that these objects were revered; they were perceived as religious relics.[235] Whereas Rösel claims that there is nothing novel in this plus in relation to Josh. 5,[236] it is apparent that the emphasis on the importance of the objects, namely the flint knives, is new here. This point alone would be enough for a late editor to omit this plus, since the reverence of an object could be perceived as idolatry by later editors.

In the plus of OG Josh 24:31a, the second claim is that it was Joshua who brought the people out of Egypt and that, for this Exodus, he was given the instructions by YHWH. There is no mention of Moses here. What makes it even more significant is that the OG is missing the reference to Moses present in MT Josh 24:5. In the OG version of Josh 24, there are numerous references to the Exodus, but no references to Moses. It is plausible that an editor might have had a problem with the absence of Moses in such an important text.[237] It is possible that the same editor was responsible for omitting verse 31a from the proto-MT and adding the reference to Moses in verse 5, to introduce Moses into the Exodus and downplay the role of Joshua in it.[238]

Therefore, upon a closer examination, three arguments speak for the primary nature of verse 24:31a: (1) its omission is probably connected with the omission of 21:42d and the rewriting in the proto-MT phase of 5:2–9, (2) the reverence of the flint knives could be perceived as theologically problematic, and (3) the emphasis put on Joshua as the leader of the Exodus could be perceived as problematic. Even if one does not approve the first explanation, the theological peculiarities alone make it much more likely that verse 24:31a is an omission in the proto-MT tradition, and not a secondary addition. It is not likely that a late Hebrew editor would have added such a polemic verse.[239] Thus, OG Joshua preserves an earlier verse

---

[234] These theological peculiarities were also noted by Rofé 1982, 23–24.
[235] Thus also Rofé 1982, 24.
[236] Rösel 1980, 349.
[237] The absence of Moses in Josh 24 is corroborated as a true concern for ancient scribes dealing with the text when one looks at the variant readings of 24:8 in the LXX manuscripts. There, MSS 82 12 add μωυσης "Moses" to the text.
[238] It seems that we might have here a remnant of a differing Exodus tradition which emphasizes Joshua's role in leading the people out of Egypt. This verse could, interestingly, thus have an impact on the reconstruction of the evolution of the Exodus traditions.
[239] The verse was probably then originally written at the same time when the OG version of Josh 5:4–6 was produced, by a scribe who had not yet realized the possible theological problems that

linked with the death and burial of Joshua, while MT Joshua omits the verse as offensive, and Judges further agrees. The absence of the verse in Judges is understandable, since Judg 2:6–9 represents a later adaptation of the pericope whose aim is to reverse the theme of the fidelity of the Israelites. The burial of the flint knives or Joseph's bones is not as such of interest in this new context.[240]

Replacement of "Place"? (v. 28)

While Josh 24:28 reports that Joshua sent the people away, the MT, OG, and some Greek witnesses differ on where the people exactly went. MT Josh 24:28 reads אִישׁ לְנַחֲלָתוֹ "each to his inheritance" in the same way as Judg 2:6. OG Josh 24:28, however, reads εἰς τὸν τόπον αὐτοῦ "to his place". The MT נַחֲלָה is likely the latest reading, since instead of the general "going to a place", it highlights the land as being divided into inheritances.

The Greek τόπος in OG Josh 24:28 is not commonly used to translate נַחֲלָה. It most commonly reflects מָקוֹם. Therefore, it has been suggested that the Hebrew *Vorlage* of OG Josh 24:28 might reflect למקמו.[241] It is certainly likely that the translator was working with a different *Vorlage*, since נַחֲלָה is nearly always translated with a word deriving from κλῆρος in the book of Joshua. Elsewhere in the book of Joshua, there are 49 occurrences of נַחֲלָה and the only two exceptions to the common translation are Josh 18:7 and 24:32, where μερίς is used. A Hebrew *Vorlage* differing from the MT therefore must be assumed. That the *Vorlage* would have read למקמו is, however, not the only option. The LXX witnesses in Josh 24:28 and Judg 2:6 preserve another possibility. While in Josh 24:28 most Greek manuscripts reads "to his place", interestingly La[100] reads *in domum suam* "to their house".[242] In the parallel verse Judg 2:6, a similar double reading is reflected by the A-text τὸν οἶκον αὐτοῦ "to their house". In all the other occurrences of τόπος in the book of Joshua, La[100] uses the translation equivalent *locus*. Therefore, it is possible that La[100] indirectly preserves the Greek variant τὸν οἶκον αὐτοῦ in

---

might be connected with these texts. When the Pentateuch was given more and more authority, these problems were realized.

240 We do not know whether the editor of Judges knew OG Josh 24:31a or the other burial notices (Josh 24:31–33) when he adapted OG Josh 24:28–31 into his new composition. On the one hand, since he follows the sequence of OG Josh 24:28–31, it is possible that he was aware of the verse dealing with the flint knives. On the other hand, the verse might have been omitted at such an early stage that the Vorlage of the editor of Judges did not have access to it. In any case, the themes introduced in Judg 2:10 was the reason for including verses from the end of Josh 24 in the first place.

241 Rofé 1982, 21–22.

242 The marginal reading τὴν πολιν in MSS 85 and 344 is probably quite late.

Josh 24:28. But is this the earliest Greek translation of Josh 24:28 or a later harmonization, for example, towards OG Judg 2:6?

It is hard to evaluate what exactly has happened here, since harmonizations in several directions are possible. It seems, however, that in any case one has to speculate on the Hebrew *Vorlage* of the reading. In this regard, an intriguing suggestion has been made according to which the earliest Hebrew reading for Josh 24:28 was איש לביתו which preserved a textual link with 1 Sam 10:25.[243] The probability of such an early link is corroborated by several other affinities between Josh 24 and 1 Sam 10:17–27.[244] This original reading would first have been translated word-for-word with τὸν οἶκον αὐτοῦ in OG Josh 24:28. However, this OG reading was lost due to an early revision, which secondarily changed the Greek text into τὸν τόπον αὐτῶν. This might have been a harmonization with Josh 24:33b, and it is reflected in most Greek MSS. The OG reading of Josh 24:28 would then only be preserved indirectly in La[100] but also in the double reading τὸν οἶκον αὐτοῦ of the parallel verse in Judg 2:6. However, the weak manuscript support for τὸν οἶκον αὐτοῦ as the OG in Josh 24:28, and the possibility of a secondary harmonization, undermines this solution. Since the variant does not have major repercussions for this study, the question will remain open.

Other Minor Variants between the Four Accounts

There are three likely secondary additions in Judg 2:6–7 which highlight the secondary nature of the passage in Judges in relation to Joshua. First, in Joshua, when the people go back to their own inheritances they are referred to only as אִישׁ "each", while Judges gives a more specific בְּנֵי־יִשְׂרָאֵל "sons of Israel". This should probably be regarded as a later addition harmonizing the text with other verses in the context of Judges (Judg 2:4, 11).[245] It is also possible that the phrase was missing from OG Judg, as attested by its absence in the B-text. If this is the case, this Greek text might reflect a different Hebrew *Vorlage*. In any case, "sons of Israel" is a secondary addition in MT Judg. Such an addition could have easily emerged as a marginal gloss. Second, the verse in Judges includes a report that the Israelites went to take possession of the land (לָרֶשֶׁת אֶת־הָאָרֶץ). This expression

---

243 See Koopmans 1990, 263–264. Although Koopmans falsely suggests that τὸν οἶκον αὐτοῦ in Judg 2:6 could be a later revision towards the original reading in Josh 24:28. This does not accord with what we know about the *Kaige* revision in Judges. It is most probable that τὴν κληρονομίαν αὐτοῦ is not the earliest reading, but a *Kaige* reading that is common to the B-text.
244 See section 4.2.6.
245 It would be harder to explain why בְּנֵי־יִשְׂרָאֵל would have been omitted in Joshua. There are no possible stylistic reasons or ideological motives that would cause such an omission.

is likely a late Deuteronomistically inspired insertion.[246] The shorter version preserved in Joshua would be good soil for such an addition.[247] Third, in Judg 2:7, there is the plus הַגָּדוֹל in both the OG and the MT versions of Judges. It seems to be a late addition, with the motive of further emphasizing the mightiness of YHWH's works. It is, as Hartmut Rösel puts it, "eine sekundäre Verstärkung".[248]

Besides these additions, the reading in MT Josh 24:28 does not contain וַיֵּלְכוּ which is present in all the other versions. There is no ground for *parablepsis* in MT Joshua, thus the omission in the MT could be intentional. The omission could be related to the replacement of "place" (OG) with the more specific "inheritance" (MT), since it can be interpreted as highlighting Joshua as the divider of the land into inheritances. It is, however, also possible that the omission is stylistically motivated, removing an unnecessary verb.[249]

In the second verse (OG Josh 24:29, MT Josh 24:31 / Judg 2:7), there is also variation between the verbs רָאוּ and יָדְעוּ. The *Vorlage* of OG Joshua probably reflects רָאוּ since the verb יָדַע is never translated with ὁράω in Joshua.[250] MT Judg has also רָאוּ, while MT Josh and OG Judg read יָדְעוּ (OG Judges ἔγνωσαν). It is not easy to decide which one is the more original, since these verbs can be used synonymously and the motives for this interchange cannot be deduced from the larger context of the chapters (both variants are present in Joshua and Judges). Still, the verb ראה might well be the more original, because the elders concerned are perceived as eyewitnesses to the deeds of YHWH. The verb ידע would then be a later change to a verb with a wider semantic field, which would include even people who have not seen the deeds of YHWH but know of them. This hypothesis would corroborate my previous conclusions that the OG Josh

---

246 The verb ירש occurs 34 times in Deuteronomium. Compared to the second largest occurrence rate of 8 in Joshua, the concept of "taking possession of the land" is clearly linked with Deuteronomistic ideology. See Knoppers 2005, 147–148. This expression is also seen as a late addition by Rösel 1980, 344.

247 If not, one would have to argue why MT and OG Joshua omits this expression. A *parablepsis* is not possible here. Thus, the omission would be intentional. Auld (2005, 82) argues that Joshua indeed omits this phrase, which belongs to the more original reading. According to Auld, the omission was made because the book of Joshua aims to give the impression that the settlement of the land was completed before Joshua's death. One has to ask: would this expression, situated right before the narration of Joshua's death, not convey exactly that? The expression could be seen as reminding the reader that the "taking possession of the land" was finished before the leader's death.

248 Rösel 1980, 344.

249 One could also argue that the MT of Joshua presents the more original reading. It would, however, be hard to conceive of why and how an editor would insert a verb that usually begins a new sentence in the middle of a sentence in both OG Josh and OG/MT Judg.

250 The most common equivalent for יָדַע in Joshua is γινώσκω.

holds the more original text of this verse, which has been further edited in MT Josh and – in this case – OG Judg. Some minor support for this line of argument comes from La[100] which supports the MT Judg reading with *viderunt*. This conclusion should, however, be viewed with caution, as these verbs can be used quite synonymously.

In the last verse reporting Joshua's burial, Joshua and Judges differ on the name of the burial place. Where MT Joshua reads תִּמְנַת־סֶרַח, MT Judges has תִּמְנַת־חֶרֶס. This could be a simple metathesis either way. In OG Joshua, B reads Θαμναθασαχαρα and A θαμνασαχαρ. Whichever is the correct OG reading, it still probably reflects the Hebrew תִּמְנַת־סֶרַח since in Judges תִּמְנַת־חֶרֶס is transcribed with either Θαμναθαρες (B) or Θαμναθαρεως (A). If the change was intentional, the more original reading would probably be תִּמְנַת־חֶרֶס since it can be perceived as more offensive.[251] This, however, is speculative, as it is not clear whether the place name would have really been perceived as offensive. Thus, either one could be the more original reading.

The Extended Ending in the OG (v. 33a, b)

In the OG, verse 24:33 begins with the introductory formula Καὶ ἐγένετο μετὰ ταῦτα "And it happened after these things", which is not present in the MT. Both versions then report the death of Eleazar and his burial to Gibeah, which is in the hill country of Ephraim. MT Josh ends there, but the OG continues with two distinct verses. Verse 33a reports that the Israelites carried the ark of YHWH in their midst while Eleazar's son Phinehas served as the priest, until he also died and was interred in Gibeah. In verse 33b, the tone of the chapter suddenly changes as the Israelites, after departing each to their own place, start to worship Astarte, Astaroth, and the gods of the surrounding nations. Because of this, the Lord delivers the Israelites into the hands of Eglom for eighteen years. In other words, while Josh 24 ends in the MT with the Israelites remaining loyal to YHWH, the OG concludes with the typical vicious circle of the Israelites who break their promise to worship YHWH alone.

The longer ending of Josh 24 in the OG has received some discussion in the scholarly literature, but the various solutions remain inconclusive. In my opinion, the earlier text-critical models have been too quick to judge the whole ending either as a later addition or omission, without giving enough attention to the intricacies in the content of these two separate verses. Two influential opposing solutions were presented in the 1980s by Rösel and Rofé. I will briefly

---

[251] As argued by Auld 1975, 264. The offensiveness comes from it being connected with the worship of the sun (חֶרֶס).

summarize these solutions, since they illustrate the simplifications usually made when dealing with the extended ending of Joshua.

In his 1980 article, *Die Überleitungen vom Josua ins Richterbuch*, Rösel defended the traditional view, stating that the MT contains the most original shorter reading. Rösel's argument consists of four observations that speak for the secondary nature of the plusses in the OG. First, the introductory formula (ἐν ἐκείνῃ τῇ ἡμέρᾳ) in verse 33a raises the suspicion that we might be dealing with a later addition. Second, the verse has a clear connection with Judg 20:27–28 that reports Phinehas serving as a priest in front of the ark, and which also is probably a later addition in its contexts.[252] This, according to Rösel, also casts doubts on the originality of 24:33a. Third, the place name ἐν Γαβααθ τῇ ἑαυτοῦ seems to be an *ad hoc* formulation created "besides a writing table". Fourth, the beginning of verse 33b includes a repetition from verse 28 (ἕκαστος εἰς τὸν τόπον αὐτοῦ) and could thus be a sign of being a later addition.[253] The editorial technique utilized here is resumptive repetition (*Wiederaufnahme*). I will return to this fourth claim below since it is, in my opinion, the most persuasive part of Rösel's argument.

The priority of the longer ending in the OG has been defended by Rofé in his article *The End of the Book of Joshua According to the Septuagint*. His proposal has been relatively influential and has been adapted by, for example, Tov in his introductory work to the textual criticism of the Hebrew Bible.[254] Rofé argues that the version in the OG includes in its entirety an earlier version of Joshua's ending. The mention of Eglom at the end originally linked the book of Joshua with Judg 3:12, where Israel's apostasy and deliverance into the hands of Eglom is narrated. Thus, Rofé argues that the OG ending of Joshua preserves the lost link between the once unified books of Joshua and Judges. This link was lost when the longer ending was omitted in the MT version of Joshua, during the separation of the books and the addition of late material in Judg 1:1–3:11. In addition to a text-critical evaluation, Rofé introduces external evidence for the priority of the OG Joshua ending. The Damascus Document mentions in the same context five items present in the longer ending of Joshua: the Ark, the death of Eleazar and Joshua,

---

[252] There are at least two problems with these verses in the context of Judg 20. First, it is the only passage in the book of Judges where the Ark of the Covenant appears. Second, it is chronologically awkward to introduce Phinehas at such a late point in the narrative of Judges, since he was supposed to have already lived in the times of Moses and Joshua (see, for example, Num 25 and Josh 22). Against the conclusion that Judg 20:27–28 is a later addition see, for example, Butler 2009. 447.
[253] Rösel 1980, 349.
[254] Tov 2012, 298.

the elders, and the worship of Astaroth. This, according to Rofé, is evidence that the ending of Joshua in the OG was known to the author of the Damascus Document in its original Hebrew form.[255]

Already at this point it should be noted that this external evidence does not solve whether the text of the OG is earlier or not. If these two verses were secondarily added to the Hebrew, the author of the Damascus Document may have simply used the version that had gone through the addition of these verses. Thus, the evaluation should be done based on internal arguments.[256]

The main problem with these and other past explanations is that they attempt to explain both verses of the extended ending together. When one compares verses 33a and 33b, it is apparent that they differ markedly in their tone and content. First, verse 33a is firmly linked with the earlier verses where the Israelites are still faithful to YHWH and the burial of an important figure is narrated. Verse 33b, conversely, disrupts this continuity and introduces a surprising and abrupt abandonment of YHWH. Second, the mention of Phinehas in 33a further underlines the different tone between 33a and 33b. In the book of Joshua, Phinehas the son of Eleazar is a zealous defender of the correct worship of YHWH. In Josh 22, it is Phinehas who leads the convoy to remind the tribes east of Jordan, in accordance with Deut 12, that there can only be one true altar for YHWH. Moreover, elsewhere in the Hebrew Bible Phinehas serves as a model of a faithful servant of YHWH for subsequent generations (see, for example, Num 25:1–13, Ps 106:28–31, and 1 Macc 2:26).[257] After such an emphasis on the fidelity of the Israelites in 33a, the sudden apostasy in 33b seems surprising. Therefore, due to the different content and tone, these verses should be considered separately.

Verse 24:33a is text-historically probably earlier than 24:33b, since it belongs closely together with the preceding verses 28–33. There are at least five arguments supporting this claim. First, it has been noted by several scholars that chapter 24 is related to verses 8:30–35.[258] Both describe an event taking place in Shechem, both describe a ceremonial act involving all the tribes of Israel led by Joshua, both include the book of law, and – as concluded in section 3.2.2 – the list of elders in the opening verse 24:1 was in its earliest form (OG) identical with the list of elders in 8:33. What is missing from MT Josh 24 is the ark, which plays a pivotal role in 8:30–35. Josh 24:33a in the OG, however, links the ark to the

---

255 Rofé 1982.
256 Some criticism against arguing with the Damascus Document was also raised by Rösel 2002.
257 For an analysis of figure of Phinehas in the Hebrew Bible, see Spencer 1992, 346–347.
258 Soggin 1972, 241–244 and Mayes 1983, 50–51.

covenant chapter 24. Considering the other parallels with 8:30–35, this supports the originality of verse 33a.

Second, the notion that Phinehas succeeded as priest after the death of his father is not found anywhere else in the Hebrew Bible.[259] However, in light of the prominence of Phinehas in Joshua (Josh 22), such a mention is suitable at the end of Joshua. By mentioning him as a priest and reporting his burial, Phinehas is envisioned as one of the elders "that outlived Joshua" (MT Josh 24:31), during whose lifetime the Israelites remained faithful to YHWH. The argument that the succession of the priesthood to Phinehas is an early part of Josh 24 is strengthened by the presence of such traditions in two other sources. After having reported the death of Joshua, Josephus tells that around the same time Eleazar died "leaving the high priesthood to his son Phineas" (Ant. 5.119).[260] In addition, SamJosh, which also has many other parallels with the OG, likewise reports that Phinehas continued as a priest after the death of Joshua (SamJosh 23:16).[261] When one considers all the scant mentions that Phinehas continued as a priest after the death of his father (OG Josh 24:33a, Judg 20:27–28, Josephus, and SamJosh), Josh 24 is certainly the most plausible original context for the provenance of such a tradition. There, he was included among the elders during whose time the Israelites remained loyal to YHWH. Therefore, it is likely that the OG, Josephus, and SamJosh preserve here an early tradition lost from the MT.

Third, the Greek language of this verse is Hebraistic, and its possible retroversion fits stylistically well into the context.[262] For example, the Greek ἐν ἐκείνῃ τῇ ἡμέρᾳ clearly reflects בַּיּוֹם הַהוּא in a Hebrew *Vorlage*, a phrase which also links it directly with the event in the last verse.

Fourth, as Rösel noted, Josh 24:33a is closely connected with Judg 20:27–28, where Phinehas serves as the priest in front of the ark. These verses in the context of Judg 20 are probably a late addition.[263] If we assume that the depiction of Phinehas serving as the priest in front of the ark originates from

---

259 In Judg 22:27–28 it is assumed that Phinehas had inherited the priesthood from Eleazar, but the actual succession is not narrated.
260 Even though Josephus seems to follow the MT more closely than the LXX in his retelling of the book of Joshua, it is possible that he derived this information from the LXX. See Begg 2007, 129–145 for more on this issue and a thorough analysis of Ant. 5.115–119 in relation to MT and OG Josh 23–24, Pseudo-Philo, and the Samaritan Joshua material.
261 This was noted already at the beginning of 20th century by Gaster (1909, 120), but has not been taken into account by subsequent scholars dealing with the extended ending in OG Josh 24. See also Tov 2015a, 215–216.
262 See the retroversion below.
263 Also Guillaume 2004, 207.

Josh 24, it is possible to explain where the secondary addition Judg 20:27–28 was taken from. It is conceivable that a later scribe took this depiction from the earlier ending of Josh 24 and inserted it into Judg 20, where it clearly is an interpolation. Such an assumption fits well together with the other occasions where the book of Judges would have secondarily taken ideas from the book of Joshua.[264]

Fifth, there are two possible reasons for the omission of verse 33a in a later proto-MT phase. On the one hand, it is possible that the mention of the death of Phinehas was omitted to harmonize it with information found in the book of Judges. After Judg 20:27–28 had at some point been secondarily added to Judg 20, an editor might have concluded that the death of Phinehas should not be reported at the end of Josh 24, since he is still alive in Judges. Thus, ironically, verses Judg 20:27–28, which were originally created based on Josh 24:33a, later caused the omission of Josh 24:33a. On the other hand, it is also possible that the omission is related to the struggles related to the purity of the priesthood in the Second Temple period. While Phinehas indeed belonged to the "correct" Aaronide line of priests, there might have been a concern that Phinehas the son of Eleazar could be mixed up with Phinehas the son of Eli. Phinehas the son of Eli, together with his brother Hophni, were bad priests (1 Sam 2:12–36) to whom the editors of the Hebrew Bible attributed the elimination of the priestly line of Eli (1 Kgs 2:27). Thus, the omission of the verse dealing with Phinehas (OG Josh 24:33a) in a late textual phase might have been motivated by concerns arising from the later historical books. Since the ending of Josh 24 was also otherwise subjected to heavy editing, the secondary omission of Josh 24:33a due to one of these reasons is more than plausible.

Verse 24:33b in the OG, conversely, is more problematic, and it has all the features of a later harmonizing addition. At least four arguments support this claim. First, as already mentioned, it begins by repeating an element taken from verse 28 (ἕκαστος εἰς τὸν τόπον αὐτῶν "each to their place"), thus forming a resumptive repetition. This was the editorial technique with which a later scribe inserted this verse into the text. Second, verse 33b is in contradiction with the movements of the people in Josh 24. The chapter first presents a dialogue in Shechem between Joshua and the people in which the Israelites give a threefold promise to worship YHWH alone. This dialogue ends in verse 27 with the erection of a stone as a witness to the promise. In verse 28, the people return each to their own places. When verse 33b reports again that the Israelites

---

[264] The death and burial of Joshua, for example, was secondarily adapted from Josh 24 to Judg 2:6–9. See 3.4.2.

returned to their own places, it assumes that the people were gathered in one place, when the chapter has already started reporting on the deaths and burials of great men.

Third, the content of the verse is abrupt, and contradicts with what has been concluded in the chapter. Suddenly, the Israelites start to worship forbidden gods. Such a contrast between the fidelity and apostasy of the Israelites is a central structure in Judges. The theme might therefore have been imported into the end of Joshua from the book of Judges. In fact, when studied more closely, the added verse 33b does seem to be borrowed from the book of Judges. It contains many elements found in Judges 2:6, 11–13, and 3:12–14.[265] Hence, the purpose of the addition might be related to an aim of bringing the ending of the book of Joshua into closer conformity with the history of deterioration, as reported in Judges.

Fourth, it is peculiar that the gods Astarte and Astaroth are mentioned together. The Greek words Ἀστάρτη and Ασταρωθ are both used to translate the Hebrew עשתרות. Only in 2 Chr 15:16 is Ἀστάρτη used for אֲשֵׁרָה.[266] Rofé suggests that this is a rendition of the Hebrew עשתרת ואת עשתרות but nowhere in the Hebrew Bible do we find these words presented as they are here.[267] These linguistic peculiarities, together with the arguments mentioned earlier, corroborate the lateness of this verse.

Finally, it is probable that verse 33b was already present in the Hebrew *Vorlage* of the OG. The translation technique of Joshua is varying, but while the translator does take some liberties, as I have concluded earlier, he would not have made such radical additions, but remained quite loyal to the Hebrew source text.[268] Verse 33b is also relatively Hebraistic, which supports the claim that it was added by a Hebrew scribe and merely translated into Greek.

A possible retroversion from the OG text into Hebrew further illustrates the point that verses 33a and 33b were both originally composed in Hebrew.[269] Although such a retroversion is not without problems, it illustrates how relatively easily the Hebrew source text can be deduced from the type of Greek that the translator used.

---

[265] Trebolle 2016, 192–193. The connections of Josh 24:33b with Judg 2 undermines the argument by Rofé that 24:33b would preserve the original ending linking with Judg 3:17.
[266] Thus also Rösel 2002, 18.
[267] Rofé 1982, 21.
[268] See section 2.3.2.
[269] This point is elaborated by Rofé (1982, 21), who also gave a possible retroversion of these verses.

3.4 Joshua 24:28–33: Text and Apparatus

Vorlage of OG Josh 24:33a-b	OG Josh 24:33a-b
33a ביום ההוא	33a ἐν ἐκείνῃ τῇ ἡμέρᾳ
לקחו בני ישראל	λαβόντες οἱ υἱοὶ Ἰσραήλ
את ארון האלהים	τὴν κιβωτὸν τοῦ θεοῦ
וישאו	περιεφέροσαν ἐν ἑαυτοῖς,[1]
ויכהן פינחס	καὶ Φινεες ἱεράτευσεν
תחת אלעזר אביו	ἀντὶ Ελεαζαρ τοῦ πατρὸς αὐτοῦ,
עד אשר מת ויקבר	ἕως ἀπέθανεν καὶ κατωρύγη
בגבעה אשר לו	ἐν Γαβααθ τῇ ἑαυτοῦ.
33b ובני ישראל הלכו	33b οἱ δὲ υἱοὶ Ἰσραήλ ἀπήλθοσαν
איש למקומו	ἕκαστος εἰς τὸν τόπον αὐτῶν
ולעירו	καὶ εἰς τὴν ἑαυτῶν πόλιν.
וייראו בני ישראל	καὶ ἐσέβοντο οἱ υἱοὶ Ἰσραήλ
את עשתרת ואת עשתרות	τὴν Ἀστάρτην καὶ Ασταρωθ
ואת אלהי העמים	καὶ τοὺς θεοὺς τῶν ἐθνῶν
אשר סביבותיהם	τῶν κύκλῳ αὐτῶν·
ויתנם יהוה	καὶ παρέδωκεν αὐτοὺς κύριος
ביד עגלון מלך מואב	εἰς χεῖρας Εγλωμ τῷ βασιλεῖ Μωαβ,
וימשל בהם שמנה עשרה שנה	καὶ ἐκυρίευσεν αὐτῶν ἔτη δέκα ὀκτώ.

Note
[1] ἐν ἑαυτοῖς is likely an interpretive addition made by the translator.

To sum up, OG verses Josh 24:33a and b probably derive from the hands of different Hebrew scribes. Verse 33a is likely earlier and better linked with the rest of the chapter, while verse 33b creates a secondary link with Judges. It is another question which text should be reconstructed as earliest in textual criticism. If the argument presented in my preceding discussion is accepted, there are two solutions.

First, it could be concluded that the ending reflected by the Hebrew *Vorlage* of the OG, along with 24:31a and 24:33a–b, is the best text-critically recoverable text. In this case, Josh 24:33b would be the latest verse added to the chapter in its literary growth. The MT would then be regarded as preserving an even later textual form, which has gone through omissions and a reorganizing of the ending due to the reasons discussed earlier.

Second, it is possible that the common archetypal text form behind the endings of MT and OG Josh 24 ended with the Hebrew *Vorlage* of OG Josh 24:33a. This text was heavily edited in the proto-MT phase, changing the order of the text and omitting two verses. The Hebrew *Vorlage* behind the OG is then closer to this earliest text form, but at some point a scribe secondarily added verse 24:33b to it, and in this way harmonized the text closer to the book of Judges. Since the verse is missing from the MT, the MT is earlier in this regard.

The only difference between these two solutions is whether the proto-MT editors knew the late verse 24:33b or not. In other words, did they omit it, or did it not yet exist? This issue can probably not be solved with the preserved evidence. Nevertheless, from the point of view of editorial history, two conclusions remain: first, the ending of Joshua in the MT witnesses to omissions and reorganizing and, second, the OG contains early material missing from the MT and a late addition harmonizing the ending with the book of Judges.

3.5 Text-Critical Conclusions

To sum up, the results of the text-critical analysis are gathered in the table below. The table is not a presentation of all individual textual variants – instead, it presents an overview of *significant content related differences* between the textual witnesses. The primacy between the OG and the MT is indicated with an X either column.

ID	Verse	Variant	The OG is earlier	The MT is earlier
1	24:1	Alignment of the list of leaders	X	
2	24:1, 25	Replacement of Shechem with Shiloh		X
3	24:3	Addition of Canaan	X	
4	24:4–5	Secondary harmonizing additions towards towards 1 Sam 12 in MT	X	
5	24:4–5	Original link with Deut 26:5–6 in OG lost due to a scribal mistake	X	
6	24:5–13	Change of speaker from Joshua to YHWH	X	
7	24:6	Addition of fathers	X	
8	24:7	Change of subject from "we" to "they"	X	
9	24:8	Change of the subject of destruction from you to YHWH	X	
10	24:9	Addition of Balaam's title	X	
11	24:11	Rearrangement of the list of seven nations with transpositions	X	
12	24:12	Change of two kings to twelve kings		X
13	24:14	Addition of "foreign"		X
14	24:15	Addition of "gods of your fathers"	X	
15	24:15	Omission of "because he is holy"	X	
16	24:17	Scribal mistake omitting "he is God"	X	
17	24:17	Large Exodus related addition	X	

3.5 Text-Critical Conclusions — 157

ID	Verse	Variant	The OG is earlier	The MT is earlier
18	24:18	Transposition of Amorites/people	X	
19	24:22	Addition of "we are witnesses"	X	
20	24:24	Addition of "our God"	X	
21	24:25	Addition of the tent		X
22	24:26	Omission of "the sanctuary"		X
23	24:27	Addition of "today"		X
24	24:27	Softening rewriting at the end of the verse	X	
25	24:29 OG	Transposition of a whole verse	X	
26	24:31a	Omission of the flint knives	X	
27	24:33a	Omission of the ark and Phinehas	X	
28	24:33b	Addition linking with Judges		X

There are significant differences between OG and MT Josh in almost every verse of chapter 24. The key differences are quantified in the table above. The focus is on *significant content related differences*; that is, specific differences in meaning between the textual traditions are labeled under one ID. A single ID might contain various numbers of textual variants, as long as the variants relate to the same phenomenon. For example, the change of speaker in Josh 24:5–13 (ID 6) consists of over ten textual variants, while the replacement of Shechem with Shiloh (ID 2) only relates to two variants. Another quality of a single ID is that the difference was achieved through a specific editorial technique (addition, omission, rewriting, and transposition). This links the summary to the upcoming section 5. This categorization is dependent upon my qualitative analysis of the variants in the preceding sections.[270]

According to this classification, there are 28 *significant content related differences* between the MT and the OG of Josh 24. In majority of the differences – that is in 21 cases (75%) – the OG should be preferred. In 7 instances, the MT (25%) probably contains the earlier reading. Thus, in majority of the cases, the OG should be preferred as preserving the earlier textual form.[271]

---

[270] Admittedly, the categorization could be done in various other ways depending on different research questions. My approach here should be understood in the wider context of this study. Because of my approach, many textual variants are also left out from this table. For instance, the stylistic omission of "I gave" in OG Josh 24:4 does not count as a significant content related variant, since it is minor and does not affect the meaning of the verse.

[271] Note that here the quantification of variants is based on content, not the amount of text. Therefore, the numbers should not be understood in the latter way; in other words, the OG does

Prior to this study, several scholars have argued that the OG reflects a Hebrew version of the book of Joshua that is not only different but also earlier than the MT.[272] My textual analysis of Josh 24 mostly substantiates this claim. However, OG Josh 24 also contains elements that should be regarded as secondary in relation to the MT. Most notable are the change of location and the late verse 33b. These changes are so substantial that they should not be attributed to the translator, but to editing behind the Hebrew *Vorlage* of the OG. Thus, one needs to assume that both the Hebrew *Vorlage* of the OG and the proto-MT version once split from a common archetypal Hebrew text form. After this split, both have been exposed to various editorial intrusions. Nevertheless, when one compares the secondary editorial intrusions in the MT with those in the OG it becomes clear that the OG is much closer to this archetypal text form. To simplify: if we only had the OG, and the MT was not preserved, we would be closer to the earlier text form of Josh 24 than if we only had the MT and the OG was not preserved.

Based on this analysis, a model of the textual history of Josh 24 as attested by text-critical evidence can be constructed as illustrated in the chart below.

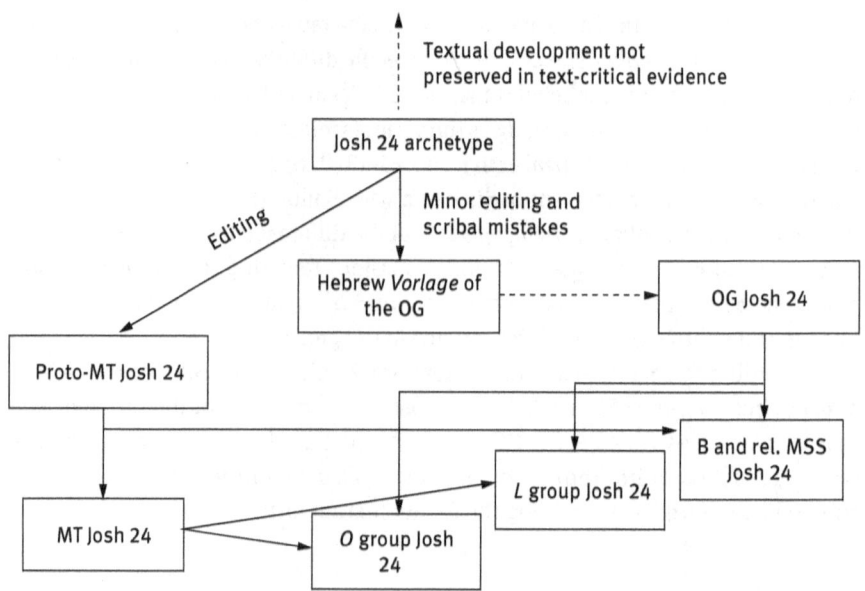

Chart: Textual development of Josh 24 as attested by documented evidence

---

not hold the earliest reading in 75% of the amount of text, but rather 75% of the cases of significant content-related variants.

272 See section 2.3.3.

How does this model of textual growth in Josh 24 relate to the book of Joshua? Naturally, one cannot generalize the text-critical findings from Josh 24 to the whole book as such. However, the model put forth here corroborates the conclusions made by Lea Mazor after an analysis of material from the book of Joshua. According to her analysis, the proto-MT and the Hebrew *Vorlage* of the OG have a common source from which both eventually diverged and developed independently.[273] This common source corresponds to the "Josh 24 archetype" in the model above and, in the light of the thorough analysis of Mazor, I would assume that the situation in Josh 24 is not radically different from the whole composition. In addition, my analysis of Josh 24 aligns with a significant amount of research, beginning in 1914 with the work of Samuel Holmes, that suggests that OG Joshua generally preserves an earlier text of the book of Joshua when compared to the MT.[274] Therefore, studies aiming to reconstruct the textual and editorial history of the book of Joshua cannot afford to dismiss the OG; it needs to be considered as a valuable textual witness.

The editorial intrusions behind the proto-MT text of Josh 24 are not random. Two possible editorial motivations can be discerned behind these changes.[275] The first motivation is ideological, and the second more textual or literary in nature.

First, behind the proto-MT editing there seems to have been nomistic motivations at play. This nomistic editing sought to align texts in the book of Joshua with important texts and concepts in the Pentateuch.[276] The authority of the Pentateuch was derived from Moses. Especially the book of Deuteronomy is often behind the secondary nomistic editorial intrusions observed in Josh 24.[277] In the preceding analysis, the following variants reflect this editorial motive.

- The rewriting behind Josh 5:4–6 and its connection with the omission of 21:42d and 24:31a. A later editor or a group of editors wished to align the circumcision accounts with legal material found in the Pentateuch.[278] The aim of this editing was to ensure that Joshua and the Israelites were faithful to the Torah and their actions did not contradict central claims of the

---

[273] Mazor 1994, 38.
[274] This research has been summarized in section 2.3.3.
[275] It is another question whether this editing can be labeled as a redaction. Probably not, if the term redaction refers to a consistent creation of a literary whole as envisioned behind the Deuteronomistic history.
[276] This was also recently noted—referring to Josh 5 and 20—by Finsterbusch 2016: "- - tendency to connect and conform legal material to (different) pentateuchal legislation."
[277] On the popularity of Deuteronomy in the late Second Temple Judaism, see Crawford 2005.
[278] See section 3.4.2.

Pentateuch. Specifically, a key concern behind the proto-MT editing relates to the conquest of the Promised Land. In Josh 5 it was highlighted that the Israelites were faithful to the law before the conquest. Also, the question of which generation did conquer the Promised Land was important. According to Deuteronomy, nobody from the Exodus generation should have seen the Promised Land (Deut 34–46). In the proto-MT editing of Josh 5:4–6, the distinction between the two generations was sharpened by reporting the death of the older generation to execute the sanction ordered by YHWH. In addition, concerns of ritual purity led to rewriting in the circumcision account. This motivation might have also been at play in the earlier editorial history of Josh 24, as will be illustrated in section 4.

- In verse 24:8, the editor wanted to highlight that all war activities should be attributed to YHWH. Being successful in battle was not a merit of the people. This was achieved by changing the subject of the ban from the people to YHWH.[279]
- In verse 24:15, an editor softened the reference to the polytheism of the patriarchs by changing the possessive expression to a relative clause.[280]
- In verse 24:17, a large addition ("from the land of Egypt, the house of slavery where he performed these great miracles before our very own eyes") filled in language from Deuteronomy into the Exodus remembrance. This gave the verse a much more Deuteronomistic flavor than in the earlier text preserved by the OG.[281]
- The role of Moses has been subtly increased in the proto-MT editing of Josh 24. In Josh 24:5, the phrase "and I sent Moses and Aaron" was added. Josh 24:31a was omitted, deleting the emphasis on Joshua (rather than Moses) as the leader of the Exodus. The sequence of events in the death and burial account of Joshua (MT Josh 24:28–31) was aligned with the sequence of events in the death and burial account of Moses (Deut 34:5–9). This editorial motive is not limited only to Josh 24. In the book of Joshua, there are six instances where Moses in mentioned in the MT but not in the earlier text of the OG (Josh 1:14; 4:10; 13:33; 14:2, 3; 24:5). In addition, the title of Moses as a "servant of YHWH" is secondarily added in four verses in the MT (Josh 1:1, 15; 12:6; 22:4). It is probably not a coincidence that the several variants pertaining to the role of Moses are concentrated in the first and last chapter of the book of Joshua. One would expect that an editor wanting to increase the authority of the book of Joshua by appealing to Moses would focus especially on editing

---

279 See section 3.2.2.
280 See section 3.3.2.
281 See section 3.3.2.

3.5 Text-Critical Conclusions — 161

the beginning and ending of the composition. In a way, such editing envelopes the book with the authority derived from Moses.[282]

It should also be noted that some ideological motivations can be observed behind the minor secondary features in the Hebrew *Vorlage* of OG Josh 24. In Josh 24:1 and 24:25–26, several variants were explained together. The change from Shechem to Shiloh was done to harmonize the chapter with earlier passages in Joshua, and to highlight a separation from the Samaritan community of faith. The addition of the tent of YHWH strengthened the view that the covenant making took place at Shiloh. Along with the change of the locale, theological problems were removed that arose from the statement that holy stones and trees were present in the sanctuary of YHWH.[283] The notion that ideological concerns have led to editorial intrusions not only in the proto-MT editing, but also to a smaller degree in the Hebrew *Vorlage* of the OG, emphasizes that such editing is not limited to one-time editorial intrusions or certain communities. In the later part of the Second Temple period, there were probably several scribal circles that wanted to make minor ideological changes to the texts they were transmitting.

This editorial motivation is related to recent discussion concerning the nomistic editors of the Second Temple period. In the Deuteronomistic paradigm, it is often assumed that one of the latest redactional layers of the historical books were nomistic in nature. Several scholars have tried to differentiate between different nomistic editors (e.g. DtrN^1, DtrN^2, DtrB).[284] My textual analysis of Josh 24 reveals that sporadic nomistic editing took place even in the latest stages of the textual history attested by documented evidence. Since the beginning of the nomistic movement is usually dated to the late 6th century, it seems that we are not dealing with a clearly defined redaction but with an editorial process extending over several hundreds of years. The process is apparently linked with the rising authority of Moses and the Torah in the Second Temple period.

Second, aside from the Pentateuch, the proto-MT editing introduced some secondary alignments towards other texts and phrases in Joshua and the Hebrew Bible. Such an increase of inner-biblical connections strengthened the character of Josh 24 as a text referencing to various books in the Hebrew Bible.[285] These

---

[282] See also Finsterbusch 2016: "The intention was obviously to underline that Joshua was totally dependent upon Moses and his Torah."
[283] See section 3.3.2.
[284] For a helpful summary of the discussion see Pakkala 2008, 251–268.
[285] See section 4.2.

editorial intrusions could also be seen as an attempt to integrate Josh 24 more closely into a larger literary corpus (possibly the Deuteronomistic history), and to strengthen literary connections within such a corpus. The following variants were observed in the textual analysis of this study.

- The earlier list of leaders in OG Josh 24:1, which was similar to Josh 8:33, was reorganized to accord with the list of leaders in Josh 23:2.
- In Josh 24:3, "Canaan" בִּכְנַעַן was added to align the verse with idiomatic phrase אֶרֶץ כְּנַעַן "land of Canaan" found elsewhere in the book of Joshua (Josh 5:12; 14:1; 21:2; 22:9–11, 32).
- Four added secondary elements in the MT missing from the OG were secondary alignments towards the farewell speech of Samuel in 1 Sam 12.[286]
- Several secondary features in the MT are connected with Mic 6:4. The addition of the sending of Moses and Aaron to Josh 24:5 is similar to the sending of Moses, Aaron, and Miriam.[287] Also, the added phrase "from the land of Egypt, the house of slavery" in Josh 24:17 is a phrase found in Mic 6:4. In this instance, it is hard to imagine that an editor would have wanted to bring Josh 24 closer to Mic 6:4. It is more probable that both the secondary features in MT Josh 24 and the phrases in Mic 6:4 employ common language that was used by Second Temple scribes. Therefore, we might speak of a larger phenomenon of bringing the books in the Hebrew Bible closer one another by employing idiomatic language.

Not all secondary features in the proto-MT editing can be characterized as deriving from ideological, nomistic, harmonistic, or other significant motivations. Many editorial intrusions seem to be *ad hoc* in character, and may have been made by single scribes noticing gaps or problems in the text they were transmitting. For example, the addition of the title "son of Beor" in 24:9 is an addition based on traditional language that any scribe could have made as a part of the transmission process.[288] Due to the random nature of many editorial intrusions, one should not automatically attribute all changes to specific editors. The secondary changes observed in the OG and the MT may have accumulated over a longer period, and during several instances of copying. Therefore, the chart above is also necessarily a simplification. In the tree of the development of Josh 24 there may have been several branches that cannot be reconstructed due to the random nature of the preserved evidence.

---

286 See section 3.2.2.
287 See section 3.2.2.
288 See section 3.2.2.

Textual criticism reveals that Josh 24 was heavily edited even in the latest stages visible in the textual evidence. Since the preservation of textual evidence is due to random chance, it is probable that editing also took place that is not preserved in the evidence from different textual traditions. In the next section 4, I will apply the editorial patterns visible in the documented evidence to the evaluation of the various proposed literary and redactional developments in Josh 24. Before this literary and redaction critical analysis, however, a brief look at the Samaritan version of Joshua's farewell speech is in order, since it contains several interesting readings and has not yet been integrated into the discussion in past research.

3.6 The Samaritan Farewell Speech of Joshua

Although the nature of the Samaritan versions of Joshua is disputed, a closer examination of the Samaritan farewell speech of Joshua is interesting, coming after the textual analysis of the major textual witnesses. Contrary to the MT and the OG, SamJosh does not contain two distinct farewell speeches by Joshua. Instead, SamJosh 22 presents a combination of the beginning of Josh 23, the key parts of Josh 24, and an addition from Deut 4 dispersed with unique Samaritan additions. While SamJosh 22 presents many passages of Josh 24, it does not contain many parts: these missing parts might be interesting, since they overlap significantly with material that is often regarded as late additions in literary criticism. The text of SamJosh 22 is next presented, together with a brief analysis.

In the following table, SamJosh 22 is presented together with a translation following the edition by Gaster.[289] The farewell speech can also be found in *Sepher Hayamim* with minor variants, suggesting that at least this part of the Samaritan book of Joshua has a longer history.[290] The text with no markings follows both the MT and the OG, agreements with the OG are boxed, and agreements with the MT are marked with **bold**. The unique readings of SamJosh are highlighted with a gray background.

---

[289] For the text of SamJosh see Gaster 1908, 273–275 and section 2.5.2. For the text of *Sepher Hayamim* see Macdonald 1969, 98–99; 29–31.
[290] The Arabic Samaritan book of Joshua does not contain the farewell speech.

v.	SamJosh 22	MT	Translation
1	ויהי מקץ ימים רבים אחרי הניח יהוה לישראל מכל איביהם מסביב	Josh 23:1	This happened after a long time when YHWH had given rest to Israel from all their enemies around
2	ויהושע בן נון זקן בא בימים		and Joshua, son of Nun, was old in years.
3	ויאסף יהושע את כל שבטי ישראל שכמה	Josh 24:1	And Joshua gathered all the tribes of Israel to **Shechem**
4	ויקרא לכל זקני בני ישראל ולראשיהם ולשופטיהם ולשוטריהם		and summoned all the elders of the sons of **Israel** their heads their judges their scribes
5	ויעלו אליו אל המקום המבחר הרגריזים בית אל ויתיצבו לפני האלהים בפתח אהל מועד		and they went up to the chosen place at Mount Gerizim in Bethel and they set themselves before God at the entrance of the tent of meeting.
6	ויאמר אליהם יהושע בן נון אנכי מת והלך מעמכם	Josh 23:14	And Joshua, son of Nun, said to them: "I am about to die and depart from you.
7	ואתם ידעתם את כל אשר עשה יהוה לכם	Josh 23:3a	You know all that YHWH has done for you.
8	ויוצא את אבותיכם מארץ מצרים באותות ובמופתים ובמלחמה וביד חזקה ובזרוע נטויה ובמראים גדלים ותעברו את ים סוף ביבשה	Josh 24:6 Deut 4:34	He brought your fathers out of the land of Egypt with signs, wonders, war, a strong and outstretched hand, and great miracles; you crossed the Sea of Reeds on dry land
9	ויתן לכם את הארץ אשר לא יגעתם בה והערים אשר לא בניתם ותשבו בהם כרמים וזיתים אשר לא נטעתם אתם אכלים	Josh 24:13	and he gave you the land which you did not labor and the cities that you did not build and you live in them; of vineyards and olive yards that you did not plant, you will eat.
10	ועתה יראו את יהוה אלהיכם ועבדתם אתו בתמים ובאמה והסירו את אלהי הנכר מבניכם ולא תעבדו כי אם את יהוה אלהיכם לבדו	Josh 24:14	And now fear YHWH your God and serve him in sincerity and in faithfulness. And put away the foreign gods from among you and do not serve them for YHWH your god you shall serve.

3.6 The Samaritan Farewell Speech of Joshua — 165

v.	SamJosh 22	MT	Translation
11	ואם רע בעיניכם	Josh 24:15	If it is bad in your eyes
	לעבד את יהוה אלהיכם		to serve YHWH your God
	בחרו לכם היום		choose for yourselves today
	מי תעבדון		whom you will serve,
	אם את יהוה אלהיכם		either YHWH your god
	אם את אלהי הגוים		or the gods of the nations
	אשר אתם יושבים בארצם		in whose land you are living.
	ואנכי וביתי		But I and my household
	לא נעבד		will not serve them
	כי אם את יהוה אלהינו לבדו		for we will serve YHWH our God."
12	ויען כל העם ויאמר	Josh 24:16	And all the people answered and said:
	הלילה לנו מעזב		"Far be it from us that we forsake
	את יהוה אלהינו		YHWH our God
	לעבד אלהים אחרים		to serve other gods
13	כי יהוה אלהינו נעבד	Josh 24:21b	for YHWH our God we will serve
	כי הוא אלהינו	Josh 24:18b	for he is our God
	ואלהי אבותנו		and the God of our fathers."
14	ויאמר יהושע אל העם	Josh 24:22	Then Joshua said to the people:
	עבדים אתם בכם		"You are witnesses against yourselves
	כי אתם בחרתם לכם		that you have chosen to yourselves
	את יהוה לעבד אתו		YHWH, to serve him."
15	ויאמרו עדים		And they said: "(we are) witnesses!"
16	ויכרת יהושא בן נון	Josh 24:25	So, Joshua, son of Nun, made
	ברית לעם ביום ההוא		a covenant with the people that day
	וישם לו חק		and gave them statutes
	ומשפט		and ordinances
	בעיר שכם הקדושה		in the holy city Shechem
	אשר היא מתחת		which is at the foot
	להר גריזים בית אל		of Mt. Gerizim, Bethel,
	וישמה כסא המשפט		where he set the judgment throne.
17	ויכתב את הדברים האלה בספר	Josh 24:26	And he wrote these words in a book
	ויתנו אל הכהנים בני לוי		and gave it to the Levite priests.
	ויאמר אליהם		And he said to them:
	לקחו את הספר הזה		"Take this book
	ושמרתם אתו		and keep it safe."
	ויקחו אבן גדולה		And he took a large stone
18	ויקימה שם תחת האילה		and set it there under the oak
	אשר ביסיד הר גריזים		which is at the foot of Mount Gerizim
	מקום מקדש יהוה		in the site of the sanctuary of YHWH.
19	ויאמר יהושא אל העם	Josh 24:27a	And Joshua said to the people:
	הנה האבן הזאת		"Look, this stone

(Continued)

v.	SamJosh 22	MT	Translation
20	תהיה בנו לעדה ויבן שם מזבח תחת ההר ויקח איל אחד מן הצאן ויקריבו על הברית הזה אשר כרתו בני ישראל עמו		shall be a witness against **us**." Then he built there an altar at the foot of the mountain and he took a ram from the cattle and offered it for the covenant which the Israelites had made with him.
21	ואחרי כן בחר יהושע בן נון שנים עשר נשיא מן נשיאי בני ישראל איש אחד לשבט		After this Joshua, son of Nun, chose twelve rulers from the rulers of the Israelites, one man from each tribe.
22	וישלך עליהם גורל על פי אלעזר בן אהרן הכהן במקום המדבר הר גריזים בית אל לפני יהוה ויצא גבול המלכות על בני ישראל לאיש שמו נתנאל בן אחי כלב משבט יהודה וימליכו על בני ישראל		And the lot was tossed by Eleazar, the son of Aaron, the priest of the chosen place at Mt. Gerizim in Bethel before YHWH. And fell the lot of kingship over the Israelites to the man called Nathaniel, the son of Caleb's brother from the tribe of Judah. And he was chosen as king over the Israelites.
23	ויהי אחר הדברים האלה וימת יהושע בן נון עבד יהוה בן מאה ועשר שנים	24:30	And it happened after these things that died Joshua, son of Nun, the servant of YHWH, one hundred ten years old.
24	ויקברו אתו בגבעה אשר היא מול המקום המבחר הר גריזים בית אל בתמנת סרח ויבכו אתו בני ישראל שלשים יום ויתמו ימי בכיתו	24:31[1]	And they buried him at Gibeah which is opposite to the chosen place, Mt. Gerizim, Bethel[2], in Timnat-serah And the Israelites cried for him for 30 days. Then he days of grief became full.

Notes

[1] The location of the following verse (MT Josh 24:32) reporting the burying of Joseph's bones in Shechem is different in SamJosh. It is situated earlier in the composition, just before the incident with the Gibeonites (MT Josh 9) and after the conquest of Ai (MT Josh 8). At this juncture, SamJosh also contains a markedly expanded and ritualized version of the altar scene (MT Josh 8:30–35).

[2] The only other textual witness that mentions Bethel in this instance is the Sahidic daughter version of the LXX. According to the edition by Maspeo, it adds at the end of the verse "near Baethel which is Magdaritis Baithon".

The text of SamJosh 22 can be analyzed in three stages, mirroring the possible layers in the text. First, there are several secondary Samaritan additions that are probably quite late. Second, there is the text running parallel to the biblical text of Josh 24, which accords mostly with the earliest text-critically recoverable form of the chapter. Third, much material is missing when contrasted with the biblical text, which might be interesting given the nature of the missing material.

The secondary expansions in SamJosh 22 accord with typical secondary Samaritan elements.[291] First, SamJosh 22:5, 16, 18, and 24 make additions specifying the location of the scene at Mt. Gerizim in Bethel. According to the Samaritans, this was המקום המבחר "the chosen place" (SamJosh 22:5, 22, 24). It is also specified that this is where the tent of meeting was held (SamJosh 22:5). Second, there is an attempt to fill out gaps in the historical remembrance at the end of SamJosh 22:8, where a phrase is added concerning the crossing of the Sea of Reeds. Third, in SamJosh 22:10–13 there are several additions which fill out formulaic language used in the commitment scene. Fourth, in SamJosh 22:17 there is an addition highlighting the role of the Levites by recalling that Joshua gave the book of the law to them to guard and keep safe. Fifth, the longest addition can be found in SamJosh 22:20–22. There, the building of an altar for sacrifice is reported and a new king is chosen for Israel by lot. These five types of secondary material in SamJosh 22 are easy to recognize, since they accord largely with the typical secondary Samaritan material in the Samaritan Pentateuch.[292]

Most of the material following the biblical account of Josh 24 is common to both the MT and the OG. However, there are nine significant variants. In five instances, SamJosh follows the MT against the OG. First, the scene in SamJosh takes place at Shechem. In the text-critical analysis above, it was concluded that this is the earlier reading and that the OG location of Shiloh is a secondary development.[293] Therefore, SamJosh together with the MT preserves the earlier tradition. Second, SamJosh agrees with the MT against the OG at the beginning, where we are told that Joshua gathered זקני בני ישראל "the elders of the sons of Israel" (SamJosh 22:4). Here the shortest form "their elders" (OG) is likely the earliest.[294] The MT together with SamJosh contains the addition of ישראל "Israel", while SamJosh expands even further by adding בני "the sons of". This seems to be

---

291 Overall, the large amount of Samaritan secondary features in SamJosh and *Sepher Hayamim* have probably grown in several stages, and originate from the fourth century CE onwards. See Macdonald 1969, 8.
292 For the expansions in the Samaritan Pentateuch see, for example, Tov 2012, 87–90 and Pakkala 2013, 93–97.
293 See section 3.2.2.
294 See section 3.3.2.

typical secondary specification in the Samaritan version (cf. SamJosh 22:2, 6, 16). Third, SamJosh 22:15 contains the secondary plus "And they said: 'We are witnesses!'" also present in MT Josh 24:22 but missing from the OG. Fourth, SamJosh 22:18 contains the sanctuary also present in MT Josh 24:26, which was likely secondarily removed from the Hebrew *Vorlage* of the OG. Fifth, SamJosh 22:19 reads together with MT Josh 24:27 the first-person plural, stating that the large stone will be a witness "against us", while the OG uses the second-person plural.

In four cases, SamJosh follows the OG against the MT. First, SamJosh 22:10 together with OG Josh 24:14 specifies that the Israelites should put away אלהי הנכר "the foreign gods", while the MT mentions only gods. Here הנכר is likely a secondary addition. SamJosh strengthens the argument that it was not done by the Greek translator, but likely already present in his Hebrew *Vorlage*.²⁹⁵ Second, SamJosh 22:9 together with OG Josh 24:13 reads the verbal form referring to the acts of YHWH in the third-person ויתן לכם את הארץ "and he gave you a land". This is important, since earlier it was argued that the third-person formulations in OG Josh 24:5–13 reflect an earlier Hebrew text where the historical summary was presented not as a direct speech by YHWH but as the speech of Joshua, referring to YHWH in the third-person.²⁹⁶ SamJosh gives some corroboration to this argument. Third, SamJosh 22:17 follows the OG in Josh 24:26, where both are missing "Joshua", which is likely secondarily added in the MT in order to make the implicit subject explicitly clear. Fourth, SamJosh 22:19 together with OG Josh 24:27 reads "and Joshua said to the people", while the MT contains a minor secondary addition reading אֶל־כָּל־הָעָם "all the people".

When the MT and the OG disagree in the farewell speech, SamJosh preserves the likely earlier reading in over half of the readings (five out of nine). When considered together with the several notable similarities between SamJosh and the OG,²⁹⁷ these minor variants strengthen the assumption that the Samaritan tradition is not only medieval reception history of the Masoretic book of Joshua but also reflects ancient readings.

The biblical material missing from SamJosh 22 constitutes most of Josh 23, most of the historical summary in Josh 24:2–12, several elements from the commitment scene (Josh 24:17–18a, 19–21, 23–24), and much of the material connected with the burial of Joshua (Josh 24:28, 31). One could explain the absence of this material as resulting from a creative use of the material present in Josh 23–24 by the Samaritan author. However, it would be peculiar that the material was omitted, since it does not contain any polemical content from a Samaritan point

---

295 See section 3.3.2.
296 See section 3.2.2.
297 See section 2.5.2.

of view. Material similar to that which is being "omitted" is also being added (SamJosh 22:8). It is therefore also possible that the author of the Samaritan farewell speech did not have some of this material at his disposal. It is striking that when one removes the secondary Samaritan material from the text and compares it with the earliest basic text of Josh 24 as recovered by several literary and redaction critics, the texts are strikingly similar in their main parts.[298] It is then possible that SamJosh reflects in its earliest core a text that had not yet undergone all the secondary expansions that are present in the MT and the OG. As far as I know, this possibility has not been yet discussed in research. I will return to this issue in the next section dealing with the editorial developments of Josh 24.

In the light of these brief observations on SamJosh, it seems that the Samaritan Joshua traditions should be given more attention in text-historical research. The Samaritan Joshua traditions should perhaps not be discarded as simply late medieval texts, but might in fact also partly reflect ancient traditions. The utilization of the Samaritan material in textual criticism, however, should always begin with the analysis of the principal textual witnesses (OG, MT, and Qumran). In the future, a comparison of SamJosh with these principal textual witnesses may yield new and interesting results.

---

[298] See section 4.3.3.

4 Literary and Redaction Criticism of Joshua 24 in the Light of Documented Evidence

4.1 Introduction

> Dieses Kapitel gehört zu den schwierigsten Texten des Alten Testaments und wird in der Forschung entsprechend divergierend beurteilt.[1]

> Genau besehen ist bei keinem grösseren Abschnitt des Hexateuchs die Frage der literarischen Vorgeschichte und der Quellenzusammenhänge so schwierig, wie bei den Sagen der ersten Hälfte und der Schlusskapitel des Josuabuches.[2]

These two quotations from different scholars, each giving their own literary and redaction critical theories on the origin and growth of Josh 24, illustrate the difficulties involved in this endeavor. The research literature concerning Josh 24 is full of similar quotes. There is a multitude of models explaining the literary growth and development of chapter 24 and its relationship to other material in the Hebrew Bible.[3] One is easily – and rightfully so – struck with bewilderment when trying to make sense of the literary and redaction history of Josh 24 after reading the scholarly literature on the subject from 19th century onwards. In this section, my aim is not to put forth yet another completely new diachronic model on the development of Josh 24. Instead, I wish to integrate the documented evidence discussed in the previous section more closely with the scholarly discussion about the composition of Josh 24. In this way, I will offer what is in my eyes the most plausible way forwards. To achieve this goal, I will proceed in three steps.

First, the textual and literary connections of Josh 24 with other texts in the Hebrew Bible are analyzed in some detail (section 4.2). These connections also constitute in a wider sense documented evidence. Different explanations of these connections form the basis of all the literary and redaction critical models.

Second, the most important arguments used in reconstructing the literary and redaction history of Josh 24 are put forth and evaluated (section 4.3). Here, I do not attempt to introduce the whole state of research, since that would entail an entire study of its own. Rather, I wish to highlight the most advocated lines of development

---

[1] "This chapter belongs to one of the most difficult texts in the Old Testament and has accordingly been divergently judged in the research." Kreuzer 1989, 183.
[2] "The question of literary history and source connections is not, strictly speaking, in any other portion of the Hexateuch as difficult as in the legends of the first half and the final chapter of the book of Joshua." Möhlenbrinck 1938, 238.
[3] The same applies to other theologically central chapters in the historical books, such as 2 Sam 7 and 2 Kgs 17.

that are present in modern scholarly literature.⁴ At the same time, I will argue for what is, in my estimation, the most plausible line of development in the light of the documented evidence. In this evaluation, it will become increasingly clear that the starting point for many literary and redaction critics, namely a preference of the MT, is in many respects problematic, and biases several compositional theories. If literary and redaction criticism wishes to illuminate the historical development of texts, it needs to consider the textual growth already preserved in documented evidence. One of the serious problems in this respect is the neglect of all Greek witnesses.⁵ This discussion will result in a theory of the different literary layers in Josh 24.

Third, I will suggest a synthesis of the most plausible line of the literary growth of Josh 24 (section 4.4). A model assuming a nomistic Persian period commitment narrative which has been supplemented and edited by various scribal circles during the Second Temple period turns out to be most plausible explanation for the evolution of Josh 24. I will argue that this model best serves as a continuum for the development visible in the documented evidence. However, in this section, I will also discuss the overall methodological possibilities, difficulties, and limitations of literary and redaction criticism in light of what has been learned from analyzing documented changes. What exactly are the possibilities for discovering the editorial prehistory of Josh 24 – or any text in the Hebrew Bible for that matter? Should such hypothetical work even be carried out? The answer given in this section is: yes, but only to a certain degree. I will argue that the best way forward for uncovering editorial histories is to devote more attention to specific editorial techniques and processes attested in documented evidence.

Thus, the overall aim of this section is to serve as a necessary starting point for future scholarly work carried out with the editorial history of Josh 24 and related texts. In addition, it will offer a case study through which one can reflect on the viability of the methods of literary and redaction criticism overall. After reading this section, it should be clear that the compositional history of the texts in the Hebrew Bible cannot be studied reliably without beginning from documented cases of editing. In addition, I will hopefully demonstrate that the diachronic

---

4 As a supplement, other overviews and critical evaluations of the research history of Josh 24 can be found, for example, in Koopmans 1990, 1–163 and Noort 1998.
5 I am not the first one to point out this flaw. The neglect of the LXX in the literary and redaction criticism of Joshua has been pointed out by, for example, Auld 1998, 103 and De Troyer 2010. Dozeman (2011, 189–190) has correctly noted: "The tendency among redaction critics is all too often to privilege or even limit research to the MT in determining the final form of Joshua or any book for that matter." In respect to the books of Samuel, Edenburg and Pakkala (2013, 12–13) correctly state that "it is necessary to bring the text-critical evidence to the fore in the discussion about redactions." This agenda is followed in this section.

study of texts should still be regarded as necessary basic research if one wishes to use the Hebrew Bible critically.

4.2 A Complex Web of Literary Connections

Josh 24 is crafted out of several literary and thematic connections with different books in the Hebrew Bible. Generally, it seems to be the case that Josh 24 secondarily utilizes material from several sources. In some cases, it is hard to evaluate whether Josh 24 secondarily refers to other texts, or whether other texts are dependent on Josh 24. In some instances, the relationship might even be reciprocal. Often it is enough to merely state that they operate on a similar literary level or are dependent on a similar tradition. The difficulty of these connections has contributed to the existence of diverse literary and redaction critical models for Josh 24. Before delving into those models, it is helpful to clarify the web of connections Josh 24 has with other texts in the Hebrew Bible. Such an analysis of connections, together with the text-critical analysis in the previous section, builds an important groundwork for evaluating the various compositional models. In addition, the aim of this analysis is to illuminate how problematic and complex the literary questions in Josh 24 are, and to reveal that no simple solution suffices in the text-historical study of Josh 24.[6]

4.2.1 Joshua 24 and Genesis

There are three parts in Josh 24 that probably refer to various texts in Genesis. These are the beginning of the historical summary (Josh 24:2–4), the mention of the "sword and bow" (Josh 24:12), and the putting away of foreign gods (Josh 24:14). In addition, the place name Shechem has connotations with Genesis. Together with the other Pentateuchal references, the connections with Genesis are concentrated mostly in the first part of Josh 24, which is the historical summary (Josh 24:2–13).

---

[6] This analysis of literary connections is by no means exhaustive. I will, however, attempt to mention all of the most important connections. For a similar analysis, see Koopmans 1990, 345–414. I am aware that this analysis could be improved by utilizing a stricter theoretical framework pertaining to theories of intertextuality. However, for the purposes of this study, it is not necessary to describe more carefully how and why the writers of texts use other texts. The main purpose is to sketch a wider outline of the possible textual backdrop of Josh 24. Therefore, it is enough to operate on a general level and use the term "literary connection" in a wider sense. The exact relationship depends on the text in question, and will be discussed case by case.

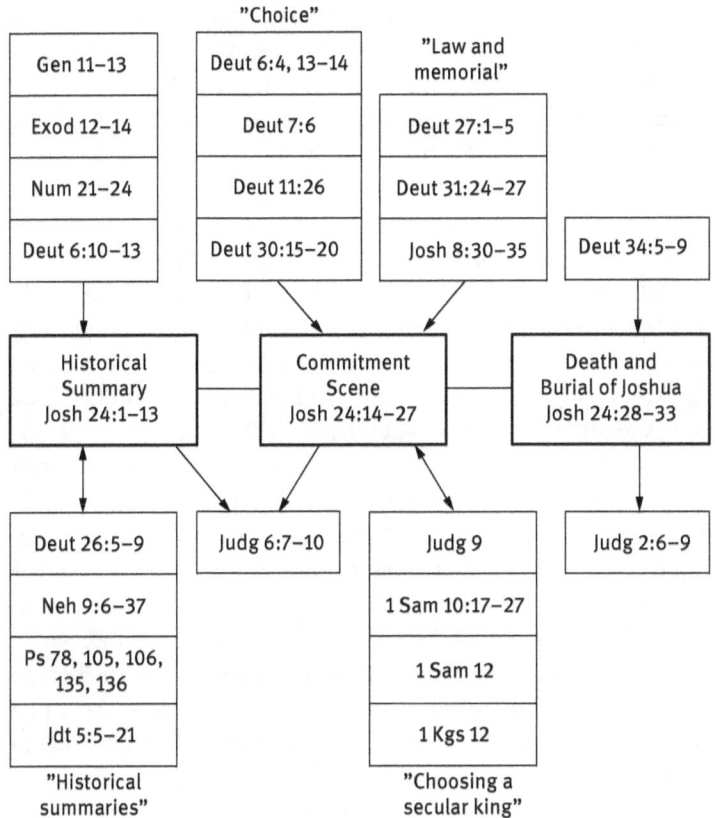

Chart: Literary Connections of Josh 24

In Josh 24:2–4, the prophetic speech consisting of a historical summary begins with a reference to the ancestors of the Israelites on a general level. Then Terah, the father of Abraham and Nahor, is mentioned by name. According to Josh 24:2, these ancestors served other gods "beyond the river". This is the first allusion to Genesis in Josh 24. More specifically, the text alludes to the list in Gen 11:26–32. The serving of other gods, however, is not related in Gen 11. As noted by Knauf, Genesis lets us believe quite the opposite, since Abraham is the one chosen by YHWH (Gen 12:7) who did not serve other gods.[7] Soggin states that

---

[7] Knauf 2008, 195. Nevertheless, there might be some traces of polytheism left in the Genesis accounts related to Abraham. For instance, in Gen 14:22 the tetragrammaton in the MT is likely a secondary addition, since it is missing from the OG. The addition could be seen as a way of softening the polytheistic imagery related to the reference to only "El Elyon" in the earlier text of the OG.

"the description of the religion of Israel's ancestors in Mesopotamia is much more realistic here than in the Pentateuch."[8] Most probably the explication of the past polytheism of the fathers should be understood as emerging from the overall dichotomy between YHWH and other gods present throughout Josh 24. In this way, the situation addressed in Josh 24 affects how the author interprets Israel's past. Such a usage, in other words, reveals that Josh 24:2 represents a later interpretation of the Patriarchal story in the light of new historical contexts.[9] Moreover, the tradition that Terah served other gods is explicated in detail in the book of Jubilees (Jub 12:1–12), dating to 160–150 BCE.[10] Jubilees emphasizes that while Terah and his other sons worshipped hand-made gods, Abraham recognized that these gods were not real and burned them. This tradition seems to be an even later attempt to purge the reputation of Abraham from the reference in Josh 24:2 implying that he served other gods.[11] Hence, both Josh 24:2 and Jub 12:1–12 probably preserve later stages in the development of the Abraham traditions, as is seen in the addition of details to the life of Abraham before he left Ur.

Josh 24:3 relates the movements of Abraham. The verse can be viewed as an abbreviation of Gen 12–13. Scholars often note that the phrase "in all the land of Canaan" derives from Priestly texts (cf. Gen 17:8).[12] However, it is more probable that the reading in the OG ("in all the land") is earlier, making "Canaan" a secondary addition in the proto-MT editing.[13] Therefore, it seems that the phrase has taken on a Priestly nature because of later scribal activities. Here, then, one is cautioned not to derive a Priestly provenance for the whole text simply due to phraseology that has been filled out by later scribes.

In Josh 24:12, the phrase "it was not by your sword or by your bow" can be read as an antithesis for Gen 48:22 in which Jacob gives one portion – that is שְׁכֶם "Shechem" – to Joseph, which he claims to have taken from the hands of the Amorites with his sword and bow. In the light of the other Genesis connections in Josh 24, the textual connection between these verses is likely, and the phrase in Josh 24:12 can be characterized as a quotation which turns the meaning of the

---

[8] Soggin 1972, 232.
[9] After the publication of *The Historicity of the Patriarchal Narratives: The Quest for the Historical Abraham* (Thompson 1974) and *Abraham in History and Tradition* (Van Seters 1975) many scholars have argued that the patriarchal narratives are also themselves quite late literary products drawing from exilic themes.
[10] VanderKam 2001, 17–21.
[11] Thus also VanderKam (2001, 47) when referring to the relationship of Josh 24:2 with Jubilees: "Jubilees, while admitting the problem in the patriarchal family, absolves Abram of guilt in the matter, although it does not explain how the child came to his early monotheistic views."
[12] Rösel 2011, 366.
[13] See section 3.2.2.

donor text upside-down.[14] Otherwise in the Hebrew Bible, the combination of the sword and the bow is also known also elsewhere (2 Kgs 6:22, Hos 1:7). Also common is the notion that the conquest of the land was not due to the merits of Israelites (Deut 9:1–5, Ps 44:3).

Gen 48:22	Josh 24:12
וַאֲנִי נָתַתִּי לְךָ שְׁכֶם אַחַד עַל־אַחֶיךָ אֲשֶׁר לָקַחְתִּי מִיַּד הָאֱמֹרִי בְּחַרְבִּי וּבְקַשְׁתִּי	וָאֶשְׁלַח לִפְנֵיכֶם אֶת־הַצִּרְעָה וַתְּגָרֶשׁ אוֹתָם מִפְּנֵיכֶם שְׁנֵי מַלְכֵי הָאֱמֹרִי לֹא בְחַרְבְּךָ וְלֹא בְקַשְׁתֶּךָ

In Josh 24:14 and 23, the putting away (סור hiphil) of foreign gods echoes the order by Jacob to his household to put away the foreign gods in their midst (Gen 35:3).[15] The connection is even more probable since the scene in Genesis also takes place at Shechem (Gen 35:4).[16] Due to this connection, earlier scholars assumed that Josh 24:14, together with Gen 35:1–5, might reflect an ancient ceremony.[17] Such an assumption, however, is not needed to explain the connection on a literary level. The most important observation is that the latter part Josh 24:14b seems to originate from a different literary horizon than the first part, which includes the call to serve YHWH alone. In addition to Gen 35:3, it is similar to Judg 10:16 and 1 Sam 7:3–4, which are often held as belonging to the later layers of these books.[18] Therefore, instead of emphasizing the connection with Genesis too much, it seems that the putting away of foreign gods is best understood in the context of the later layers in Josh–Sam.[19]

Finally, Shechem (MT Josh 24:1, 25) is mentioned several times in the Patriarchal stories in Genesis.[20] The first appearance of Shechem in the Hebrew Bible can be found in the already mentioned Gen 12:6–8. There, YHWH appears to Abraham at the tree of Moreh. The mention of Abraham right after Shechem at the

---

14 Nielsen (1955, 90) calls Josh 24:12 a reaction against the "military" version of Gen 48:22.
15 The verb סור hiphil is used for putting away other gods elsewhere in Judg 10:16; 1 Sam 7:3–4; 1 Kgs 15:12; 2 Kgs 3:2; 2 Chr 33:15, 34:33; Is 36:7.
16 For other possible connections between Gen 35 and Josh 24, see Koopmans 1990, 349–353.
17 Alt 1953, 79–88.
18 Rösel 2011, 370. According to Veijola (1977, 30–38), 1 Sam 7:2–17 belongs to the later Deuteronomistic editors.
19 See also Nielsen 1955, 102–103. Even though his historical conclusions are outdated, he correctly emphasizes that while Gen 35:1–5 is a concrete text dealing with "Aramean house-gods", the horizon of Josh 24:14, Judg 10:16, and 1 Sam 7:3ff. is more on theologizing that reflects later situations.
20 For an extensive analysis, see Nielsen 1955, 213–286.

beginning of Josh 24 (MT) would have evoked the Patriarchal stories in the heads of the ancient readers. The terebinth in 24:26 would have been likened to the tree of Moreh. While Josh 24:2–5 is largely dependent upon Genesis, it is certainly even possible that Josh 24 may have affected late editing of Genesis.[21] However, one should not make too much of Shechem in Genesis when interpreting Josh 24. This is due to the vast literary and text-critical problems related to the chapter.

Text-critically, the variation between Shechem (MT) and Shiloh (OG) has been discussed in section 3.2.2. The more probable earlier setting at Shechem is surprising, since it is not mentioned in Josh 1–11 or in the land lists in 13–19. Otherwise in the book of Joshua, Shechem is mentioned as a city of refuge (20:7) and as a Levitical city (21:21).[22] In the Former Prophets, two scenes take place at Shechem (Judg 9 and 1 Kgs 12), both dealing with the themes of kingship. That Shechem was, in the historical books, understood as the place where kings were made, is probably more relevant to the interpretation of the chapter than the meaning of Shechem in Genesis.[23] A closer analysis of these and other texts mentioning Shechem would warrant a study of its own.

Overall, the references to Genesis in the historical summary of Josh 24:2–13 should be regarded as late interpretations of the Patriarchal narratives in a new literary context. The centralization of these references to Josh 24:2–13 hints that the historical summary might have a different provenance than the commitment scene in Josh 24:14–27. At the least, the literary character of these two parts is different.

4.2.2 Joshua 24 and Exodus

As was the case with Genesis, the references to Exodus are limited to the historical summary in Josh 24:2–13. The most important section relying heavily on Exodus is 24:5–7. In addition, there are some sporadic references in vv. 11–12 which, however, do not constitute material unique to Exodus.

As seen in the text-critical section, in Josh 24:5 the major differences between the OG and the MT begin. The common text behind both traditions relies

---

[21] See Koopmans 1990, 351–353, who characterizes the relationship as reciprocal.
[22] Butler 1983, 269.
[23] According to Levin (1985, 117–118) the readers of Josh 24 probably had the two mentions of Shechem in their minds when approaching this text: Judg 9 dealing with the kingship of Abimelech, and 1 Kgs 12 where Rehoboam is made the king. This theme, according to Levin, connects with Josh 24, since here YHWH is chosen as the king of Israel. Thus, we are dealing with the concept of divine kingship. While in Josh 24 the people faithfully choose YHWH as their king, later in Judg and 1 Kgs the people unfaithfully choose secular kings. I will return to this important observation later.

on various parts of the Exodus, as is revealed by several textual details. The notion that YHWH smote (נגף) Egypt is present in the Exodus-traditions only in connection with the last plague and the Passover (Exod 12:23, 27), and it is probable that Josh 24:5 alludes to this text. This is strengthened by the observation that the verb form used for bringing the people out of Egypt is in both chapters the *hiphil* form of יצא (Exod 12:51).[24] That Exod 12 probably served as an inspiration for the author of Josh 24:5 also supports our earlier text-critical conclusion that the third-person formulation preserved in the OG is original.

The common text of MT and LXX Josh 24:6–7 relies extensively on Exod 14.[25] As seen in the table below, these connections are so extensive that it is apparent that there is a literary connection between the two passages.

Exod 14	Josh 24
⁹ וַיִּרְדְּפוּ מִצְרַיִם אַחֲרֵיהֶם "And the Egyptians pursued after them"	⁷ וַיִּרְדְּפוּ מִצְרַיִם אַחֲרֵי אֲבוֹתֵיכֶם "And the Egyptians pursued after your fathers"
כָּל־סוּס רֶכֶב פַּרְעֹה "all of the horses and chariots of Pharaoh"	בְּרֶכֶב וּבְפָרָשִׁים יַם־סוּף "with chariots and horsemen to the Sea of Reeds"
¹⁰ וַיִּצְעֲקוּ בְנֵי־יִשְׂרָאֵל אֶל־יְהוָה "And the sons of Israel cried out to YHWH"	⁷ וַיִּצְעֲקוּ אֶל־יְהוָה "And they cried¹ out to YHWH"
²⁰ וַיָּבֹא בֵּין מַחֲנֵה מִצְרַיִם וּבֵין מַחֲנֵה יִשְׂרָאֵל "And it came between the camp of the Egyptians and between the camp of the Israelites"	⁷ וַיָּשֶׂם מַאֲפֵל בֵּינֵיכֶם וּבֵין הַמִּצְרִים "And he gave a darkness between you and between the Egyptians"
²⁸ וַיָּשֻׁבוּ הַמַּיִם וַיְכַסּוּ "And the sea returned and covered them"	⁷ וַיָּבֵא עָלָיו אֶת־הַיָּם וַיְכַסֵּהוּ "And he brought the sea upon them and covered them"

(Continued)

---

24 This is a significant connection, since the verb used for the deliverance from Egypt varies between two different traditions. For the most part, two different verbs are used throughout the Hebrew Bible for the narration of the deliverance from Egypt. These are the hiphil forms of יצא and עלה. On their differences see Wijngaards 1967, 91–102. Josh 24 in its current form is a mixture of both of these traditions, since in Josh 24:17 the latter is used. The different verb used for the Exodus in the historical summary, and the commitment scene hints at the literary-critical solution that they belong to different editorial hands.
25 See also Koopmans 1990, 119 and Nihan 2013, 263–265.

Exod 14	Josh 24
³¹ וַיַּרְא יִשְׂרָאֵל אֶת־הַיָּד הַגְּדֹלָה אֲשֶׁר עָשָׂה יְהוָה בְּמִצְרַיִם	⁷ וַתִּרְאֶינָה עֵינֵיכֶם אֵת אֲשֶׁר עָשָׂה יְהוָה בְּמִצְרַיִם
"and Israel saw the great work that YHWH did to Egypt"	"and your eyes saw what YHWH did² to Egypt"

Notes

1 The earlier verbal form is probably "and we cried" which links with Deut 26:7 and is preserved by the OG. See section 3.2.2.

2 Here I follow the original third-person formulation preserved by the OG. See section 3.2.2.

The Exodus narrative in Josh 24:6–7 reads as a brief summary of Exod 14:9–31.[26] Scholars who differentiate between Priestly (P) and non-Priestly (non-P) elements in the Pentateuch have pointed out that Josh 24:6–7 fuses elements from both editorial strands. For example, while the motive of a darkness separating the people and the Egyptians is non-P (Exod 14:20), the basic description of events is taken from the P material (Exod 14:9).[27] Therefore, it has been suggested that "the composition of Josh 24 took place in a context in which the Priestly and non-Priestly traditions were no longer separated, and had begun to merge one with the other."[28] This observation strengthens the impression that the historical summary in Josh 24:2–13 is a particularly late part of Josh 24.

Without going too deep into the distinction between the Pentateuchal P and non-P elements and the evolution of these traditions, two observations should be kept in mind. These caution against too rigid redaction-critical conclusions based on single phrases in Josh 24:6–7. There are complex textual problems in the key passages that are attributed to either P or non-P. The word מַאֲפֵל "darkness" is not used in Exod 14:20, and it seems that the OG secondarily brings the text closer to the passage in Exodus by using νεφέλην καὶ γνόφον "a cloud and darkness".[29] The expression "they cried out" links with Exod 14:10 only in the MT, and the earlier reading "we cried out" is connected with Deut 26:7. In fact, there are also other links with Deuteronomy in Josh 24:6–7. In Josh 24:7, such a link is preserved in the phrase וַתֵּשְׁבוּ בַמִּדְבָּר יָמִים רַבִּים "and you lived in the wilderness for a long time". This phrase is probably connected to Deut 1:46

---

26 Accordingly, Koopmans (1990, 119) notes that "Josh 24:6–7 gives the impression of a free condensing of the Exodus account."

27 For the source division in Exod 14 see Noth 1962, 104–106 and Durham 1987, 189–190.

28 Nihan 2013, 265.

29 See section 3.2.2.

וַתֵּשְׁבוּ בְקָדֵשׁ יָמִים רַבִּים "and you lived in Kadesh for a long time". Also, the phrase "and your eyes saw" in Josh 24:7, referring to the deeds of YHWH, is common in Deuteronomy (e.g. Deut 4:9, 7:19, 10:21, 29:2). Therefore, Josh 24:6–7 seems to be a fusion of several elements owing both to Exodus and Deuteronomy. Due to the fluidity present in the textual evidence, it seems that different phrases in vv. 6–7 cannot be used as evidence for recovering the conventional redactional strands P, non-P or Dtr.[30] In any case, it does seem that the creative mixture of intertextual connections in the historical summary confirms the late provenance of this part of Josh 24.

In Josh 24:11–12, there are two minor connections with Exod 23:23, 28. First, there is the list of the seven nations in v. 11. To be sure, the list of the seven defeated nations is formulaic. Similar lists are found throughout the Hebrew Bible. As concluded in section 3.2.2, it is probable that the earlier version of the list in Josh 24:11 is preserved in the OG, and the list is secondarily harmonized in the MT towards other similar lists (Exod 23:23, Deut 7:1, Judg 3:5). In any case, the list in Josh 24:11 is altogether often correctly interpreted as a later gloss, since it does not make sense in the context of fighting against one city ("the Lords of Jericho fought against you"), nor does it correspond with the kings mentioned in 24:12.[31] The list therefore reflects later tendencies to "subsume the entire conquest of the land" into the story of particular victories.[32] Second, another connection with Exod 23 can be found in the sending of the "hornets" (or "terror"[33]) before the Israelites (Josh 24:12 / Exod 23:28).[34] Josh 24:11–12 appears to be the execution of the word of YHWH in Exod 23:28. The sending out of the "hornets" is also present in Deut 7:20. However, Exod 23:28 is closer to Josh 24:11–12, as is seen in both use the verb גרשׁ "drive out" and the *qal* form of the verb שׁלח "send" in connection with the hornets.[35]

---

30 See also the critical notes by Carr 2011, 134–137 who argues that "Joshua 24 has been identified as post-Priestly on insufficient grounds."
31 See, for example, Boling & Wright 1982, 536; Becker 2006, 157; Müller 2004, 253; Rösel 2011, 369. It is notable that even Sperling (1987, 127), who argues for the literary unity of Josh 24, interprets the list as a gloss.
32 Butler 1983, 272.
33 As mentioned earlier, the meaning of צִרְעָה is unclear. It occurs only in Exod 23:28, Deut 7:20, and Josh 24:12. The interpretation "hornet" is based on ancient translations (LXX, Vulgate, and Peshitta), but meanings such as "fear", "terror", and "discouragement" are often used following the suggestion made by Köhler 1936, 291. See also Butler 1983, 264 and Rösel 2011, 369.
34 Perlitt 1969, 254.
35 Deut 7:20 does not contain the verb גרשׁ and utilizes the *piel* form of שׁלח for sending out the "hornets". In addition, it should be noted that the verb גרשׁ never occurs in Deuteronomy. See also Koopmans 1990, 332.

4.2.3 Joshua 24, Numbers, and Deuteronomy

The influence of Deuteronomy on Josh 24 is significant both in the historical summary and the commitment scene. The passages influenced by Deuteronomy are found at the end of the historical summary (Josh 24:8–10, 13), at the beginning of the commitment scene (24:14–15), and scattered in the later parts of the commitment scene (24:17, 20, and 25–27).³⁶ It seems that there could be no Josh 24 without Deuteronomy. Moreover, some passages identified as secondary developments in the text-critical evidence, most notably the addition in MT Josh 24:17, are the result of later harmonization towards Deuteronomy. Therefore, the influence of Deuteronomy on Josh 24 cannot be isolated to any single editorial intrusion or redaction, but the harmonization of the text towards Deuteronomy has rather been an ongoing process in the gradual editing of Josh 24.

From Josh 24:8 onwards, the historical summary proceeds to describing various victorious battles that took place when the Israelites took possession of the Promised Land. Verse 8 describes the defeating of the Amorite kings east of Jordan. It should probably be regarded as a concise summary of the events in Num 21:21–25, in which the defeat of the Amorite kings Sihon and Og is described.³⁷ However, there is also the phrase "I gave them into your hands" (וָאֶתֵּן אוֹתָם בְּיֶדְכֶם), which is common in Deuteronomy (Deut 2:24, 30; 3:2; 7:24; 20:13; 21:10).³⁸

Josh 24:9–10 refers to the traditions concerning Balaam and Balak. These traditions are exceedingly complex in the Hebrew Bible. The seer Balaam and the hostile Moabite king Balak appear most prominently in Num 22–24, a text which is echoed in Josh 24:9–10. The text-critical analysis in this study, however, revealed that the beginning of the earliest textual form of Josh 24:9 was identical to Deut 23:6 ("and YHWH your God would not listen to Balaam").³⁹ Therefore, Josh 24:9–10 is textually connected to the Balaam tradition in Deut 23, which can be added to the list of several other connections of Josh 24:2–13 with key texts in Deuteronomy. The direction of the dependence is hard to reconstruct. This would require a detailed study of the various Balaam traditions. It might be, as

---

36 The relationship of the historical summary in Josh 24 with Deut 26:5–8 is dealt in section 4.2.7, together with other historical surveys.
37 Thus also Koopmans 1990, 328–329.
38 Koopmans (1990, 329) notes that this phrase should not be seen as part of a Deuteronomistic redaction, since the "stereotypical phrase describing the actions of a deity giving the enemy into the hands of his people" was common in the ancient Near East. He refers to several texts supporting this claim. Indeed, the identification of specific redactors based on individual phrases is on shaky grounds.
39 See section 3.2.2.

4.2 A Complex Web of Literary Connections — 181

Butler suggested, that Josh 24:9–10 is based on Deut 23:6, which in turn is based on Num 22–24.[40] However, since Josh 24 is connected with Num 21, it is likely that the author of Josh 24:9–10 knew both of the traditions in Deut 23:6 and Num 22–24.[41] Moreover, if one takes into account the textual variation between MT and OG Josh 24:9–10 and the supposed literary layers in each individual Balaam text,[42] it becomes increasingly clear that we might not be able to give a straightforward answer to the question of the direction of the textual dependence between the various Balaam texts. It is also possible that the various texts have reciprocally influenced each other in separate phases of their textual history.

As a general notion, the diachronic development of the Balaam and Balak traditions in the Hebrew Bible seem to have moved from presenting Balaam in a positive light towards presenting him in a negative manner. This development can already be distinguished in the various literary layers of Num 22–24, although the literary history of the passage is disputed.[43] In Josh 24:9–10, Balaam is portrayed as cursing the Israelites and trying to advance the hostile plots of Balak, which aligns vv. 9–10 with the other late negative portrayals in the Hebrew Bible (Num 31:16, Deut 23:5–6, Josh 13:22, Neh 13:2). Therefore, the Balaam material presented in Josh 24:9–10 is probably quite late.

It seems that Josh 24:8–10 is an interesting mixture of references to Numbers and Deuteronomy. While Josh 24:8–10 utilizes the phraseology of Deuteronomy, it makes several references to Numbers. These mixed literary connections are enough to make Auld conclude that Josh 24:8–13 is a "blend of Deuteronomistic and Priestly terminology".[44] Thus, once again it seems that a creative blend of different kinds of material from the Pentateuch is common to the historical summary in Josh 24:2–13.

Josh 24:13 is an interesting but polemic verse that has been attributed to several different sources in research.[45] The most obvious textual connection is with Deut 6:10–13. Both passages mention cities, vineyards, and olive groves (Deut 6:10–11), and both mention that the Israelites did not build the cities or plant

---

40 Butler 1983, 264.
41 It could also be argued that Deut 23:6 is based upon a combination of Num 22:5 and Josh 24:9–10 as Koopmans (1990, 331) does.
42 For instance, Noth (1971, 404) differentiated a secondary layer in Josh 24:9–10 based on assumptions regarding the direction of the textual dependence with Num 22–24 and Josh 24:9–10.
43 Olson 2011.
44 Auld 1980, 74–75. However, while some phrases in Josh 24 are like Priestly terminology, the contents of Josh 24 are not markedly Priestly. Carr (2011, 136), for example, notes that "the chapter lacks links to specifically Priestly texts". The few Priestly elements in Josh 24 seem to be rather late harmonizations towards certain texts, sometimes lacking from the earlier textual witness (e.g. the mention of Aaron in MT Josh 24:5, see section 3.2.2).
45 See Koopmans 1990, 333–334.

the harvest that they enjoyed (Deut 6:10–11). Deut 6:10–13 also combines other themes present in the historical summary of Josh 24. For example, the Exodus (Deut 6:12) and the fearing and serving of YHWH (Deut 6:13). The direction of textual influence has been argued in both directions. Sperling claims that Deut 6:10–13 was dependent upon Josh 24:13. His main argument is that the picture in Deut 6:10–13 is taken much further than that in Josh 24:13. The Israelites do not merely eat the harvest of the land, but they enjoy it in abundance. According to Sperling, the author of Deut 6:10–13 adds several things to the "houses filled with all sorts of good things" (Deut 6:11), while the picture in Josh 24:13 is much more realistic.[46] This argument could, however, also be turned around to argue that Josh 24:13 tones down the abundance present in Deut 6:10–13. In fact, Josh 24:13 can be read as a shortening of Deut 6:10–13.[47] This would be understandable, considering the general nature of the historical summary (Josh 24:2–13) as referring in a brief form to various passages in the Pentateuch. Ultimately, the evaluation of the textual dependence comes back to the various assumptions about the literary history of both texts. In the light of the other references to the Pentateuch in Josh 24, it is more probable that Josh 24:13 secondarily refers to Deut 6:10–13.

Josh 24:14 begins a new section in Josh 24, moving from the historical summary to a choice given to the Israelites present at the holy place. The first part of the verse presents an exhortation to the people to fear and serve YHWH. The concept of fearing (ירא) YHWH occurs frequently in Deuteronomy (see, for example, Deut 4:10, 6:2, 13, 24). In fact, Josh 24:14 resembles the similar exhortation in Deut 6:13–14.[48] It is sometimes claimed that the presentation of a choice to serve either YHWH or other gods (Josh 24:14–15) is a combination unique to Josh 24.[49] However, the inspiration for the author of Josh 24:14–15 to present such a choice must have come from Deuteronomy, where Israel is presented with similar important choices (Deut 11:26, 30:15–20).[50] The author probably builds upon the notion that YHWH has chosen (בָּחַר) Israel as his people (Deut 7:6), and now it is time for Israel to choose whom she wants to serve.[51] Therefore, the choice which is at the core of Josh 24 builds upon ideas that would have already existed in Deuteronomy when the text of Josh 24:14–15 was written.

The commitment scene in Josh 24:14–27 refers in several parts to Deuteronomy. First, it has been noted that the short credo at the beginning of 24:17 יְהוָה אֱלֹהֵינוּ

---

46 Sperling 1987, 128.
47 Knauf 2008, 197.
48 Rösel 2011, 370.
49 Koopmans 1990, 346–347.
50 The same idea is also taken from Deuteronomy in 1 Kgs 18:21.
51 Aurelius 2008, 102.

"YHWH is our God" resembles Shema Israel found in Deut 6:4. This is probably not a coincidence, since earlier parts of Josh 24 are also dependent upon Deut 6. Furthermore, the documented evidence revealed that Josh 24:17 has been even further edited towards Deuteronomy, with the large insertion "from the land of Egypt, out of the house of slavery, and who did those great signs in our sight."[52] The phraseology used in the addition can also be found in Deut 6 (vv. 12 and 22). Therefore, while Josh 24:17 was in its earliest text form (OG) dependent upon the credo in Deut 6, it has been further edited (MT) to conform even more closely with language found in Deut 6. Second, 24:24 utilizes the expression וּבְקוֹלוֹ נִשְׁמָע "his voice we will listen", which probably derives from Deut 13:5.[53] Third, in Josh 24:25–27 the report that Joshua makes a covenant with the people and sets up the stones of witness is reminiscent of some passages in Deuteronomy. The phrase חֹק וּמִשְׁפָּט "statue and ordinance" is used, for example, in Deut 4:1; 45, 6:1 (in plural form). The proceedings of putting the covenant document in a safe and holy place recalls Deut 31:24–27,[54] and can also be read as an execution of the command in Deut 27:1–8. That a literary connection is perceived between Josh 24:25–27 and Deut 31:24–27 is strengthened by the late addition in SamJosh 22:17, which reports that the written law was given to the Levites to guard (cf. Deut 31:25–26).

In sum, some of the most central elements of the commitment scene in Josh 24 are built upon phraseology and themes in Deuteronomy. One could therefore argue that the core of Josh 24 represents, in a way, a reception history of Deuteronomy. The choice presented gives the people a possibility to respond to the choice made by YHWH as envisioned by Deuteronomy. This is, however, not the whole story. Connections with later historical books reveal that the choosing of YHWH is also related to a wider perspective of the future unfaithful choices made by the Israelites.

4.2.4 Joshua 24 and Joshua

The loose character of Josh 24 in the composition of the book of Joshua has puzzled scholars for a long time.[55] The clearest textual connections with other parts of the book of Joshua are with chapter 23 and 8:30–35. These, however, might be connections born quite late in the transmission history of the book of Joshua.

---

52 See section 3.3.2.
53 Thus also Rösel 2011, 373.
54 Rösel 2011, 357.
55 Noort 1998, 205: "Jos 24 steht einsam in der Meereslandschaft." See also Perlitt 1969, 241 and Hoffman 1980, 301.

The relationship of Josh 24 to Josh 23 is notoriously difficult, and much has been written on it. Therefore, at this point, it is not necessary to solve all the problems pertaining to their relationship.[56] In terms of textual and thematic connections, however, it should be highlighted that Josh 23 and 24 are only loosely connected. They differ in several key issues. First, Josh 23 can be read as a summary of the book of Joshua, giving a review of the occupation of the land. Josh 24, conversely, recalls longer trajectories of history from the Patriarchs to the Promised Land.[57] Second, while Josh 23 utilizes language borrowed from Deuteronomy, the phraseology in Josh 24 is a mixture of various sources.[58] Third, the focus of Josh 23 is on the observance of the law and the relationship with the nations remaining in the land, while Josh 24 deals with a choice presented to the Israelites to serve either YHWH or other gods.[59] Fourth, there are surprisingly few textual details that show direct textual influences between Josh 23 and 24. In addition, some of these textual details have been produced only in the latest proto-MT editing of Josh 24. I will analyze some of these details below.

Josh 24:1 begins with a gathering of the Israelites. This beginning fits poorly in its current literary and narrative context. The assembly of the people in the previous chapter (Josh 23) has not been ended in any way. There are no narrative links to the present context in the book of Joshua.[60] This has contributed to the models positing that the original introduction of Josh 24 is to be sought at the beginning of Josh 23.[61] At the beginning of Josh 24:1, Joshua gathers all the tribes of Israel. The expression "all the tribes of Israel" seems to suppose the system of the twelve Israelite tribes. The phrase is not used in the gathering of the Israelites in Josh 8:30–35 or Josh 23:2. We find the expression mainly within the Deuteronomistic literature, conveying a concept of a large Israel with all of its tribes (e.g. Deut 29:20; Judg 20:2, 10, 12; 21:5; 1 Sam 2:28; 10:19–20).[62] Thus, the verse seems to suppose that the division of the land to the various tribes of Israel (Josh 13–19) has taken place.[63] Its literary horizon is wider than just the current context.

---

[56] The question will be revisited in relation to literary and compositional issues in sections 4.3.3 and 4.3.5. For helpful discussions of the key issues and theories on the relationship of Josh 23 and 24, see Koopmans 1990, 396–399; Popović 2009, 87–98; Römer 2010, 91–99.
[57] Nelson 1997, 266.
[58] Römer 2010, 91. Almost every verse in Joh 23 utilizes language taken from Deuteronomy. See the helpful table in Butler 2014, 269–271.
[59] Popović 2009, 87.
[60] Perlitt 1969, 241.
[61] See section 4.3.3.
[62] Perlitt 1969, 249–250.
[63] A section which is often designated as a late post-exilic addition to the book of Joshua. See, for example, Otto 2009, 392–393 and Levin 2013, 128. For the connection of Josh 24:1 and 13–19, see also Rösel 2011, 364.

The list of leaders found in the MT version of Josh 24:1, "Israel's elders, their heads, their judges, and their scribes" is identical to that in Josh 23:2. This, however, was found in the text-critical analysis to be a later harmonization towards chapter 23.[64] The earlier list of leaders, "their elders, their scribes, and their judges" in Josh 24:1 (OG) accorded with Josh 8:33, which strengthens the observation that chapters 24 and 8:30–35 have a close literary connection with each other.[65] Furthermore, since Josh 8:30–35 has such close affinities with Deut 27, which also contains the same conception of the large state of Israel with twelve tribes as in Josh 24:1, both Deut 27 and Josh 8:30–35 should be seen as a literary backdrop for understanding Josh 24.[66]

It has also been suggested that another point of contact between Josh 23 and 24 is that they both include obedience to the covenant (בְּרִית).[67] This theme, indeed, is not present anywhere else in the book of Joshua, where "covenant" is only mentioned as an attribute of the ark.[68] However, in Josh 23:16 the tone is negative, preparing the Israelites for a future transgression of the covenant, while Josh 24:25 reports the actual making of a covenant. Furthermore, a closer analysis of Josh 23:16 reveals that the verse is dependent on Deut 11:16–17 and not Josh 24:25. In the MT in relation to the OG, this connection is even stronger, as seen in the table below.

OG Josh 23:16	MT Josh 23:16	Deut 11:16–17
¹⁶ ἐν τῷ παραβῆναι ὑμᾶς τὴν διαθήκην κυρίου τοῦ θεοῦ ὑμῶν, ἣν ἐνετείλατο ὑμῖν, καὶ πορευθέντες λατρεύσητε θεοῖς ἑτέροις καὶ προσκυνήσητε αὐτοῖς.	¹⁶ בְּעָבְרְכֶם אֶת־בְּרִית יְהוָה אֱלֹהֵיכֶם אֲשֶׁר צִוָּה אֶתְכֶם וַהֲלַכְתֶּם וַעֲבַדְתֶּם אֱלֹהִים אֲחֵרִים וְהִשְׁתַּחֲוִיתֶם לָהֶם וְחָרָה אַף־יְהוָה בָּכֶם	¹⁶ הִשָּׁמְרוּ לָכֶם פֶּן יִפְתֶּה לְבַבְכֶם וְסַרְתֶּם וַעֲבַדְתֶּם אֱלֹהִים אֲחֵרִים וְהִשְׁתַּחֲוִיתֶם לָהֶם ¹⁷ וְחָרָה אַף־יְהוָה בָּכֶם וְעָצַר אֶת־הַשָּׁמַיִם וְלֹא־יִהְיֶה מָטָר וְהָאֲדָמָה לֹא תִתֵּן אֶת־יְבוּלָהּ

(Continued)

---

64 See section 3.2.2.
65 Soggin (1972, 220–244) even postulates that verses 8:30–35 originally followed Josh 24:1–27.
66 On the possible connections between Deut 27, Josh 8:30–35, and Josh 24:1–28 see, for example, Soggin 1972, 220–244; Nielsen 1955, 50–141; and Koopmans 1990, 353–356.
67 Koopmans 1990, 397.
68 "Covenant" is also mentioned in Josh 7:15, but there it refers specifically to the transgression of Achan during the conquest of Jericho.

OG Josh 23:16	MT Josh 23:16	Deut 11:16–17
	וַאֲבַדְתֶּם מְהֵרָה מֵעַל הָאָרֶץ הַטּוֹבָה אֲשֶׁר נָתַן לָכֶם	וַאֲבַדְתֶּם מְהֵרָה מֵעַל הָאָרֶץ הַטֹּבָה אֲשֶׁר יְהוָה נֹתֵן לָכֶם
when you transgress the covenant of YHWH your God which he commanded you and go and serve other gods and bow down to them.	When you transgress the covenant of YHWH your God which he commanded you and go and serve other gods and bow down to them, then the anger of YHWH will be kindled against you	Take care of yourselves that your heart will not be deceived, so that you turn away and serve other gods and bow down to them, then the anger of YHWH will be kindled against you. He will shut up heavens, so that there will be no rain, the ground will not give fruit
	and you will perish quickly from the good land which he gave you.	and you will perish quickly from the good land which he gave you.

While the beginnings of MT Josh 23:16 and Deut 11:16 are different, the latter parts accord word for word: "and serve other gods and bow down to them, then the anger of YHWH will be kindled against you". Deut 11:17 then contains additional material about the heavens closing, so that the land will be left without fruit. After this, both continue with the consequences of serving other gods: "and you will perish quickly from the good land which he gave you." The shorter version in OG Josh 23:16 could be earlier.[69] If this is the case, Josh 23:16 has been secondarily brought even closer to Deut 11:16–17. However, it is also possible that the end of the verse has been lost in the Hebrew *Vorlage* of the OG due to haplography (between לָהֶם and לָכֶם).[70] A secondary omission could even be intentional, since a late editor could have perceived the highlighting of the anger of YHWH as problematic before Josh 24. In any case, while Josh 23:16 is clearly modeled upon Deut 11:16–17, the latter does not contain the covenant. Therefore, it is possible that 23:16 may have been created as a combination of Josh 24:25 and Deut 11:16–17. In fact, verse 23:16 is probably a secondary addition to Josh 23, intended to bring Josh 23 closer to Josh 24 with the inclusion of the covenant. This hypothesis is

---

69 Holmes (1914, 78) argues that the secondary insertion was made because a Hebrew editor did not understand that 23:16a is the protasis of 23:15. Also Latvus (1998, 32–33) follows the OG reading in this instance.
70 Nelson 1997, 255.

4.2 A Complex Web of Literary Connections — 187

corroborated by the *Wiederaufnahme* repeated in 23:16 from the end of 23:15 (אֲשֶׁר נָתַן לָכֶם).[71]

Two conclusions can be drawn concerning the relationship (or lack thereof) of Josh 24 and Josh 23. First, in their current form the bulk of these chapters have been written and expanded by different authors, for different purposes, and with different literary horizons.[72] It is probable that parts of these chapters at one point constituted a single ending for the book of Joshua. In their current form, the double ending is a product of expansions in several directions in two separate farewell speeches. Therefore, chapters 23 and 24 as independent units should probably be considered as one of the later developments in the composition of the book of Joshua. Second, in a late stage, the chapters have been brought closer one another with minor adjustments, including the change in the list of leaders identified with the help of documented evidence, and the assumed addition of Josh 23:16 containing the covenant.

It was noted above that the earlier version of the list of leaders in Josh 24:1 (OG) was connected with the list of leaders in Josh 8:30–35. This is not the only connection between these texts. Josh 24 and Josh 8:30–35 both contain the book of the law (Josh 24:26 בְּסֵפֶר תּוֹרַת אֱלֹהִים / Josh 8:31 בְּסֵפֶר תּוֹרַת מֹשֶׁה),[73] both have stones at the center of their ritual action (Josh 24:26 / Josh 8:31), both report the presence of all the Israelites (Josh 24:1 / Josh 8:32), both include the ark of the covenant (OG Josh 24:33a / Josh 8:33), and both report a ritual act in which the Israelites devote themselves to YHWH. The similarities between Josh 24 and Josh 8:30–35 were already noted by Von Rad. Even though his reconstruction of a cultic *Sitz im Leben* is outdated, his observation that Josh 24, Josh 8:30–35, and Deut 27, 11:29–32 are somehow connected, and are all abruptive in their literary contexts, is still relevant.[74] In fact, the observation is far more interesting in the light of recent text-critical discussion related to Josh 8:30–35. Josh 8:30–35 – or parts of it – can be

---

71 Latvus (1998, 32–33) regards all of 23:15–16 as secondary in relation to the basic text of Josh 23. He also points out that the opening וְהָיָה כַּאֲשֶׁר is clumsy and that 23:15 repeats אֲשֶׁר דִּבֶּר יְהוָה אֱלֹהֵיכֶם אֲלֵיכֶם from 23:14.
72 See also Römer 2010, 91: "It is also clear that these two testaments of Joshua cannot be the work of one author (otherwise one should definitely give up the historical investigation of the Hebrew Bible!)". The prehistory of these chapters is probably quite complicated. Since they perform the same function (summary of a whole) with a different scope, it is possible that the chapters originated in different literary traditions and have only later been incorporated together to form the literary form now present in the MT and the OG. It is interesting that SamJosh does not contain most of Josh 23.
73 In the historical books, the "book of the law" is mentioned elsewhere only in Josh 23:6 and 2 Kgs 14:6.
74 Von Rad 1938, 34–43.

found in three various locations in different textual witnesses (OG, MT, 4QJosh[a]).[75] The peculiar text-critical situation suggests that Josh 8:30–35 has been inserted only at quite a late stage into the book of Joshua, and it has not found a fixed place in the composition.[76] It is therefore hard to say whether Josh 24 or Josh 8:30–35 came first, and which has influenced which. In any case, the loose character of both texts in their literary contexts suggests that we are dealing with late material.

Once again, besides the textual connection with Josh 8:30–35 and Josh 23, Josh 24 is curiously loose in the context of the book of Joshua.[77] It makes no references to the conquest accounts in Josh 1–12. The only possible reference to the division of the land in 13–22 is that the introduction supposes the concept of a large Israel being present at Shechem. Even the mention of Moses in Josh 24:5, which might be likened to the several mentions of Moses in Josh 1, is a later addition in the proto-MT phase. In the case of Josh 24:11, the chapter even contradicts Josh 6 by giving an alternative account of the conquest of Jericho. The loose relationship of Josh 24 with the book of Joshua points towards its function not as a part of the book of Joshua as such but as a conclusion or transition in a larger narrative of the history of Israel. Therefore, it is understandable that scholarship on Josh 24 frequently links the text to the idea of a Hexateuch, Enneateuch, or DtrH. I will return to these redactional questions later in section 4.3.

4.2.5 Joshua 24 and Judges

At least three texts in the book of Judges are relevant for the study of Josh 24. These are the parallel death and burial notice of Joshua in Judg 2:6–9, the speech of the unknown prophet in Judg 6:7–10, and the failed kingship of Abimelech in Judg 9. To put things into a larger perspective, it is important to note that the books of Joshua and Judges have several literary connections. For example, Judg 1, while offering a very different picture of the conquest, contains plenty of material already presented in Joshua.[78] It is often the case that the parallel texts in Judges are dependent on Joshua, but there is also influence in the other direction.[79]

The relationship of the parallel passages Josh 24:28–31 and Judg 2:6–9 plays a crucial role as evidence for various models of the composition of the historical books. The textual evidence pertaining to Josh 24:28–31 and Judg 2:6–9 was

---

[75] See De Troyer 2005b, 141–164 and Feldman 2013, 116–118.
[76] According to Auld (1998, 110), Josh 8:30–35 is a "latecomer looking for a suitable home."
[77] See also Noort 1998, 205–206.
[78] Rake 2006.
[79] Spronk 2009, 145–147.

discussed in section 3.4.2. From a text-critical point of view it seems most probable that OG Josh 24:28–31 holds the earliest form of this passage, which was further edited in MT Josh 24:28–31 and secondarily adapted to Judg 2:6–9. This is especially true of Josh 24:28, of which Judg 2:6 contains a more expanded form. Since this text is so closely connected with literary and redaction critical models, I will also return to it in section 4.3.5 when discussing the transition from Joshua to Judges.

Josh 24:2 begins with Joshua speaking to the people and utilizing the messenger formula "thus says YHWH, the God of Israel". This formula is, of course, most widely used in prophetic literature, and it is often used as a redactional tool for adding more texts to the prophetic literature.[80] Thus, the historical summary presented here is envisioned as a prophetic speech, and Joshua is the prophet.[81] A close parallel is found in Judg 6:7–10, where the Israelites cry out to YHWH, who sends an unknown prophet whose speech also begins with the messenger formula. In addition, the content of the unknown prophet's speech is quite similar to the content of Josh 24. Both give a historical summary recalling the Exodus (Judg 6:8–9 / Josh 24:5–7), both include a dichotomy between YHWH and other gods (Judg 6:10 / Josh 24:14–24), and both mention the gods of the Amorites (Judg 6:10 / Josh 24:15).[82] A direct textual dependence is corroborated by the observation that almost every strophe in Judg 6:8b–10 finds a counterpart in Josh 24:2–24.[83] The key difference between the passages is that while Josh 24 ends with people being loyal to YHWH, Judg 6:7–10 ends by noting that the people could not serve YHWH. A similar difference in content was also observed between the parallel passages Josh 24:28–31 and Judg 2:6–10.[84]

It is most probable that Josh 24 is earlier than Judg 6:7–10, and that Josh 24 played a significant role in shaping Judg 6:7–10. Three observations support this claim. First, Judg 6:7–10 is a relatively late insertion to the text of Judges, as is revealed by textual evidence. The passage is missing from 4QJudg^a which preserves a textual tradition of Judges to which the passage was not yet added.[85] In addition, literary-critical research has shown that the passages is abrupt and does not fit in the context of Judg 6.[86] Second, the gods of the Amorites are not mentioned

---

80 This is often the case in the book of Jeremiah. See, for example, Sweeney 2010, 110–112.
81 Woudstra 1981, 344; Butler 1983, 270; Rösel 2011, 365.
82 Rösel 2011, 365.
83 This was illustrated by Koopmans 1990, 373.
84 See section 3.4.2.
85 Ulrich 2008, 489–506.
86 Several scholars have addressed the textual and literary issues. That 4QJudg^a preserves here an earlier text than the MT is the best explanation for the lack of Judg 6:7–10 in the Qumran scroll. Judg 6:7–10 is a late insertion, as was already assumed by literary-critical research. For a good

elsewhere in the book of Judges. They fit poorly in the context of Judges, while in Josh 24 the Amorites have a much more significant role.[87] Third, the anonymity of the prophet in Judg 6:8 might speak for its dependence on Josh 24:2, since the prophetic messenger formula is usually reserved for the identifiable men of YHWH.[88]

Lastly, there is a thematical connection between Josh 24 and the story of the failed kingship at Shechem in Judg 9. First, in both chapters the scene takes place at Shechem. Second, the crowning of the wicked Abimelech as king takes place "by the oak of the pillar at Shechem" (עִם-אֵלוֹן מֻצָּב אֲשֶׁר בִּשְׁכֶם, Judg 9:6). This is probably a reference to the oak in Josh 24:26, and further to the original oak in Shechem in Gen 12:6. Third, while in Josh 24:14 the Israelites are urged to serve YHWH in "sincerity and in faithfulness" (בְּתָמִים וּבֶאֱמֶת), in Judg 9:16, 19 these same qualities (אִם-בֶּאֱמֶת וּבְתָמִים) are expressed towards the human king.[89] The closeness of the promise to worship YHWH alone at Shechem (Josh 24) with the serving of Baal-berith (Judg 9:4) and El-Berith (Judg 9:46) at Shechem suggests that the author of either text (or both texts) deliberately juxtaposed the choice of the Israelites with the infidelity. The connections between these chapters also raises the observation that Josh 24:1–28 is linked with the idea of divine kingship. According to Levin, Josh 24 relates to Judg 9 in this manner. The choice to serve YHWH as the true king in Josh 24 is a preamble to the subsequent failures to do so in Judg 9 and 1 Kgs 12.[90] While the composition history of Judg 9 is complicated,[91] one cannot escape the idea that at some point Josh 24 and Judg 9 were together understood as emblems for the failure of the Israelites to keep their promise. This theme is probably already at the core of the earliest text form of Josh 24, and I will return to this question in later sections.

In the case of Judg 2:6–9 and Judg 6:7–10, it seems that these texts were secondarily influenced by Josh 24. In this regard, the statement by Koopmans may be justifiable: "Josh. 24 played a conspicuous role in the shaping of the present form of Judges."[92] Even if one sees the direction of influence as being in the other direction, it remains valid to note that later editors sought to bring the books of Joshua and Judges closer one another. This suggests a developmental trajectory for the

---

summary of the literature and an articulation of this well-supported thesis, see Ausloos (2014, 358–476), who also demonstrates why other explanations are not convincing.
87 See also Koopmans 1990, 375–377.
88 These are, most prominently, Moses and Aaron (Exod 5:1, 32:27), Joshua (7:13, 24:2), Samuel (1 Sam 10:18), Nathan (2 Sam 12:7), Ahijah (1 Kgs 11:31, 14:7), a student of Elisha (2 Kgs 9:6), Huldah (2 Kgs 22:15), Isaiah (Isa 37:21), and Jeremiah (e.g. Jer 11:3, 24:5, and 30:2).
89 Koopmans 1990, 379.
90 Levin 1985, 117–118.
91 See, for example, Müller 2004, 93–118.
92 Koopmans 1990, 370.

development of the books of Joshua and Judges: the texts began as fragmentary units and were, over the course of time, harmonized with each other and brought closer one another to form compositions and larger literary units. In addition, the relationship of Judg 9 and Josh 24 might have to do with a wider literary perspective relating to the theme of divine versus human kingship. This issue will be discussed in detail later in the study.

4.2.6 Joshua 24 and Samuel-Kings

There are several texts in Samuel-Kings that are somehow connected to Josh 24. The most notable are the selection of Saul as the king in 1 Sam 10:17–27, the farewell speech of Samuel in 1 Sam 12, and the choosing of Jeroboam as the Israelite king in 1 Kgs 12. There are also other possible connections, but they do not need to be dealt with here.[93]

Many scholars have noted that there is some kind of a thematic and/or structural connection between Josh 24 and 1 Sam 10:17–27.[94] The similarities between Josh 24 and 1 Sam 10:17–27 can be found especially in the frames of the narrative: they both begin with the leader summoning the people to a holy site (1 Sam 10:17 / Josh 24:1), both introduce the protective acts of YHWH with the formula "thus says YHWH the God of Israel" כֹּה־אָמַר יְהוָה אֱלֹהֵי יִשְׂרָאֵל (Josh 24:2 / 1 Sam 10:18), both speeches include a historical recollection making a reference to the Exodus (1 Sam 10:18 / Josh 24:5–6), and both end with a reference to a book that is placed in a sanctuary (1 Sam 10:25 / Josh 24:26).[95] Also, the expression "they stood themselves before YHWH" (*hitpael* form of יצב) in Josh 24:1 finds a counterpart in 1 Sam 10:19 "stand yourselves before YHWH". Koopmans has noted that structurally the choosing of Saul as king 1 Sam 10:24 is close to the choosing of YHWH as Lord in Josh 24:22. In both cases, the verse begins with the leader presenting to the people the result of a choice. Both verses end with the people confirming the choice with a short exclamation. In terms of vocabulary, both utilize the verb "to choose" בחר and both introduce the thing to be witnessed with a כִּי-clause.[96] To be sure, there are not enough textual connections to argue for a literary dependence. However, both texts seem to utilize a type of a legal form which is also reflected in other texts (e.g. Ruth 4:9–12 and 1 Sam 12:8). The similarities in the form of these texts are not enough for arguing an early dating or speculating on a common ancient *Sitz im*

---

[93] For further possible connections see, for example, Koopmans 1990, 379–398.
[94] See, for example, Levin 1985, 116–119 and Koopmans 1990, 380–386.
[95] For further analysis on the connections between these chapters see Koopmans 1990, 380–386.
[96] Koopmans 1990, 384.

Leben.⁹⁷ However, based on the thematic similarities with 1 Sam 10:17–27 and the above mentioned Judg 9, it seems even more probable that in Josh 24 the commitment scene is paralleled with a procedure for choosing a king. Josh 24 underlines that the Israelites chose YHWH as a king for themselves. This, in turn, underlines the wickedness of the people when they later choose a human king for themselves.

Among the several links between Josh 24 and 1 Sam 12, some are presented by both the OG and the MT, while some are secondary additions to the MT. As noted earlier, in Josh 24:5 the MT creates a secondary link with 1 Sam 12:8 with the addition of "I sent Moses and Aaron". Similar secondary alignments in the MT are found in 24:6, 7, and 22.⁹⁸ Thus, documented evidence reveals that Josh 24 has been secondarily aligned with 1 Sam 12. While this has not been taken into account by scholars thus far, the connections between Josh 24 and 1 Sam 12 have been recognized by many. There are several similarities present in both textual traditions: both present the farewell speeches of an important figure, 1 Sam 12:5 and Josh 24:22 (MT) are structurally similar, 1 Sam 12:6–8 recalls the fathers in Exodus much like Josh 24:5–7, and both give a historical summary with several parallels (1 Sam 12:8–12 / Josh 24:2–13).⁹⁹ The most important difference of 1 Sam 12 with Josh 24 is that it incorporates the theme of the infidelity of the Israelites into the historical summary (1 Sam 12:10) and links the choosing of a king with this infidelity (1 Sam 12:7). There might be a subtle reference to Josh 24 in 1 Sam 12:12, were it is said that the people wanted a king to reign over them even though "YHWH your God was your king" (וַיהוָה אֱלֹהֵיכֶם מַלְכְּכֶם).

In terms of the direction of influence, it is usually argued that Josh 24 has served as one source for the author of 1 Sam 12, which seems to be the most probable alternative.¹⁰⁰ Veijola correctly attributed the whole chapter 1 Sam 12, which presents a negative attitude towards monarchy, to the late DtrN redactor.¹⁰¹ Nihan argues that 1 Sam 12 was composed as part of a revision that sought to align the traditions concerning the origins of kingship with the conception of choosing between serving YHWH or the other gods in Josh 24. According to Nihan, this revision was part of an attempt to align the books of the Hexateuch with the latter historical books.¹⁰² While these are possible conclusions, the textual evidence analyzed in this study has shown that the relationship of Josh 24 and 1 Sam 12 is

---

97 Contra Koopmans 1990, 386.
98 See section 3.2.2.
99 For other analyses of the connections between Josh 24 and 1 Sam 12 see Koopmans 1990, 390–391; Müller 2004, 181–186; Nihan 2013, 259–262.
100 Nihan 2013, 261.
101 Veijola 1977, 83–99.
102 Nihan 2013, 265–266.

more complicated and reciprocal. While 1 Sam 12 might have originally used some form of Josh 24 as one of its sources, Josh 24 has undergone harmonization towards 1 Sam 12 in the proto-MT phase of its editing. Therefore, one should be careful in making overly broad conclusions based on the complex relationship of Josh 24 and 1 Sam 12.[103] The key point for the study of editorial techniques is that secondary harmonization of parallel texts is not limited to one or the other. In the case of parallel texts, both may have been secondarily harmonized closer to one another. This makes the evaluation of the textual dependence between similar texts more complicated. Furthermore, Josh 24 and 1 Sam 12 are both related to a negative attitude towards human kingship, as was revealed already in the comparison with 1 Sam 10:17–27.[104] Therefore, it is possible that both texts may have been written and subsequently harmonized by the same editorial groups that had a negative view of kingship.

The last relevant text in Samuel-Kings for understanding Josh 24 is 1 Kgs 12:1–19, with the division of the kingdom and the failure of the Northern kingdom to come under the kingship of Rehoboam. It should be noted up front that 1 Kgs 12:1–19 is an extremely complex text due to its textual and literary problems, that cannot be dealt with in this study.[105] It is enough to make a few observations on the similarities with Josh 24. In addition to taking place at Shechem, Josh 24 and 1 Kgs 12:1–19 both have several points of connection: they are structured as a dialogue between the leader and the people,[106] they utilize the verb עבד "to serve" in relation to serving either YHWH or the king (Josh 24:14–21 / 1 Kgs 12:4, 7), they explicate that "the whole Israel" was present (Josh 24:1 / 1 Kgs 12:1), and they include the elders (הַזְּקֵנִים) among the people (Josh 24:1 / 1 Kgs 12:6). It would not be sustainable to argue for a direct textual and literary dependence between the passages. Rather, the linguistic and thematical similarities of Josh 24 with 1 Kgs 12:1–19 and Judg 9 strengthens the earlier conclusion that the commitment scene in Josh 24 is modeled as a contrast to the upcoming events. In Shechem, "the whole people" dedicated themselves to serve YHWH (Josh 24). In Shechem, the

---

[103] The picture becomes even more complicated when one takes the LXX version of 1 Sam 12 into account. For some of the text-critical problems present in 1 Sam 12 see, for example, Aejmelaeus 2010, 200–205.
[104] See also Kratz 2002, 303.
[105] For a brief description of the literary and textual problems and further studies related to 1 Kgs 12 see Witte 2010, 91–93. For literary criticism of 1 Kgs 12, see Würthwein 1977, 150–166.
[106] Koopmans (1990, 395): "This account is of considerable importance regarding the poetic narrative of Josh. 24:1–28 because it demonstrates that the enthronement negotiation in Shechem as narrated in 1 Kgs 12:1–17 also employs poetic discourse (cf. the enthronement negotiation at Shechem in Judg. 9)."

Israelites tried to choose a human king instead of YHWH, but failed miserably (Judg 9). Finally, in Shechem, "the whole Israel" fell apart (1 Kgs 12).[107]

Therefore, the commitment scene in Josh 24 seems to represent Second Temple reception of key texts in Deuteronomy (e.g. Deut 7:6, 11:26, 30:15–20) in the light of a wider "historical" and literary perspective (Judg 9, 1 Sam 10:17–25, 1 Sam 12, 1 Kgs 12). In this regard, it differs fundamentally from the historical summary at the beginning of the chapter.

4.2.7 Joshua 24 and Other Historical Summaries

The last literary connection to be noted is the close relationship of the historical summary in Josh 24:2–13 with very late historical summaries in the Hebrew Bible and beyond. When analyzing these similar historical summaries, some scholars even speak of a "sub-genre of sorts".[108] It seems to be practically justifiable to loosely use the term literary genre when referring to this type of a historical summary. The texts in question are, most notably, Deut 26:5–9, 1 Sam 12:6–17, Neh 9:6–37, Ps 78, 105, 106, 135, 136, Jdt 5:5–21, and Acts 7.[109] All the above-mentioned texts present a selective summary of the history of Israel to enforce their own message. It is not necessary to analyze all the textual connections between Josh 24:2–13 and these texts in detail, since these texts have a long history of research. However, I will briefly survey some of these key features of the texts to gain a deeper understanding of Josh 24:2–13.[110]

Some of the textual connections between Josh 24:2–13 and Deut 26:5–9 have already been referenced to. The most remarkable feature is the plus in the earlier text OG Josh 24:5–6 ("and became there a great and populous and mighty nation, and the Egyptians afflicted them"), which is an almost word-for-word reference to Deut 26:5–6. This link was lost in the MT due to a scribal mistake. OG Josh 24:7 preserved another earlier reading ("and we cried out to the Lord") which is a reference to Deut 26:7 lost in the proto-MT editing.[111] While the OG preserves a text closer to Deut 26, whether one reads the OG or the MT, the connections between these texts are clear. To name a few, both refer to the fathers moving

---

[107] Levin 1985, 177; Schmid 1999, 230; Kratz 2002, 303; Müller 2004, 226.
[108] Gera 2014, 201.
[109] For a brief overview of these and other summaries of history in the Hebrew Bible and early Jewish literature, see Wischmeyer 2006, 348–353.
[110] The connections between Josh 24 and 1 Sam 12 have already been analyzed in the previous section.
[111] See section 3.2.2.

down to Egypt (Deut 26:5 / Josh 24:4), both refer to YHWH leading the Israelites out of Egypt with signs and wonders (Deut 26:8 / Josh 24:5, 17), and both refer to YHWH giving them a land full of good things (Deut 26:9 / Josh 24:13). It was Von Rad who first observed the connections between these historical summaries, called them "small historical creeds", and proposed that they contain traces of an ancient cultic creed.[112] While the observations on the connections remain valid, in modern research Deut 26:5–9 is usually regarded as a late exilic supplement to the book of Deuteronomy.[113] This is seen especially in the way that the text creatively utilizes older material from Num 20:15ff. and other sources.[114] Since it is probable that Josh 24:2–13 secondarily refers to Deut 26:5–9, it seems that Josh 24:2–13 should be seen as an even later passage. While the relationship between Deut and Josh remains complex, and it is impossible to untangle all the intricacies here, it is safe to assume that both Deut 26:5–9 and Josh 24:2–13 are representatives of late Second Temple period efforts to concisely present a history of Israel to rationalize a specific message.

The connections between Josh 24:2–13 and Neh 9:6–37 are numerous. To name a few, both begin their historical summary with the selection of Abraham (Josh 24:3 / Neh 9:7), both contain a summary of what YHWH did in Egypt (Josh 24:5–6 / Neh 9:9–10), both recall the events at the Sea of Reeds (Josh 24:6–7 / Neh 9:11), both recall a long period in the wilderness (Josh 24:7 / Neh 9:21), both contain a reference to Sihon and Og (Josh 24:12 / Neh 9:22), and both reference all the good things mentioned in Deut 6:10–12 (Josh 24:13 / Neh 9:25). To be sure, Neh 9:6–37 contains a much longer summary of the history of Israel, together with an emphasis on the constant rebelling of the people. In other words, the literary and chronological perspective of Neh 9:6–37 is much wider than in Joshua. Neh 9, in fact, belongs to the youngest sections in the Hebrew Bible. It is a product of late *Fortschreibung* expanding upon themes in the earlier layers of Ezra-Nehemiah.[115] Much like Josh 24:2–13, it utilizes material found in various parts of the Hebrew Bible. Arguably, Neh 9 goes even further in its intertextual connections, and is probably an even later version of the historical summary than the one found in Josh 24:2–13. In any case, the connections between Josh 24:2–13 and Neh 9 corroborate the conclusion that the historical summary as a genre is a very late literary creation.

In addition to narrative material, the group of psalms often labeled as "historical psalms" (Ps 78, 105, 106, 135, 136) has close affinities with the historical summary in Josh 24:2–13. Parallel to Josh 24:2–13, the main stages of a historical

---

[112] Von Rad 1938, 3–8.
[113] See, for example, Lohfink 1994, 265–289; Gertz 2000, 30–45; Kratz 2005, 133.
[114] Kreuzer 1996, 99–101.
[115] Pakkala 2004, 180–184.

summary can be found in these psalms: the Israelites in Egypt, the Exodus, the desert wandering, and settlement in the Promised Land. Psalm 105 is the only one that, like Josh 24, begins the summary from the times of Abraham (Ps 105:9). Therefore, Ps 105 seems to be closest to Josh 24:2–13. In addition, both contain the sending of Moses and Aaron (Ps 105:26 / MT Josh 24:5) and refer to Deut 6:10–13 (Ps 105:44 / Josh 24:13). All the historical psalms contain a far more elaborate recollection of the history of Israel than Josh 24:2–13. Several detailed analyses have been made of these psalms by various scholars.[116] For the purposes of this study it is enough to note that these psalms are probably late Second Temple texts, which once again points towards Josh 24:2–13 belonging to this late scribal tradition.[117]

Differing from the historical summaries in the previous texts, the book of Judith inserts the historical summary into the mouth of a gentile called Achior. Jdt 5:5–21 contains several elements present also in Josh 24:2–13. Many phrases in Judith even accord word-for-word with OG Joshua, including: "the gods of your / their fathers" τοῖς θεοῖς τῶν πατέρων ὑμῶν / αὐτῶν (Josh 24:15 / Jdt 5:7), "they went down to Egypt" κατέβησαν εἰς Αἴγυπτον (Josh 24:4 / Jdt 5:10), "and became there a great, many, and mighty nation" καὶ ἐγένοντο ἐκεῖ εἰς ἔθνος μέγα καὶ πολὺ καὶ κραταιόν (Josh 24:5) / "and became there very large in number" καὶ ἐγένοντο ἐκεῖ εἰς πλῆθος πολύ (Jdt 5:10), "and he struck" καὶ ἐπάταξεν (Josh 24:5 / Jdt 24:12), καὶ ἀνεβοήσαμεν πρὸς κύριον "and we cried out to the Lord" (Josh 24:7) / "and they cried out to their God" καὶ ἀνεβόησαν πρὸς τὸν θεὸν αὐτῶν (Jdt 5:11), and "you / they destroyed completely" ἐξωλεθρεύσατε / ἐξωλέθρευσαν (Josh 24:8 / Jdt 5:15).[118] As is the case with Neh 9 and the "historical psalms", Jdt 5 presents a more detailed summary of the history than Josh 24:2–13. It is likely that the author knew and intentionally utilized Josh 24:2–13, among other texts. The dating and original language of the book of Judith is still a matter of controversy, but most likely it is a composition written in the late Second Temple period.[119] Thus, it is another witness for the popularity of the historical summary as a literary genre

---

116 See, for example, Fensham 1981, 25–51; Anderson 1988, 59–62; Gärtner 2015, 373–399.
117 For example, Klein (2015, 420–422) highlights that the historical psalms should be understood as "a literary search for identity." They draw from both Priestly and non-Priestly narratives, and have been placed in redactional turning points in the Psalter. Consequently, Klein notes that "it can be assumed that the historical psalms go back to scribal circles that – similar to the Qumran community – transmitted and continued the later biblical texts in order to re-establish identity after the catastrophe of exile."
118 For other similarities and connections of Jdt 5:5–21 with other historical summaries, see Gera 2014, 199–217.
119 For a discussion see, for example, Gera 2014, 79–97.

in the late Second Temple period and, together with the other texts, suggests that Josh 24:2–13 is also a product of this late literary environment.

Finally, the lateness of the historical summary as a literary genre is evidenced by the usage of the literary form in Acts 7, written at the end of the first century CE. The analysis by Wischmeyer reveals that the author of Acts 7 portrays the speech of Stephen as a historical summary, which is a direct continuation from the tradition of Josh 24:2–13 and other similar summaries.[120] Like the other summaries, the author of Acts 7 uses a selective retelling of the history of Israel, emphasizing the turning away of the Israelites from the true God. In this case, the strategy inherited from the Hebrew Bible is used to link the Israelite's rejection of God in history with their first century rejection of Jesus.[121] The usage of the literary form of a historical summary in the New Testament reveals that it was a popular literary genre even at the end of the Second Temple period.

4.2.8 Three Interim Conclusions for Literary and Redaction Criticism

The analysis of the literary and thematical connections of Josh 24 with other texts forms a basis for the evaluation of literary and redaction critical models. Three key issues should especially be kept in mind when moving on to the next section. First, whereas Josh 23 could function as a conclusion to the book of Joshua, the literary horizon of Josh 24 is wider. It is only loosely anchored in the context of the book of Joshua, and makes several references to the preceding and following books. Therefore, it has been possible to use it as evidence for different, larger compositional models (e.g. Hexateuch and DtrH). Second, the mixture of intertextual connections in Josh 24 makes it impossible to characterize the chapter with any single label. It is not dependent on any single text or literary layer, but presents a creative blend of various kinds of sources. While it is possible that one very late author could have utilized diverse material, taken together with the existence of variant textual editions, this rather suggests a literary development in several subsequent stages. Third, in terms of literary connections, Josh 24 is made up of three parts. The historical summary in Josh 24:2–13 is connected with other very late historical summaries in the Hebrew Bible and beyond. It makes several connections with the history of Israel as found in the Pentateuch, and gives the text a "Hexateuchal" flavor. The commitment scene in 24:14–27, on the

---

120 Wischmeyer 2006, 341–358. For an analysis of the most notable Old Testament quotations in Acts 7, see Arnold 1996, 311–319.
121 Arnold 1996, 312.

other hand, is mostly dependent upon themes and ideas from Deuteronomy and other historical books (Judg 9, 1 Sam 10:17–27, 1 Kgs 12). Lastly, the death and burial scene in Josh 24:28–33 is a flexible unit, and could function as a possible ending or transition in various literary wholes. This is seen, for example, in that it has been secondarily adapted by Judges.

4.3 Literary and Redaction Criticism of Joshua 24

4.3.1 Introductory Remarks

I will now turn to reconstructing the literary history of Josh 24. There are several literary-critical models pertaining to Josh 24 that have support in modern research. These models range from assuming one author to postulating several subsequent layers. In this study, they will be evaluated in the light of the documented evidence analyzed in previous sections. To understand and appreciate the state of research today, however, some phases in the early history of this research need to be surveyed. Following the typology in the recent commentary by Dozeman, the history of literary and redaction critical research into the book of Joshua can be divided into four phases.[122]

First, nineteenth century research was dominated by the concept of the Hexateuch. In this paradigm, the book of Joshua was regarded in its earliest form as a supplement to the Pentateuch, which formed an ending for the sources in the Pentateuch. Among the most prominent scholars within this paradigm were Wellhausen and Kuenen.[123] Their key observation was that the book of Joshua attests to several stages of editing. At least three phases can be distinguished: (1) an original Hexateuchal ending for the sources of the Pentateuch, (2) a Deuteronomistic rewriting of Joshua, and (3) the Priestly version of the story of the conquest and division of the land.[124] In this manner, these scholars also separated various sources and stages of development in Josh 24. The core of the chapter was a continuing source from the Pentateuch. The kernel of the chapter was attributed to the Elohist (E). The E source, however, was preserved in Josh 24 through a complex process of editing. While Wellhausen supposed Deuteronomistic editing, which utilized both Jahwist (J) and E elements in shaping the chapter, Kuenen also regarded many of the elements as Deuteronomistic additions.[125]

---

[122] Dozeman 2015, 5–32.
[123] Wellhausen 1899 and Kuenen 1886.
[124] Dozeman 2015, 6.
[125] Wellhausen 1899, 133–134 and Kuenen 1886, 155–159.

Several key critical observations from the early Hexateuchal scholarship remain relevant to the study of Josh 24.[126] However, the conclusion that the book of Joshua reveals an early continuation of the sources of the Pentateuch is not held anymore. As revealed by my study of the literary connections, it is clear that Josh 24 preserves complex connections with the Pentateuch. However, assuming a continuing early E source is problematic since, as my analysis revealed, many of these connections are probably very late and may even be results of later harmonization, as revealed by some variants between the MT and the OG. Here one can also point to the critique by Koopmans, who demonstrates that the manner in which the Pentateuch is used in Josh 24 does not show preferences following the classic JE distinctions.[127] Moreover, the whole attempt to establish ancient J and E sources that expand themselves over various books is often based on weak grounds utilizing assumptions made on the basis of single phrases or words.[128]

Second, in the first half of the 20th century research was more focused on the search for the historical realities behind the events described in the book of Joshua than on the compositional or textual history. It was generally accepted that the book of Joshua did not report history as such. However, there was a belief that preliterary etiological stories, in the spirit of form-criticism, could be traced behind the text. These quests were driven by the increasing exposure of biblical scholars to the archaeology of Syria-Palestine, and the formation of several international archaeological institutes. One of the main discussions pertained to the historical realities behind the conquest of the land by the Israelites, and especially a debate between the "infiltration theory" (Albrecht Alt) and "unified conquest theory" (William F. Albright).[129] Josh 24 was not at the center of this discussion. Several scholars, however, gave reconstructions of the ancient *Sitz im Leben* behind Josh 24. The chapter was explained, for example, in the light of an assumed ancient amphictyonic cultic tribal gathering at Shechem,[130] assumed

---

126 These are, for example, the notion that the book of Joshua is a product of subsequent stages of editing, the observations concerning the textual connections between the book of Joshua and the Pentateuch, and the conclusion that the historical value of the conquest accounts in the book of Joshua is dubious (Dozeman 2015, 6–8).
127 Koopmans 1990, 118–128.
128 See, for example, Carr 2011, 110. On the various way that the "Yahwist" is understood in modern research see Römer 2006, 9–27.
129 For a brief review see Dozeman 2015, 8–16.
130 Noth 1930, 85–97. Also, Mowinckel (1958, 137–150; 1964, 48), who however argued that the original cultic event at Shechem consisted of ten tribes, and that the tradition of twelve tribes emerged at the earliest in David's times.

ancient cultic creeds,[131] and Hittite treaty texts.[132] This phase of research on Josh 24 can be described, in the words of Koopmans, as "a search for literary correlations between biblical, covenantal texts and ancient treaty documents, which led to the assertion of a specific OT genre, a covenant formulary dependent upon the treaty form."[133]

The search for the historical events behind the book of Joshua has continued in some circles, but generally scholarship has taken the direction summarized by Richard Nelson: "Joshua is fundamentally a theological and literary work. Hardly any of the material it preserves is of the sort that can be directly used for historical reconstruction".[134] In the light of the most recent summaries of archaeological findings, the reports in the book of Joshua have been shown to have little or no basis in describing how Israel actually came into being, as an indigenous development through a complex social transformation among the pastoral people of the Canaanite highlands.[135] In addition, modern scholarship is usually skeptical towards the possibility of recovering the ancient cultic settings or people behind the texts in Joshua, since the various sagas probably reflect later traditions. As Nelson aptly continues: "Joshua's true historical value consists of what it reveals about the social and ideological world of those who told these stories, collected and redacted them".[136] When one adds to this discussion the complex set of text-critical variants and literary connections that were uncovered in the preceding sections, it seems that Josh 24 as such does not provide information on pre-exilic historical creeds or cultic moments.[137] Therefore, as Dozeman has noted, "the impasse in recovering the history of the tribal period from the book of Joshua has redirected research back to the question of its literary composition."[138]

The last two phases in the literary and redaction critical research of the book of Joshua are, according to Dozeman, the hypothesis of a Deuteronomistic history and the view that Joshua is an independent book.[139] This statement, however,

---

131 Von Rad 1938.
132 Mendenhall 1955.
133 Koopmans 1990, 61.
134 Nelson 1997, 2–3.
135 Nelson 1997, 3–4; Finkelstein & Silberman 2002, 97–122; Dever 2003.
136 Nelson 1997, 4.
137 After Perlitt (1969, 239–247) it has been hard to argue that the scene taking place in Josh 24 is any more than literary fiction. See also, for example, Hoffman 1980, 305–306; Levin 1985, 114; Aurelius 2008, 95. Of course one cannot rule out the possibility that such texts might contain echoes of older traditions. Even later writers may have known and utilized such traditions – at least as distant memories.
138 Dozeman 2015, 16.
139 Dozeman 2015, 16–32.

simplifies current research. The situation in modern research seems to be more complicated and varied. For example, there are several models of subsequent redactions that break away from the Deuteronomistic history hypothesis.[140] In this study, I will now move from a chronological review to evaluating the most prominent compositional positions that are held in respect to Josh 24.

The most important aim of the following critical evaluation is to integrate the documented evidence of editing into the discussion. One of the key features of my argument in the following evaluation is: documented evidence sets boundaries for what can be argued in literary and redaction criticism. This argument follows logically from my text-critical analysis, which revealed that the latest literary growth of Josh 24 was visible in documented evidence. Therefore, documented evidence overrules some possibilities for what can be argued in terms of the compositional history of Joshua.[141] On the other hand, documented evidence corroborates the assumptions and arguments presented in literary and redaction criticism. In this way, some existing literary-critical arguments and models gain support from textual evidence. When the evidence has been considered in this manner, we will have an outline of the literary history of Josh 24.

The following analysis of literary and redaction critical possibilities is divided under three headings, following the main traits of each theory or paradigm. The first two stages are related to the literary criticism of the chapter. First, I will evaluate the arguments put forth for the original literary unity of Josh 24 (section 4.3.2). Second, after having overruled this possibility, I will argue that the assumption of a basic commitment narrative expanded in several stages best accords with the documented evidence (section 4.3.3). The next two stages relate to redaction criticism and larger compositional issues. Can Josh 24 be explained within the framework of Deuteronomistic redactions (section 4.3.4)? What is the best explanation for the transition from Joshua to Judges (section 4.3.5)? Since these questions are related to many other texts in the Hebrew Bible, the discussion is much more modest than one would hope. Nevertheless, I believe it adequately illuminates the problems and possibilities in using Josh 24 as a part of larger compositional models. Finally, I will propose a synthesis of the discussed themes which, in my opinion, best illuminates the literary development of Josh 24 in the light of documented evidence. In this context, I will also discuss the overall

---

140 For example, Becker 2006 and Knauf 2008.
141 Similarly, also Auld (1998, 17) regarding LXX Joshua: "Many more textual cruces could be studied, some of them with significance for the literary criticism of the book: normally only negative significance, in that they foreclose options." In my opinion, however, textual criticism also has a positive significance for literary criticism. Literary-critical arguments often find support from text-critical arguments.

viability of the methods of literary and redaction criticism in uncovering editorial intrusions, together with methodological insights from my analysis of Josh 24.

4.3.2 A Late Literary Unity

The main task of literary criticism is to determine the possible unity or disunity of a given text. In recent scholarship, there has been an increasing trend towards regarding Josh 24 as a literary unity. These models are often connected with the larger compositional theory positing that in the late (Persian or Hellenistic) stages of the literary growth of the Hebrew Bible there was an editorial movement towards creating a large compositional unity (Hexateuch or even Enneateuch).[142]

In the light of the analysis of documented evidence, it can be stated already at the outset that the assumption of a literary unity in Josh 24 seems unfounded. Text-critical evidence reveals that there were already several stages of editing in the latest literary growth of Josh 24. While both the OG and the MT exhibit later editorial intrusions, especially the latter reflects several secondary elements. This documented evidence raises the suspicion that such editing has also taken place in Josh 24, the traces of which are not preserved in the textual evidence. In my opinion, the overall methodological conclusions by Müller, Pakkala & Haar Romeny also apply in the case of Josh 24: "…we can assume that these documented cases attest to merely a fraction of the actual changes that have taken place in the transmission… there are good reasons to assume that similar editorial processes took place during the earlier periods of the textual transmission that are largely undocumented by variant editions."[143] The models assuming a late literary unity suffer from a wide neglect of the documented evidence provided by the OG.

Despite this suspicion raised by text-critical observations, it is necessary to analyze some of the arguments used in models postulating a basic unity of Josh 24. This is because these models are quite influential in modern research. The main claim of these theories is that Josh 24 is a late post-exilic and post-Deuteronomistic composition. The beginnings of this line of interpretation can be attributed to the studies of John Van Seters,[144] Erhard Blum,[145] and Moshe Anbar.[146] The

---

[142] See, for example, Römer & Brettler 2000, 408–416. They attribute this endeavor to a Deuteronomistic-Priestly minority who had come together in their attempt to promote the publication of a Hexateuch.
[143] Müller, Pakkala & Haar Romeny 2014, 9.
[144] Van Seters 1984, 139–158.
[145] Blum 1990, 363–365; 1997, 194–206.
[146] Anbar 1992.

4.3 Literary and Redaction Criticism of Joshua 24

basic view of Josh 24 as a late literary composition has been adopted in several studies.[147] The various formulations of this theory are not uniform, and there are disagreements in details. One of the main debates, for example, is whether Josh 24 is not only post-Deuteronomistic but also post-Priestly, as argued by Anbar and Nihan.[148]

The main arguments for this theory emerge from various details in the text. These have been interpreted as evidence for the literary unity and late provenance of Josh 24. Moreover, according to Römer & Brettler, the assumption of a late Hexateuch "solves the various critical problems associated with the chapter."[149] However, my text-critical analysis sheds doubts on many of these observations.

First, within the theory of a late and unified Josh 24, the beginning verses Josh 24:1–2 are explained as an opening statement that is modeled upon a Deuteronomistic parenesis. The beginning of the chapter, which combines the assembly of the people with an introduction of divine speech ("thus says YHWH, the God of Israel") would have been created following late Deuteronomistic texts, specifically in Josh 23:2 and 1 Sam 10:17–18. Based on this observation, Van Seters concludes that 24:1–2 is modelled on "the kind of prophetic style that is the hallmark of the Dtr tradition both in DtrH and in the late prophetic works."[150] From these observations it would then follow that the author who created such an introduction was aware of several late traditions. However, Van Seters does not note the variants in the OG. My text-critical analysis revealed that these textual connections are more complicated than merely stating that Josh 24:1–2 was modelled upon other late introductions. The evidence from the OG revealed that Josh 24:1 has been secondarily harmonized towards Josh 23:2. Before this harmonization, Josh 24:1 was connected with Josh 8:33.[151] Therefore, in order to explain all of the textual evidence, we have to assume at least two editorial phases at the beginning of Josh 24:1. It is then not probable that the beginning verses as we have them in the MT have been modelled by one author, but rather that they have probably undergone several stages of editing with respect to similar texts.

Second, the historical summary in Josh 24:2–13 is explained as a late composition deliberately combining several elements. Van Seters links the historical

---

[147] For example, Mayes 1983, 51; Römer & Brettler 2000; Finsterbusch 2012, 190. In conformity with these models, Sperling (1987 and 2000) argues that most of Josh 24:1–28 is a literary unity and the work of a single author. Sperling, however, argues that the text should be dated to early pre-exilic times.
[148] Nihan 2013, 265.
[149] Römer & Brettler 2000, 409.
[150] Van Seters 1984, 146–147.
[151] See section 3.2.2.

summary to various recitals of YHWH's protective actions in the history of Israel resembling Deut 26:5–9 (Judg 6:7–9, 10:11–12, 1 Sam 10:18, 12:8–12). Such historical summaries usually begin with the Exodus and somehow bring the historical happenings into the time of the speaker. They are significantly free adaptions of the events. In terms of Josh 24:2–13, Van Seters notes that the historical summary does not merely repeat the traditional elements of these historical summaries, but adds several new elements from the "pre-Priestly" traditions (e.g., the patriarchal history, additional information on the Exodus, Balaam-narrative). This, according to Van Seters, does not speak for the presence of older traditions, but of the late nature of the text. The late author could take the Deuteronomistic traditions and inflate them with other traditions. According to Van Seters, these later inflations (e.g., the sea event in Josh 24:6–7) cannot be late additions, but they are integral to the story itself, which is seen in the adapting of the literary form of the story presented by the "Yahwist" in Exod 12–14.[152]

The basic observations related to the lateness of the historical summary are correct, as was also concluded earlier in this study. With respect to the historical summary, the case for literary unity is however problematic, since the documented evidence preserves such a complicated picture of the latest literary growth. While the earlier OG text presents the historical summary as a prophetic speech of Joshua, the MT secondarily transforms it to a divine speech. It also expands the historical summary with elements taken from 1 Sam 12 (MT) and softens some theological concepts that are perceived as problematic.[153] These variants are not merely sporadic glosses, and their satisfactory explanation demands assuming several developmental phases in the development of the Hebrew text of the historical summary. Neglecting this evidence altogether is the only way of preserving an assumption that we are dealing with a literary unity. For instance, when Van Seters compares the literary form of Josh 24:5–7 to that of Exod 12–14, he does not consider that some similarities between the passages are not original, but were created secondarily as revealed by textual evidence.[154] Hence the textual evidence preserved in the historical summary presents a significant obstacle for scholars who wish to maintain the literary unity of Josh 24.

Moreover, the lateness of the historical summary is a different issue than the date of the commitment scene. As have been shown earlier in this section, these contain quite different literary connections and ideas, and have probably not been created by the same author. I will, however, return to this question later.

---

[152] Van Seters 1984, 147–149.
[153] See section 3.5.
[154] Van Seters 1984, 149. For an evaluation of the connections with Exodus, see section 4.2.2.

Third, several details in the textual argumentation for a unified Josh 24 created to conclude a late Hexateuch reveal that relevant textual evidence is neglected in these theories. Römer & Brettler notes that Josh 24 employs Priestly as well as Deuteronomistic language, and refer to the expression "land of Canaan" in Josh 24:6. However, text-critical evidence reveals that "Canaan" is a later insertion in v. 6.[155] It has also been argued that the "inclusive" location of the covenant scene at Shechem would speak for a coalition of Deuteronomistic and Priestly authors,[156] but the text-critical uncertainty related to the location of the scene undermines such an assumption.[157] In addition, the connotations of Shechem in the Hebrew Bible are ambiguous, especially in the late stages of the growth of the text.[158] It is equally possible that such a coalition would have wanted to exclude the Samaritans from the covenant, and utilized Shiloh as the location for the covenant making. This underlines the problems related to deducing such a historical coalition from ambiguous textual evidence. Lastly, the case of Josh 24:17 should be pointed out. The verse is part of a section (24:16–18) containing the answer of the people, which, according to Van Seters, corresponds rather closely to the Deuteronomistic "pattern of the recital of history as confessional."[159] This close correspondence, however, is not modeled by a single author; in the MT there is a considerable late addition drawing from formulaic language in various sections of the Deuteronomy.[160] Once again, one cannot speak of a late author who composed the text from various Deuteronomistic and Priestly materials, as documented evidence reveals that there was an earlier text which has been later harmonized towards Deuteronomy.

Several other problems with the textual arguments could be pointed out in the endorsement of a late literary unity in the case Josh 24. Yet, the main observation is clear: the documented evidence of editing does not allow for an assumption of literary unity. When one begins the study of Josh 24 by comparing the extant textual versions, it becomes clear that several subsequent scribal hands are needed to explain the genesis of the chapter. Furthermore, is safe to assume that the documented history of the textual development is only the tip of the iceberg. Other changes have probably taken place that have not left traces in variant textual versions. Only by excluding the OG can one uphold the position of a unified text. This is indeed done, for example, in the article by Van Seters,

---

155 See section 3.2.2.
156 Römer & Brettler 2000, 413.
157 See section 3.2.2.
158 See sections 4.2.5 and 4.2.6.
159 Van Seters 1984, 149.
160 See section 3.3.2.

which does not make any mention of the LXX.¹⁶¹ To be sure, it is still possible that the latest literary stages in Josh 24 reflect editorial motivations towards creating a Hexateuch of some sort. At least there are several documented cases where the text has been secondarily harmonized towards other Pentateuchal texts. However, the textual arguments in these recent compositional models need to be refined so that they better take into account the multifaceted documented evidence preserved in Josh 24.

4.3.3 A Basic Commitment Narrative Expanded in Several Stages

Josh 24 cannot have been written by one author at one point in time. This has already been demonstrated by the analysis of the variant versions preserved in the MT and the OG. Once it has been agreed that Josh 24 has developed in several stages, of which documented evidence for some has likely not been preserved, one should proceed with analyzing the various signs of diachronic development. This, however, cannot be done solely on the basis of the MT, and one should simultaneously keep all the textual evidence on the table.

I will now put forth the most convincing literary-critical arguments and conclusions, drawing also from the arguments by other scholars who advocate for a model of gradual literary growth in Josh 24.¹⁶² This model – presented with some degree of variation in the literature – assumes that a basic narrative of Josh 24 was first created, which then grew through gradual accretion. This, in my opinion, is the most likely model for the literary development of Josh 24. While the proponents of this model do not generally take the OG into account, the evidence from the OG fits quite well with the main arguments. I wish to demonstrate this during the following analysis.¹⁶³

---

161 Van Seters 1984, 139–158.
162 Most notably Levin 1985, 114 & 2013, 125–128; Müller 2004, 251–254; Kratz 2002, 299–307 & 2005, 198–200; Becker 2006, 139–162; Aurelius 2008, 95–114. These scholars build upon earlier scholarship, especially the works of Noth (1938, 1953) and Perlitt (1969). Some might characterize this paradigm as the Göttingen school of literary and redaction criticism. However, for example, Becker (2006, 150–153) subscribes to a model of subsequent editing akin to the Göttingen School, but forcefully distances his analysis from the Deuteronomistic history model. The Deuteromistic history model and its relationship to Josh 24 will be discussed further below, in section 4.3.4. In this section, I will concentrate on the literary-critical evidence concerning various literary strata in Josh 24.
163 While the text-critical analysis carried out in section 3 left many questions open, assuming editorial processes without variant versions is subject to even more uncertainty. However, documented evidence has shown that such an analysis is justifiable when the limitations of the approach are kept in mind. These limitations will be further discussed at the end of this section.

Besides the documented evidence, the argument that Josh 24 has developed in several stages begins with the observation that Josh 24 consists of many difficult readings, tensions, intertextual references, and repetitions. It also includes theologically diverse concepts, which cannot be ascribed to a single historical author or community.[164] In terms of content, there are three main parts in Josh 24. First, the historical summary in 24:1–13 is a recollection of the salvation history ranging from the patriarchs to the Promised Land. This historical summary builds upon earlier texts in the Pentateuch. Second, the commitment scene in 24:14–27 is read as a repetitious dialogue which has, in contrast to the historical summary, many affinities with Deuteronomy and the following historical books.[165] Third, the death and burial accounts at the end of the chapter (24:28–33) are not directly connected with the content of the chapter. The main aim is to report the death of the hero of the conquest of the land, which could have originally emerged in several literary contexts, as is also seen in the documented evidence offered by Judg 2:6–9.

It is most probable that the commitment scene in Josh 24:14–28 holds the earliest basic narrative of Josh 24. The historical summary has been added later as an introduction to this commitment narrative, which has also resulted in various additions to the basic commitment narrative.[166] These additions have secondarily given Josh 24 a Hexateuchal flavor.[167] In the table below, the most common attempts to reconstruct the basic narrative in Josh 24 are presented. The basic commitment narrative running from 24:14a to 24:28 is almost similar in the analysis of several scholars. The main disagreement between scholars relates to what originally came before the commitment narrative, and whether some form of the introduction in vv. 24:1–2 belonged to the basic commitment narrative, or whether it was added later. I will next put forth the key textual arguments for this basic literary critical division in Josh 24.

When the three basic parts of Josh 24 have been established, the literary-critical argument continues with the observation that there seems to be a literary seam between 24:13–14. Verse 14 begins with the introduction וְעַתָּה "and now", and the subject matter changes from the protective actions of YHWH in history to a choice which Joshua presents to the people.[168] To be sure, the literary seam is even stronger in the MT tradition, which secondarily gives vv. 5–13 as the speech

---

164 Becker 2006, 143.
165 Becker 2006, 144.
166 Kratz 2005, 199 and Becker 2006, 144. The arguments for this claim will be discussed further.
167 Aurelius 2008, 107–114.
168 The introduction וְעַתָּה as a literary marker is highlighted by many scholars. See, for example, Kratz 2005, 199; Becker 2006, 144; and Aurelius 2008, 99. See also the comments by Butler (1983, 272): "The text abruptly changes speaker and mood." There are several models on whether

Previous suggestions for the basic commitment narrative

[¹³:¹ᵃ Now Joshua was old and advanced in years ²³:²ᵃ and Joshua summoned all Israel ²³:²ᵇ* and said to them: "I am now old and well advanced in years ²³:³ and you have seen all that YHWH your God has done to all these nations for your sakes. For it is YHWH your God who has fought for you.]¹

[²⁴:¹ᵃ And Joshua gathered all the tribes of Israel to Shechem ²⁴:¹ᵇ And set them before Lord. ²⁴:²ᵃ And Joshua said to all the people:]²

²⁴:¹⁴ᵃ *Now fear YHWH and serve him in sincerity and in faithfulness.* ²⁴:¹⁵ᵃ *Now if you are unwilling to serve YHWH,*³ *choose yourself today whom you will serve.* ²⁴:¹⁵ᵇ* I and my household, we will serve YHWH ²⁴:¹⁶ Then the people answered and said: "Far be it from us that we would abandon YHWH to serve other gods. ²⁴:¹⁸ᵇ also we will serve YHWH, for he is our God." ²⁴:²² Then Joshua said to the people: "You are witnesses against yourselves that you have chosen YHWH, to serve him." And they said: "We are witnesses!" ²⁴:²⁸ *So Joshua sent the people away, each to their inheritances.*⁴

Notes
1 The beginning according to Kratz 2005, 199 (23.1b–2, 3) and Aurelius 2008, 102. In this model, it is assumed that the basic commitment narrative was originally linked with Josh 13:1a. Thus 13–22 is late material.
2 The beginning according to Becker 2006, 157; Müller 2004, 252–253; Levin 2013, 126.
3 Müller (2004, 253) does not include the cursive 14a–15a in the earliest commitment narrative.
4 While Becker (2006, 159) and Aurelius (2008, 102) include Josh 24:28 to the basic commitment narrative, Müller (2004, 253–254) and Levin (2013, 126) posit that Josh 24:28 is an even earlier verse which belonged to the early transition of Joshua and Judges (Josh 11:23b-24:28-Judg 2:8–9). The latter theory will be discussed below after the basic literary-critical solutions of Josh 24 have been made.

of YHWH.¹⁶⁹ This literary-critical notion alone could lead scholars to prefer the textual form of the MT in the historical summary. However, a text-critical analysis seems to tip the scale towards the OG preserving the earlier third-person form of the speaker in the historical summary. Therefore, the change in person emerged secondarily in the proto-MT editing. It is, however, noteworthy that the proto-MT editor changed the person of the speech to first-person speech of YHWH only in vv. 3–13 and not in v. 14ff. This observation from text-critical evidence, then, strengthens the assumption that ancient editors perceived a change in content, and a seam of some sort between vv. 13–14. Furthermore, the possibility that the historical summary in vv. 2–13 can be isolated from the commitment scene, and

---

וְעַתָּה was originally connected with the speech introduction in Josh 24:1–2 or Josh 23:2–3. The above tables summarize the main models. See also the discussion by Müller 2004, 220–221.
169 See section 3.2.2.

may have been secondarily added as an introduction to the commitment scene, gains indirect support from the growing body of documented evidence suggesting that ancient texts were often revised through adding introductions.[170]

If the historical summary was added secondarily, the earliest text form of Josh 24 is then found by discerning the later material in the commitment scene of vv. 14–27. The identification of resumptive repetitions (*Wiederaufnahme*), together with other literary-critical arguments, offers a relatively solid possibility for identifying the later additions made to the basic commitment narrative.[171] On the basis of disruptions in content, repetitions, and other criteria, five likely expansions can be discerned from the basic commitment narrative: Josh 24:14b, 15*, 17–18a, 19–21, and 23–27.[172] In addition, other observations discussed below expose them as *Fortschreibung*, and strengthen the argument for their lateness in relation to the commitment narrative.

First, Josh 24:14b ("put away the gods that your fathers served beyond the river and in Egypt, and serve YHWH") has been added by repeating וְעִבְדוּ אֶת־יְהוָה in a transposed form from the beginning of v. 14.[173] In terms of content, the order

---

170 See Milstein 2016.
171 *Wiederaufnahme* has been assumed as an editorial technique already early in literary-critical research. The usage of resumptive repetitions by ancient scribes to expand texts has been corroborated by documented evidence from both biblical and other ancient Near Eastern textual material. See, for example, Tigay 1982, 74–76; Carr 2011, 44; Müller, Pakkala & Haar Romeny 2014, 22–25. Some scholars even promote resumptive repetitions as an "objective criterion" for determining various literary sources in the biblical texts (Talmon 1981, 58–59). However, *Wiederaufnahme* can also be used as a stylistic device by a single author. Therefore, it should not function as the sole argument for identifying secondary additions.
172 These are, in my opinion, the most likely secondary additions. Other parts have also been suggested, and I will discuss them in the footnotes and further in the section.
173 Thus also Levin 1985, 114 and Müller 2004, 216. According to Müller (2004, 221–224) the whole 24:14–15a is a secondary addition inspired by the addition of the historical summary. He notes that the *parenesis* "now fear YHWH and serve him" (24:14a) does not fit well with the call to "choose yourself today whom you will serve" (24:15aα2). These cannot have stood together in the basic narrative, and the latter cannot be removed as secondary since that would remove the core idea of the text reflected also in 24:22. Furthermore, according to Müller, the clause "now if you are unwilling to serve YHWH" (24:15a) cannot be a reference to anything else but the secondarily added other gods in 24:15*. It is easy to agree with Müller that "choose yourself today whom you will serve" cannot be removed as secondary, since it is at the core of the choice presented in Josh 24. Müller also correctly notes the parallels for this "juridical" formulation hanging on the verb בחר (Ruth 4:9, 1 Sam 12:5). However, I do not think that there is a problem in including both 24:14a and 24:15a in the basic text. The idea that the Israelites might be unwilling to serve YHWH does not have to refer specifically to the gods mentioned in 24:15*, but is already embedded into the idea that the Israelites can choose to either serve or not to serve YHWH. In the light of Deut 30:15–20, which I have already discerned as one of the sources for the choice, the basic text of

to put away foreign gods does not follow from what has been stated earlier. The putting away of foreign gods (סור *hiphil*) is elsewhere connected with situations where there are physically foreign gods among the people (Gen 35:2–3, 1 Sam 7:3–4), and not to a situation of *a priori* choice between YHWH and other gods. The plea to put away other gods is understood better in a context such as Judg 10:16, and in Josh 24:14 it could be explained as an addition, together with 24:23, motivated by a later situation in which the temptation to serve foreign gods is among the people.[174] The assumed addition of v. 14b also links the secondary historical summary with the commitment scene, by making a reference to its beginning in 24:2. Furthermore, textual variants offer some evidence that the phrase might be a secondary addition. Namely, the Hebrew *Vorlage* of OG secondarily adds that the gods served by the fathers were "foreign".[175] This is a harmonization with the phrase in verse 23 אֶת־אֱלֹהֵי הַנֵּכָר and should be understood as a later attempt to integrate the loose phrase in 14b more tightly with the context in Josh 24.

In addition, the middle part of v. 15 ("whether the gods *of your fathers* that were beyond the river or the gods of the Amorites in whose land you are living") can be regarded as an addition together with 14b, since it introduces the same themes and uses similar vocabulary.[176] In the MT, v. 15* has been harmonized even further with 14b by changing the possessive form of the gods of the fathers to the expression (אֶת־אֱלֹהִים אֲשֶׁר עָבְדוּ אֲבוֹתֵיכֶם) taken from 14b.[177]

Second, verses 19–21 have been added by repeating אֶת־יְהוָה נַעֲבֹד in a transposed form from v. 18b. Also, אֱלֹהֵי נֵכָר is repeated from the added v. 14b. These verses introduce the surprising statement by Joshua that the people cannot serve YHWH. Many scholars note that such a statement is not likely to have originally belonged to the themes of Josh 24. This is because it severely interrupts the content of the commitment scene; the certainty of the choice presented in v. 22 seems banal coming right after such a notion.[178] The incoherence of vv. 19–21 with the context is also seen in the light of the preceding material. As Noth already noted, the content of vv. 19–21 is very peculiar after the positive invitation in v. 14.[179] The theme of the incompetency to serve YHWH should therefore be seen as a note

---

Josh 24:14–15a is likely. Removing 24:14a as secondary would also remove some key references to Deuteronomy, which are probably at the core of the choice presented in Josh 24:14–15.
174 Aurelius 2008, 100.
175 See section 3.2.2.
176 Becker 2006, 145 and Aurelius 2008, 100.
177 See section 3.3.2.
178 Levin 1985, 114; Müller 2004, 217; Aurelius 2008, 100.
179 Noth 1953, 263.

leading to the upcoming historical books: a late redactor wanted to highlight that the story of the Israelites ends in infidelity, and created a proleptic statement at this point.[180]

Third, verses 23–24 have been added by repeating נַעֲבֹד אֶת־יְהוָה כִּי־הוּא אֱלֹהֵינוּ in the slightly modified form אֶת־יְהוָה אֱלֹהֵינוּ נַעֲבֹד from v. 18b.[181] In addition, the order to put away the foreign gods (הָסִירוּ אֶת־אֱלֹהֵי הַנֵּכָר) is repeated from the added v. 14b. Moreover, later editing in 22–24 is revealed by the literary device וְעַתָּה and the sudden change of speaker from the people (v. 22b) to Joshua (v. 23b). When the speaker changes to Joshua elsewhere in the dialogue of Josh 24, it is always introduced with a formula (vv. 19, 22, 27). The addition needs to be explained together with the addition of 14b, since they both introduce the idea of foreign gods being amid the Israelites.

Fourth, verses 25–27 have been added by repeating several times the idea of something (the Israelites themselves or stones) being a witness against the Israelites from v. 22.[182] The secondary addition of the scene with the witness stones is also implied by the phrase בַּיּוֹם הַהוּא used at the beginning of v. 25.[183] The added verses introduce the new themes of covenant making and law-giving into Josh 24, which hints towards its lateness in relation to the basic narrative, which does not yet include the concept of law.[184] In this way, a continuum was drawn from the Sinai covenant to the commitment scene. Here one can also see the influence of Josh 8:30–35, which is a latecomer in the book of Joshua, also strengthening the lateness of vv. 25–27.[185] Several scholars now hold that the unique reference to סֵפֶר תּוֹרַת אֱלֹהִים "the book the Torah of God" was coined by late Hexateuch-redactors as an attempt to include the book of Joshua into the Torah.[186] This conclusion is based, for example, on the notion that Joshua writes הַדְּבָרִים הָאֵלֶּה "these words", that is the words of Joshua, as an addition to an existing scroll. Joshua

---

[180] Becker 2006, 145. It is noteworthy that Römer (2006, 539), who otherwise holds Josh 24 as a literary unity, also regards vv. 19–21 as a secondary redactional addition.
[181] Thus also Müller 2004, 216 and Becker 2006, 144.
[182] Becker 2006, 146 and Aurelius 2008, 101.
[183] Müller 2004, 218
[184] Although Finsterbusch 2012, 196 holds Josh 24 a late literary unity, she argues that this is the latest reference to the Torah in the diachronic development of the book of Joshua.
[185] Becker 2006, 146. Documented evidence of Josh 8:30–35 reveals that its position was not yet fixed at quite a late stage. See section 4.2.4.
[186] See, for example, Blum 1997, 204; Römer and Brettler 2000, 415; Aurelius 2003, 176; Finsterbusch 2012, 193. The phrase is used elsewhere only in the late verses Neh 8:8, 18. See Pakkala 2004, 136–179, who argues that the verses with the references to the book of the Torah of God belong to the later additions in Neh 8.

is therefore imagined as a lawgiver akin to Moses, who also spoke הַדְּבָרִים הָאֵלֶּה, a phrase last mentioned in Deut 32:45.

At this point it should be noted that the cumulative argument for the secondary nature of the material in vv. 23–27 is strengthened by the observable literary strategy behind the *Fortschreibung*. In the earlier commitment narrative, continued from v. 22 to v. 28, the dialogue with the people ended in the idea that the people themselves functioned as a witness to the decision. This witnessing was the last thing mentioned before the dispersal of the people. The secondary addition of the material in vv. 23–27 preserved this literary form: the last thing mentioned before the dispersal of the people (v. 28) was that there is a witness to the commitment of the people. The original literary idea that the witness is the last thing mentioned in such a commitment scene was preserved by later editors. Therefore, the texts before and after the *Fortschreibung* both follow the same literary strategy.

Fifth, vv. 17–18 begin and end with the designation of YHWH as אֱלֹהֵינוּ "our God". This is not a traditional resumptive repetition, but it is possible that the first "our God" is a sign of an addition. Based on content, vv. 17–18a stick out as a short historical summary which remembers the Exodus and the driving out of the Amorites. The mention of אֶת־אֲבוֹתֵינוּ fits the context poorly, since the fathers are not mentioned elsewhere in the commitment narrative. Also, the הָאֱמֹרִי יֹשֵׁב הָאָרֶץ "the Amorites that lived in the land" is only loosely connected to the commitment scene.[187] Both, in fact, already assume the presence of the historical summary in Josh 24:2–13; thus, the addition of 17–18a may be seen as an editorial attempt to integrate the commitment scene with the secondarily added historical summary. The nature of vv. 17–18a as *Fortschreibung* is corroborated by documented evidence: in the proto-MT phase of editing, the happenings in Egypt were narrated further with the long addition ("from the land of Egypt, out of the house of slavery, and who did those great signs in our sight.") missing from the earlier OG text.[188] Thus the added historical summaries were likely subjected to *Fortschreibung* in several stages, the development of which may possibly never be reconstructed in full.

The identification of vv. 14b, 15*, 17–18a, 19–21, and 23–27 as probable secondary additions is corroborated by the traditional *Gegenprobe*; that is, the basic commitment narrative flows smoothly without these additions.[189]

---

[187] See Müller 2004, 217–218.
[188] See section 3.3.2.
[189] Van Seters (1984, 149–150) argues against regarding some of these verses as secondary additions: "The unit Joshua 24.19-24 has often been judged a Dtr additions, but its removal would make the transition from v. 18 to v. 25 too abrupt." The secondary nature of Josh 24:19-24 was, indeed, suggested by Noth 1953, 136–137. Van Seters is correct in arguing against this solution,

4.3 Literary and Redaction Criticism of Joshua 24

Translation	Basic commitment narrative
24:14a And now fear YHWH	וְעַתָּה יְראוּ אֶת־יְהוָה
and serve him in sincerity and in faithfulness.	וְעִבְדוּ אֹתוֹ בְּתָמִים וּבֶאֱמֶת
24:15a If it is bad in your eyes to serve YHWH,	וְאִם רַע בְּעֵינֵיכֶם לַעֲבֹד אֶת־יְהוָה
choose for yourselves today whom you will serve.	בַּחֲרוּ לָכֶם הַיּוֹם אֶת־מִי תַעֲבֹדוּן
24:15b* I and my household will serve YHWH	וְאָנֹכִי וּבֵיתִי נַעֲבֹד אֶת־יְהוָה
24:16 And the people answered and said:	וַיַּעַן הָעָם וַיֹּאמֶר
"Far be it from us that we forsake YHWH	חָלִילָה לָּנוּ מֵעֲזֹב אֶת־יְהוָה
to serve other gods.	לַעֲבֹד אֱלֹהִים אֲחֵרִים
24:18b We will also serve YHWH for he is our God."	גַּם־אֲנַחְנוּ נַעֲבֹד אֶת־יְהוָה כִּי־הוּא אֱלֹהֵינוּ
24:22 Then Joshua said to the people:	וַיֹּאמֶר יְהוֹשֻׁעַ אֶל־הָעָם
"You are witnesses against yourselves	עֵדִים אַתֶּם בָּכֶם
that you have chosen YHWH,	כִּי־אַתֶּם בְּחַרְתֶּם לָכֶם אֶת־יְהוָה
to serve him."[1]	לַעֲבֹד אוֹתוֹ
24:28 And Joshua sent the people away,	וַיְשַׁלַּח יְהוֹשֻׁעַ אֶת־הָעָם
each to their inheritances.[2]	אִישׁ לְנַחֲלָתוֹ

Notes
1 Thus far, literary critics have often also included the answer of the people ("And they said: "We are witnesses!") in the basic narrative. See, for example, Müller 2004, 253. However, as I have shown in section 3.3.2, this answer is missing from the OG, and is probably a late secondary addition. Therefore, it should not be included in the earliest text.
2 While Becker (2006, 159) and Aurelius (2008, 102) include Josh 24:28 in the basic commitment narrative, Müller (2004, 253–254) and Levin (2013, 126) posit that Josh 24:28 is an even earlier verse which belonged to the early transition of Joshua and Judges (Josh 11:23b-24:28-Judg 2:8–9). The latter theory will be discussed below after the basic literary critical solutions of Josh 24 have been made.

Furthermore, the basic commitment narrative consists of text present both in the OG and the MT, which means that documented evidence does not rule out the possibility that such a basic text once existed.[190] As a matter of fact, documented evidence supports the identification of these verses as secondary additions. Many textual variants reflect attempts to either smoothen out traces of earlier redaction or integrate the added verses to the context with more additions. It seems that, in the case of Josh 24, textual variants concentrate in places that have already been edited in earlier times. It seems therefore likely that a conglomeration of textual

---

since 24:22 likely belongs to the earliest basic text of Josh 24. However, the criticism by Van Seters does not apply to the more sophisticated model created after Noth and presented in this section.
190 Except for the variants Shechem (MT) / Shiloh (OG) which, as concluded in the text-critical analysis, probably represents secondary developments in the OG. It is also possible that the original commitment narrative did not read any parts of 24:1–2, and began with parts of 23:2–3 (see the table above), which would mean that the scene was not localized in its earliest form.

variants could serve as an indicator that a text has also been subjected to editing in the prehistory of the text.

Next, while the historical summary in vv. 2–13 has already been argued to be a secondarily added introduction to the commitment narrative, the question remains whether it was added in one or several stages. For example, Müller recognizes several additions to the historical summary. For instance, the Balaam scene in 24:9–10 is seen in his model as a secondary addition.[191] Moreover, several scholars note single glosses to the historical summary. For example, the list of the Amorite kings in 24:11 is often explained as a gloss, since it cannot specify the Lords of Jericho mentioned earlier.[192] Overall, it seems that one should be cautious in trying to identify too rigidly the developmental stages in the historical summary. This is because the text seems to be composed of scattered intertextual references to various parts in the Pentateuch. Such references may together give the impression of a loosely knit whole, and it might be tempting to recognize literary strata based on references to other texts. This impression, however, might already be the result of the work of the first author of the summary. Therefore, there should be several good reasons for separating episodes such as the Balaam tale from the historical summary.

That being said, the documented evidence has already shown that the historical summary has been supplemented with other texts in later phases. Both the OG and MT reveal that intertextual references have been added between verses 4 and 5. While the OG adds material from Deuteronomy, the MT adds material from 1 Sam 12.[193] It is then probable that several sporadic glosses have been made to the historical summary in various phases of its copying history. The list of the Amorite kings in 24:11 might be one such gloss. While such glosses do not relate to any larger redactions, the mention of the fathers by the sea in vv. 6b–7a is the only addition to the historical summary which is likely related to a larger redactional aim.

> **Josh 24:5.** And *YHWH smote* Egypt *with miracles* that he did in their midst and afterwards *he* brought you out **6.** of Egypt.
>
> > And you came to the sea. And the Egyptians pursued after your fathers with chariots and horses to the Sea of Reeds. 7. And *we cried* out to the Lord and he put darkness between *us* and the Egyptians and he brought the sea upon them and covered them.
>
> And your eyes saw what *YHWH did in the land of* Egypt. Then you lived in the wilderness many days.

---

[191] Müller 2004, 252–253.
[192] Thus, for example, Boling & Wright 1982, 536; Sperling 1987, 127; Becker 2006, 157; Müller 2004, 253; Rösel 2011, 369.
[193] See section 3.2.2.

4.3 Literary and Redaction Criticism of Joshua 24 — 215

It can be assumed, as was the case with the commitment narrative, that the earliest form of the narrative did not yet have any references to the fathers. The fathers have been secondarily added to differentiate between the old unfaithful and the new faithful generation. When one reads the events in Josh 24:5–7 without the scene dealing with the fathers at the Sea of Reeds, the narrative merely recalls the phases in the journey of the people, addressed to "you". The assumably added narrative dealing with the fathers at the Sea of Reeds disrupts this flow, since the text changes to referencing "the fathers" instead of "you".[194] The nature of vv. 6b–7a as an added scene is corroborated by the surprising personal form "we", which gives the feeling of a flashback. This formulation is not use elsewhere in Josh 24, in either one of the textual traditions. In addition, the proto-MT editor tried to integrate the scene closer to the historical summary by adding at the beginning of v. 6 וָאוֹצִיא אֶת־אֲבוֹתֵיכֶם "and I took your fathers" which is missing from the earlier OG text.

The addition of 6b–7a is probably the only identifiable secondary addition to the historical summary related to wider redactional aims. Together with the added verses 14a, 15b, and 17–18a, it brings out the differentiation between the generation present at Shechem and the generation of the fathers to Josh 24. The sharpening of this division is a late motif, as seen in the documented editing of the circumcision scene in Josh 5.[195] That the additions of the fathers take place both in the commitment scene and the historical summary corroborates their lateness: they were made in a phase when the text of Josh 24 already constituted of both the historical summary and the commitment scene. It is probably not possible to say whether all the additions pertaining to the fathers were made by the same redactor or by subsequent editors. The latter is more probable, since in Josh 5:4–6 the same phenomenon is visible in late documented evidence.

Having discerned the late material from the basic commitment narrative, the question of the beginning and the end of Josh 24 remains open. The ending verse 24:28 belongs, according to some scholars, to an earlier ending of a conquest account or the first transition between Joshua and Judges, which was followed by the earlier death account of Joshua in either Josh 24:29–30 or Judg 2:8–9.[196] This question will be revisited in the upcoming sections. The evaluation of the beginning of Josh 24, on the other hand, is dependent partly on how one understands its relationship with Josh 23. One possibility is that the gathering

---

[194] Aurelius 2008, 108. The Sea of Reeds episode is also identified as an addition by Fritz 1994, 238 and Carr 2011, 135.
[195] See section 3.4.2.
[196] See, for example, Müller 2004, 253–254 and Levin 2013, 126. See also Knauf 2008, 18–20 who assumes that Josh 24:29 ended the original Exodus-Conquest account.

in 24:1*.2a is earlier, and the basic commitment narrative did not begin with the gathering in Josh 23:1–2.[197] The gathering in 24:1–2 was later aligned with Josh 8:33 with the secondary addition of the list of leaders (OG), and secondarily aligned by modifying the list closer to that in Josh 23:2 (MT). Both alignments with other texts in Joshua are late. Conversely – and a bit more likely – Josh 23:1, referring to the successful conquest of the land and the old age of Joshua, would be a good candidate for the beginning of the earliest ending scene of a conquest narrative. This proposition relates to larger compositional issues, since 23:1b can be understood as a *Wiederaufnahme* of 13:1a, with which one of the latest sections in the book (Josh 13–22) was added.[198] Moreover, it is hard to regard the introduction in Josh 24:1 as original, since it does not give any apparent narrative reason for a gathering and is only loosely connected with the narrative of the book of Joshua. Therefore, it seems more probable that some form of Josh 23:1–3 constituted the original introduction to the basic narrative of the commitment scene in Josh 24.[199] In any case, the question of the beginning of the original commitment narrative is related to the wider compositional issues, and a more detailed account would require a larger analysis of the texts. At this point, it suffices to conclude that the basic commitment narrative originally began with a gathering of the people, and the doubling of this gathering (Josh 23:2–3 and Josh 24:1–2) is probably a result of later redactional activity that created two separate endings with separate functions.

Lastly, I am not aware of any scholar that has noted that SamJosh corresponds in remarkably many details with the model of the basic narrative proposed in literary-critical research. A more detailed textual analysis of SamJosh 22, the chapter parallel to Josh 24, was carried out in section 3.6. In this context, it is enough to point out four similarities between SamJosh and the literary-critical model posited in this section. First, the late historical summary in Josh 24:2–13 is missing almost in its entirety from SamJosh 22. Only Josh 24:13, referring to Deut 6:10–13, is present before the commitment narrative. In other words, as is the case with the postulated earliest basic text of Josh 24, SamJosh lacks all the references to the early stages of the story of Israel, and therefore does not contain a wider Hexateuchal perspective. Second, as concluded before, it is possible that the earliest commitment scene began with a single introduction retained in Josh 23:1–3. This is also the case in SamJosh, which begins with an introductory formula combining elements of Josh 23:1–2a and Josh 24:1. Both the introduction of the

---

197 As reconstructed by Becker 2006, 157; Müller 2004, 252–253; Levin 2013, 126.
198 Kratz 2005, 193 Levin 2013, 128.
199 As suggested by Kratz 2005, 199.

assumed basic commitment narrative and the introduction of SamJosh contain a reference to the old age of Joshua. After a single introductory formula, the text of SamJosh continues to Josh 24:13–14, as is also the case with the assumed basic narrative (although excluding 24:13). Third, many passages considered late in the commitment narrative in Josh 24:14ff. are missing from SamJosh. This includes the short historical summary (24:17–18), the claim that the Israelites cannot serve YHWH (24:19–21), and the repetitive exhortation and answer before the covenant making (24:23–24). Fourth, it is interesting that the "movable unit" in MT Josh 24:31 (OG 24:29), emphasizing the fidelity of the Israelites after the death of Joshua, is missing from SamJosh.

How should one explain these similarities? There are two possibilities. The first explanation attributes the differences to a late – ancient or medieval – Samaritan writer. Given the selective nature of the retelling of the biblical book of Joshua in SamJosh, it is possible that a Samaritan writer would have wanted to harmonize the two farewell speeches into one. It would have then been only natural that the Samaritan writer would not choose to retain Josh 23, but instead Josh 24, since it takes places at Shechem. The assumed late writer would have worked in quite the same manner as a modern literary critic, removing repetitions and abruptive passages from a redacted text. This explanation, however, is not without problems. First, there are no other texts in which an ancient writer would have matched the conclusions of a modern literary critic in so many instances. Therefore, one would have to assume an improbable coincidence. Second, much of the material that the editor would have removed is not likely to have been removed by a Samaritan author, or any other late author for that matter. For example, the historical summary in Josh 24:2–12 does not contain any anti-Samaritan or theologically polemic themes.[200] In addition, an author wishing to create a unified farewell

---

[200] Macdonald (1969, 5–6) also cautions against too easily assuming ideological omissions in *Sepher Hayamim*, since in many passages the text contains material from the biblical text that explicitly condemns the Northern rulers and the Samaritans. One would assume that a Samaritan editor attuned to ideological omissions would have deleted these passages. However, according to Macdonald (1969, 14–15) there is probably also deliberate altering of the source text, and the texts should always be evaluated on a case-by-case basis. In the case of the farewell speech, Macdonald (1969, 23) argues that the elements missing are secondarily omitted for various reasons. The reasons given by Macdonald are not satisfactory, however. For instance, Macdonald notes that the short historical summary in Josh 24:17–18a was omitted since it is "of secondary importance." No other arguments are presented. Furthermore, Macdonald argues that some parts were removed since they accuse the Israelites of serving other gods. If this was true, it would be peculiar that the editor preserved in several instances the possibility that the Israelites might choose to serve foreign gods (e.g. SamJosh 22:11). Furthermore, as a slight contradiction to his argument, Macdonald (1969, 24) assumes that in the Judges part of *Sepher Hayamim* the editor did not omit

speech would not have had any reasons to remove the historical summary, which is presented as an integral part of the speech in Josh 24. Third, as is also the case with the Samaritan Pentateuch, the nature of the Samaritan Joshua text seems to be generally expansionistic. Since the assumed secondary omissions do not seem to be related to any systematic motivations, the expansionistic nature of the text speaks against the argument for omissions.[201]

The second explanation is that SamJosh 22 retains echoes of an old tradition of the farewell speech of Joshua that has yet not been subjected to the latest stages of the expansive editing visible in MT and OG Josh 24. One would then have to assume that the Samaritans would have possessed a version of the book of Joshua in the late Second Temple period.[202] According to this model, the textual histories of SamJosh 22 and MT/OG Josh 24 would have been separated at an early phase of the literary growth of the farewell speech. Both have independently gone through expansive editing. While OG/MT Josh 24 exhibits editing in relation to the Pentateuch and other historical books, SamJosh 22 has been expanded with large scale Samaritan additions. If this explanation is correct, the farewell speech of Joshua known from Samaritan sources is based on an early version of Joshua 23–24. The biggest problem for accepting this explanation is the fact that the manuscript material containing the farewell speech of Joshua is only known from modern times.[203] However, since the farewell speech exists in several MSS and has notable parallels with the LXX and Josephus, one should not abandon the possibility that the text might ultimately go back to an ancient version. After all, the best manuscript of the MT has also preserved a good text for well over a thousand years.

---

the Deuteronomistic parts, noting that the Israelites "did evil in the sight of the Lord" but that they might have possessed a tradition of Judges that did not yet contain these remarks.

201 In a similar vein, one could explain the omissions by returning to the explanation that SamJosh is a late forgery that the Samaritans made *ad hoc* for curious western scholars. However, in this case one would have to assume that the forgery utilized not only the MT but also the LXX, Josephus, and achieved many of the same results as later 20th century literary critics. In addition, SamJosh is not the only manuscript retaining the unified farewell speech corresponding to the assumed basic commitment narrative. The farewell speech of Joshua in the Samaritan Chronicles or *Sepher Hayamim* and all its MSS corresponds closely to the farewell speech in SamJosh 22 with only minor textual variants.

202 This is likely, since Joshua is the greatest hero of the Samaritans after Moses. See Macdonald 1969, 3: "…it is not at all unlikely that the Sams., before Roman times, had a book – uncanonical but valued – which chronicled the deeds of Joshua…"

203 However, according to Macdonald (1969, 69–70) the manuscript is clearly a copy of a much earlier copy. Cohen (1981, 187) also notes appropriately, considering *Sepher Hayamim*: "The fact that we acknowledge – that our copy was made in 1908, in no way forces us to the conclusion that it is a 'modern Chronicle' with no historical or literary value as an independent source."

In the light of the preceding discussion, it is possible that SamJosh 22 is based on a version of Josh 24 which had not yet been subjected to all the additions present in the MT/OG.[204] In addition, literary criticism of Josh 24 contributes to the scholarly understanding of the nature of SamJosh. The observations made here suggest that this text should probably be researched more carefully in future research. A thorough textual analysis of the possible editorial tendencies in SamJosh would either substantiate or undermine the hypothesis put forth here.[205]

To sum up, a model of literary growth in Josh 24 which began from a basic commitment narrative that was expanded in several stages is compelling. This model, extending its roots back to the research of Noth, convincingly explains both the documented evidence and the internal features of the text. Two major editorial intrusions have been the addition of the historical summary (Josh 24:2–13), which led to additions in the commitment scene, and the addition of the fathers in several instances. Therefore, one can probably distinguish at least three phases in the literary prehistory of Josh 24. Nevertheless, many glosses and isolated editorial intrusions may have left little traces in the text. Therefore, the literary history of Josh 24 is likely more complicated than we can reconstruct.

Are these literary layers in Josh 24 connected with specific redactions? The first basic text can be connected with the so-called nomistic Deuteronomistic editing (DtrN), but one has to be flexible in the understanding of this "redaction". This will be discussed further in section 4.3.4.[206] The addition of the historical summary creates wide connections with the Pentateuch, and might be

---

[204] If not, SamJosh has secondarily – through omissions – created a text which does not have all the secondary additions discerned in literary criticism. In this case, thus, it also lends support to the literary-critical model presented in this section.

[205] The possible connections of SamJosh with the various Qumran Joshua texts also remain unexamined. Feldman 2013, 195–197 has noted that some striking parallels between 4Q378 and 4Q379 and Samaritan Joshua traditions.

[206] This opens up once again the relationship of Josh 23 with Josh 24, since many scholars attribute Josh 23 to DtrN (Schmid 1999, 216–217). According to Latvus (1998, 31–36), however, Josh 23 also has a complicated history of subsequent editing. In his model, the basic text layer of Josh 23 is dependent upon ideas in DtrH but is earlier than the DtrN-texts, which have been added secondarily to Josh 23. If this is true, the editorial histories of Josh 23 and Josh 24 are intertwined in a complex way. It is possible that the nomistic Deuteronomistic editors first brought out their ideas about the end of the book of Joshua by creating the basic text of Josh 24. This would have led to secondary nomistic additions in Josh 23. However, the process may also have proceeded the other way around. In any case, both texts have probably been subsequently edited in several stages that cannot be uncovered due to the lack of documented evidence. The key point is this: the relationship of Josh 23 and Josh 24 cannot be answered in a simplistic manner. They both have complex textual histories and have been subsequently edited by nomistically motivated

connected to the so-called Hexateuchal redaction, which is assumed to have the aim of integrating the book of Joshua into the Pentateuch.[207] However, this is not necessary, since the addition of the historical summary might simply be connected with a wider scribal motivation of creating larger presentations of the salvation history of Israel, as visible in other similar historical summaries.[208] This, in turn, might be related to the beginning canonization process of some texts. In late Second Temple Judaism, some texts (e.g. the Pentateuch and most notably Deuteronomy) would have achieved a proto-canonical status, and their content would have affected editing in other texts and the creation of new literary compositions. Therefore, I am not sure whether the evidence from Josh 24 is enough for arguing for a unified Hexateuchal redaction. All the other secondary additions in Josh 24 are also related to these two motivations. Since late documented evidence reveals similar editing, I would hesitate in connecting the additions further with any specific redactions. One might simply speak of a nomistically motivated *Fortschreibung* which took place in several stages. It should be kept in mind that the literary development likely was more complex than the evidence allows us to reconstruct. This is evident when one compares, for example, the intricacies of the various models that propose different amounts of later additions to the basic commitment narrative. It seems to me that a rigorous literary division resembling Swiss clockwork cannot be done, but it is enough to sketch the major outlines of the literary developments in Josh 24.

4.3.4 Deuteronomistic Redactions

The second significant compositional trend in modern theories on Josh 24 emerges from considering the book of Joshua within the framework of Deuteronomistic redactions. The work of Noth laid the foundation for this paradigm. Before Noth, Deuteronomistic editing was recognized in the later phases of the development of the composition. After Noth, the first author of the book of Joshua has often been identified as the Deuteronomist.[209] When one looks at the reception of his model, the first commentary on Joshua by Noth can undoubtedly be called

---

editors. It is likely that both texts are related to DtrN, but how consistently one understands the editing connected with DtrN is another question, which is discussed below in section 4.3.4.

207 See, for example, Knauf 2008, 20–21.

208 See section 4.2.7.

209 Dozeman 2015, 16. Also, the time period for interpreting the book of Joshua was changed: while earlier scholarship often attributed the monarchy as the most crucial part for interpreting the book, after Noth the exile became the key for the composition.

4.3 Literary and Redaction Criticism of Joshua 24

"the most influential book on the book of Joshua in the twentieth century."[210] As Dozeman has noted, most of the major commentaries on the book of Joshua in the late twentieth century "build on the hypothesis of Noth, while offering only minor variations on the history of composition."[211] The belief that major parts of Joshua derived from various Deuteronomistic redactors has been maintained in several investigations in the 21st century.[212]

However, the place of Josh 24 in the assumed Deuteronomistic history has been interpreted in diverse ways. While it is usually argued that the basic text of Josh 24 should not be attributed to the original Deuteronomist,[213] interpretations of the chapter and the literary connections of its various parts differ. Already for Noth, the interpretation of Josh 24 and the relationship of Josh 23 with Josh 24 was problematic, and he modified and altered his view several times. In the earliest treatment of Josh 24 in *Das System der Zwölf Stämme Israels*, Noth accepted the premise that the core of Josh 24 should be attributed to E, but that it was also supplemented with a Yahwistic source. In addition, there was a number of later Deuteronomistic glosses in the chapter.[214] These source distinctions were often based on conclusions drawn on the basis of single phrases, many of whose text-critically problematic nature I have demonstrated in my analysis.[215] In his later work in *Das Buch Josua*, Noth still maintained that there was a pre-Deuteronomistic core to Josh 24, but he put more emphasis on the Deuteronomistic redaction.[216] In the second edition of the commentary in 1958, he emphasized the Deuteronomistic nature of Josh 24 even further by attributing more textual details to this redactor.[217] In terms of the relationship of Josh 23 and 24, there were considerable changes in Noth's view. In the first commentary (1938), Josh 1–12 and Josh 24 were interpreted as evidence for Joshua preserving a pre-Deuteronomistic tradition of the conquest. Noth argued that Josh 24 served as a model upon which the Deuteronomist created Josh 23.[218] In 1943,

---

210 Dozeman 2015, 11. Also Noort 1998, 92.
211 Dozeman 2015, 18. The commentaries mentioned by Dozeman are Soggin 1972, Boling & Wright 1982, Butler 1983, and Fritz 1994.
212 For example, Nentel 2000, 66–96; Pressler 2002, 1–8; Müller 2004; Aurelius 2008; Levin 2013.
213 See, for example, Nelson 1981a, 94 and Nihan 2013, 263.
214 Noth 1930, 133–139.
215 For example, Noth (1930, 139) maintained that the list of leaders in Josh 24:1 is a gloss taken from the list of leaders in the Deuteronomistic verse Josh 23:2. Our analysis has shown that the MT reading in Josh 24:1 is a later harmonization towards Josh 23:2. In the earlier reading, there was a connection with Josh 8:33.
216 Noth 1938, 105–140.
217 Noth 1953, 140.
218 Noth 1938, xiii, 101.

Noth explicitly renounced this position. According to him, a literary dependence between these chapters could not be proven, since their textual connections are of such a general nature. Instead of assuming that Josh 24 was part of the pre-Deuteronomistic conquest narrative, he assumed that it derived from an independent tradition which was only later redacted in a Deuteronomistic style, and added at the end of the book of Joshua.[219] In the second edition of his commentary (1953), he reverted back to the earlier position that Josh 24 served as a model for Josh 23 but maintained – in line with his 1943 argument – that Josh 24 originally came from an independent tradition which was added to the book of Joshua, and already at this point had its Deuteronomistic shape.[220]

The ambiguity in the work of Noth on how to correctly interpret Josh 23–24 as part of an assumed Deuteronomistic history has not been resolved within the paradigm of a Deuteronomistic history, and various contradictory models still prevail.[221] While some argue that some parts of Josh 24 date back to the original Deuteronomist,[222] many deny this possibility altogether.[223] At the same time, the whole theory of a thoroughgoing initial Deuteronomistic history (DtrH) spanning from Deut to Kings has come under severe criticism. Several analyses of the textual evidence have illustrated that it is increasingly hard to assume a single author-editor and original literary unity behind Deut–Kings.[224] Several other explanations have emerged instead. It has been argued that the core of the first mid sixth-century BCE Deuteronomistic history is found only in some of the pro-monarchic and temple-related texts in 2 Kings. The wider profile and literary unity of Deut-Kings is then attributed to later authors. Among these are the nomistically oriented editors who may have also been responsible for connecting the separate texts and compositions together. Moreover, the work of the nomists (or DtrN) would not have constituted a single well-defined redaction, but is instead characterized by flexible and gradual editorial intrusions taking place in an undefined amount of stages.[225] Many have argued that the various literary connections between Dtr–Kings have emerged only in later times, and that the earlier phases of literary development were more fragmentary than assumed by the traditional model of DtrH. For example, Lohfink has proposed that the core of

---

[219] Noth 1943, 9. A view which Nelson (1981a, 94–95) characterized as a consensus in 1981.
[220] Noth 1953, 139.
[221] See, for example, Kratz 2005, 206–207.
[222] For example, Fritz 1994, 235–249 and Nentel 2000, 66–96.
[223] For example, O'Brien 1990, 77–81 and Nihan 2013, 263.
[224] See, for example, Edenburg & Pakkala 2013, 1–2 and Dozeman 2015, 18–22.
[225] Pakkala 2008, 257–266. See also, for example, Kratz 2005, 216–221, 326 and Edenburg & Pakkala 2013, 9.

4.3 Literary and Redaction Criticism of Joshua 24 — 223

the Deuteronomistic history lies in an early narrative of the conquest (DtrL) found in Deut 1–Josh 22, from the time of Josiah. In addition, there was a Josianic edition of Kings, but this separate composition became connected only in later times.[226] Thus, maintaining an early continuous Deuteronomistic history seems to be more and more problematic.

The most obvious issue related to the traditional understanding of DtrH is at the end of Joshua. Were Joshua and Judges originally bound together as part of a larger presentation of the history of Israel? In recent scholarship, most scholars who adhere to a traditional view of DtrH only include Josh 24:28 in the work of original Deuteronomist. This dismissal notice was then followed by the death and burial account of Joshua in Judg 2:8–9, together with the rise of a new unfaithful generation in Judg 2:10.[227] This created the original link between Joshua and Judges. This question will be dealt separately below in section 4.3.5, when the transition between Joshua and Judges is discussed.

Among those who have attributed Josh 24 to the original Deuteronomist, one could mention Rudolf Smend. The argument put forth by Smend is dependent upon his analysis of Josh 23 and the beginning of Judges. As many others, Smend regards Josh 21:43–45 as the original conclusion of the conquest of the land in DtrH.[228] However, contrary to many earlier scholars, Smend argues extensively that Josh 23 cannot be regarded as belonging to the original DtrH. According to him, textual observations suggest that Josh 23 should rather be attributed to the later nomistic Deuteronomistic editor (DtrN). Especially the emphasis put on law (e.g. 23:6) and the connections with Josh 1:7–9 demonstrate that we are more likely dealing with a later nomistic editor than the original Deuteronomist. Moreover, Josh 13:1–6 contains a later view of the conquest and is connected with Josh 23 through the notion that Joshua had become old (Josh 13:1a, Josh 23:1b). Since Josh 23 is late, and Josh 23 and 24 contain many similarities, Smend deduces that Josh 24 had to belong to DtrH and serve as a model for DtrN for the writing of Josh 23.[229] After the scene at Shiloh, the original DtrH continued from Josh 24:31 to Judg 2:10. Smend does not give any detailed textual arguments on Josh 24, and it seems that his views on broader redactional trajectories led to the appraisal of Josh 24 as belonging to DtrH. Therefore, his view on Josh 24 does not accord with the textual evidence. Nevertheless, following the valid argument that Josh 23 should be attributed to DtrN, it seems that Josh 24 might also belong to nomistically inspired

---

[226] Lohfink 1991, 125–42
[227] See section 4.3.5.
[228] Also, Mayes 1983, 55 and O'Brien 1990, 74. Noth (1981, 40) did not attribute this passage to DtrH.
[229] For more detailed arguments see Smend 1971, 497–504.

"Deuteronomistic" redaction. Smend operated with a more rigid understanding of the DtrN than is currently accepted in the literature.

A more flexible understanding of nomistic editing offers the possibility to extend DtrN to Josh 24 as well. While several scholars have discerned well-defined phases of Deuteronomistic nomistic editing (DtrN[1], DtrN[2], DtrB), Pakkala has argued that the differences are so small that it is hard to discern between the editors. Rather, DtrN or the designation "nomistic" should be understood as a wider umbrella term for various Second Temple editorial groups, or one group that was later imitated. The nomistic perspectives are so widely distributed in the current textual forms of the historical books that one might speak of a "very dynamic and creative movement". Typical themes of nomistic thinking are seeing the king in a negative light, ignoring or undermining the temple, exclusive devotion to YHWH, law as the center of Israel's religion, Moses as the symbolic mediator between YHWH and Israel, and emphasis on the tablets of law.[230]

In fact, all of the above discerned phases in the literary growth of Josh 24 can be somehow connected with nomistically inspired redaction. Already the basic commitment scene in Josh 24 contains two key features of the nomistically motivated editors. First, it is born out of the idea that Israel should serve YHWH exclusively. Second, as illustrated in the analysis of textual connection, the idea behind the basic commitment scene is dependent upon texts (e.g. Judg 9, 1 Kgs 12) that attach negative attitudes towards monarchy. Choosing YHWH as the divine king is meant to undermine the choosing of human kings. This point has been most profoundly stressed by Levin, who regards the basic text of Josh 24 as belonging to the second phase of Deuteronomistic editing, which added an anti-monarchic layer to several texts. This criticism of monarchy was related to the consolidation of Persian power in Palestine, which transformed the hopes for a Judean king to theology concerning the kingship of YHWH.[231]

Some of the later additions discerned in the literary and textual analysis of Josh 24 are also nomistic in nature. The additions pertaining to the Israelites serving other gods and the strong plea to abandon them (24:14b, 15*, 19–21, 23–24) only strengthens the exclusivity of serving YHWH related to nomistic ideology. The making of a covenant and references to the book of the law (24:25–27)

---

[230] Veijola 1977, 119–122 and Pakkala 2008, 262–266.
[231] Levin 1985, 114–119. Also, Schmid (1999, 212) and Müller (2004, 215) connect Josh 24 with negative attitudes towards monarchy. Referring to the work of Joachim J. Krause, Cynthia Edenburgh and Konrad Scmid in the June 2017 issue of *Hebrew Bible and Ancient Israel*, Thomas Römer (2017, 203–216) considers the dating of Josh 24 to the Persian period a growing consensus. See Schmid 2017, 148–160 for a helpful analysis of the evidence pointing to an early Second Temple Period date.

also serve nomistic ideas. Moreover, several secondary additions and corrections in the MT – as revealed through a comparison with the earlier text of the OG – are nomistically motivated in nature as was concluded in section 3.5. Among these, one should highlight the addition of the role of Moses in the proto-MT editing of Josh 24.

Since the influence of nomistic editing in Josh 24 extends from its beginnings to the latest proto-MT editing, it seems that a flexible view of DtrN or nomistic editing best explains the evolution of the text. Several editors or groups of editors in the Second Temple period worked with this key text to make it better reflect and accord with nomistic ideals. There are no signs of characteristics conventionally attributed to the DtrH in Josh 24.[232] Josh 24 is rather a gradually growing and evolving product of the Second Temple nomistic scribal circles. Therefore, the framework of a Deuteronomistic history helps in understanding Josh 24 only if it is understood in the flexible way that many scholars understand it in recent scholarship. Josh 24 is an example of a text that has been written and successively edited to create connections with other texts and crystallize nomistic thinking.

4.3.5 The Transition from Joshua to Judges

The Possibilities
In studying the relationship of various books in the Hebrew Bible, substantial attention has been focused on the seams of different books. The seam between the books of Joshua and Judges is a particularly debated topic, which stems from the ambiguous textual parallels between the first two chapters of Judges and the ending of the book of Joshua. The main questions are: were the books of Joshua and Judges, in a much shorter and earlier literary form, originally joined, as is assumed in the traditional model of DtrH? Conversely, have they always been separate entities, and only secondarily been brought closer to one another?

The main solutions to the problem in the scholarly literature have been: (1) there used to be an original connection between Joshua and Judges, but the compositions were separated at some point and continued developing on their own, (2) most of the book of Judges was inserted between Joshua and Samuel at a late stage, and only after this insertion were the books brought closer one another, (3) most of the book of Joshua was inserted between Deuteronomium and Judges at a late stage, and only after this insertion were the books brought closer one another, and (4) the books of Joshua and Judges have

---

232 Excluding possibly 24:28 which is dealt with below.

separate literary histories, and have been harmonized closer one another in the latest stages of their literary and textual growth. These solutions will next be evaluated in the light of the documented evidence. Since documented evidence related to the ending of Joshua sets limits for what can be argued in literary and redaction criticism, it is assumed that it may help in evaluating what the possible solutions are.[233]

The question is also related to the issue of physical copies of compositions in scrolls. If scholars argue for an original connection between books, they must assume that they were originally written in some form on one scroll. Moreover, if we assume that some compositions were originally read in sequence, they would have been written on different scrolls but organized, read, and stored in a specific order. We do not possess physical evidence of any of these practices in relation to the historical books.[234] Therefore, the matter remains speculative but needs to be considered.

Original Book Connection

As noted before, redaction-critical models assuming an early DtrH ranging from Deut to 2 Kgs assume that the books of Joshua and Judges have only secondarily been separated, and that this separation has led into substantial editorial expansions to both books. This view goes back to the work of Noth, who assumed that the original book connection ran from Josh 23 to Judg 2:6–9. The original purpose of Judg 2:6–9 was to serve as a conclusion to the story of the conquest and the occupation of the land. After the books were separated, the death and burial account of Joshua was repeated at the end of Josh 24.[235]

Several scholars have advocated this basic view, with some variation, between the verses attributed to the original book connection.[236] The most recent version of this view has been presented by Levin, who argues that it presents the most plausible explanation for the double account of Joshua's

---

[233] At several points in this section, I will refer to the findings in section 3.4.
[234] As mentioned in section 2.4, the Qumran evidence of Joshua is scarce. The evidence pertaining to Judges is even scarcer. Only small parts of Judges have been preserved in 4QJudg^a, 4QJudg^b, and 1QJudg. See Ulrich 2010, 254–258. It might be notable that the books of Joshua and Judges in Qumran have been preserved in different scrolls that have apparently been written by different scribes. So, in the earliest extant textual evidence, these compositions were treated as different entities.
[235] Noth 1943, 8–9.
[236] The most common connection – Josh 24:28–Judg 2:7–10 – is articulated by, for example, Latvus 1998, 36; Müller 2004, 251–254 and Rake 2006, 127. An alternative view is argued by O'Brien 1990, 81: Josh 24:29–31–Judg 2:10.

death.²³⁷ Building partially on the textual analysis of Auld,²³⁸ Levin argues that the original report of Joshua's death is to be found in Judg 2:8–9. In the original Deuteronomistic account, this report of the death of Joshua proceeded after the land had rested from the war (Josh 11:23b), and Joshua had sent every man back to their inheritance (Josh 24:28). The next stage in the textual growth of a combined Joshua–Judges was when the story of the angel of YHWH (Judg 2:1–5) was added between the story of conquest and the death account of Joshua. The addition was enveloped with a resumptive repetition when Judg 2:6 was repeated from Josh 24:28. Several minor additions were made to the book of Joshua while Joshua and Judges were still a single composition. Most notably, Josh 24 was added in its earliest short form.²³⁹

A decisive moment in the literary development took place when the single composition Joshua-Judges was separated into two different books. After the separation, several editorial intrusions took place which, according to Levin, indicates that the separation took place relatively early on. The death and burial account of Joshua was repeated in Josh 24:29–31 to give a conclusion to the newly separated book of Joshua. The earliest elements of Judg 1 were added. The new beginning of Judg in chapter 1 (וַיְהִי אַחֲרֵי מוֹת יְהוֹשֻׁעַ "And it happened after the death of Joshua") is an important detail in this argument, since it parallels with the beginning of the book of Joshua (וַיְהִי אַחֲרֵי מוֹת מֹשֶׁה "And it happened after the death of Moses"). Quantitatively, the most significant editorial activity after the separation of the books relates to the book of Joshua. The whole distribution of the land to the different tribes of Israel in Josh 13:1–21:42 and chapter 22 was interpolated. This material was better fitted into the context by repeating the beginning of the account (Josh 13:1) in Josh 23:1. In this model, it is assumed that most of the parallels of Judg 1 with Josh 13–22 can only be explained when Judg 1 is regarded as the source text for those parts in Joshua.²⁴⁰

This line of development is, according to Levin, part of a literary and redactional phenomenon in which the separation of books results in considerable editorial activities in the new, now separate, compositions. "The expansion as a whole comprises 303 Masoretic verses, exactly the same length as the first twelve chapters of the book. This means that, apart from the last two chapters, half of today's book came into being after the separation. Once again we see that it was

---

237 Levin 2013, 125.
238 See Auld 1975.
239 Levin 2013, 125–128.
240 Levin 2013, 126–128. Here Levin builds on the study of Rake (2006), although he also differs with the study on several details. See also the review of Rake's work by Levin (2007).

the separation into independent books that provided the precondition for the later growth of the text."[241]

The theories postulating an original book connection between Joshua and Judges go well beyond the documented evidence preserved in variant textual witnesses. To argue for such a model, one has to make several literary-critical assumptions about the complex relationship of various verses in Josh 23–Judg 2. Therefore, documented evidence cannot settle the question of an original book seam. The textual analysis of the death and burial accounts of Joshua, however, does help in critically evaluating the strengths and weaknesses of this model.[242] In general, it shows that these models do not adequately take documented evidence into account, and should therefore be modified in order to better account for the text-critical evidence. This is evident in at least two textual details.

First, my analysis of documented evidence revealed that OG Josh 24:29–31 likely preserves the earliest form of the death and burial account of Joshua. This account has been secondarily modified in MT Josh 24:29–31 by reversing the sequence of verses and omitting the mention of the burial of the flint knives. Moreover, while Judg 2:7–9 preserves the earlier sequence of events taken from OG Josh 24:29–31, its nature as a later selective adaptation can be seen in several secondary additions and features. Therefore, MT Judg 2:7–9 as such cannot be held as the earliest account of Joshua's death and burial, which would have then served as an ending to the Deuteronomist's conquest and occupation story. Since, according to my analysis of the text-critical evidence, the earlier death and burial account is to be found in OG Josh 24:29–31, an earlier and original book connection between Joshua and Judges would have to be modified to take this evidence fully into account.[243]

Second, a comparison of the different endings between OG Josh 24 and MT Josh 24 revealed complicated traces of editing already present in the documented history of the ending of Josh 24. The Hebrew *Vorlage* of OG Josh 24 preserves material (vv. 31a, 33a) that has been lost in the rewriting of the ending in MT Josh 24. However, there is also a secondary addition (v. 33b) that brings the Hebrew *Vorlage* closer to the book of Judges. To integrate this multifaceted editing at the end of Josh 24 with a model of an early book connection between Joshua and Judges, one would have to assume several phases in the early literary development. While the model of a DtrH book connection assumes at least four stages of editing, documented evidence reveals three independent phases of editing.

---

[241] Levin 2013, 128.
[242] For a detailed textual analysis, refer to section 3.4.
[243] One possibility for preserving the model could be building on the idea of O'Brien (1990, 81) that the original book connection ran from Josh 24:29–31 to Judg 2:10.

Moreover, the model of a DtrH assumes that the books were once connected and secondarily separated, but documented evidence reveals that the books were brought closer one another. Therefore, one should ask what the explanatory power of such a complicated model would be. In the light of the limited amount of evidence, is it really credible to reconstruct a model in which the book seam of Joshua and Judges has been exposed to seven phases of literary development that have both moved the compositions further apart and brought them closer one another? A simpler explanation would be that the books have a separate literary history, and have only secondarily been brought closer to one another at the seam. In this case, all the evidence could be explained under one developmental trend.

Nevertheless, one key observation of this theory gains support from documented evidence which revealed that the dismissal in Judg 2:6 is secondary in relation to Josh 24:28. This is also assumed in the model as articulated by Levin. It is probable then, as Levin argued, that the secondary addition of the mention of the angel of YHWH in Judg 2:1–5 was the reason that the dismissal notice was repeated in Judg 2:6. This argument could be taken even further by claiming that all the elements in Judg 1–2:5 have been secondarily added by means of a resumptive repetition. In other words, that the death and burial of Joshua is repeated in Judg 2:6–9 affirms that resumptive repetition was used as an editorial technique to add even large sections of text at the beginning of a composition.

Finally, more attention should be paid to the uncertain evidential value of the repetition preserved in Josh 24:28–31 and Judg 2:6–9. It seems that this doubling does not unambiguously solve the transition from Joshua to Judges. An important perspective from documented evidence is that this passage seems to be extremely flexible in its function. It serves well as a conclusion for Josh 24, but with some modifications equally well as a transition in the story of Judg 2. The passage still functions either as a conclusion or a transition even if the order of the verses is altered. Consequently, it is equally possible that some form of the death and burial account of Joshua originally served as a transition in DtrH, just as it may have originally served as a conclusion for an early conquest account.[244] This passage is a "flexible and movable unit" in the textual witnesses, and it might be impossible to attribute such units to a single better or more original narrative context.[245] Therefore, the model of an original connection from Joshua to Judges as part of the original DtrH does not gain unequivocal support from this passage. If one wishes to argue for this model, the basis of the argument should probably be in other texts.

---

244 As argued by Knauf, see section 4.3.5.
245 Another, even more flexible unit is Josh 8:30–35. See section 4.2.4.

Secondary Insertion of Judges
The hypothesis that the book of Judges was inserted between Joshua and Samuel-Kings at a late stage (Persian or Hellenistic era) is currently supported by several scholars. The support for this model is so widespread that Knauf labeled it in 2013 "a growing consensus".[246] In some sense, the model of a secondary insertion of Judges into the Former Prophets is a result of scholars looking at these books from a new perspective. Unlike Noth, who interpreted the books from Joshua to Kings looking forwards from Deuteronomy, this model entails looking backwards from Kings.[247] Consequently, Judges is regarded as a kind of a "protokings" which sets the stage for various themes present in Samuel-Kings.

There are several variants of this model entailing elaborate literary and redaction critical assumptions about the prehistory of various books. As was the case in the previous section, all the evidence cannot be considered within the limits of this study. What follows is an analysis of three different versions of this model so far as they pertain to the seam of Joshua and Judges.

In order to argue for the secondarity of Judges, one has to show that Judges is secondarily depended upon material in the surrounding books. This is exactly the way in which Spronk forms his argument.[248] In terms of the seam of Joshua and Judges, Spronk argues that the material in Judg 1–2 is dependent upon various material in Joshua. According to him, the episode of the angel at Bochim (Judg 2:1–5), together with the report of the death and burial of Joshua (Judg 2:6–9), mirrors Josh 24. Like Joshua in Josh 24, the angel reminds the people of the protective actions of YHWH in the history of the Israelites, also referring to the Exodus (Judg 2:1). However, the outcome of the infidelity in Judg 2:2 is contrasted with the answer of the people in Josh 24:24 that they will serve YHWH.[249] The argument by Spronk gains support from the textual analysis, which revealed that Judg 2:6–9 is dependent upon Josh 24:28–31. As Spronk assumed was the case with Judg 2:2, the death report is also appended with Judg 2:10, which adds the infidelity of the people to the picture. It is therefore possible that Judges 2:1–9 was organized by an editor to relate to and contrast with Josh 24. When one adds to this the secondary parallel of Judg 1:1a with Josh 1:1a, it seems likely that the beginning of Judges has been harmonized at a late stage with arrangements found in Joshua. However, this does not support or disapprove the suggestion that the whole book

---

[246] Knauf 2013b, 154. In addition to Knauf, the view is held in some form by, for example, Kratz 2005, 195–198; Guillaume 2004, 260; Spronk 2009, 137–150; Bieberstein 2011, 170; Groß 2011, 177–206.
[247] As noted by Spronk 2009, 140–141.
[248] Spronk 2009, 137–149.
[249] Spronk 2009, 147.

of Judges would have been added at a late stage. From the evidence at the seam presented by Spronk, one can only observe how editors harmonized the beginning of a composition by reference to another composition.[250]

A more sophisticated version of this model has been proposed by Kratz in *The Composition of the Narratve Books of the Old Testament*.[251] According to him, Judges represents a secondary literary bridge that joined together two earlier larger historical accounts. The origins of the Israelites were reported in the Exodus narrative, which is found in the earliest continuing layer of Exod 2–Josh 11/12. The other historical account reported the origins of the kingdoms of Israel and Judah, in the annalistic source of the earliest layer of Samuel-Kings, which for Kratz presents the Deuteronomistic history. It was only the addition of the book of Judges that joined these sources together and created an "Enneateuch" ranging from Exod 2 to 2 Kgs 25.[252] As for the seam of Joshua and Judges, Kratz abandons all of Josh 13–21, Josh 23–24, and Judg 1–2:5 as later material. This also includes the overlapping text in Josh 24:28–31 and Judg 2:6, 7, 10. When the core of Judges was added between Joshua and Samuel, the link between the Exodus narrative and Judges was made from Josh 11:16aα, 23b to Judg 2:8–9, 3:7ff.[253] The translation of this link would have looked like this:

> [11:16aα] So Joshua took all that land [23b] and Joshua gave it for an inheritance to Israel according to their tribal allotments. And the land had rest from war. [Judg 2:8] Joshua son of Nun, the servant of YHWH, died at the age of one hundred ten years. [2:9] So they buried him within the bounds of his inheritance in Timnat-heres, in the hill country of Ehpraim, north of Mount Gaash. [3:7] The Israelites did what was evil in the sight of YHWH...

The seam between Joshua and Judges has later been filled out with various material in at least four stages, creating various kinds of links between the two books. First, the basic text of the farewell discourse in Josh 23–24 was attached to Josh 11–12. Meanwhile Judg 2:7, 10, 11–19 were added to Judg 2. Second, the tribal geography in 13:1–23:1a was added in between. Third, Judg 2:1–5, 6 was added between the basic text of Josh 23–24 and Judg 2:7. Judg 2:7 was also augmented with Judg 2:20–3:6. At the same time, Josh 23:4–16 was added to the basic text of the farewell speech. Fourth, the historical summary in Josh 24:1–13 was added,

---

250 See also the critical remarks against Spronk's model by Wright 2010, 164–165. Spronk's larger argument, of course, relies on much more textual evidence. Therefore, the argument cannot be evaluated further within the limits of this study.
251 Kratz 2005, which is an English translation of the original study Kratz 2000.
252 For a helpful overview of the model see Kratz 2005, 326.
253 Kratz 2005, 197–198.

and the death account was repeated in 29–33. Judg 1 was also added in this latest stage.²⁵⁴

The model proposed by Kratz overlaps in many instances with the observations made in this study. The historical summary in Josh 24 is likely one of the latest elements in the chapter. The reconstruction of the earliest basic text of Josh 23–24 is almost identical to what was considered most probable in the literary-critical analysis above. However, a more detailed analysis of the OG reveals some problems for the model. The death and burial account of Joshua in MT Josh 24 is indeed a late modification, but the version in the OG revealed many signs of being the source of the repeated death and burial account in Judg 2:6–9. In addition, the analysis of the death and burial account should include an appraisal of the burial of the flint knives (OG Josh 24:31a) and the mentioning of Phinehas and the ark (OG Josh 24:33a). Also, the addition of the infidelity of the Israelites (OG Josh 24:33b) should play a role in the analysis of the seam. Kratz does not integrate these into the model, nor does he mention any variants in the OG.²⁵⁵

Furthermore, the same critical remarks apply that were made with respect to the model of an original DtrH connection. Documented evidence illustrates the flexibility of the death and burial account of Joshua. The model by Kratz accentuates this point even further. If Josh 24:23b was secondarily linked to Judg 2:8, we have to assume that the death and burial account of Joshua in Judg 2:8–9 once served as the beginning of the book of Judges. If the same passage can easily function as a beginning, conclusion, or transition, it cannot be used as evidence for any particular theory. It is a piece of the puzzle that can be fitted to support any number of different theories.

Finally, while I cannot evaluate all of the intricacies of the model proffered by Kratz, it serves as an excellent illustration of a conclusion arising already from documented evidence. Namely, the seam between Joshua and Judges has been subjected to remarkably high volumes of editing in many separate phases of its textual and literary history. Kratz overlooked the latest editing preserved in the documented evidence, and did not consider the evidence preserved in the OG. Whether he correctly uncovered all the literary phases is hard to evaluate, since the evaluation of the text-critical evidence can only be carried out to a limited degree of probability. Because of the complexities already related to the documented editing of this seam, it is likely that all the editorial stages simply cannot be uncovered.

---

254 Kratz 2005, 198.
255 Nevertheless, in other studies he discusses the OG variants in some detail. See Kratz 2002, 300, 304–305.

Lastly, also Knauf assumes that Judges is a late addition. However, this suggestion should be seen in a larger context in his model. The model put forth by Knauf assumes that there were seven literary phases in the development of the book of Joshua. He attributes the textual growth of Josh 24 to the latest of these layers. According to Knauf, the book of Joshua began as part of a written Moses-Joshua narrative in about 600 BCE. This Moses-Joshua narrative was built of the basic narratives in Exod 14, Josh 6 and 10. This first written story, the "first draft"[256] of Joshua, can be dated, according to Knauf, to the kingship of Josiah or shortly after that.[257] This story went through a Deuteronomy or Pentateuch-redaction (Exod 2–Josh 11), which in turn saw minor redactional responses from the Priestly circles beginning from the inauguration of the second temple, which, according to Knauf, took place in 515 BCE. At the Priestly phase of editing, we encounter the earliest element present in Josh 24, that is the death notice in MT Josh 24:29.[258] In the second half of the fifth century, when Jerusalem had gained back its authority, the book of Joshua went through a Hexateuchal redaction which combined P- and D-elements. The aim was to produce a Hexateuch spanning from Genesis to the H-additions of Josh 18:1 and 21:43–45.[259] An important moment in creating an independent book was the next redaction, dated to 400 BCE, where most of Josh 1 and 24 were added to the book to create an independent "supplement to the Torah". This phase in the model is called the book redaction.[260] According to Knauf, the book redaction offers the framework for the interpretation of Josh 24. One of the most interesting features in the model of Knauf is the sixth phase in the redaction, which resulted from a late insertion of the book of Judges between Joshua and Samuel. The addition of Judges after Joshua resulted in the addition of Josh 18:2–19:48 and 23, which aim at bringing Joshua closer to Judges. This is the first point in history at which we have, according to Knauf, all the books attributed to a traditional Deuteronomistic history together. The last redaction in the book of Joshua is a late second century BCE anti-Samaritan and pro-Hasmonean polishing, which is visible most notably in the replacement of Shiloh with Shechem in Josh 24:1, 25.[261] For this last "redaction", according to Knauf, there is therefore textual evidence in the OG.

---

[256] Knauf 2010, 131.
[257] The similarities between the names Joshua and Josiah constitute one argument for this dating (Knauf 2008, 16–18). There is, in fact, plenty of evidence to assume that the figure of Joshua in the book of Joshua has been modelled as a forerunner of King Josiah. See, for example, Nelson 1981b.
[258] Knauf 2008, 18–20.
[259] Knauf 2008, 20–21.
[260] Knauf 2008, 21–22.
[261] Knauf 2008, 22.

Knauf interprets Josh 24 as an attempt to reconcile various competing views in the second half of the fifth century. The rhetoric of choosing between the God of the Torah and other gods is a solution to the conflict between various parties: those that returned from the exile, the Benjaminites who stayed in the land, the Idumean and Egyptian Jews, and the Samaritans. According to Knauf, Josh 24 aims at bringing these different factions together under the same Torah. By fusing various traditions, including the forefathers and the Exodus, it wishes to include all the Israelites under the same covenant.[262] In line with his method of not assigning too diligently every single word to various compositional phases in a diachronic model, Knauf does not give a detailed diachronic analysis of Josh 24. Instead, he points to some P-, D-, and H-elements in the chapter and deems some details, for example the mentioning of the forefathers by name, as late additions.[263] Therefore, when approached only in the context of Josh 24, the model of Knauf is quite close to the models that assume a late literary unity in Josh 24.[264]

Many of the critical remarks made earlier also apply to the model by Knauf. In addition, it is interesting how selectively, on the one hand, and with how far-reaching compositional conclusions, on the other hand, Knauf uses the textual evidence preserved in the OG of Josh 24. The earlier setting for the covenant making in the analysis of Knauf was Shiloh, as indicated by the OG of Josh 24.[265] In the diachronic model of Knauf, this is a natural choice for the book redactor, who took it up from the H-redactor's addition in Josh 18:1. Moreover, since at the time of the book redaction there was no Judges after Joshua, it created a continuum with 1 Sam 1, where the sanctuary in Shiloh is a key element.[266] Therefore, the text-critical evaluation of the primacy of Shiloh over Shechem plays a key role in the larger compositional conclusions made by Knauf. It corroborates the hypothesis that Judges is a late addition between Joshua and Samuel. In my text-critical analysis, I have shown that the choice between Shiloh or Shechem as the earlier reading is fraught with problems. When everything is considered, Shechem is the most probable earlier reading, and Shiloh presents a secondary move away from the inclusion of the Samaritans in the covenant. Moreover, it is methodologically untenable to choose one minor variant from the OG and ignore the other more significant variants. Many parts of the verse-by-verse analysis in the commentary of Knauf would have benefited from a closer observation of the

---

[262] Knauf 2008, 192–194.
[263] Knauf 2008, 195–196.
[264] See section 4.3.1. Hence my main criticism of not taking the documented evidence of literary development adequately into account applies to the model of Knauf.
[265] For a detailed discussion of this variant see section 3.2.2.
[266] Knauf 2013a, 120.

4.3 Literary and Redaction Criticism of Joshua 24 — 235

OG.[267] Since the model of Knauf accurately remarks that text-critical evidence reveals editing of the book of Joshua as late as in the second century BCE, a more in-depth text-critical scrutiny would develop his model on the composition of Joshua to a new level.

Secondary Insertion of Joshua

One of the most recent models on the composition of the book of Joshua and the transition from Joshua to Judges was presented by Dozeman in the introduction of the new Yale series commentary (2016).[268] According to Dozeman, the book of Joshua was written as an independent document apart from the other historical books. It is the work of a post-exilic Samarian (not Samaritan[269]) author. Joshua presents a Samarian myth of origins which is critical towards the Judean emphasis on Jerusalem, but still presents a story of conquest pertaining to the whole Israel. The Northern perspective is seen from the narrative structure of the book. It presents a total conquest of the land, which results in the bringing of the ark to its central location at Shechem (Josh 8:30–35). This is where the book also ends in a renewal of the covenant (Josh 24). This Samarian myth of origins was later inserted between the books of Deuteronomy and Judges, resulting in DtrN additions (Josh 1:7–9, 13:1–6, 23) aiming at integrating the book closer with its new literary context.[270]

A central argument in Dozeman's model relates to the five death and burial accounts in Deuteronomy, Joshua, and Judges. When one reads the present sequence of books in the MT, various death accounts create problems in the plot of the book. The death of Moses is first reported in Deut 34:5–9, creating a transition to the time of Joshua. However, the death of Moses is then disturbingly repeated in Josh 1:1a. The problems continue in the transition from Joshua to Judges. The death of Joshua is reported in Josh 24:28–31, immediately repeated in Judg 1:1a, and taken up once again in Judg 2:6–9. According to Dozeman, these problems are resolved if one regards the book of Joshua as a secondary insertion between

---

[267] For example, Knauf comments on the literary connections of the term "house of slavery" in Josh 24:17 without noticing that it is, in fact, together with a large part of the verse a later addition in the MT.
[268] Dozeman 2015.
[269] The model relies on a late Hasmonean dating of the schism between the Jews and Samaritans. Following recent research, Dozeman (2015, 30–31) correctly assumes that in the Persian period the relationship of Judean and Samarians was more complex, and had not yet reached polemical magnitudes. The Samarians were not a sectarian movement, as was the case with the Samaritans.
[270] Dozeman 2015, 28–32.

Deuteronomy and Judges. Without the book of Joshua, the death of Moses in Deut 34:5–9 is read sequentially to the death of Joshua in Judg 2:6–9. Both serve a transitional function in the story: the leader dies (Deut 34:5 / Judg 2:8), his age and burial are reported (Deut 34:5–6 / Judg 2:8–9), and a transition is made to a new generation (Deut 34:9 / Judg 2:10). Therefore, the original link between compositions was not from Joshua to Judges, but from Deuteronomy to Judges. Together, they created a unified narrative in which Moses and the first generation of Israelites left Egypt, Joshua and the second generation began the conquest of the land, and finally the Judges and their generation failed to conquer the land.[271]

The model put forth by Dozeman suffers from the same shortcomings as the models analyzed above. It does not adequately take the evidence from the OG into account. The textual analysis in section 3.4 revealed that the death and burial account of Joshua in Judg 2:6–9 is likely a secondary adaptation from OG Josh 24:28–31. It is true, as Dozeman notes, that while Judg 2:6–9 serves a transitional function in the context of Judges, Josh 24:28–31 serves as a conclusion in the context of Joshua. However, my textual analysis demonstrated that the adaption of the conclusion to serve as a transition might be secondary. On the other hand, the secondary addition of the infidelity of the Israelites in OG Josh 24:33b might be interpreted as lending some support to the model by Dozeman. OG Josh 24:33b clearly serves as a secondary link with the book of Judges. An editor may have wanted to soften the problems of sequence between Joshua and Judges by bringing the ending of Joshua closer to Judges. However, this function of the addition lends an equal amount of support to the hypothesis that Judges was secondarily added after Joshua, or that the seam between these books was subjected to harmonization in late times.

Moreover, the model proposed by Dozeman does not take into account that many or all the death and burial accounts might simply be later additions to existing compositions or beginnings and endings of books. By assuming that most of the material in the beginning of Judges (including both of the death reports of Joshua) are secondarily added, the narrative problems in the sequence from Joshua to Judges are removed. From a wider perspective, it is not likely that the textual history of Joshua can be explained by assuming only two editorial phases: a unified Samarian composition, and some additions made after the insertion of Joshua between Deuteronomy and Judges. Dozeman refers in passing to Rofé, who has isolated some nomistic additions in the proto-MT editing of Joshua and argues that these might be integrated into the latter editorial phase of Joshua.[272]

---

[271] Dozeman 2015, 22–28.
[272] Dozeman 2015, 32.

However, the differences between the MT and the OG are far more pervasive and complex, and they represent only the documented phase of editing. As I have demonstrated in the literary analysis of Josh 24, earlier editing was even more radical. Therefore, it seems that a two-step editorial history for the whole book of Joshua, as assumed in Dozeman's model, is too simplistic.

The most innovative aspect of the model by Dozeman is the suggestion that the book of Joshua was originally a Samarian composition. This suggestion is especially compelling in the light of the possible textual value of the Samaritan Hebrew book of Joshua noted earlier in this study. Nevertheless, this issue cannot be explored further within the confines of this study.

Harmonizing Separate Compositions at their Seam
As I hope to have shown, none of the above-mentioned solutions take the documented evidence adequately into account. The evidence from the OG is either completely ignored or used selectively. However, they all have merits and propose many probable developments. Based on this concise survey and the evidence observed in the textual and literary analysis of this study, I would base my own proposal on the transition from Joshua to Judges on the following observations.

First, there is an editorial phenomenon at the seam of the books of Joshua and Judges which can be observed from the textual evidence. Namely, the ending of Joshua and the beginning of Judges have both been radically edited and expanded in several stages. The latest stages of this editing are visible in the documented evidence (e.g. the addition of OG Josh 24:33b and the secondarity of Judg 2:6–9), and earlier stages can be reconstructed quite reliably (e.g. additions to the basic commitment narrative in Josh 24, the secondarity of the material in Judg 1–2:5).[273]

Second, most of the editing at the seam is motivated by a desire to harmonize the contents between the books. The secondary repetition of Judg 2:6–9 links the beginning of Judges more closely to the ending of Joshua. The late addition of the infidelity of the Israelites in OG Josh 24:33b is a reference to what follows in Judges. Secondary textual developments in the Greek revisions of LXX Josh 24:28–31 and LXX Judg 2:6–9 reveal that these parallel passages have been harmonized towards each other even in late stages of textual transmission.[274]

Third, the editing at the seam of Joshua and Judges is exceedingly complex. Documented evidence revealed that while many things were added,

---

[273] Many scholars conclude that the material in Judg 1–2:5 is late. See, for example, Kratz 2005, 198.
[274] See section 3.4.1.

even substantial portions have been omitted. In addition, a whole verse was transposed, and some element replaced. The complicated and sophisticated model proposed by Kratz hints that the editorial intrusions in the prehistory of the text are also complex. However, while Kratz only assumes elaborate additions, it is also likely that in the earlier editorial history passages were omitted, transposed, and rewritten.

In the light of these three observations, I would argue for the simplest solution. It is likely that the books of Joshua and Judges have originally separate literary histories. They have been harmonized closer one another at their seam by late Second Temple editors, who sought to construct wider narratives of the history of Israel and created links between books. The seam of these books also served as a fruitful place to add short and long passages. Building a more detailed model would entail an analysis of more key texts. It is, however, already clear that much of the secondary material in Joshua and Judges are written so that one has used the other as its source (e.g. Judg 1 in relation to Josh 13–22).[275] This exemplifies the same late harmonizing tendency that is visible in the documented evidence at the seam of the books.

Models arguing for the secondary insertion of Joshua or Judges have moved in the right direction in assuming independent histories and late adjustments between these books. However, they often do not take enough into account that the compositions are products of several subsequent editorial intrusions. On the other hand, models arguing for an original link between Joshua and Judges as part of a DtrH make important observations on the complicated literary history of these texts. However, the passages used as evidence for an original link between these books are flexible, and can be adapted to several differing models. Thus, here we run into an interesting dilemma: while the evidence corroborates that the editorial intrusions were complex, it also illustrates that they were too complex to be reliably uncovered.

The problems related to assuming early links and connections between different compositions are severe. One can always postulate possible original narrative sequences between books by discarding material that does not fit one's model. Many texts, such as the death and burial account of Joshua, are so flexible that they can simply be fitted into any model. We should be increasingly careful that assumptions rising out of the order of compositions in our modern books do not influence our theories. When working with separate scrolls containing various early textual forms of compositions, the ancient readers may well have in practice imagined several possible sequences between the texts. The problems

---

[275] Rake 2006, 34–60.

we perceive when reading the books in the MT in sequence may not always be the same as the problems the ancient readers perceived. In the light of these observations, it is better to assume a fragmentary emergence of separate compositions of Joshua and Judges, rather than impose a rigid order or sequence as a starting point for their development.[276]

That this is the most probable model explaining the seam of Joshua-Judges undermines the traditional model of a Deuteronomistic history, which would have originally spanned from Deuteronomy to Kings. To be sure, the traditional DtrH model relies on several other texts that have not been explored in this study. But if the assumption that there was an original link between Joshua and Judges relies on weak textual evidence, one loses a central part of the DtrH model. The discussion in this section provides more support for a model of Deuteronomistic redactions that supposes that the literary connections between the historical books are products of later Second Temple editing, seeking to create wider literary wholes.[277]

4.4 Literary and Redaction Critical Conclusions

4.4.1 Joshua 24 – A Gradually Evolving Late Nomistic Text

Josh 24 has likely undergone several stages of editing that are not visible in variant textual versions. Its literary history may have been even more complicated than the documented history of editing, which leads me to conclude that many of the editorial intrusions simply can not be reconstructed. This is especially the case with small additions and harmonizations, which may have been made by single scribes in different phases without any wider redactional motivations. In addition, due to omissions and rewriting we may have lost some of the material related to Josh 24.

However, at least four stages in the literary development can be reconstructed with a modest degree of probability. Note that the linear presentation of these stages below does not preclude that the text may have developed in a multilinear fashion in different scribal circles. It is probable that different forms of the text were in simultaneous use in different circles. In addition, these editorial stages should be understood as loosely defined intrusions in the assumed literary

---

[276] If we ever discover fragments of scrolls containing texts that clearly link the ending of Joshua with the beginning of Judges, the situation will need to be assessed anew.
[277] See, for example, Kratz 2005, 326.

growth. It is a rough outline of the possible compositional phases, but the reality has probably been more complicated.

First, the death and burial account of Joshua (OG Josh 24:30–31[278]) may have originally been part of some other literary work than an independent book of Joshua. As has been illustrated, it is a flexible passage which would have functioned well in different contexts. Some have suggested that it may have ended some form of an early conquest narrative.[279] Many questions concerning a postulated early Exodus-Conquest narrative remain open within the limits of this study: which parts of the book of Joshua belonged to this original conquest narrative? What preceded the conquest? What followed the conquest? Regarding the last question, I have demonstrated the problems in assuming that the death of Joshua was followed by the book of Judges in an early DtrH, which would have preserved an original link between these books. My text- and literary-critical observations seem to point in the direction that the books of Joshua and Judges have separate histories, and have only in later times been brought closer one another through several complex editorial intrusions. The secondary adaptation of the death and burial of Joshua in Judg 2:8–9 is one example of this development. Thus, the evidence analyzed in this study gives some support to fragmentary theories of the prehistory of the historical books, rather than an early continuous narrative such as the DtrH. Moreover, the texts analyzed in this study do not permit giving any precise dating for an assumed early conquest narrative since it depends upon many other texts. However, the similar age of death with Joseph (Gen 50:22) might hint that the conquest narrative ending in the death of Joshua might have been born out of the early Second Temple period Priestly circles.[280]

Second, the earliest farewell speech containing the basic narrative of the commitment scene was created and inserted before the death of Joshua in order to include the theological theme of exclusive fidelity to YHWH. As noted earlier, the commitment scene mirrors larger literary and theological issues related to the negative evaluation of kingship in the history of Israel. Thus, the best framework for explaining the birth of the basic commitment narrative is a group of Second

---

278 The burial of the flint knives may have been reported already in this early account, or it may have been added by a scribe at some point. Whether the burial of the flint knives in LXX Josh 24:31a was originally connected with the death account depends on when the circumcision account at Gilgal entered the account of the crossing of the Jordan. Most probably they did not belong to the earliest literary strata.
279 Possibly not the earliest version of a conquest narrative. See also Müller 2004, 231: "Die Entlassung des Volkes und der im Abschluß daran berichtete Tod Josuas (Jos 24,28–30/Jdc 2,8.8f) könnten für sich genommen zwar einmal das Ende einer Landnahmeerzählung gebildet haben –"
280 In addition, further evidence is presented by Knauf 2008, 19–20, 199.

4.4 Literary and Redaction Critical Conclusions — 241

Temple nomistic editors. The choice of the people to serve only YHWH made it possible to highlight the wickedness of the people when they later chose a human king for themselves, and whenever they chose to worship other gods instead of YHWH. At this point, one can speak of a Deuteronomistic nomistic (DtrN) horizon encompassing wider insights into the history of Israel and stressing the faults of the people that led to the exile. This horizon is not merely a single redaction, but refers to a longer process which affected several texts in the Hebrew Bible.[281]

Third, at some point the historical summary (24:2–13) was added as an introduction to the basic commitment narrative. This addition utilized a common literary genre used in late Second Temple period, and introduced a Hexateuchal perspective to the farewell speech of Joshua.[282] Moreover, the addition of the historical summary as an introduction to the commitment narrative led to additions to the commitment scene (vv. 19–21, 23–27). These may have been done by the same scribal circles who wanted to emphasize the Hexateuchal horizon of the book of Joshua, and maybe even add the book of Joshua to the "book of the Torah of God". While these additions may have taken place in several stages by several authors, it is probably not methodologically sound to differentiate between various editors or redactions.

Fourth, in very late Second Temple times, probably the third and second centuries, the text continued to grow towards a greater harmony in relation to the authority gained by Moses and the Pentateuch. Nomistic editing seemed to have been a flexible process that continued for a long time. Probably the last recoverable phase in the literary growth of Josh 24 consists of the additions of the infidelity of the fathers to several parts of the historical summary, and the commitment narrative (vv. 6b–7a, 14b, 15*, 17–18a). These additions were made to sharpen the differentiation between the faithful generation present at Shechem and the unfaithful generation of the fathers. This was a necessary differentiation, since Deuteronomy demanded that the generation that went to conquer the land was different from the Exodus generation, which should have died out before the conquest. The lateness of this motive in the text of Josh 24 is revealed by the

---

[281] For example, the nomistic text 1 Sam 12 (especially 1 Sam 12:12) belongs to this editorial horizon (Veijola 1977, 83–99). The complex relationship of Josh 24 and 1 Sam 12 (see section 4.2.6) illustrates that DtrN cannot be regarded as forming one single coherent redaction. It is exceedingly difficult to discern temporal relations within various texts of the DtrN – it is possible that some texts belong to the earliest DtrN texts, while others are nomistically inspired. However, I am not sure whether one can reliably discern which is which. Within the same nomistic horizon as the basic text of Josh 24, one could also mention the dynastic promise, which is conditioned by fidelity to YHWH (e.g. 1 Kgs 2:4, 8:25, 9:4–5; Veijola 1975, 127–142).
[282] Thus also Müller 2004, 231–232.

observation that similar rewriting is attested by the text-critical evidence preserved from the circumcision account in Josh 5.[283]

These four loosely defined phases in the editorial history of Josh 24 have led to the archetypal text form from which the OG and MT of Josh 24 once split. Both textual traditions continued to be edited in the manner that was revealed by the text-critical analysis in section 3. Moreover, it is possible that the Samaritan version of Joshua's farewell speech ultimately goes back to a version of Josh 23–24 that had not yet been exposed to all these editorial phases. Nevertheless, SamJosh has a subsequent transmission and editorial history of its own.

4.4.2 Literary and Redaction Criticism in the Light of the Documented Evidence

The texts in the Hebrew Bible are a result of complex editing. The methods of literary and redaction criticism have been developed to uncover this editing and describe the history of the formation of these texts. This methodology, however, has come under severe criticism. The analysis of Josh 24 partly corroborates and partly counters this criticism. Ultimately, the future of literary and redaction criticism lies in insights gained from documented evidence.

Documented evidence affirms that literary and redaction criticism should be carried out. In the analysis of documented evidence from Josh 24, it has become obvious that literary and redaction criticism has not produced only false results. Josh 24 is a heavily edited text, and cannot be considered a literary unity. Documented evidence presents the latest phases in this editing. Several secondary elements revealed by the documented evidence could also have been discerned without this documented evidence. For example, if we only had OG Josh 24, verse 24:33b could have been recognized as a secondary addition due to its many peculiarities in relation to the context. In addition, it is important that documented evidence revealed nomistic editing, missing from the OG, made to the proto-MT text in the last centuries of the Second Temple period. This corroborates the assumption in some current redaction-critical studies that nomistic ideology had a major influence on different editorial groups in Second Temple Judaism.

Textual variants and later scribal corrections are often situated in passages that have been also previously edited. Therefore, text-critical variants may serve as indicators that a text has undergone also earlier editing. Since Josh 24 (and Josh 8:30–35, Judg 6:7–10) are late texts containing several textual variants, it can be assumed that late texts often attracted editing in the textual transmission.

---

[283] See section 3.4.2.

4.4 Literary and Redaction Critical Conclusions — 243

In this way, even if documented evidence does not preserve direct evidence of earlier literary phases, it can serve as an indirect marker for suspecting earlier editing.

Documented evidence complicates literary and redaction criticism. The analysis of Josh 24 and related texts also revealed that many of the editorial intrusions are exceedingly complex. There are not just additions but also omissions, transpositions, and rewritings. Literary critics would have, for example, not been able to completely reconstruct the text preserved in OG Josh 5:4–6 if they only had MT Josh 5:4–6. The older ideas have simply been removed and replaced with corrected ones. Another example is that without OG Josh 24 many elements connected with the death and burial of Joshua in the Hebrew *Vorlage* would simply be missing from us. A literary critic would possibly not have suggested that some Hebrew writers thought that the flint knives from the Gilgal circumcision were buried with Joshua. Documented evidence has also shown that texts were harmonized towards other texts. Thus, when scholars see connections between texts and base their theories on these connections, it is always possible that the connections have come about through later harmonization. Since the editorial processes in documented evidence are so complex, we may assume that the earlier editorial processes were as well. Therefore, it seems that the texts should not be divided into different layers too rigorously. It is often enough to describe the most likely outlines of the editorial history, keeping in mind that these reconstructions are based on lower probabilities than those based on documented evidence.

Documented evidence shows the way forward. The differentiation between textual, literary, and redaction criticism is arbitrary. Documented evidence reveals that radical intentional editing took place also in the late textual transmission of the Hebrew Bible. In the case of Joshua and several other books, the latest editorial intrusions can be discerned when comparing extant textual witnesses. Therefore, the methodology of literary and redaction critical studies concentrating mainly on the MT is biased. From documented evidence, it is also clear that textual variants may often be related to redactional issues. Therefore, insights gained from textual criticism help in literary and redaction criticism. When certain patterns of editing are visible in textual evidence, one can sometimes deduce that similar editorial patterns were at play already in the literary prehistory of the text. For example, the text-critical evidence from Josh 5 revealed that behind the proto-MT editing there was a need to differentiate between the present faithful generation and the previous unfaithful generation of the fathers. This separation was not yet so strict in the earlier text of the OG. This editorial pattern was, in turn, recognized also in the earlier literary and redactional history of Josh 24. It presented a case of continuum within the nomistic editorial groups of the Second Temple period.[284] Furthermore, insights gained from literary and redaction criticism may help in evaluating between textual variants. Since textual variants often accumulate in places that have been heavily edited, the assumed earlier editing should be considered when evaluating the variants. There are often instances where it is hard to decide the earlier reading using only text-critical principles. In such instances, literary and redaction critical insight may be of help.[285]

It should also be highlighted that boundaries between methods are often practical rather than theoretical. This implies that scholars should increase their collaboration with other scholars working with other methods and fields. For example, the textual criticism of the Septuagint is often so specialized that scholars working with the redaction of a Hebrew text might not see the connections with their own work. A stronger focus on creating effective dialogue is greatly needed. For example, organizing hands-on workshops that gather people with different sets of expertise would best serve in breaking the barriers between methods and different research traditions. This is even more important in relation to the education of future scholars, who should get a good training in different methods. It is also a question of identity and social groups within the scholarly world. When scholars identify themselves within a single field or method, it might sometimes limit their judgment. As a young scholar, I feel that it is more helpful to identify oneself broadly as a text-historical scholar rather than as based on a single method (e.g. "I am a textual critic").

Finally, documented evidence provides signposts for future literary and redaction critical research, because it offers evidence for editorial techniques used by ancient scribes. More attention should be paid on the ways that editorial techniques are used in documented cases. This can also serve as a way of establishing "more controls for literary-historical analyses."[286] Such research should be done both with a qualitative and a quantitative approach. Qualitative research should focus on thoroughly answering questions related to single editorial techniques. For example, when examining a single addition, identified with the help of documented evidence, attention should be paid to several aspects. How and why was the addition made? How does the addition change the nature and flow of a text? Does the addition create problems in the resulting text? How is new material connected to an earlier text in terms of language and content? What happens at the seam of the earlier and the added text? Would it be possible to recognize the addition without documented evidence? Quantitative research in turn should

---

284 See sections 4.3.3 and 4.4.1.
285 See, for example, the variant discussed in section 5.3.3.
286 Milstein 2016, 28.

survey, collate, and categorize various editorial techniques visible in the documented evidence. In this way, we could describe editorial processes on a more general level. What is the most used editorial technique? How often does transpositions occur? Are editorial techniques genre-specific? When encountering a repetition, what is the probability of it being a sign of an editorial intrusion rather than a stylistic device? Through such quantitative and qualitative research, we would gain a more thorough picture of ancient editorial processes. This would also provide a stronger basis for literary and redaction critics to discern various editorial intrusions when documented evidence is not preserved.

Following these remarks, in the next section I will gather and analyze the most important editorial techniques discerned in Josh 24. This section, combining a qualitative approach with some very elementary quantitative data, will serve as one example and starting point for the framework of research outlined here.

5 Evidence of Editorial Techniques Used by Ancient Scribes

5.1 How and Why Did Scribes Edit Texts?

The documented evidence of editing analyzed and discussed in the previous sections revealed several types of editorial intrusions into the texts of the Hebrew Bible. In this section, these editorial processes are compiled, classified, and analyzed from an explanatory point of view: *how* (technical aspects) and *why* (motivations for editing) did ancient Second Temple Jewish scribes change sacred texts? Although this study has focused on Josh 24 and related texts, the discussion is not only relevant to the book of Joshua. Based on past research on the editing of biblical texts,[1] I would assume that the editorial processes observed in Josh 24 and related texts have been at play, in various degrees, throughout the history of the biblical texts. Therefore, scholarship concentrating on the textual history of any texts in the Hebrew Bible – and even other ancient texts[2] – can benefit from

Table: Frequencies of text-critically verifiable intentional editorial intrusions in Josh[1].

Technique	N	%
Addition	12	46
Omission	4	15
Rewriting	7	27
Transposition	3	12
Total	26	100

Note

[1] For the analysis, grouping, and calculation of this data, see the table in section 3.5. I have only included intentional editorial intrusions and not scribal mistakes.

---

[1] Many of the relevant studies have been surveyed in the introduction of this study in section 1.2.
[2] Similar editorial processes can be observed in the textual histories of many ancient works. For example, the Gilgamesh Epic (Tigay 1982) and the Diatessaron (Donner 1985). There is also a long scholarly tradition of studying the editorial processes of the books in the New Testament. Pakkala 2013, 45 interestingly notes: "There is no reason to assume that the editorial processes of the Hebrew Bible were fundamentally different than those of the New Testament." See section 1.2 for more examples.

https://doi.org/10.1515/9783110602241-005

this discussion.³ Of course, one should be careful when generalizing the results, since every text has its own character and social background.

The table presents frequencies of various editorial techniques used by the editors behind the differences between the MT and OG of Josh 24. Note that the quantification is not based on the length of the textual variants, but on the categorization of *significant content related differences* presented in section 3.5. The editorial intrusions vary significantly in their size and the amount of words they affect. For instance, the different rewritings analyzed in this study include editorial intrusions ranging from replacements of single words to rewriting of larger sections. The main reason for categorizing different editorial intrusions under one ID is that they likely represent editorial intrusions made by the same scribe in the same sitting, due to a specific editorial motivation.

As seen from the table, four types of editorial intrusions can be observed in the textual history of the Hebrew Bible: additions, omissions, rewritings, and transpositions. The use of these editorial techniques has been motivated by stylistic concerns, explanatory needs, the aim of harmonizing texts with other important texts, nomistic motivations, and the wish to expand upon notable events in the history of Israel. The overall motivation for editorial intrusions could be characterized as a *wish to preserve the relevance of sacred texts for the religious communities of the scribes*. The usage of various techniques for updating sacred texts that were in the toolbox of the scribes working in Second Temple Judaism has been the focus of studies working with documented evidence for some time.⁴ Based on these studies, the techniques could be further divided into several subcategories. In the following discussion I will, however, deal with the four main types found in our textual material.

5.2 Editorial Processes at the End of a Book

As it now stands in the extant textual witnesses, the covenant scene in Josh 24 forms the ending for the book of Joshua. In addition, in its wider literary perspective it can be characterized as a change of epochs: the history of salvation (*Heilsgeschichte*) gives way to the upcoming history of disaster (*Unheilsgeschichte*) in the following historical books. In terms of mapping ancient edito-

---

3 This section is directly dependent on the textual and literary-critical analyses in the earlier sections of this study. Thus, I will not repeat my arguments, nor give detailed tables of the original texts, but merely make use of the results. In the footnotes, I will refer to the sections where the more detailed argumentation can be followed.
4 See the discussion in section 1.2.

rial processes, the position of the chapter at the end of the composition and at the turning point in history should be highlighted.[5] The vast number of textual variants preserved at the end of Joshua points towards the conclusion that book endings may have specifically attracted the activity of editors. This finding strengthens several other scholarly investigations on different books in the Hebrew Bible, which conclude that book endings typically attracted considerable amounts of editing.[6]

A well attested type of editorial intrusion at the end of a composition is simply adding new material to an existing text. Physically, this might have been easy to accomplish. At the end of manuscripts there may have often been additional space left, which would make it easy for editor-scribes to add new material to the composition. This allows for editing the end of a composition without having to produce a new manuscript.[7] OG Josh 24:33b – highlighting the apostasy of the Israelites after the death of Joshua – may have come into existence in this way.[8] As can be seen from its content, its aim was to harmonize the book of Joshua towards the book of Judges. Therefore, it might have been a simple addition at the end of an existing Hebrew scroll, made at a stage of the composition history of the Hebrew Bible in which the scrolls of Joshua and Judges were ordered successively.

---

[5] See also, for example, Becker 2006, 149: "Jos 24 liefert ein weiteres Beispiel für die vielfältig anzutreffende Tendenz, die Epochenwechsel immer stärker literarisch auszugestalten und theologisch aufzuladen." See also the comments by Römer 2006, 523–525 highlighting the importance gained by the book endings in the Hebrew Bible.

[6] Several book endings in the Hebrew Bible could be mentioned. Many regard Lev 27 as an addition to a composition that originally ended with Lev 26 (Römer 2010, 86). Also, the endings of Judges (Judg 17–21) and the books of Samuel (21–24) should probably be regarded as miscellaneously organized, added sections at the end of a composition (see, for example, Soggin 1981, 261 on Judges and McCarter 1984, 16–19 on 2 Samuel). Carroll (1986, 857–858) regards the last chapter of Jeremiah (Jer 52) as an added appendix which serves a specific function. This is apparent since the earlier chapter ends with: "Thus far are the words of Jeremiah" (Jer 51:64). That this added appendix has been edited in several stages is apparent from the documented evidence: in addition to many textual variants, several whole verses present in the MT are missing from the LXX (Jer 52:2–3, 15, 28–30). For the complicated editorial processes in Jer 52, see Tov 1999f, 368 and Müller, Pakkala & Haar Romeny 2014, 109–125. Pakkala (2013, 343–349) notes that several successive editors added new endings to the book of Esther. While the MT reveals that the book ending in Esth 9 has been expanded by many scribes, the LXX preserves a text in which many signs of this earlier editing have been removed. Lastly, Mal 3:22–24 may have been added at the end of the book of Malachi as a conclusion to a corpus of prophetic books (Reventlow 1993, 160–161).

[7] Thus also Pakkala 2013, 343. Unfortunately, not many scroll endings are preserved among the Dead Sea Scrolls. According to Tov (2004, 105–106), only 29 scrolls (3.1%) have their ending preserved. They do not contain any clear secondary additions. Therefore, this claim cannot be substantiated with material evidence.

[8] See section 3.4.2.

The editorial processes attested at the end of the book of Joshua, however, go beyond the notion of simply expanding the ending of a manuscript. Many changes at the end of Josh 24 are so complicated that they probably were designed before copying the manuscript. Already the documented evidence in MT Josh 24:28–33 reflects the radical redesign of the earlier ending preserved in the Hebrew *Vorlage* of the OG, which was achieved through omissions, a transposition, and other minor adjustments.[9] In addition, if one accepts the model of literary growth presented earlier, it is clear that the large additions of material in Josh 24 could not have been done *ad hoc* in any remaining space at the end of a manuscript, but would instead have been planned beforehand.

Lastly, it is important that the documented evidence preserved of Josh 24: 28–33 reveals that the death of a hero attracted various amounts of editing, even at a relatively late stage. The comparison of the MT and OG reveal that both small and large textual units were added in various phases of the development of the Hebrew text, before and after the death of Joshua. Noth already claimed in his redaction-critical model that miscellaneous textual material was often cumulatively added right before the death of a hero.[10] This argument is seen, for example, in the literary-critical assumptions that the poetic material in Deut 32, Gen 49:1–27, and 2 Sam 20:23–24:25 were added in a position preceding the deaths of Moses, Jacob, and David.[11] These turning points in history may have been especially compelling sections for subsequent editors. To be sure, I have not discovered any additions of poetic material before or after Joshua's death; however, the phenomenon of adding textual material around the deaths of prominent figures gains solid support from the documented evidence of Joshua's death.

5.3 Additions

It is often assumed that additions are the most common editorial intrusions in the textual history of the Hebrew Bible.[12] This is corroborated by the documented evidence analyzed in this study. Among the intentional changes in Josh 24, 46% (n = 12) were either small or large addition, making it the single most common

---

9 See section 3.4.
10 Noth 1981, 35.
11 McCarter 1984, 17–18.
12 Thus, for example, Carr 2011, 65–88 and Pakkala 2013, 16.

editorial intrusion.¹³ It is understandable that additions are the most common editorial technique, since it is a conservative practice. The work of a scribe usually entails preserving and transmitting traditions. It can be assumed that in this process ancient scribes were less likely to omit text than to supplement them. Following the idea put forth by Pakkala, it may be argued that additions were made not just in connection with major paradigm changes (e.g. the destruction of the temple and the exile), but also when texts were transmitted in times of continuity.¹⁴ More radical editorial intrusions that require deleting older texts would have probably needed more compelling justification. Thus, they were more connected with times of unrest, when theology needed to be rethought.

5.3.1 Harmonizing Additions

One of the central features of the secondary additions revealed by the documented evidence in Josh 24 is that they frequently harmonize the chapter with other key texts. While the additions often understandably harmonize Josh 24 with the Pentateuch, connections are also made with other historical books. As already seen in the literary and redaction critical part of this study, such secondary harmonizations obscure the separation of well-defined literary strata in the text. For example, it seems that scribes responsible for the secondary features in the MT made additions not only to Josh 24, but also to the rest of the book of Joshua, which could be described as Deuteronomistic.¹⁵ These are sporadic nomistic corrections that may be impossible to attribute to a specific literary layer. Two of these secondary harmonizing additions revealed by documented evidence will now be discussed further, focusing on how and why the editorial technique was used.

First, some of the harmonizing additions in Josh 24 seem to be phrases that were in wider use by late Second Temple scribes. These formulaic phrases draw

---

13 Compared to many other biblical texts, however, the percentage seems rather low. For instance, when one compares the MT and OG of the book of Jeremiah it seems that most variants are additions in the MT version. This highlights the fact that every text and book should be approached on their own merits. Even though it may be true that ancient scribes followed a "trend toward expansion" (Carr 2011, 65–88), this principle cannot be applied slavishly to explain the textual evidence of individual texts.
14 Many literary critics also falsely assume that this is almost the only editorial intervention, since the scribes supposedly would not have omitted texts that were perceived as normative or sacred. See, for example, Becker 2011, 86. See also the critical discussion of this assumption in Pakkala 2013, 16–25.
15 As noted briefly also by Tov 1999c, 394.

from key texts in Exodus and Deuteronomy. The secondary introduction of Moses and Aaron into the Exodus aligns the Exodus remembrance with the narrative in the book of Exodus. In the earliest text form, as attested by the OG, Moses was not in any way connected to the Exodus allusions in Josh 24. In addition, MT Josh 24:17 significantly expands the brief Exodus allusion with formulaic material from Exodus and Deuteronomy.[16] That we are dealing with a wider phenomenon of scribes harmonizing various Exodus accounts by expanding them with formulaic language is suggested by the striking similarity of these additions with Mic 6:4. Mic 6:4 recalls the sending of Moses, Aaron, and Miriam (MT Josh 24:5), together with the designation of Egypt as the house of slavery out of which YHWH brought the Israelites (MT Josh 24:17). Based on these similarities, and the observation that the elements in MT Josh 24 are late harmonizing proto-MT additions, one can assume that these themes were regularly added by scribes to existing texts. Therefore, the dating of Mic 6:4 to pre-exilic or exilic times based on Deuteronomistic language, should also be regarded with high skepticism, since such formulaic language was also common for scribes in late Second Temple times.[17]

There is documented evidence for the editorial technique of harmonizing various Exodus remembrances with one another in Josh 24. A significant amount of the details in this editing were mediated through Deuteronomy. That we are dealing with a wider scribal phenomenon in Second Temple Jewish literature is also seen in other sources. The phenomenon is, for example, prominent in the harmonizing tendencies of the pre-Samaritan Pentateuch.[18] In several pre-Samaritan texts, elements are imported from one part of the text to another part of the text, for example, to remove contradictions from the narrative. Many such harmonizations pertain to the Exodus narratives. Therefore, the harmonizations in MT Josh 24 fit together with the conclusion that in the Second Temple period there was "a wider tradition of scribal interventions for harmonization and content editing", which might in many cases manifests itself even only in single manuscripts.[19] The observation that the harmonizing additions in Josh 24 are taken from Deuteronomy fits well with the overall observation that Deuteronomy

---

16 See sections 3.2.2 and 3.3.2.
17 An early dating is argued by, for example, Mays 1976, 30.
18 Pre-Samaritan refers to the earlier layer witnessed by the SP, which goes back to a different tradition of the Pentateuch that was circulating in the last centuries BCE. The SP has a late veneer of sectarian editing, but behind to this sectarian editing is an early variant version of the Pentateuch. The existence of such a textual tradition was confirmed by the finding of several proto-Samaritan texts from Qumran. See Tov 2012, 79.
19 Crawford 2005, 131–132.

was a popular book at the end of the Second Temple period.[20] The editors responsible for many of the secondary additions throughout the Hebrew Bible may have therefore been especially guided by Deuteronomy.

From a technical point of view, the addition of Moses and Aaron in Josh 24:5 could have been made as a longer marginal gloss, while the expansion of the Exodus allusion in Josh 24:17 would have required more effort, as seen below. The addition is not a simple gloss, but envelopes the word "Egypt", which is found in the common textual tradition behind the OG and the MT. The text highlighted in the table below represents the added material. If the material was added in one sitting, it could be labeled as an enveloping addition using "Egypt" as an anchor word. However, it is possible that the addition took place in two phases. First, some earlier scribe changed "from Egypt" to "from the land of Egypt". Second, a subsequent scribe inserted the long phrase after "from the land of Egypt". In this case, the first developmental phase would be missing missing from our textual evidence.

Before (OG *Vorlage*)	After (MT)
הוא המעלה אתנו	הוּא הַמַּעֲלֶה אֹתָנוּ
ואת אבותינו	וְאֶת־אֲבוֹתֵינוּ
ממצרים	מֵאֶרֶץ מִצְרַיִם מִבֵּית עֲבָדִים וַאֲשֶׁר עָשָׂה
	לְעֵינֵינוּ אֶת־הָאֹתוֹת הַגְּדֹלוֹת הָאֵלֶּה

Moreover, the complexity of the addition is seen in that the expansion combines material from various texts in Deuteronomy, and yet is not a verbatim repetition of any single text. These observations together suggest that the addition was not made to an existing scroll, but when a new copy of the text was produced. The similarity of the additions in 24:5, 17 together with the parallel verse Mic 6:4 suggests that the additions may have been made by the same scribe when he was copying a new scroll of the text. However, this is not necessary: every time a new copy of a text was produced, scribes may have potentially added new elements to the text. When dealing with formulaic language, it is even more probable that such additions have been made in several stages. In fact, it is impossible to say whether the large addition in 24:17 was made at one sitting or whether it too has grown in stages.

In addition to harmonizing with Deuteronomy and the rest of the Pentateuch, the additions in Josh 24 also provide evidence for the harmonization of similar texts closer one another. As demonstrated in section 4.2.6, it is likely that Josh 24 served

---

[20] In the caves Qumran, Deuteronomy was the second most attested book of the Hebrew Bible. See Crawford 2005, 127–128.

as one basis of 1 Sam 12. However, the additions in Josh 24 revealed by the documented evidence also illustrated that these similar texts were also brought closer to one another in later times. Most remarkably, 1 Sam 12 inspired small secondary additions in the proto-MT editing of Josh 24. This underlines a central problem in analyzing literary connections between texts. When two texts look similar, it does not necessarily mean that they are originally dependent on each other. They may have also been harmonized towards each other in later times. Therefore, it is not enough to build text-historical models simply by observing inner-biblical quotations and allusions, but the analysis of similarities should be carried out in connection with a thorough text, literary, and redaction critical analysis.

5.3.2 Small Additions and Marginal Glosses

There are several small secondary additions in both the MT and the OG of Josh 24. It is hard to pinpoint any specific moment in the textual history of Josh 24 for these additions, since they are often so general in content. Moreover, several scribal mechanisms could be imagined for the emergence of the small additions. It is possible that many of the small additions came about as marginal glosses or notes between the lines, and ended up in the main text when later copies were made. However, the small additions may have also been inserted into the text on the spot, while writing a new copy. Minor additions would not have needed major planning or the support of a community, but could have simply been conjured up by single scribes as clarifications of harmonizations.

The clearest external evidence for marginal glosses in Josh 24 comes from the Greek manuscript material of the LXX.[21] Manuscripts 85 and 344 contain several readings added as notes to the margin of the text by a later scribe. These marginal notes contain principally Hexaplaric readings.[22] For example, in Josh 24:24 manuscripts 85 and 344 add τω θῶ ημων "our God" after Κυρίῳ "the Lord". This is a Hexaplaric reading that aligns the Greek text with the expression אֱלֹהֵינוּ אֶת־יְהוָה "YHWH our God" in the MT. The reading is also found in the main text of

---

[21] Beyond Josh 24, the clearest Hebrew evidence for glosses and corrections inserted in the margins or between the lines comes from the Great Isaiah Scroll found in Qumran. There one can observe that even long sentences could be added between the lines. See, for example, Callaway 2011, 84–86.

[22] An analysis of the marginal readings in 344 is presented in a forthcoming article by Kristin De Troyer in a collection of studies based on the symposium "From Scribal Error to Rewriting: How (Sacred) Texts May and May Not Be Changed" (Tbilisi 2015). The volume will be published in the *De Septuaginta Investigationes* -series (Göttingen: Vandenhoeck & Ruprecht).

manuscripts 19 82 120 130 509. In these cases, it is not probable that the readings would have first emerged as marginal notes and later been adopted into the main text in the process of copying. They have more probably come about as part of the Hexaplaric revision process. Manuscripts 85 and 344 have been later supplemented with marginal notes correcting the main text. Therefore, while these manuscripts attest to the phenomenon of adding notes to the margins of the text, they do not offer external evidence for new material being added to the text through margins.

There are at least 13 cases of documented minor secondary additions revealed by the comparison of MT and OG Josh 24. In the MT, the small additions are the words and phrases כְּנַעַן "Canaan" (24:3), וָאֶשְׁלַח אֶת-מֹשֶׁה וְאֶת-אַהֲרֹן "and I sent Moses and Aaron" (24:5), וָאוֹצִיא אֶת-אֲבוֹתֵיכֶם "and I took your fathers" (24:5), וַיִּלָּחֲמוּ אִתְּכֶם "and they fought against you" (24:8), בֶּן-בְּעוֹר "son of Beor" (24:9), אֱלֹהֵינוּ "our God" (24:24), יְהוֹשֻׁעַ "Joshua" (24:26), כָּל "all" (24:27). These are missing from the earlier version preserved by the OG. In the OG, the small additions that either reflected a different Hebrew *Vorlage* or were made by the translator included τὴν ἐρυθράν "Red" (24:6), τοὺς ἀλλοτρίους "foreign" (24:14), ἐνώπιον τῆς σκηνῆς τοῦ θεοῦ Ἰσραήλ "before the tent of the God of Israel" (24:25), Ἰησοῦς "Joshua" (24:26), and ὁ ἀρχιερεὺς "the high priest" (24:33). These are missing from the earlier version preserved by the MT.

The small additions can be roughly divided into four categories. First, there are some additions of titles of important characters in the text. For example, "son of Beor" is added to describe Balaam, and "high priest" is added as an attribute of Eleazar. The phenomenon of scribes adding titles to characters is well-attested in other texts.[23] These kinds of additions could have been easily made as a marginal gloss in any phase of the transmission of the text. Second, there are stylistic additions that make explicit elements that are already implicitly assumed when reading the text. For example, "Joshua" has been added in two different locations in OG and MT Josh 24:26. The agent of the verse would have been understood as Joshua even without these additions. Third, there are some theological stock phrases that are added to the speeches in Josh 24. For example, "our God" heightens the sense of sacredness in the text. These stock phrases may have their roots in liturgical practice. The phrases are so common that the scribes would have known them by heart, and they would have likely been a part of their own religious practices and prayers. Fourth, some small additions are related to redactional issues. The addition of "and I sent Moses and Aaron", for instance, relates

---

23 For example, when comparing the OG and the MT of the book of Jeremiah, one can observe that several titles were added in the proto-MT editing. See Janzen 1973, 69–86.

to larger nomistic concerns. Some small additions might also be connected with earlier redaction. This is the case of "and I took your fathers", which will be analyzed below.

For the purposes of literary and redaction criticism, these results have three implications. First, it seems that some of the small additions in Josh 24 could have been recognized without documented evidence. The clearest example is the addition "and I sent Moses and Aaron". The phrase is a loose element in the historical summary, which emphasizes the actions of YHWH alone in guiding the Israelites in their history. Moses does not appear anywhere else in the chapter, in which Joshua functions as the mediator between YHWH and the Israelites. This would have alerted the redaction critic that Moses might be a later import into the chapter. From other texts, he would have known that in later times the authority of texts was derived more and more from the figure of Moses. In addition, when reading only the MT one can notice that there are several formulaic phrases beginning with *wayyiqtol* forms. The addition of a phrase in this link of similar sentences could have been easily made in a later phase by repeating the same formula. Second, some small additions mimic phraseology that is often attributed to specific editors. For example, "land of Canaan", used in MT Josh 24:3, is a typical Priestly phrase. If one does not compare the MT with the OG, the nature of "Canaan" as a later addition may bias the redaction-critical analysis into attributing the text to the Priestly editor. Third, many of the small additions are so minor that redaction critics would not recognize them as secondary without documented evidence. There are no criteria for recognizing which instances of "all" or "foreign" are secondary and which original in a given text. Therefore, one must accept that while many small additions may have made to texts in several phases, most of these cannot be reliably uncovered.

Finally, in the compositional history of the book of Joshua many marginal glosses have been assumed without documented evidence. The evidence from Josh 24 corroborates that this is possible. Tov, for example, introduces two instances where short explanations of names and words may have been first added to the margin and later been integrated to the running texts of new copies.[24]

Josh 18:13 וְעָבַר מִשָּׁם הַגְּבוּל לוּזָה אֶל־כֶּתֶף לוּזָה נֶגְבָּה [הִיא בֵית־אֵל]
"From there the boundary passes towards Luz, to the shoulder of Luz southwards [that is Bethel]"

Josh 15:8 אֶל־כֶּתֶף הַיְבוּסִי מִנֶּגֶב [הִיא יְרוּשָׁלָםִ]
"... to the shoulder of the Jebusites [that is Jerusalem]"

---

24 Tov 1999e.

Both cases have to be assumed without text-critical evidence, since the readings are present in all the witnesses. They are, however, hard to explain otherwise. In the former, "that is Bethel" refers to Luz, and is therefore placed in an awkward position at the end of the sentence. Such a position in the sentence would easily result from a marginal gloss. The latter, in turn, is confirmed by documented evidence, since the explanatory gloss is missing from the parallel verse in Josh 18:16.

5.3.3 Small Addition to Smooth Out Tensions Created by an Earlier Large Addition

The addition of "and I brought your fathers out" in MT Josh 24:6 could at first sight seem to be an isolated gloss.[25] After surveying the compositional history of Josh 24:5–7, however, there seems to be a clear connection with this small addition revealed by textual criticism and an addition assumed by literary criticism. Considering these additions together illustrates how textual and literary criticism overlap in this instance. It also sheds light on how modern scholars can recognize later additions.

> **Josh 24:5.** And *YHWH smote* Egypt *with miracles* that he did in their midst and afterwards *he* brought you out **6.** [And I brought your fathers out] of Egypt.
>
>> And you came to the sea. And the Egyptians pursued after your fathers with chariots and horses to the Sea of Reeds. **7.** And *we cried* out to the Lord and he put darkness between *us* and the Egyptians and he brought the sea upon them and covered them.
>
> And your eyes saw what *YHWH did in the land of* Egypt. Then you lived in the wilderness many days.[26]

The basic narrative of YHWH's deeds, told by Joshua, concerns the Israelites who are being referred to as "you". In verses 5–6, the speech recalls how "he (YHWH) brought you out of Egypt". The possible earlier form of the narrative, constructed with the help of literary criticism, then continues narrating how the Israelites moved in their journey: "your eyes saw", "you lived in the wilderness". The sudden shift from "your" to "your fathers" in verse 6b interrupts this basic narrative. Thus, the incident involving the fathers of the Israelites at the sea seems to

---

[25] For the text-critical arguments see section 3.2.2.
[26] Here the secondary addition is indicated with a different indentation. Minor secondary additions are printed in [square brackets]. The translations are the ones introduced already in the earlier analysis sections. The text is the earliest text-critically attainable form, and cursive is used to highlight that the reading is preserved only in the OG.

be a later intrusion into the basic narrative concerned with the Israelites.[27] Furthermore, as has already been noted, the added material abounds with allusions to Exodus 14, which signals that it probably was the source and inspiration for the addition: וַיִּרְדְּפוּ "and they pursued" (Exod 14:9, 23), בְּרֶכֶב וּבְפָרָשִׁים "with chariots and horses" (Exod 14:9, 28), צעק "to cry out" (Exod 14:10), "darkness between" (Exod 14:20), and וַיְכַסֵּהוּ "and it covered them" (Exod 14:28; 15:10).[28] Thus, the large addition might have been motivated by a desire to bring the prophetic speech closer to the well-known Exodus account.

In the light of this assumed large secondary addition, the short addition in the proto-MT phase of 24:6 does not seem loose anymore. It is connected with the earlier large literary addition, since it anticipates the theme of the fathers. This connection can be explained in two ways. First, it is possible that the large addition and the short addition were made by the same scribe, who wanted to introduce the incident with the fathers into the historical summary. If this was the case, it would be hard to explain why the OG preserves a version in which the large addition is preserved but the short addition is not.

Second, it is more probable that the short addition was made in the proto-MT editing of Josh 24 to tie the large addition more closely to the historical summary. The fathers were introduced at the beginning of verse 6, smoothening out the tension between "you" and "your fathers" created by the earlier large addition in the OG 24:6. This was, in fact, not the only way that the proto-MT editor smoothened the large addition. Also, the change of the personal form and the pronoun from "we cried ... us" (OG) to "they cried ... you" (MT) is a way of making the text flow smoother with the added material. The first-person "flashback"-form of the verb, derived originally from Deut 26:7, was secondarily connected more tightly with the fathers in the proto-MT editing. This was motivated by the verbal form present in 1 Sam 12:10.

The literary addition of the fathers is so large and significant that it has probably been made at a point in the textual history when a new copy or version of the text was being produced. In theory, the small addition of three words could have been first written in the marginal or between rows in a scroll, and then inserted in the main text when a scribe copied a new scroll. It is, however, also more probably connected with the larger proto-MT editing of the book of Joshua, which must have been a more thorough process than just a mere copying with minor addition. The change made to the verbal form used in the historical summary also suggests this.

---

[27] See section 4.3.3.
[28] See section 4.2.2.

In this instance, the overlap of the observations of textual criticism and literary criticism are intriguing. It is, however, interesting to note that if the text-critical evidence was not preserved, a careful literary critic might have noticed that "and I brought your fathers out" is a secondary addition. There are at least three reasons for this. First, it is clearly connected to the insertion of the incident with the fathers. Second, the connection with 1 Sam 12:8 would help the literary critic in making the conclusion that a basic narrative has been expanded to bring it closer to similar material elsewhere in the Hebrew Bible. Third, the small addition creates a disturbing repetition in the text וְאַחַר הוֹצֵאתִי אֶתְכֶם וָאוֹצִיא אֶת־אֲבוֹתֵיכֶם (Josh 24:5–6) with the doubling of the verb יצא. These traces of editing may have alerted the literary critic that we are dealing with a minor addition. Hence, this instance strengthens the notion that literary and redaction criticism is possible, and can produce correct results when different arguments accumulate.

5.4 Omissions

Documented evidence preserved from Josh 24 has illustrated that scribes sometimes omitted even whole verses from the text they were transmitting. Omissions are almost impossible to detect without documented evidence. Peculiarities in a text might hint towards earlier editing that omitted passages from the text. However, if something is deleted it cannot be observed anymore. Therefore, it is understandable that literary and redaction criticism has mostly assumed that texts have developed through additions. This tendency in research has been recently analyzed in detail by Pakkala in *God's Word Omitted*. Pakkala also presents an important case for the recognition of omissions as an editorial technique in the diachronic development of the texts in the Hebrew Bible.[29] The documented evidence in Josh 24 revealed four omissions which can be divided into two subcategories: minor stylistic deletions and theological omissions.[30]

There are not many stylistic omissions in Josh 24. The omission of the second וָאֶתֵּן "and I gave" from the sentence "and I gave him Isaac, (and I gave) to Isaac Jacob and Esau" (24:3–4) can be counted as a purely stylistic omission witnessed by the OG. Such an omission could have been made either by the translator or by a Hebrew editor working with the *Vorlage*. Moreover, the omission of "because he is holy" at the end of MT Josh 24:15 revealed that stylistic omissions could be

---

[29] Pakkala 2013. See also section 1.2.
[30] Since I am dealing with intentional editorial techniques, I exclude from the discussion unintentional omissions that emerged due to scribal mistakes.

connected with earlier redaction. The phrase was likely removed as an unnecessary doublet for material that was secondarily added (v. 19) in the history of the text.[31] That there are not many stylistic omissions speaks for the conclusion that scribes and the OG translator were usually not that keen on correcting stylistic problems in a text through omitting material. For text-critical argumentation, this means that theological explanations should not be seen as secondary to stylistic or linguistic explanations. When something was omitted from a text, it was often done with good reasons.

The theologically motivated omissions in Josh 24 reveal that intentional omissions are often connected with more comprehensive rewriting. While additions could have been made lightly on separate occasions, omissions seem to relate to editing that changes the meaning of the text. The major omissions at the end of Josh 24 are connected with wider editorial activities elsewhere in the composition. Josh 24:31a was likely removed by the same editor who highlighted the fidelity of the Israelites to circumcision in Josh 5. The omission of 24:33a was connected with wider issues of continuity between the books of Joshua and Judges.[32] The relationship between Joshua and Judges was indeed a motivating factor for several editorial intrusions at the end of Joshua and beginning of Judges. It is also important to highlight that the omission of these two verses at the end of Joshua is connected with a radical reworking of the ending of Joshua. These omissions were not isolated incidents, but closely related with a systematic restructuring of the ending. Therefore, this evidence suggests that book endings have sometimes been reworked more radically than just through additions.

Based on the documented evidence attested in Josh 24, three conclusions may be drawn concerning omission as an editorial technique. First, omissions were not made as frequently as additions. Whereas additions could have been easily motivated, theologically motivated omissions may have entailed much more deliberation. One could speculate that a single scribe would not have omitted whole verses from a text, but that omissions needed to be discussed between different scribes and within the whole community of the scribe. When something was removed from a text, it might have required wider approval of the religious leaders. This, however, is only a working hypothesis derived from Josh 24, which would have to be examined in more detail. Second, omissions are usually connected with other rewriting. The deletion of older texts and ideas is connected with a shift in thinking. For example, the rewriting of Josh 5, together with the omission of 24:31a, represents a major shift in ideas connected with the

---

31 See section 3.3.2.
32 See section 3.4.2.

Gilgal circumcision. It is a rewriting of history. This might be the reason why we see fewer omissions in the development within single compositions (e.g. book of Joshua) than in the creation of new compositions (e.g. the "rewritten" Joshua books). Omissions are probably more usual within major paradigmatic changes in a community, or in the creation of new compositions. Third, the omissions revealed by documented evidence could not have been recovered without documented evidence. There would be no reason to assume that a tradition of burying flint knives with Joshua was once connected with the burial account if the OG would not have preserved such a text. This adds a note of caution to the usage of literary and redaction criticism. Because addition is the most common editorial technique, we may probably quite reliably recover earlier forms of certain texts without documented evidence. Yet it is probable that, because of omissions, we are missing much of the material once connected with our texts. Therefore, overly rigid reconstructions of editorial developments remain questionable.

5.5 Rewriting

In its basic meaning, rewriting refers to the scribal phenomenon of replacing at least one unit of a text with another unit. In practice, scholars usually focus on the rewriting of larger textual units such as verses, chapters, or even whole compositions. However, the replacement of a single word with another word carrying a different meaning can also be considered rewriting. The term itself has been traditionally used with respect to "non-canonical" texts, such as the Joshua scrolls 4Q378 and 4Q379, written on the basis of "canonical" books.[33] In recent scholarship, however, it has become more and more clear that a strict separation between the scribal techniques used in producing the "canonical" books and the so-called "rewritten" biblical texts is an arbitrary one. Both scribal processes belong "to the same dynamic process of retelling, writing, and rewriting tradition during Second Temple times."[34] Besides the fact that there was no strict canon in Second Temple times, documented evidence has revealed that even heavy rewriting has taken place in the textual history of the now canonical books. The textual analysis in this study has confirmed this state of research by observing several documented cases of rewriting in Josh 5 and 24. I will now turn to the most important cases, proceeding from small to larger instances.

---

33 See section 2.5.1.
34 Debel 2011, 67.

The first case of rewriting observed in the documented evidence is the secondary change of location of the scene in the OG. If this is considered an isolated variant, as many commentators do, it appears to be a fairly small relocation. However, the secondary change of location to Shiloh is probably connected to the editorial motivation of diminishing the Samaritans claim to importance. This motivation also resulted in the omission of the "sanctuary" from Josh 24:26 and the addition of the tent of YHWH in 24:25.[35] These text-critical conclusions have implications for how the replacement of Shechem with Shiloh was achieved. If it was an isolated replacement, it could have been made easily at any point of the transmission of the text. For instance, since the location in Josh 18 is Shiloh, any scribe proceeding to the copying of the end of the book could have simply made a harmonizing correction in Josh 24:1, 25. However, since we are dealing with a wider editorial aim, it is more probable that the rewriting was planned. Moreover, it is linked to socio-historical issues connected with the relationship of the Samaritans and the Judeans in the late Second Temple period. In other words, the rewriting was made to update the important covenant text to take into the current societal situation.

Other small rewritings in Josh 24 may be connected to locally perceived problems in the text that the scribe was copying. For example, in Josh 24:12, the earlier text (MT) had the problematic reading "the twelve kings of the Amorites". Any scribe could have regarded the number "twelve" as a problem, or even a mistake, since it does not accord with any other record of the number of Amorite kings. The scribe responsible for replacing "twelve" (MT) with "two" (OG) probably considered the near context which refers to Sihon and Og. This small correction could have been made at several points in the textual history of Josh 24:12: in the transmission of the Hebrew *Vorlage* of the OG, in the translation process, or even in later revisions of the original translation. Such a replacement may have also grown in several steps. One scribe could have made the correction to the margins of a manuscript, while a later scribe would have replaced it in the main text. In any case, once again it is clear that such small scribal alterations are impossible to date and describe exactly. Moreover, these types of rewritings may have taken place multiple times in the earlier prehistory of any given text, without any trace in our scarce documented evidence.

A larger rewriting in Josh 24 pertains to the speaker of the historical summary. In its earlier form (OG), the recollection in 24:5–13 was given as the speech of Joshua, who refers to YHWH in the third-person. Later (MT), the speech was harmonized with the beginning (24:2–4) and presented thoroughly as the first-person speech of YHWH. As observed in the textual analysis, the phenomenon of rewriting

---

35 See section 3.2.2 and 3.3.2.

speeches to take on the aspect of a direct speech from YHWH is also known from the Temple Scroll.[36] There were probably stylistic and ideological reasons behind this rewriting. In terms of style, the text in the MT is more unified, as it follows the first-person formulation in almost every verse. The earlier reading is more cumbersome, since it alternates between different persons. In terms of meaning, the first-person formulation was better suited to several details in the text. For example, later editors wanted to attribute the active role in the ban in Josh 24:8 to YHWH, rather than to the people themselves. Moreover, attributing the speech directly to YHWH increased the authority and impact of the text. The confession of faith became a prophecy in which Joshua assumed the role of a prophet.

In terms of technique, the rewriting was achieved through two kinds of editorial intrusions. First, every verbal form in the third-person was simply replaced with a verbal form in the first-person. In addition, some of the connected pronouns needed to be changed. Interestingly, in the case of the complicated verse Josh 24:7, the scribe did not change the expression "he put darkness", which remains the only third-person formulation in the MT. This scribal lapse illustrates that attempts to harmonize a text would not always produce perfect results. Second, all the mentions of "the Lord" were omitted, although technically they could have also worked in the rewritten text (e.g. Josh 24:5 could have read "I, the Lord, smote Egypt"). Since the rewriting is not technically complicated, it is possible that it may not have required a great deal of planning. It is possible that a scribe reading the passage, for example in light of the beginning verses, simply assumed that the speech leading up to the covenant should be a direct speech from YHWH. Therefore, this rewriting can be considered a minor improvement taking place at some point in the proto-MT editing. Since the phenomenon of changing the speaker is known elsewhere, the scribe could have had a precedent for making the change.

Lastly, in Josh 5:4–6, relating to the omission of the flint knives in Josh 24:31a, heavy rewriting was observed. The rewriting was guided by three ideological motivations: reinterpreting history so that the Israelites were faithful to circumcision in Egypt, dissolving the continuity between the generation of the fathers and the generation that conquered the land, and making sure that everyone participating in the Passover celebrations were ritually pure.[37] The complex rewriting cannot be characterized with the usage of any single editorial technique. It was achieved with a creative mix of additions, omissions, replacements, and reordering of the text. In the table below, it can be seen that the rewritten text, especially

---

36 See section 3.2.2.
37 See section 3.4.2 for the precise arguments and the reconstruction of the Hebrew *Vorlage*.

in verses 5:4–5, does not have many counterparts with the text that preceded it. However, looking at the similar expressions highlighted in the table below and the relocated expressions marked with a textbox, the rewriting does not seem to be random, but seems to have been guided by some strategy.

Before (*Vorlage* of OG)	After (MT)
⁴ וזה הדבר אשר מל יהושע	⁴ וְזֶה הַדָּבָר אֲשֶׁר־מָל יְהוֹשֻׁעַ
את בני ישראל	כָּל־הָעָם הַיֹּצֵא מִמִּצְרַיִם
כל הילדים בדרך	הַזְּכָרִים כֹּל אַנְשֵׁי הַמִּלְחָמָה מֵתוּ
ובלי הערלים היו	בַמִּדְבָּר בַּדֶּרֶךְ
בצאתם ממצרים	בְּצֵאתָם מִמִּצְרָיִם
⁵ את כל אלה מל יהושע	⁵ כִּי־מֻלִים הָיוּ כָּל־הָעָם הַיֹּצְאִים
	וְכָל־הָעָם הַיִּלֹּדִים בַּמִּדְבָּר בַּדֶּרֶךְ
	בְּצֵאתָם מִמִּצְרַיִם לֹא־מָלוּ
⁶ כי ארבעים ושתים שנה	⁶ כִּי אַרְבָּעִים שָׁנָה
הלכו ישראל במדבר	הָלְכוּ בְנֵי־יִשְׂרָאֵל בַּמִּדְבָּר
לכן ערלים היו רבים	עַד־תֹּם כָּל־הַגּוֹי
אנשי המלחמה היצאים	אַנְשֵׁי הַמִּלְחָמָה הַיֹּצְאִים
מארץ מצרים	מִמִּצְרַיִם
אשר לא שמעו בקול אלוהים	אֲשֶׁר לֹא־שָׁמְעוּ בְּקוֹל יְהוָה
אשר נשבע להם	אֲשֶׁר נִשְׁבַּע יְהוָה לָהֶם
לבלתי הראותם את הארץ	לְבִלְתִּי הַרְאוֹתָם אֶת־הָאָרֶץ
אשר נשבע יהוה לאבותם לתת לנו	אֲשֶׁר נִשְׁבַּע יְהוָה לַאֲבוֹתָם לָתֶת לָנוּ
ארץ זבת חלב ודבש	אֶרֶץ זָבַת חָלָב וּדְבָשׁ

The expansive rewriting in 5:4–5 has been achieved through reorganization and replacing some elements in the shorter text. In verse 4, the first and last phrases remained intact, and the material in between was replaced with the notion that everyone coming out of Egypt was circumcised. The augmented verse 5 in the MT, on the other hand, was created by taking elements from the earlier verse 4, moving them further along in the new text, and adding new material in between. The expression בְּצֵאתָם מִמִּצְרַיִם "when they came out of Egypt" was placed at the end of the new rewritten text as a resumptive repetition. This binds the new augmented verse closely with what had been said earlier. The expression כל הילדים בדרך "everyone born on the way" from OG verse 4 was taken up in a longer form in the rewritten MT verse 5. The expression בני ישראל was also taken from OG verse 4 and inserted at the beginning of the rewritten MT verse 6. In this way, the scribe preserved the main elements of the older text, but gave them a new meaning by inserting new material around and between them. Lastly, in verse 6 all of the main elements remained intact, but the phrase לכן ערלים היו רבים "for many of them were uncircumcised" was perceived as problematic and was simply replaced with the new phrase עַד־תֹּם כָּל־הַגּוֹי "until all the people had died". This expression was not taken from the earlier text of Josh 5:4–6, but was probably imported from passages such as Num 32:13 or Deut 2:14–15.

The rewriting observed in Josh 5:4–6 with the help of documented evidence is so creative and complex that all its intricacies could not have been uncovered if we only had the MT. In theory, the rewriting observed here follows the basic assumptions of textual and literary criticism. Namely, shorter texts are often earlier, and texts have mostly grown through additions. However, the additions are not achieved simply by keeping the earlier text intact, but the text it is reorganized, and elements are dispersed in the new text. However, the situation would not have been completely hopeless without the OG. The resumptive repetition of בְּצֵאתָם מִמִּצְרָיִם "when they came out of Egypt" at the end of MT Josh 5:5 could have alerted the literary critic that the verse might be a later addition.[38] With this observation, the literary critic could have removed the later idea in verse 5 that all the people coming out of Egypt were circumcised, and Joshua only circumcised those born in the wilderness. This would have brought the literary critic closer to the earlier idea of the text. Yet the ideas, completely omitted from the earlier text, would have been harder to reconstruct. Thus, to some degree it is possible to uncover traces of secondary rewriting, especially when it is expansive in nature. However, due to the creativity of ancient scribes and the lack of comprehensive documented evidence, many aspects of complex rewritings will inevitably remain unattainable.

5.6 Transpositions

Transposition is a technical term for the phenomenon of a scribe changing the location of one or more textual units.[39] The inclusion of the evidence from the OG into textual criticism of the Hebrew Bible has introduced a large amount of evidence that scribes sometimes reordered textual units during the transmission of texts. The presence of transpositions in textual evidence illustrates that

---

38 Indeed, Josh 5:5 has been regarded as a secondary addition by, for example, Steuernagel 1900, 167–168 and Noth 1953, 39.
39 Some scholars use other terms such as "relocation" or "change in sequence".

reordering took place even quite late in the transmission of the Hebrew Bible.⁴⁰ The documented evidence from Josh 24 attests to some such editorial intrusions. There seems to be two types of transpositions. First, the locations of two words, sentences, or verses may have been swapped. Such small interchanges were present in Josh 24:18 and in the Greek manuscript material.⁴¹ Second, a textual unit may have been relocated to a new location. This is the case with the transposition of MT Josh 24:31, which highlights the fidelity of the Israelites.

The first type of transposition is widely attested in the textual witnesses of the Hebrew Bible. This is especially true when referring to small transpositions of single words within a phrase.⁴² In Josh 24:18, there is a transposition in the proto-MT phase which is related to a small addition. The earlier text read "the Amorites and all the people that inhabited the land" (OG Josh 24:18), with the reference "and all the people" being a secondary interpolation, as revealed by the context. The editor behind the MT secondarily changed the order to "all the people and Amorites that inhabited the land" in order to better integrate the loose addition to the context. Moreover, as attested by MSS 15 19 376 426, the Hexaplaric reviser transposed the Greek text again to make it accord with the Hebrew text.⁴³ In Josh 24:19, in turn, the MT reads לְפִשְׁעֲכֶם וּלְחַטֹּאותֵיכֶם "your transgressions or your sins", while the OG has a different sequence, reading τὰ ἁμαρτήματα καὶ τὰ ἀνομήματα ὑμῶν "your sins or your transgressions". Once again, the Hexaplaric reading in MSS 15 19 376 426 corrects the Greek order toward the Hebrew. In this case, it is hard to say which tradition made the transposition, since it does not really affect the meaning of the text.

These small stylistically motivated transpositions, attested by a difference in the MT and the OG, could have been made at any point during the copying of the text to a new scroll. In addition, they could have been either intentional or unintentional. The scribe could have memorized a larger section of the text he was copying, kept and contemplated it in his working memory, and accidentally produced a transposed text in the new copy. In other words, the transposition could have taken place in the mind of the scribe. On the other hand, the scribe may have deliberately reordered the phrase, and may even have been aware of earlier editing such as the secondary addition in Josh 24:18. These possibilities highlight the ambiguity related to small transpositions; it is not possible to pinpoint the exact date or mechanism of these transpositions. If the transposition is not

---

40 Tov 1999d, 411–418 and Mäkipelto, Tekoniemi & Tucker 2017.
41 This may have also happened with larger textual units. For example, Josh 8:30–35 and 9:1–2 are situated in opposite locations between the MT and the OG. See section 4.2.4.
42 Tov 2012, 239.
43 See 3.3.1.

connected to theological or narrative issues in a text, one should not give too much weight to it.

Minor transpositions were also common in the later secondary Greek revisions, and apparently especially the *L* group of manuscripts. In Josh 24:14 the OG reads "put away the foreign gods that your fathers served beyond the river and in Egypt", reflecting the MT. There are no stylistic reasons for transposing this Greek text. Apparently, later revisers understood "beyond the river" as referring to Jordan, as seen by the transposition guided by the idea that first the Israelites left Egypt and then crossed the river Jordan (*L:* "put away the foreign gods that your fathers served in Egypt and beyond the river").[44] In this way, minor transpositions could be made to the text even in the late Christian revisions, guided by the conviction of the reviser concerning the correct meaning of the text.

The second type of transposition is more uncommon, but often has more implications for the meaning of the text. As concluded in the text-critical analysis, the earliest location of the verse highlighting the fidelity of the Israelites (OG Josh 24:29 or MT Josh 24:31) is preserved in the OG.[45] This verse was transposed in the proto-MT reworking at the end of the book of Joshua, probably to bring the death of Joshua closer to the death of Moses in Deut 34. In other words, we are dealing with a late harmonizing transposition which aims at bringing the two endings closer one another. In the case of such transpositions, we might already carefully speak about a beginning canonization of some scriptures. The rising authority of Deuteronomy gave scribes an incentive to also reorganize the texts of other historical books. This editing is taken even further in 4QJosh[a], where the reading of the law (Josh 8:34–35) is moved between Josh 4–5 so that it would have taken place during the crossing of Jordan.[46]

In terms of scribal practice, the latter type of transposition, in which a textual unit is moved to another location, was probably part of a carefully planned editorial intrusion in most cases. Since this kind of a relocation affects several aspects of the text, the decision to transpose would have most probably been made already in the planning stages, and not on an impromptu basis while copying. The transposition of one verse observed in Josh 24 is not as such extremely radical, but it is related to various other editorial intrusions, such as the omission of OG Josh 24:31a, affecting the length of the text. Therefore, the scribe would have had to plan the length of the new scroll, and thus probably also needed the support of a wider community. A case in point for the carefully planned nature of

---

[44] See section 3.3.1.
[45] See section 3.4.2.
[46] See section 4.2.4.

this type of a transposition is found in the textual history of Jeremiah, where the Oracles Against the Nations (MT Jer 46–51) are in completely different locations between the MT and the OG. Such a radical transposition affects the whole literary nature of the composition, and therefore needs careful planning beforehand. On a smaller scale, taken together with the other editorial intrusions, this probably also applies to the transposition of OG Josh 24:29.

Finally, documented evidence of transpositions has implications for literary and redaction criticism. Many scholars have assumed that transpositions have taken place in the editorial history of the books in the Hebrew Bible without text-critical evidence. Sometimes scholars aim at reconstructing these transpositions without documented evidence. For instance, several scholars have argued for the possibility that Josh 24 and Josh 8:30–35 would have originally formed a literary unity. This is mainly because both describe a ritual ceremony at Shechem, and both Josh 8:30–35 and Josh 24 are loosely and illogically connected to their current contexts. In these models, the transposition of either one is then a secondary feature achieved by later editors. Simpson, for example, argued that in an early pre-Dtr document the command to build an altar, that is the basic text of Deut 27, was related in a text consisting of Josh 24:1–18, 25; 8:30–34. During later editing, this text grew and was further moved about, so that Josh 8:30–35 and Josh 24 were transposed to different parts of the composition.[47] Another suggestion was made by Soggin, who suggested that Josh 8:30–35 may have originally been connected with Josh 24 at the end of the composition. Even though he notes that "we do not have any definite proof of the original unity", on a practical basis he treats the texts as having once formed a literary whole.[48] Since both models assume that a more logical text is the earliest, they are not very compelling. Accordingly, the models have not received much corroboration from other scholars.[49] However, it is worth considering that since several transpositions are visible in documented evidence, it is possible and even probable that this editorial technique was also used in the literary prehistory. Therefore, to suggest that the location of some early form of Josh 8:30-35 or Josh 24 may have originally been in a different part of the composition is not without merit. It is, however, another question whether we can reasonably uncover this location. In any case, documented cases of transposition reveal that it is probably not possible to reconstruct all the intricacies of the editorial histories of our texts.

---

[47] Simpson 1948, 316–322.
[48] Soggin 1970, 230–231.
[49] In the light of these suggestions, however, it is striking that the altar scene in MT Josh 8, or at least verses 8:34–35, are found in a completely different location in 4QJosh^a. Therefore, the basic assumption of these models – that certain texts may have originally been situated in different locations – is valid.

5.7 Editorial Techniques and the Creativity of Ancient Scribes

From its earliest phases to the latest documented editing, Josh 24 can be used as evidence for the editorial techniques utilized by Second Temple Jewish scribes. The most common editorial intrusions have been the additions of new material. This editorial technique is easiest to uncover, even in instances where documented evidence is not preserved. It has been shown that minor additions and the addition of material at the end of the chapter could have been made to an older copy of the text without having to produce a completely new manuscript. Therefore, additions were often economical. However, more radical editorial techniques have also been at play. Omissions, transpositions, and rewriting together constitute about half of the editorial intrusions observed in the textual history of Josh 24. The observations made from the mechanics of these editorial intrusions led to the conclusion that such editorial techniques fundamentally change aspects of a text. Therefore, while some of these editorial intrusions could have been uncovered without documented evidence, they would mostly remain unattainable without traces in textual witnesses. These radical editorial intrusions often require careful deliberation and material planning, which means that they probably also required wider support from the leaders and communities of the scribes. They would have been done almost solely when a new copy of the manuscript was produced.

It is also necessary to briefly put the observations in this section into a wider perspective. Josh 24 is a product of the creative scribal environment of the Second Temple period. Several studies have explored and described this creative milieu. Debel, for one, notes: "In a nutshell, the Second Temple period now appears as a time of unprecedented scribal creativity and socio-religious dynamics, during which the scriptural text was still organically developing and in a pluriform state."[50]

What exactly does it mean when we describe ancient scribes as creative? In modern creativity research, creativity is often defined by referring to its three components. First, creative ideas and products are original, that is somehow new or innovative. Second, they are of high quality. Third, creative ideas and products have to be suited either to the task at hand or some other future purpose of that task.[51] These categories apply to various stages of editing observed in the textual evidence of Josh 24. To ensure that Josh 24 remained of high quality and suitable for its changing audiences, scribes had to continue making changes to

---

50 Debel 2011, 67.
51 Stenberg & Kaufman 2010, xiii.

the text. Moreover, it is clear from modern research that creativity is an immensely multifaceted phenomenon. There are several "individual, situational, social, and cultural factors" that affect the creative process and its outcomes.[52] Each of these facets are in and of themselves complex and contain many overlapping processes. From this complexity related to creativity as a human process, it follows that creative processes cannot be understood mechanically. In other words, it is not enough to simply describe the technical aspects of scribal work and imagine that these techniques were always applied as such. Several variables in the cognition of the scribes, the dynamics of their communities, and their historical realities were present in their everyday creative work. Therefore, one should not be surprised if evidence suggests that scribes did not follow the patterns we would expect from research on editorial techniques. Furthermore, this means that a complete understanding of the development of texts needs to be embedded in a holistic model that takes psychological and socio-historical realities seriously.[53]

Therefore, analyzing evidence of editorial techniques and describing how these were used constitutes only one part in understanding the creative efforts of ancient scribes. However, it should be highlighted that this is an immensely important part of the task. The vast majority of earlier studies have been either narrow text-critical work aiming at recovering some early text, or literary and redaction criticism concentrating only on one textual witness. The aim of text-historical work should be to describe what has happened to a text as truthfully as possible. To achieve this goal, we need a detailed understanding of how ancient scribes handled texts. This understanding can be best obtained from analyzing documented evidence beyond canonical boundaries. These findings can be further applied to the assumed earlier changes in any text. Since the importance of Second Temple creative scribal work has turned out to be pivotal for the study of the Hebrew Bible, much future research is needed in describing the editorial aspects of the transmission of texts and traditions in this period.

---

[52] Ward & Kolomyts 2010, 93.
[53] Even though the field of biblical studies has seen growth in these themes, there have been relatively few attempts to integrate psychological and sociological perspectives into the study of scribal work or textual transmission. For one example, see Vroom (2016, 259–279) for an initial application of cognitive psychology of memory to the understanding of textual transmission, and specifically the copying error of haplography. Another example is the plea by Brooke (2014, 119–136) to integrate aspects from memory research to better understand the processes of rewriting.

6 Conclusions and Discussion

This study presented an in-depth text-historical analysis of Josh 24 and related texts, which allowed a critical discussion of recent methodological issues in biblical studies. The overall aim was to describe ancient editorial processes in the light of documented evidence and refine the basic methodology of studying the textual and editorial history of the Hebrew Scriptures. I will now recap the conclusions of this study and discuss its methodological implications. Finally, I will highlight some issues for future scholarship in the field.

6.1 Documented Evidence of Changes in Joshua 24

At the end of the Second Temple period, the book of Joshua was circulating in different textual forms. In this late period, it was still subjected to creative editing by various groups seeking to update its message for their audiences. The principal witnesses for studying the editorial history of the book of Joshua are the MT, LXX, biblical and rewritten Dead Sea scrolls, and possibly the Samaritan sources. While these sources exhibit a high amount of unity, they also witness to the textual plurality of the book of Joshua in ancient Judaism. The principal witnesses for Josh 24 are the MT and the OG. My analysis of Josh 24 strengthened the text-critical view which posits that the Hebrew *Vorlage* of the OG presents a text that is mostly earlier than the MT. However, the OG also contains secondary readings which led to the conclusion that the Hebrew *Vorlage* of the OG and the proto-MT once split from a common archetypal text form. Even though the OG is closer to this archetype, every variant must be analyzed critically on its own merits.

Secondary readings in the MT, revealed through a comparison with the OG, are not random, but exhibit ideological tendencies characterizing the proto-MT editing. First, there are nomistic tendencies seeking to align Josh 24 with the Pentateuch and the authority of Moses. One notable example is the proto-MT editing that corrected the meaning of the circumcision performed by Joshua at Gilgal (Josh 5:4–6) in the light of legal issues emerging from the Pentateuch. In Josh 24, this editing led to the omission of an earlier verse, preserved in the OG, commemorating the flint knives with which the circumcision was performed (OG Josh 24:31a). The proto-MT editing also introduced Moses to Josh 24:5 through a minor addition, and aligned the death and burial account of Joshua with the death account of Moses (Deut 34:5–9). Second, there is a harmonistic tendency to introduce elements to Josh 24 from the near context and other historical books. This is visible, for example, in the secondary harmonization of the list of leaders in Josh

24:1 with the list in Josh 23:2, or the introduction of several elements from 1 Sam 12 to Josh 24 which are missing from the OG. Overall, the documented cases of harmonization illustrate that at a late stage the ending of Joshua was brought closer to the books preceding and following it. Apparently, there was a need for creating larger literary complexes. Finally, not all secondary elements in the MT derive from wider editorial tendencies. There was much subtle editing that could have taken place on the spot when scribes were copying a new scroll.

The secondary elements in the Hebrew *Vorlage* of the OG are much more modest, but also exhibit some ideological tendencies. The clearest case is the change of location from Shechem to Shiloh and the removal of the sanctuary at Shechem from the earlier text of Josh 24:26, motivated by anti-Samaritan tendencies. Some small secondary elements in the OG also reflect stylistic corrections and minor freedoms taken by the translator. Thus, while the OG generally represents the earlier text, the MT also witnesses to earlier readings. Both witnesses together illuminate the latest editing of Josh 24.

6.2 The Literary Prehistory of Joshua 24

The documented evidence of editing pertaining to Josh 24 clearly illustrated two points that have implications for the study of the chapter's earlier editorial history. First, the book of Joshua cannot be reliably used in critical scholarship without taking all the textual evidence into account. In light of this observation, I argued that some literary and redaction critical solutions should be ruled out or refined since they do not adequately consider the textual witnesses. Many literary and redaction critical models are based only on the MT. For example, it is questionable whether the death and burial accounts of Joshua in Josh 24:28–31 and Judg 2:6–9 at the seam of Joshua-Judges can be used as evidence for an original connection between the books of Joshua and Judges, as a part of an early DtrH. The flexibility and movability of these verses in the textual witnesses demonstrates that it is equally possible that the death and burial account of Joshua originally served as a transition between Joshua and Judges, than it may have served as an ending to an early Exodus and conquest narrative. The complex editing of these verses already visible in textual evidence makes it hard to use them as evidence in such compositional models. Since the textual evidence already demands a complicated explanation, complex models of the editorial history easily lose their explanatory power. Second, textual evidence demonstrates that Josh 24 has been heavily edited even at a very late stage. Therefore, the recent trend of regarding Josh 24 as late literary unity is unfounded. Since one has to assume several editorial intrusions to explain the textual evidence, it is probable that similar editing has also taken place of which documented evidence has not survived. It is also likely that the editing visible in the textual evidence is the work of several scribes, which further undermines the unity of the text.

The literary and redactional history of Josh 24, however, does not need to be rewritten. The model of a basic commitment narrative consisting of the earliest parts of Josh 24:1–2, 14–16, 18b, 22, and 28, which has been secondarily expanded at least in two stages, is also plausible in the light of text-critical evidence. First, this basic narrative is present both in the OG and the MT, illustrating that the textual material is not secondary. Second, several textual variants can be observed at the seams of the secondarily added units. They exhibit a motivation to better integrate the added material to Josh 24. Third, the assumed additions contain themes which have also been introduced to Joshua elsewhere, as witnessed by the textual evidence. In particular, the secondary addition of the fathers to Josh 24 is strengthened by the rewriting witnessed by the OG in Josh 5:4–6, differentiating between the generation of the fathers and the present generation. The assumed additions in Josh 24 are also achieved with editorial techniques well attested by textual evidence elsewhere (e.g. additions, *Wiederaufnahme*, and revision through introduction). Fourth, some of the assumed additions are missing from the Samaritan farewell speech of Joshua, providing additional evidence for the basic outlines of the literary-critical model. This illustrates that the Samaritan material pertaining to the historical books needs to be researched more carefully.

The basic narrative of Josh 24, reconstructed with the help of textual and literary criticism, narrates the choice of the people to serve YHWH alone. It presents the commitment to divine kingship. This idea should be seen as a reception of several nomistic texts in Deuteronomy, and as a counterpart for the choice of a secular king at Shechem in texts such as Judg 9 and 1 Kgs 12. In this way, the basic text of Josh 24 contributes to the criticism of monarchy which is distinctive to the nomistic Deuteronomists. Therefore, it is likely that the origin of Josh 24 should be attributed to the nomistic circles of the early Persian period. The text has been subsequently expanded and edited during the Second Temple period, and the latest stages of this editing are visible in the differing textual witnesses. Since this editing is also partly nomistically motivated, nomistic editing should not be connected with only one distinct redaction (such as DtrN), but should rather be seen as a recurring editorial motive from the Persian period onwards. The latest stages of this editing should probably be dated to the last two centuries BCE, as is reflected in the textual evidence.[1] Hence, Josh 24 is best described as a gradually evolving late nomistic text.

---

[1] De Troyer 2003, 57. See also section 4.4.1 for a rough relative timeline.

6.3 Documented Evidence of Editorial Techniques

The analysis of the textual and editorial history of Josh 24 offered data on editorial techniques employed by ancient Second Temple scribes. The analysis of Josh 24 demonstrated that book endings may have specifically attracted extensive editing during their transmission. While book endings may have grown substantially, they also seem to exhibit more complex editorial processes.

Quantitatively, addition is the most common technique attested by textual evidence. The additions in Josh 24 often introduce new concepts to the text (e.g. the addition of Moses in Josh 24:5), or create intertextual links with other texts in the Hebrew Bible (e.g. the secondary links to Deuteronomy in MT Josh 24:17). Large additions were often made through repeating material already present in older texts, thus linking the new material more closely with the older material. Thus, documented evidence of editing corroborates that "foreign" concepts, contradictions, intertextual links, and repetitions may sometimes be traces of earlier editing. These observations strengthen the literary-critical assumption that additions may be discerned to some degree even without variant versions. If scholars suspect that something has been secondarily added, they should look for these traces. It should be kept in mind, however, that single "traces of editing" may often be simply stylistic devices. For example, *Wiederaufnahme* can be a sign of earlier editing, or a stylistic device employed by an author. Therefore, the argument for additions should always be cumulative. There must be several reasons for suspecting that something has been secondarily added. Even then, the probability of editing is usually lower than when dealing with documented evidence of editing. Yet scholars of history should also be open to accepting a lower degree of probability in such cases.

It is important that radical editorial intrusions are present in the late textual witnesses. Transpositions, rewritings, and omissions at a late stage suggest that the latest editorial intrusions in the transmission of Josh 24 were not merely conservative. Omissions could be made, especially out of theological and ideological motivations. It is often assumed that at a late stage the text of Hebrew Bible was already so sacred and authoritative that nothing could be omitted. The evidence from Josh 24 counters this claim. When theological value was placed upon texts, it did not lead only to conservative scribal practices. Josh 24 demonstrates that creative changes were made even to texts that present themselves as divine in their origin. Indeed, if the meaning of a text was regarded as sacred, it is only logical that scribes would sometimes have rewritten and deleted sections to make the text better serve the theological meanings imposed on it. It seems, then, that theological value was not placed on the immutability of the text, but rather on the tradition and meaning it was thought to represent. The text was important only as far as it witnessed to sacred traditions.

The examination of editorial processes in the light of documented evidence highlights the creativity of ancient scribes. Even though it is vital to try to better understand scribal techniques, it cannot be assumed that scribes used them mechanically. Creative human acts cannot be understood as predictable patterns that could be easily uncovered. While there are scribal habits whose examination provides opportunities for constructing hypotheses about editorial history not visible in variant versions, scholars should probably refrain from building overly rigid literary and redaction critical models. Textual scholarship should also not be done in a vacuum, and more collaboration is needed between specialists of different fields and methods. For instance, insight from the history of religion, archaeology, the cognitive science of religion, and social sciences might shed light on editorial practices. Even modern analogies or experimental research might illuminate the transmission of texts by ancient scribes.

6.4 Signposts for the Text-historical Study of the Hebrew Bible

I will now turn to discussing the methodological implications of these conclusions in light of the questions posed in the introduction.[2] Much of biblical research aims at answering the historical question: what has happened to a text over time? Text is understood as an abstract concept. It refers to a certain arrangement of words as attested by continuity in the ways that words have been arranged in various physical sources. It is assumed that there are abstract compositions that surpass physical limitations and time. Such compositions are, for example, the book of Joshua, 2 Maccabees, and the Epic of Gilgamesh. As with any academic paradigm, several epistemological assumptions are made, which will not be discussed here.[3]

Traditionally, the historical development of texts has been studied by separating the methods of textual, literary, and redaction criticism. As illustrated by the analysis in this study, the conventional separation between these methods must be questioned. As the amount of physical evidence for continuity and discontinuity regarding various texts has grown, many methodological assumptions have been outdated. First, it can probably be assumed that the editorial processes explored in

---

[2] This discussion has greatly benefited from the workshops and collaboration between teams 2 and 3 in the Centre of Excellence *Changes in Sacred Texts and Traditions* (www.cstt.fi). See also the methodological remarks by Aejmelaeus 2017b, 2–3, 10.
[3] For a discussion of key epistemological issues in textual criticism see Hendel 2016, 101–147.

textual, literary, and redaction criticism are essentially similar.[4] Second, due to the pluriformity of versions in the early history of several Judeo-Christian texts, it is now clear that the early history of these texts cannot be described in a unilinear fashion. When aiming at unbiased research, one should refrain from using terms that assume a unilinear development of texts, or an anachronistic and community-specific view of a canon (e.g. "final text" or "original text").[5]

Instead of defining the exact relationships between methods, I would prefer calling the whole endeavor *text-historical research*. The aim of text-historical research is to investigate how certain compositions have changed and stayed the same over time. Such research can illuminate various historical realities behind the societies of the scribes that created these texts. Text-historical research begins with a careful examination of all available textual witnesses. Once the unique features of specific textual witnesses (e.g. LXX and its revisional history) have been established, one can proceed to sorting out the relationships between various witnesses to a text. The aim is not just to discover the earliest textual form, but to explain the history of a text as extensively as possible. In other words, text-historical research begins with building a diachronic model of the historical development of a text based on documented evidence of editing.

The second phase of text-historical research is an examination of the earlier editorial history of a text which is not attested by variant versions. Based on insights gained from textual evidence, it is possible to reconstruct literary developmental stages in the history of a text with a lower degree of possibility. Since the probabilities for reliably recovering this prehistory of a text are lower than in the first phase of text-historical research, it is often necessary to suggest alternative models and evaluate their explanatory powers. This phase in text-historical research will certainly remain more disputed, and many scholars will refrain from it. However, I would argue that both stages of text-historical research are necessary if one wishes to use texts critically in literary research, or utilize them as sources for studying historical events behind the texts.

Finally, while the two phases of text-historical research reflect to some degree a practical separation between textual criticism and literary/redaction criticism, both phases benefit from these methods. Literary and redactional history cannot be studied reliably without taking all the textual witnesses into account, and

---

[4] This is certainly also since it is difficult, or perhaps impossible, to differentiate between the roles of authors, editors, and copyists when speaking about ancient scribes. See Van der Toorn 2007, 109–110.
[5] This does not mean that one should not describe the temporal relationship of readings. A reading might well be earlier or secondary in relation to another reading. However, in academia one should refrain from any value judgments when making these descriptive hypotheses.

sometimes textual witnesses are best explained in the light of assumed earlier editorial processes. In addition, text-historical research should openly discuss insights from history of religion, archaeology, psychology, sociology, anthropology, philosophy, and several other academic disciplines. Consequently, methods are only tools in text-historical research, and they should not dictate working procedures or scholarly identities.

6.5 Issues for Future Research

This study has revealed at least three areas that need more research in the future. First, the textual witnesses to the book of Joshua need to be examined more carefully. Since the OG has proved a valuable witness, there is a great need for the *Göttingen* critical edition of the book of Joshua. This is accompanied with a need to study the translation technique and revisions of LXX Joshua in more depth. For instance, the value of the *L* group and the Old Latin in Joshua is an issue still far from settled. While it is valuable to study LXX Joshua in its own right, these areas also carry major implications for uncovering the editorial history of the book of Joshua. Moreover, the rewritten Joshua scrolls and the Samaritan Joshua texts should be examined more carefully. This could not only provide more information on the early textual history of the book of Joshua, but also on the various editorial processes utilized by the communities responsible for the creation of these texts.

Second, as illustrated by my analysis of Josh 24, there is a growing need to research the editorial history of individual texts in the light of differing textual witnesses. There are several key texts that are used in reconstructions of the history of ancient Israel, but whose literary and redaction critical models are based solely on the MT. In this respect, there is still much basic research to do on the book of Joshua, but another important literary whole is Samuel-Kings, which holds many claims on the history of Israel. For example, in the book of Kings, many central texts are preserved in multiple forms. In these instances, the analysis of documented evidence can be complex but fruitful.[6] Another important group of texts that have not been sufficiently studied from this point of view are the poetic texts of the Hebrew Bible. For instance, 2 Sam 22 and Ps 18 reflect the same text, however in different forms in the MT, the OG, and the revisions of the OG. An

---

[6] For example, the burning of Jerusalem is depicted in 2 Kgs 25:8–12, Jer 52:12–16, Jer 39:8–10, 2 Chr 36:19–20, and 1 Esd 1:52–54. Many of these differ between the OG and the MT. See, for example, Müller, Pakkala & Haar Romeny 2014, 109–125.

examination of the editing of poetic texts in the light of the documented evidence would provide additional insights into how various editorial processes were utilized in different genres.

Third, more studies are needed focusing extensively on specific editorial techniques. The study on omissions by Pakkala, and the study on revision through introduction by Milstein are important representatives of this future trend. Such studies should not focus solely on the canonical books or Hebrew sources, but should illuminate ancient editorial processes more widely in a comparative manner. For example, there is still no in-depth study on the editorial technique of addition. It is well known that additions and expansions have regularly taken place in ancient Near Eastern literature and the textual history of the Bible. There is plenty of documented evidence of the usage of addition as an editorial technique. A broad examination of this evidence would illuminate quantitative and qualitative aspects of the usage of this editorial technique. This would, in turn, also help in discerning secondary additions in the editorial history of texts which are not attested by variant versions.

Finally, uncovering the creative work of ancient scribes should be done by formulating more creative research questions. In addition to basic textual research, insights from fields such as sociology and psychology could provide innovative ways of approaching the old evidence. I would especially like to see more studies where insights gained from the rapidly growing cognitive science of religion would be applied to theories concerning ancient textual transmission. Since we are dealing with the remains of creative human effort, it would be worth trying to better understand the social and cognitive frames of reference of these individuals.

Abbreviations

Sources

BHS	Biblia Hebraica Stuttgartensia
MT	The Masoretic text
LXX	The Septuagint
OG	The Old Greek: the assumed original wording of the LXX
OL	The Old Latin (in the case of Joshua, *Codex Lugdunensis* = La^{100})
SamJosh	The Samaritan Joshua traditions

Modern Journals and Publications

AASF	Annales Academiae Scientiarum Fennicae
BEThL	Bibliotheca ephemeridum theologicarum Lovaniensium
BBET	Beiträge zur biblischen Exegese und Theologie
BIOSCS	Bulletin of the International Organization for Septuagint and Cognate Studies
BJRL	Bulletin of the John Rylands Library
BNB	Biblische Notizen Beiheft
BZAW	Beihefte zur Zeitschrift für die Alttestamenliche Wissenschaft
CBET	Contributions to Biblical Exegesis & Theology
CBR	Currents in Biblical Research
DJD	Discoveries in the Judean Desert
DSD	Dead Sea Discoveries
FRLANT	Forschungen zur Religion und Literatur des Alten und Neuen Testaments
HeBAI	Hebrew Bible and Ancient Israel
HSM	Harvard Semitic Monographs
HSS	Harvard Semitic Studies
HTS	Hervormde Teologiese Studies
JAJ	Journal for Ancient Judaism
JBL	Journal of Biblical Literature
JNSL	Journal of Northwest Semitic Languages
JRAS	Journal of the Royal Asiatic Society
JSJSup	Journal for the Study of Judaism Supplement Series
JSOT	Journal for the Study of the Old Testament
JSOTSup	Journal for the Study of the Old Testament Supplement Series
JTS	Journal of Theological Studies
JQR	The Jewish Quarterly Review
OBO	Orbis Biblicus et Orientalis
OTE	Old Testament Essays

PEQ	Palestine Exploration Quarterly
PFES	Publications of the Finnish Exegetical Society
PSBA	Proceedings of the Society of Biblical Archaeology
SAAB	State Archives of Assyria Bulletin
SBL	Society of Biblical Literature
SBLR	Society of Biblical Literature Resources for Biblical Study
SJOT	Scandinavian Journal of the Old Testament
STDJ	Studies on the Texts of the Desert of Judah
TA	Teologinen Aikakauskirja (Finnish Journal of Theology)
TC	TC: A Journal of Biblical Textual Criticism
Text	Textus
VT	Vetus Testamentum
VTSup	Supplements to the Vetus Testamentum
ZAW	Zeitschrift für die Alttestamentliche Wissenchaft
ZDMG	Zeitschrift der Deutschen Morgenländischen Gesellschaft

Bibliography

Primary Sources

LXX
Brooke, Alan E. / McLean, Norman, 1917. *The Old Testament in Greek. According to the Text of Codex Vaticanus, Supplemented from other Uncial Manuscripts, with a Critical Apparatus Containing the Variants of the Chief Ancient Authorities for the Text of Septuagint. Vol. I, Part IV*, Cambridge: University Press.

Margolis, Max L., 1931–38. *The Book of Joshua in Greek. According to the Critically Restored Text with an Apparatus Containing the Variants of the Principal Recensions of the Individual Witnesses. Parts I–IV (Joshua 1:1–19:38)*, Paris: Publications of the Alexander Kohut Memorial Foundation in Trust at the American Academy for Jewish Research.

Margolis, Max L., 1992. *The Book of Joshua in Greek. According to the Critically Restored Text with an Apparatus Containing the Variants of the Principal Recensions of the Individual Witnesses. Part V (Joshua 19:39–24:33)*. Preface by Emanuel Tov. Philadelphia: Publications of the Alexander Kohut Memorial Foundation in Trust at the American Academy for Jewish Research.

Rahlfs, Alfred / Hanhart, Robert, 2007. *Septuaginta: id est vetus Testamentum Graece iuxta LXX Interpretes*, Stuttgart: Deutsche Bibelstiftung.

Old Latin (La[100])
Ulysse, Robert, 1900. *Heptateuchi partis posterioris versio latina antiquissima e codice Lugdunensi. Version latine du Deutéronome, de Josué et des Judges antérieure a Saint Jérôme publiée d'après le manuscrit de Lyon avec un fac-similé, de observations paléographiques et philolosiques sur l'origine et la valeur de ce texte par Ulysse Robert*, Lyon: Librairie de A. Rey et CIE.

Qumran
Feldman, Ariel, 2013. *The Rewritten Joshua Scrolls from Qumran: Texts, Translations, and commentary* (BZAW 438), Berlin: de Gruyter.

Ulrich, Eugene, 2010. *The Biblical Qumran Scrolls. Transcriptions and Textual Variants* (VTSup 134), Leiden: Brill.

Samaritan Literature
Gaster Moses, 1908. "Das Buch Josua in hebräisch-samaritanischer Rezension," *ZDMG* 62: 209–279.

Juynboll, Theodor Willem Jan, 1848. *Chronicon samaritanum, arabice conscriptum, cui titulus est Liber Josuae: Ex unico codice Scaligeri nunc primum edidit, latine vertit, annotatione instruxit*, Leiden: Luchtmans.

Macdonald, John, 1969. *The Samaritan Chronicle No. II (or: Sepher Ha-Yamim). From Joshua to Nebuchadnezzar* (BZAW 107), Berlin: de Gruyter.

Josephus
Josephus, 1930. *Jewish Antiquities, Volume II: Books IV–VI*, Translated by Henry St. John Thackeray and Ralph Marcus (Loeb Classical Library 490). Cambridge: Harvard University Press.

Secondary Literature
Abusch, Tzvi, 1990. "An Early Form of the Witchcraft Ritual *Maqlû* and the Origin of a Babylonian Magical Ceremony," in *Lingering over Words: Studies in Ancient Near Eastern Literature in Honor of William L. Moran* (HSS 37), ed. Tzvi Abusch, John Huehnergard and Piotr Steinkeller, Atlanta: Scholars Press, 1–57.

Adler, Alan D., 1908. "On the Samaritan Book of Joshua," *JRAS* 40: 1143–1147.

Aejmelaeus, Anneli, 1982. *Parataxis in the Septuagint. A Study of the Renderings of the Hebrew Coordinate Clauses in the Greek Pentateuch* (AASF 31), Helsinki: Suomalainen Tiedeakatemia.

Aejmelaeus, Anneli, 2001. "What We Talk about When We Talk about Translation Technique," in *X Congress of the International Organization for Septuagint and Cognate Studies, Oslo, 1998*, ed. Bernard A. Taylor, Atlanta: SBL, 531–552.

Aejmelaeus, Anneli, 2007. *On the Trail of the Septuagint Translators. Collected Essays. Revised and Expanded Edition* (CBET 50), Leuven: Peeters.

Aejmelaeus, Anneli, 2010. "How to Reach the Old Greek in 1 Samuel and What to Do With It," in *Congress Volume Helsinki 2010* (VTSup 148), ed. Martti Nissinen, Leiden: Brill, 185–205.

Aejmelaeus, Anneli, 2012. "Corruption of Correction? Textual Development in the MT of Samuel 1," in *Textual Criticism and Dead Sea Scrolls Studies in Honour of Julio Trebolle Barrera* (JSJSup 157), ed. Andres Piquer Otero and Pablo A. Torijano, Leiden: Brill, 1–18.

Aejmelaeus, Anneli, 2017a. "*Kaige* Readings in a Non-*Kaige* Section in 1 Samuel," in *The Legacy of Barthélemy: 50 Years after Les Devanciers d'Aquila* (DSI 9), ed. Anneli Aejmelaeus and Tuukka Kauhanen, Göttingen: Vandenhoeck & Ruprecht, 169–184.

Aejmelaeus, Anneli, 2017b. "What Happened to the Text in Jer 25:1–7?" *TC: 22*, 1–10.

Alt, Albrecht, 1953. *Kleine Schriften zur Geschichte des Volkes Israel, Vol 1*, ed. Martin Noth, München: C. H. Beck.

Anbar, Moshe, 1992. *Josué et l'alliance de Sichem: Josué 24:1–28* (BBET 25), Frankfurt: Peter Lang.

Anderson, A. A., 1988. "Psalms," in *It Is Written: Scripture Citing Scripture. Essays in Honour of Barnabas Lindars, SSF*, ed. Donald A. Carson and Hugh G. M. Williamson, Cambridge: University Press, 56–66.

Anderson, Robert T. / Giles, Terry, 2012. *The Samaritan Pentateuch: An Introduction to its Origin, History, and Significance for Biblical Studies*, Atlanta: SBL.

Arnold, Bill T., 1996. "Luke's Characterizing Use of the Old Testament in the Book of Acts," in *History, Literature, and Society in the Book of Acts*, ed. Ben Witherington, Cambridge: University Press, 300–323.

Auld, Graeme A., 1975. "Judges 1 and History: A Reconsideration," *VT* 25: 261–285.

Auld, Graeme A., 1979. "Joshua. The Hebrew and Greek Texts," in *Studies in the Historical Books of the Old Testament* (VTSup 30), ed. John A. Emerton, Leiden: Brill, 1–14.

Auld, Graeme A., 1980. *Joshua, Moses and the Land. Tetrateuch-Pentateuch-Hexateuch in a Generation since 1938*, Edinburgh: T&T Clark.

Auld, Graeme A., 1986. "Reviewed Work: Textual Studies in the Book of Joshua by Leonard J. Greenspoon," *JBL* 105/1: 134–136.
Auld, Graeme A., 1998. *Joshua Retold: Synoptic Perspectives*, Edinburgh: T&T Clark.
Auld, Graeme A., 2005. *Joshua. Jesus son of Naue in Codex Vaticanus*, Leiden: Brill.
Aurelius, Erik, 2003. *Zukunft jenseits des Gerichts: Eine redaktionsgeschichtliche Studie zum Enneateuch* (BZAW 319), Berlin: de Gruyter.
Aurelius, Erik, 2008. "Zur Entstehung von Josua 23–24," in *Houses Full of All Good Things. Essays in Memory of Timo Veijola*, ed. Juha Pakkala and Martti Nissinen, Helsinki: Finnish Exegetical Society, Göttingen: Vandenhoeck & Ruprecht, 95–114.
Ausloos, Hans, 2014. "Literary Criticism and Textual Criticism in Judg 6:1–14 in Light of 4QJudg^a," *OTE* 27/2: 358–375.
Becker, Uwe, 2006. "Endredaktionelle Kontextvernetzungen des Josua-Buches," in *Die deuteronomistischen Geschichtswerke. Redaktions- und religionsgeschichtliche Perspektiven zur "Deuteronomismus"-Diskussion in Tora und Vorderen Propheten* (BZAW 365), ed. Markus Witte, Konrad Schmid, Doris Prechel and Jan Christian Gertz with the cooperation of Johannes F. Diehl, Berlin: De Gruyter, 139–161.
Becker, Uwe, 2011. *Exegese des Alten Testaments: Ein Methoden- und Arbeitsbuch, 3. Edition*, Tübingen: Mohr Siebeck.
Begg, Christopher T., 2007. "The demise of Joshua according to Josephus," *HTS* 63/1: 129–145.
Ben Zvi, Ehud, 2005. *Hosea. The forms of the Old Testament literature. Vol. 21A/1*, Grand Rapids: Eerdmans.
Bennett, William Henry, 1895. *The Book of Joshua. Critical Edition of the Hebrew Text*, Leipzig: J.C. Hinrichs.
Bieberstein, Klaus, 1994. *Lukian und Theodotion im Josuabuch. Mit einem Beitrag zu den Josuarollen von Hirbet Qumran* (BNB 7), München: Görg.
Bieberstein, Klaus, 1995. *Joshua – Jordan – Jericho. Archäologie, Geschichte und Theologie der Landnahmeerzählungen Joshua 1–6* (OBO 143), Freiburg: Universitätsverlag.
Bieberstein, Klaus, 2011. "Das Buch Josua und seine Horizonte," in *Das deuteronomistische Geschichtswerk* (Österreichische Biblische Studien 39), ed. Hermann-Josef Stipp, Wien: Peter Lang, 151–176.
Blum, Erhard, 1990. *Studien zur Komposition des Pentateuch* (BZAW 189), Berlin: de Gruyter.
Blum, Erhard, 1997. "Der kompositionelle Knoten am Übergang von Josua zu Richter: Ein Entflechtungsvorschlag," in *Deuteronomy and Deuteronomic Literature* (BEThl 132), ed. Marc Vervenne, Chris H. W. Brekelmand and Johan Lust. Leuven: Peeters, 194–206.
Brooke, George J., 2014. "Memory, Cultural Memory and Rewriting Scripture," in *Rewritten Bible after Fifty Years: Texts, Terms, or Techniques?* (JSOTSup 166), ed. József Zsengellér, Leiden: Brill, 119–136.
Brooke, George J., 2017. "What is Editing? What is an Edition? Towards a Taxonomy for Late Second Temple Jewish Literature," in *Insights into Editing in the Hebrew Bible and the Ancient Near East. What Does Documented Evidence Tell Us about the Transmission of Authoritative Texts?* (CBET 84), ed. Reinhard Müller and Juha Pakkala, Leuven: Peeters, 23–39.
Bodine, Walter R., 1980. *Greek Text of Judges: Recensional Developments* (HSM 23), Atlanta: Scholars Press.
Boling Robert G. / Wright G. Ernest, 1982. *Joshua. A New Translation with Introduction and Commentary. The Anchor Bible 6*, Yale: University Press.
Brooke, George J., 1983. *Joshua. Word Biblical Commentary, Vol. 7*, Waco: Thomas Nelson.

Brooke, George J., 2009. *Judges. Word Biblical Commentary, Vol. 8*, Waco: Thomas Nelson.
Brooke, George J., 2014. *Joshua 13–24. Word Biblical Commentary, Vol 7b*, Grand Rapids: Zondervan.
Callaway, Phillip R., 2011. *The Dead Sea Scrolls for a New Millenium*, Oregon: Cascade Books.
Carr, David, 2011. *The Formation of the Hebrew Bible. A New Reconstruction*, Oxford: University Press.
Carroll, Robert P., 1986. *Jeremiah: A Commentary*, Philadelphia: Westminster Press.
Cohen, Jeffrey M., 1981. *A Samaritan Chronicle. A Source-Critical Analysis of the Life and Times of the Great Samaritan Reformer, Baba Rabbah*, Leiden: Brill.
Cooke, George Albert, 1918. *The Book of Joshua in the Revised Version, with Introduction and Notes*, Cambridge: University Press.
Crane, Oliver Turnbull, 1890. *The Samaritan Chronicle or the Book of Joshua the Son of Nun*, New York: John B. Alden.
Crawford, Sidnie W., 2005. "Reading Deuteronomy in the Second Temple Period," in *Reading the Present in Qumran Library: The Perception of the Contemporary by Means of Scriptural Interpretations*, ed. Kristin De Troyer and Armin Lange, Atlanta: SBL, 127–140.
Crown, Alan D., 1964. "The Date and Authenticity of the Samaritan Hebrew Book of Joshua As Seen in Its Territorial Allotments," *PEQ* 96: 79–100.
Crown, Alan D., 1972. "New Light on the Interrelationship of Samaritan Chronicles from Some Manuscripts in the John Rylands Library," *BJRL* 54: 86–111.
Crown, Alan D. / Pummer, Reinhard / Tal, Abraham, 1993. *A Companion to Samaritan Studies*. Tübingen: Mohr Siebeck.
Davis, Kipp / Rabin, Ira / Feldman, Ines / Krutzsch, Myriam / Rimon, Hasia / Justnes, Årstein / Elgvin, Torleif / Langlois, Michael, 2017. "Nine Dubious 'Dead Sea Scrolls' Fragments from the Twenty-First Century," *DSD* 24: 1–40.
Davis, Malcolm C. / Outhwaite Ben, 2003a. *Hebrew Bible Manuscripts in the Cambridge Genizah Collection, Vol. 3* (Taylor-Schechter Additional Series 1–31), Cambridge: Cambridge University Press.
Davis, Malcolm C. / Outhwaite Ben, 2003b. *Hebrew Bible Manuscripts in the Cambidge Genizah Collection, Vol. 4* (Taylor-Schechter Additional Series 21–225 with addenda to previous volumes), Cambridge: Cambridge University Press.
De Rossi, Giovanni Bernardo, 1785. *Variae lectiones Veteris Testamenti, Vol. 2*, Parma: Regio.
De Troyer, Kristin, 2003. *Rewriting the Sacred Text. What the Old Greek Texts Tell Us about the Literary Growth of the Bible* (SBL Text-Critical Studies), Leiden: Brill.
De Troyer, Kristin, 2005a. "Joshua," in *Papyri Graecae Schøyen. PSchøyen 1* (Papyrologica Florentina 35), ed. R. Pintaudi, Firenze: Gonnelli, 79–159.
De Troyer, Kristin, 2005b. "Building the Altar and Reading the Law: The Journeys of Joshua 8:30–35," in *Reading the Present in the Qumran Library: The Perception of the Contemporary by Means of Scriptural Interpretations*, ed. Kristin De Troyer and Armin Lange, Atlanta: SBL, 141–164.
De Troyer, Kristin, 2006. "Reconstructing the OG of Joshua," in *Septuagint Research: Issues and Challenges in the Study of the Greek Jewish Scriptures*, Atlanta: SBL, 105–118.
De Troyer, Kristin, 2010. "Which Text Are We Using for Our Studies of Deuteronomistic Literature?" in *Congress Volume Helsinki 2010* (VTSup 148), Leiden: Brill, 461–472.
De Troyer, Kristin, 2013. "Reconstructing the Older Hebrew Text of the Book of Joshua: an Analysis of Joshua 10," *Text* 26: 1–33.

De Troyer, Kristin, 2016. "The Textual Plurality of the book of Joshua and the Need for a Digital Complutensian Polyglot Bible," in *The Text of the Hebrew Bible and Its Editions: Studies in the Celebration of the Fifth Centennial of the Complutensian Polyglot*, ed. Andres Piquer Otero and Pablo Torijano Morales, Leiden: Brill, 330–346.

De Troyer, Kristin, 2017. "The History of the Biblical Text: The Case of the Book of Joshua," in *Insights into Editing in the Hebrew Bible and the Ancient Near East. What Does Documented Evidence Tell Us about the Transmission of Authoritative Texts?* (CBET 84), ed. R. Müller and J. Pakkala, Leuven: Peeters, 223–265.

Debel, Hans, 2011. "Rewritten Bible, Variant Literary Editions and Original Text(s): Exploring the Implications of a Pluriform Outlook on the Scriptural Traditions," in *Changes in Scripture: Rewriting and Interpreting Authoritative Traditions in the Second Temple Period* (BZAW 419), ed. Hanne von Weissenberg, Juha Pakkala and Marko Marttila, Berlin: De Gruyter, 65–92.

Den Hertog, Cornelis Gijsbert, 1996. *Studien zur griechischen Übersetzung des Buches Josua*, Justus-Liebig-Universität Gießen Dissertation.

Den Hertog, Cornelis Gijsbert, 2011. "Jesus. Josue / Das Buch Josua," in *Septuaginta Deutsch. Erläuterungen und Kommentare. Band 1: Genesis bis 4. Makkabäer*, Ed. Martin Karrer and Wolfgang Kraus, Stuttgart: Deutsche Bibelgesellschaft, 605–656.

Dever, William G, 2003. *Who Were the Early Israelites, and Where Did They Come From?* Grand Rapids: Eerdmans.

Dillmann, August, 1886. *Die Bücher Numeri, Deuteronomium, und Josua. Kurzgefasstes exegetisches Handbuch zum Alten Testament, 2. Edition*, Leipzig: Hirzel.

Dogniez, Cécile, 2016. "Judges – 4.3 Septuagint," in *Textual History of the Bible*. General ed. A. Lange. Consulted online on 3 August 2017.

Donner, Herbert, 1985. "Tatian's *Diatessaron* and the Analysis of the Pentateuch," in *Empirical Models for Biblical Criticism*, ed. Jeffrey H. Tigay, Philadelphia: University of Philadelphia Press, 243–256.

Dozeman, Thomas, 2011. "The Book of Joshua as an Intertext in the MT and the LXX Canons," in *Pentateuch, Hexateuch, or Enneateuch? Identifying Literary Works in Genesis through Kings*, Atlanta: SBL, 185–210.

Dozeman, Thomas, 2015. *Joshua 1–12: A New Translation with Introduction and Commentary. The Anchor Bible 6*, Yale: Yale University Press.

Durham, John I., 1987. *Exodus. Word Biblical Commentary, Vol. 3*, Waco: Thomas Nelson.

Edelman, Diana, 1991. "Are the Kings of the Amorites 'Swept Away' in Joshua XXIV 12?" *VT* 41: 279–286.

Edenburgh, Cynthia / Pakkala, Juha, 2013. "Is Samuel among the Deuteronomists?" in *Is Samuel among the Deuteronomists? Current Views on the Place of Samuel in a Deuteronomistic History*, Ed. Cynthia Edenburgh and Juha Pakkala, Atlanta: SBL, 1–16.

Ehrlich, Arnold B., 1910. *Randglossen zur Hebräischen Bibel. Textkritisches, Sprachliches und Sachliches. Dritter Band: Josua, Richter, I. u. II. Samuels*, Leipzig: J. C. Hinrichs.

Farber, Zev, 2016. *Images of Joshua in the Bible and Their Reception* (BZAW 457), Berlin: de Gruyter.

Feldman, Ariel, 2013. *The Rewritten Joshua Scrolls from Qumran. Texts, Translations, and Commentary* (BZAW 438), Berlin: de Gruyter.

Fensham, Frank C., 1981. "Neh 9 and Pss 105, 106, 135 and 136: Post-Exilic Historical Traditions in Poetic Form," *JNSL* 9: 35–51.

Fernándes Marcos, Natalio, 1994. *Scribes and Translators: Septuagint and Old Latin in the Books of Kings* (VTSup 54), Leiden: Brill.

Finkelstein, Israel / Silberman, Neil Asher, 2002. *The Bible Unearthed. Archaeology's New Vision of Ancient Israel and the Origin of Its Sacred Texts*, New York: Touchstone.

Finsterbusch, Karin, 2012. "Deuteronomy and Joshua. Torah in the Book of Joshua in Light of Deuteronomy," *JAJ* 3: 166–196.

Finsterbusch, Karin, 2016. "3. Joshua – 3.2.2 Masoretic Text and Ancient Texts Close to mt," in *Textual History of the Bible*, ed. A. Lange, consulted online on 27 June 2017.

Fokkelman, Jan, 1991. *Narrative Art in Genesis. Specimens of Stylistic and Structural Analysis*, Second edition, Oregon: Wipf & Stock.

Fox, Michael, 2015. *Proverbs*: An *Eclectic Edition with Introduction and Textual Commentary*, Atlanta: SBL Press.

Fritz, Volkmar, 1994. *Das Buch Josua* (Handbuch zum Alten Testament 1/7), Tübingen: Mohr.

García Martínez, Florentino, 2012. "Light on the Joshua Books from the Dead Sea Scrolls," in *After Qumran: Old and Modern Editions of the Biblical Texts – The Historical Books* (BEThl 246), ed. Hand Ausloos, Bénédicte Lemmelijn and Julio Trebolle Barrera, Leuven: Peeters, 145–159.

Gaster, Moses, 1908. "Das Buch Josua in hebräisch-samaritanischer Rezension," *ZDMG* 62: 209–279.

Gaster, Moses, 1909. "The Samaritan Book of Joshua and the Septuagint," *PSBA* 31: 115–127.

Gaster, Moses, 1925. *The Samaritans: Their History, Doctrines and Literature*, London: British Academy.

Gaster, Moses, 1930. "The Samaritan Hebrew Sources of the Arabic Book of Joshua," *JRAS* 62: 567–599.

Gera, Deborah Levine, 2014. *Judith* (Commentaries on Early Jewish Literature), Berlin: de Gruyter.

Gertz, Jan Christian, 2000. "Die Stellung des kleinen geschichtlichen Credos in der Redaktionsgeschichte von Deuteronomium und Pentateuch," in *Liebe und Gebot. Studien zum Deuteronomium. Festschrift zum 70. Geburtstag von Lothar Perlitt* (FRLANT 190), ed. Reinhard Kratz and Hermann Spieckermann, Göttingen: Vandenhoeck & Ruprecht, 30–45.

Gooding, David W., 1974. "Traditions of Interpretation of the Circumcision at Gilgal," in *Proceedings of the World Congress of Jewish Studies, Vol. 1*, Jerusalem: Hebrew University, 149–164.

Greenspoon, Leonard J., 1983. *Textual Studies in the Book of Joshua* (HSM 28), California: Scholars Press.

Greenspoon, Leonard J., 2005. "The Book of Joshua – Part 1: Texts and Versions," *CBR* 3/2: 229–261.

Groß, Walter, 2011. "Das Richterbuch zwischen deuteronomistischem Geschichtswerk und Enneateuch," in *Das deuteronomistische Geschichtswerk*, ed. Hermann-Josef Stipp, Wien: Peter Lang, 177–206.

Gryson, Roger, 1999. *Altlateinische Handschriften = Manuscrits vieux latins: répertoire descriptif. Première partie: Mss 1 – 275, d'après un manuscrit inachevé de Hermann Josef Frede*, Freiburg: Verlag Herder.

Guillaume, Philippe, 2004. *Waiting for Josiah: The Judges*, London: T&T Clark.

Gärtner, Judith, 2015. "The Historical Psalms. A Study of Psalms 78; 105; 106; 135, and 136 as Key Hermeneutical Texts in the Psalter," *HeBAI* 4: 373–399.

Hautsch, Ernst, 1910. *Der Lukiantext des Oktateuch. Mitteilungen des Septuaginta-Unternehmens der Königlichen Gesellschaft der Wissenschaften zu Göttingen, Vol. 1*, Berlin: Weidmannsche Buchhandlung.

Hendel, Ronald S., 2016. *Steps to a New Edition of the Hebrew Bible*, Atlanta: SBL Press.
Hjelm, Ingrid, 2000. *The Samaritans and Early Judaism. A Literary Analysis* (JSOTSup 303), Sheffield: Sheffield Academic Press.
Hjelm, Ingrid, 2008. "Shiloh and Shechem: Competing Traditions?" Paper presented at SBL International Berlin 2002, published online at: http://shomron0.tripod.com/articles/shilohandshechem.pdf.
Hoffman, Hans-Detlef, 1980. *Reform und Reformen. Untersuchungen zu einem Grundthema der deuteronomistischen Geschichtsschreibung* (Theologie des Alten und Neuen Testaments 66), Zürich: Theologischer Verlag.
Hollenberg, Johannes, 1874. *Die deuteronomischen Bestandtheile des Buches Josua* (Theologische Studien und Kritiken 46), Leipzig: Hinrichs, 462–506.
Hollenberg, Johannes, 1876. *Der Charakter der Alexandrinischen Übersetzung des Buches Josua und ihr textkritischer Werth*, Moers: Eckner.
Holmes, Samuel, 1914. *Joshua. The Hebrew and Greek Texts*, Cambridge: University Press.
Janzen, John Gerald, 1973. *Studies in the Text of Jeremiah* (HSM 6), Michigan: Harvard University Press.
Jellicoe, Sidney, 1993. *The Septuagint and Modern Study*, Winona Lake: Eisenbrauns.
Jericke, Detlef von, 1996. "Josuas Tod und Josuas Grab. Eine redaktiongeschichtliche Studie," *ZAW* 108: 347–361.
Kahle, Paul, 1908. "Zum hebräischen Buch Josua der Samaritaner," *ZDMG* 62: 550–551.
Kennedy, James, 1903. *The Note-Line in the Hebrew Scriptures: Commonly Called paseq or pᵉsiq*, Edinburgh: T&T Clark.
Kennicott, Benjamin, 1776. *Vetus Testamentum Hebraicum: cum variis lectionibus*. Vol. 1, Oxonii: e typographeo Clarendoniano.
Klein, Anja, 2015. "Praying Biblical History. The Phenomenon of History in the Psalms," *HeBAI* 4: 400–426.
Knauf, Ernst Axel, 2008. *Josua* (Zürcher Bibelkommentare 6, Altes Testament), Zürich: Theologischer Verlag.
Knauf, Ernst Axel, 2010. "History in Joshua," in *Israel in Transition. From Late Bronze II to Iron IIa (c. 1250–850 BCE)*, London: T&T Clark, 130–139.
Knauf, Ernst Axel, 2013a. "Remembering Joshua," in *Remembering Biblical Figures in the Late Persian & Early Hellenistic Periods. Social Memory and Imagination*, ed. Diana V. Edelman and Ehud Ben Zvi, Oxford: University Press, 106–130.
Knauf, Ernst Axel, 2013b. "Samuel among the Prophets: 'Prophetical Redactions' in Samuel," in *Is Samuel among the Deuteromonists? Current Views on the Place of Samuel in a Deuteronomistic History*, ed. by Cynthia Edenburg and Juha Pakkala, Atlanta: SBL, 149–169.
Knauf, Ernst Axel, 2014 "Kings among the Prophets," in *The Production or Prophecy: Constructing Prophecy and Prophets in Yehud*, ed. Diana V. Edelman and Ehud Ben Zvi, London: Routledge, 131–149.
Knoppers, Gary N., 2005. "Establishing the Rule of Law? The Composition Num 33,50–56 and the Relationship Among the Pentateuch, the Hexateuch and the Deuteronomistic History," in *Das Deuteronomium Zwischen Pentateuch und Deuteronomistischen Geschichtswerk*, ed. Reinhard Achenbach and Eckart Otto, Göttingen: Vandenhoeck & Ruprecht, 135–154.
Koopmans, William T., 1990. *Joshua 24 as Poetic Narrative* (JSOTSup 93), Sheffield: JSOT Press.

Kratz, Reinhard G., 2000. *Die Komposition der erzählenden Bücher des Alten Testaments: Grundwissen der Bibelkritik*. Göttingen: Vandenhoeck & Ruprecht.

Kratz, Reinhard G., 2002. "Der vor- und der nachpriesterschriftliche Hexateuch," in *Abschied vom Jahwisten. Die Komposition des Hexateuch in der jüngsten Diskussion* (BZAW 315), Berlin: de Gruyter, 295–323.

Kratz, Reinhard G., 2005. *The Composition of the Narrative Books of the Old Testament*, trans. by John Bowden from Kratz 2000, London: T&T Clark.

Kratz, Reinhard G., 2016. "Reworked Pentateuch and Pentateuchal Theory," in *The Formation of the Pentateuch. Bridging the Academic Cultures of Europe, Israel, and North America* (Forschungen zum Alten Testament 111), ed. Jan C. Gertz, Bernard M. Levinson, Dalit Rom-Shiloni and Konrad Schmid, Tübingen: Mohr Siebeck, 501–524.

Kratz, Reinhard G., 2017. "Nahash, King of the Ammonites, in the Deuteronomistic History," in *Insights into Editing in the Hebrew Bible and the Ancient Near East. What Does Documented Evidence Tell Us about the Transmission of Authoritative Texts?* (CBET 84), Leuven: Peeters, 163–188.

Krause, Joachim J. 2014. *Exodus und Eisodus. Komposition und Theologie von Josua 1–5*, (VTSup 161), Leiden: Brill.

Kreuzer, Siegfried, 1989. *Die Frühgeschichte Israels in Bekenntnis und Verkündigung des Alten Testaments* (BZAW 178), Berlin: de Gruyter

Kreuzer, Siegfried, 1996. "Die Exodustradition im Deuteronomium," in *Das Deuteronomium und seine Querbeziehungen*, ed. Timo Veijola, Helsinki: PFES, 81–106.

Kreuzer, Siegfried, 2009. "Translation and Recension: Old Greek, Kaige, and Antiochene Text in Samuel and Reigns," *BIOSCS* 42: 34–51.

Kuenen, Abraham, 1886. *An Historico-Critical Inquiry into the Origin and Composition of the Hexateuch (Pentateuch and the Book of Joshua)*, London: Macmillan.

Köhler, Ludwig, 1936. "Hebräische Vokabeln I," *ZAW* 54: 287–293.

Latvus, Kari, 1998. *God, Anger and Ideology. The Anger of God in Joshua and Judges in Relation to Deuteronomy and the Priestly Writings* (JSOTSup 279), Sheffield: Sheffield Academic Press.

Lange, Armin, 2009. *Handbuch der Textfunde vom Toten Meer. Band 1: Die Handschriften biblischer Bücher von Qumran und den anderen Fundorten*, Tübingen: Mohr Siebeck.

Law, Timothy Michael / Kauhanen, Tuukka, 2010. "Methodological Remarks on the Textual History of Reigns: A Response to Siegfried Kreuzer," *BIOSCS* 43: 73–88.

Lemche, Niels Peter, 2008. *The Old Testament between Theology and History*, Louisville: Westminster John Knox Press.

Lemmelijn, Bénédicte, 2012. "Influence of a so-called P-Redaction in the 'Major Expansions' of Exod 7–11? Finding Oneself at the Crossroads of Textual and Literary Criticism," in *Textual Criticism and Dead Sea Scrolls Studies in Honour of Julio Trebolle Barrera* (JSJSup 157), ed. Andres Piquer Otero and Pablo A. Torijano, Leiden: Brill, 203–222.

Levin, Christoph, 1985. *Die Verheißung des neuen Bundes in ihrem theologiegeschichtlichen Zusammenhang ausgelegt* (FRLANT 137), Göttingen: Vandenhoeck & Ruprecht.

Levin, Christoph, 2007. "Review of Mareike Rake, "Juda wird aufsteigen!": Untersuchungen zum ersten Kapitel des Richterbuches," *Review of Biblical Literature*, published online at http://www.bookreviews.org/pdf/5685_6001.pdf

Levin, Christoph, 2013. *Re-Reading the Scriptures. Essays in the Literary History of the Old Testament* (Forschungen zum Alten Testament 87), Tübingen: Mohr Siebeck.

Lohfink, Norbert, 1991. "Kerygmata des deuteronomistischen Geschichtswerks," in *Studien zum Deuteronomium und zur deuteronomistischen Literatur* (SBAB 12), *Vol. 2*, Stuttgart: Katholisches Bibelwerk, 125–141.
Lohfink, Norbert, 1994. "The 'Small Credo' of Deuteronomy 26:5–9," in *Theology of the Pentateuch. Themes of the Priestly Narrative and Deuteronomy*, trans. Linda M. Maloney, Edinburgh: T&T Clark.
Margolis, Max L., 1910. "The Grouping of Codices in the Greek Joshua: A Preliminary Notice," (*JQR* 1), Philadelphia: Dropsie College, 259–263.
Margolis, Max L., 1927. "Specimen of a New Edition of the Greek Joshua," in *Jewish Studies in Memory of Israel Abrahams*, New York: Press of the Jewish Institute of Religion, 307–323.
Mayes, Andrew David Hastings, 1983. *The Story of Israel between Settlement and Exile: A Redactional Study of the Deuteronomistic History*, London: SCM.
Mays, James L., 1976. *Micah: A Commentary* (Old Testament Library), Philadelphia: The Westminster Press.
Mazor, Lea, 1994. "The Septuagint Translation of the Book of Joshua. Abstract of Thesis Submitted for the Degree Doctor of Philosophy to the Senate of Hebrew University, Jerusalem," *BIOSCS* 27: 29–38.
McCarter, Kyle P. Jr., 1984. *II Samuel: A New Translation with Introduction, Notes and Commentary*, The Anchor Bible 9, New York: Doubleday.
McKenzie, Steven, 2005. "Review of Michaël Meer, Formation and Reformulation: The Redaction of the Book of Joshua in the Light of the Oldest Textual Witnesses," in Review of Biblical Literature, published online at http://www.bookreviews.org/pdf/4368_4379.pdf.
Mendenhall, George E., 1955. *Law and Covenant in Israel and the Ancient Near East*, Pittsburgh: Biblical Colloquium.
Merrill, Eugene H., 2008. *An Historical Survey of the Old Testament*, Grand Rapids: Baker Academic.
Milstein, Sara J., 2016. *Tracking the Master Scribe: Revision through Introduction in Biblical and Mesopotamian Literature*, New York: Oxford University Press.
Moatti-Fine, Jacqueline, 1996. *La Bible d'Alexandrie: Jésus (Josué)*, Paris: Cerf.
Müller, Reinhard, 2004. *Königtum und Gottesherrschaft. Untersuchungen zur alttestamentlichen Monarchiekritik* (Forschungen zum Alten Testament 2), Tübingen: Mohr Siebeck.
Müller, Reinhard & Pakkala, Juha, 2017. *Insights into Editing in the Hebrew Bible and the Ancient Near East. What does the Documented Evidence Tell Us about the Transmission of Authoritative Texts?* (CBET 84), Leuven: Peeters.
Müller, Reinhard & Pakkala, Juha & Haar Romeny, Bas ter, 2014. *Evidence of Editing. Growth and Change of Texts in the Hebrew Bible* (SBLR 75), Atlanta: SBL.
Mowinckel, Sigmund, 1958. "'Rahelstämme' und 'Leastämme'," in *Von Ugarit nach Qumran* (BZAW 77), Berlin: de Gruyter, 129–150.
Mowinckel, Sigmund, 1964. *Tetrateuch-Pentateuch-Hexateuch. Die Berichte über die Landnahme in den drei altisraelitischen Geschichtswerken* (BZAW 90), Berlin: de Gruyter.
Mäkipelto, Ville / Tekoniemi, Timo / Tucker Miika, 2017. "Large-scale Transposition as an Editorial Technique in the Textual History of the Hebrew Bible," *TC* 22: 1–16.
Möhlenbrinck, Kurt, 1938. "Die Landnahmesagen des Buches Josua," *ZAW* 56: Berlin: de Gruyter, 238–268.
Nelson, Richard, 1981a. *The Double Redaction of the Deuteronomistic History*, Sheffield: JSOT Press.

Nelson, Richard, 1981b. "Josiah in the Book of Joshua," *JBL* 100/4: 531–540.
Nelson, Richard, 1997. *Joshua*, Louisville: Westminster John Knox Press.
Nentel, Jochen, 2000. *Trägerschaft und Intentionen des deuteronomistischen Geschichtswerks. Untersuchungen zu den Reflexionsreden Jos 1; 23; 24, 1 Sam 12 und 1 Kön 8* (BZAW 297), Berlin: de Gruyter.
Nielsen, Eduard, 1955. *Shechem. A Traditio-Historical Investigation*, Copenhagen: Gad.
Nihan, Christophe, 2013. "1 Samuel 8 and 12 and the Deuteronomistic Edition of Samuel," in *Is Samuel among the Deuteromonists? Current Views on the Place of Samuel in a Deuteronomistic History*, ed. Cynthia Edenburg and Juha Pakkala, Atlanta: SBL, 207–273.
Nodet, Étienne, 1997. *A Search for the Origins of Judaism: From Joshua to the Mishnah* (JSOTSup 248), Sheffield: Sheffield Academic Press.
Noort, Ed, 1993. "Josua 24,28–31, Richter 2,6–9 und das Josuagrab. Gedanken zu einem Straßenschild," in *Biblische Welten. Festschrift für Martin Metzger zu seinem 65. Geburtstag*, ed. Wolfgang Zwickel, Göttingen: Vandenhoeck & Ruprecht, 109–130.
Noort, Ed, 1998. *Das Buch Josua. Forschungsgeschichte und Problemfelder* (Erträge der Forschung 292), Darmstadt: Wissenschaftliche Buchgesellschaft.
Noth, Martin, 1930. *Das System der Zwölf Stämme Israels* (Beiträge zur Wissenschaft vom Alten und Neuen Testament 4), Stuttgart: Kohlhammer.
Noth, Martin, 1938. *Das Buch Josua* (Handbuch zum Alten Testament 7), Tübingen: Mohr.
Noth, Martin, 1943. *Überlieferunsgeschichtliche Studien: Die sammelnden und bearbeitenden Geschichtswerke im Alten Testament, Vol 1*, Halle: Niemeyer.
Noth, Martin, 1953. *Das Buch Josua. Handbuch zum Alten Testament 7, Second Edition*, Tübingen: Mohr.
Noth, Martin, 1962. *Exodus: A Commentary* (Old Testament Library), Philadelphia: The Westminster Press.
Noth, Martin, 1971. "Israelitische Stämme zwischen Ammon und Moab," in *Aufsätze zur biblischen Landes- und Altertumskunde, Vol. 1*, Neukirchen-Vluyn: Neukirchener Verlag, 319–433.
Noth, Martin, 1981. *The Deuteronomistic History* (JSOTSup 15), trans. from German 1967, Sheffield: JSOT Press.
Odorico, Marco De, 1994. "Compositional and Editorial Processes of Annalistic and Summary Texts of Tiglath-pileser III," *SAAB* 8/2: 67–112.
Olson, Dennis T., 2011. "Balaam," in *Encyclopedia of the Bible and its Reception, Vol. 3*, Berlin: de Gruyter, 357–373.
Orlinsky, Harry M., 1968. "The Hebrew Vorlage of the Septuagint of the Book of Joshua," in *Congress Volume: Rome, 1968* (VTSup 17), Leiden: Brill, 187–195.
Otto, Eckart, 2009. *Die Tora Studien zum Pentateuch. Gesammelte Schriften* (Beihefte zur Zeitschrift für Altorientalische und Biblische Rechtsgeschichte 9), Wiesbaden: Harrasowitz Verlag.
O'Brien, Mark, 1990. *The Deuteronomistic History Hypothesis: A Reassessment* (OBO 92), Göttingen: Vandenhoeck & Ruprecht.
Pakkala, Juha, 2004. *Ezra the Scribe. The Development of Ezra 7–10 and Nehemia 8* (BZAW 349), Berlin: de Gruyter.
Pakkala, Juha, 2007. "The Monotheism of the Deuteronomistic History," *SJOT* 21: 159–178.
Pakkala, Juha, 2008. "The Nomistic Roots of Judaism," in *Houses Full of All Good Things: Essays in Memory of Timo Veijola*, ed. Juha Pakkala and Martti Nissinen, Helsinki: Finnish Exegetical Society, 251–268.

Pakkala, Juha, 2013. *God's Word Omitted* (FRLANT 251), Göttingen: Vandenhoeck & Ruprecht.
Popović, Mladen, 2009. "Conquest of the Land, Loss of the Land: Where Does Josh 24 Belong?" in *The Land of Israel in Bible, History, and Theology. Studies in Honour of Ed Noort*, Leiden: Brill, 87–98.
Perlitt, Lothar, 1969. *Bundestheologie im Alten Testament* (Wissenschaftliche Monographien zum Alten und Neuen Testament 36), Neukirchen-Vluyn: Neukirchener Verlag.
Person, Raymond F. Jr., 1997. *The Kings – Isaiah and Kings – Jeremiah Recensions* (BZAW 252), Berlin: de Gruyter.
Person, Raymond F. Jr. / Rezetko, Robert, 2016. *Empirical Models Challenging Biblical Criticism*, Atlanta: Society of Biblical Literature.
Pressler, Carolyn, 2002. *Joshua, Judges, and Ruth*, Louisville: Westminster John Knox Press.
Pretzl, Otto, 1928. "Die griechischen Handschriftengruppen im Buche Josua untersucht nach ihrer Eigenart und ihrem Verhältnis zueinander," *Biblica* 9: 377–427.
Pritchard, James B., 1954. *The Ancient Near East in Pictures, Relating to the Old Testament*, Princeton: Princeton University Press.
Rahlfs, Alfred, 1914. *Verzeichnis der griechischen Handschriften des Alten Testaments, für das Septuaginta-Unternehmen aufgestellt* (Mitteilungen des Septuaginta-Unternehmens 2), Berlin: Weidmann.
Rake, Mareike, 2006. *"Juda wird aufsteigen!" Untersuchungen zum ersten Kapitel des Richterbuches* (BZAW 367), Berlin: de Gruyter.
Reventlow, Henning Graf, 1993. *Das Alte Testament Deutsch: neues Göttinger Bibelwerk. Teilband 25/2, Die Propheten Haggai, Sacharja und Maleachi*, Göttingen: Vandenhoeck & Ruprecht.
Rofé, Alexander, 1982. "The End of the Book of Joshua According to the Septuagint," *Henoch* 9: 17–36.
Römer, Thomas, 2006. "The Elusive Yahwist: A Short History of Research," in *A Farewell to the Yahwist? The Composition of the Pentateuch in Recent European Interpretation*, ed. Thomas B. Dozeman and Konrad Schmid, Atlanta: SBL.
Römer, Thomas, 2010. "Book-Endings in Joshua and the Question of the So-Called Deuteronomistic History," in *Raising Up a Faithful Exegete: Essays in Honor of R. D. Nelson*, ed. Kurt L. Noll and Brooks Schramm, Winona Lake: Eisenbrauns, 85–99.
Römer, Thomas, 2012. "Deuteronomistic History," in *Encyclopedia of the Bible and its Reception, Vol. 6*, Berlin: de Gruyter, 648–653.
Römer, Thomas, 2017. "The Date, Composition and Function of Joshua 24 in Recent Research. A Response to Joachim J. Krause, Cynthia Edenburgh, and Konrad Schmid," *HeBAI* 6/2, 203–216.
Römer, Thomas C. / Brettler, Marc Z., 2000. "Deuteronomy 34 and the Case for a Persian Hexateuch," *JBL* 119/3: 401–419.
Rösel, Harmut N., 1980. "Die Überleitungen vom Josua- ins Richterbuch," *VT* 30/3: 342–350.
Rösel, Martin, 2002. "The Septuagint-Version of the Book of Joshua," *SJOT* 16: 5–23.
Rösel, Martin, 2011. *Joshua. Historical Commentary of the Old Testament*, Leuven: Peeters.
Schenker, Adrian, 2003. *The Earliest Text of the Hebrew Bible. The Relationship between the Masoretic Text and the Hebrew Base of the Septuagint Reconsidered*, ed. Adrian Schenker, Leiden: Brill.
Schenker, Adrian, 2008. "Altar oder Altarmodell? Textgeschichte von Jos 22,9–34," in *Florilegium Lovaniense. Studies in Septuagint and Textual Criticism in Honour of Florentino*

García Martínez (BEThL 224), ed. Hans Ausloos, Bénédicte Lemmelijn and Marc Vervenne, Leuven: Peeters, 417–426.

Schley, Donald G, 1989. *Shiloh. A Biblical City in Tradition and History* (JSOTSup 63), Sheffield: JSOT Press.

Schmid, Konrad, 1999. *Erzväter und Exodus. Untersuchungen zur doppelten Begründung der Ursprünge Israels innerhalb der Geschichtsbücher des Alten Testaments* (Wissenschaftliche Monographien zum Alten und Neuen Testament 89), Neukirchen-Vluyn: Neukirchener Verlag.

Schmid, Konrad, 2017. "Jews and Samaritans in Joshua 24," *HeBAI* 6/2, 148–160.

Schmitt, Götz, 1964. *Der Landtag von Sichem* (Arbeiten zur Theologie 15), Stuttgart: Calwer Verlag.

Schreiner, Joseph, 1957. *Septuaginta-Massora des Buches der Richter*, Rome: Pontifical Biblical Institute Press.

Sigismund, Marcus, 2012. "Der Codex Lugdunensis als textkritischer Indikator für die Old Greek des Buches Josua^{LXX}," in *Die Septuaginta – Enstehung, Sprache, Geschichte*, Tübingen: Mohr Siebeck, 626–634.

Sigismund, Marcus, 2016. "Der antiochenische Text im Buch Josua^{LXX} und seine Bedeutung für die älteste Septuaginta-Eine erste Reevaluation," in *XV Congress of the International Organization for Septuagint and Cognate Studies*, ed. Wolfgang Kraus, Michaël N. Van der Meer and Martin Meiser, Atlanta: SBL, 13–36.

Simpson, Cuthbert Aikman, 1948. *The Early Traditions of Israel. A Critical Analysis of the Pre-deuteronomic Narrative of the Hexateuch*, Oxford: Blackwell.

Sipilä, Seppo, 1993. "A Note to the Users of Margolis' Joshua Edition," *BIOSCS* 26: 17–21.

Sipilä, Seppo, 1997. "John Chrysostom and the Book of Joshua," in *IX Congress of the International Organization for Septuagint and Cognate Studies*, ed. Bernard A. Taylor, Atlanta: Scholars Press, 329–354.

Sipilä, Seppo, 1998. "Max Leopold Margolis and the Origenic Recension in Joshua," in *Origen's Hexapla and Fragments* (Texte und Studium zum Antiken Judentum 58), ed. Alison Salvesen, Tübingen: Mohr Siebeck, 16–38.

Sipilä, Seppo, 1998. "Theodoret of Cyrrhus and the Book of Joshua Theodoret's *Quastiones* Revisited," *Text* 19: 157–170.

Sipilä, Seppo, 1999. *Between Literalness and Freedom. Translation technique in the Septuagint of Joshua and Judges regarding the clause connections introduced by* ו *and* כי (PFES 75), Helsinki: Finnish Exegetical Society.

Sipilä, Seppo, 2014. "Old Latin Text of Josh. 5:4–6 and its Contribution to the Textual History of the Greek Joshua," in *In the Footsteps of Sherlock Holmes. Studies in the Biblical Text in Honour of Anneli Aejmelaeus* (CBET 72), ed. Kristin De Troyer, Timothy Michael Law and Marketta Liljeström, Leuven: Peeters, 257–272.

Smend, Rudolph, 1971. "Das Gesetz und die Völker. Ein Beitrag zur deuteronomistischen Redaktionsgeschichte," in *Probleme biblischer Theologie. Gerhard von Rad zum 70. Geburtstag*, ed. Hans Walter Wolff, München: Kaiser 1971, 494–509.

Smith, Gary Verlan, 1978. *An Introduction to the Greek Manuscripts of Joshua: Their Classification, Characteristics and Relationship*, Philadelphia: Dropsie University Dissertation.

Soggin, Alberto, 1972. *Joshua: A Commentary* (Old Testament Library), London: SCM Press.

Soggin, Alberto, 1981. *Judges: A Commentary* (Old Testament Library), London: SCM Press.

Soisalon-Soininen, Ilmari, 1965. *Die Infinitive in der Septuaginta*. Helsinki: Suomalainen Tiedeakatemia.

Soisalon-Soininen, Ilmari, 1987. "Beobachtungen zur Arbeitsweise der Septuaginta-Übersetzer," in *Studien zur Septuaginta-Syntax* (AASF 237), ed. Anneli Aejmelaeus and Raija Sollamo, Helsinki: Suomalainen Tiedeakatemia.
Sollamo, Raija, 1979. *Renderings of Hebrew Semiprepositions in the Septuagint* (AASF 19), Helsinki: Suomalainen Tiedeakatemia.
Sollamo, Raija, 1987. "Joosuan kirjan Septuaginta-käännöksen luonteesta," *TA* 92: 191–198.
Spencer, John R., 1992. "Phinehas (PERSON)," in *The Anchor Bible Dictionary, Vol 5: O–Sh*, ed. David Noel Freedman. New York: Doubleday.
Sperling, David S., 1987. "Joshua 24 Re-examined," *Hebrew Union College Annual* 58: 119–136.
Sperling, David S., 2000. "Joshua 24 Re-examined," in *Reconsidering Israel and Judah. Recent Studies on the Deuteronomistic History*, ed. Gary N. Knoppers and J. Gordon McConville, Winona Lake: Eisenbrauns, 240–259.
Spronk, Klaas, 2009. "From Joshua to Samuel: Some Remarks on the Origin of the Book of Judges," in *The Land of Israel in Bible, History, and Theology*, Leiden: Brill, 137–150.
Steck, Odil Hannes, 1998. *Old Testament Exegesis. A Guide to Methodology*, Second edition (SBL Resources for Biblical Study 39), trans. by James D. Nogalski, Atlanta: Scholars Press.
Stenberg, Robert J. & Kaufman, James C., 2010. *The Cambridge Handbook of Creativity*, Cambridge: University Press.
Stenhouse, Paul, 1989. "Samaritan Chronicles," in *The Samaritans*, ed. Alan D. Crown, Tübingen: Mohr Siebeck, 218–265.
Steuernagel, Carl, 1900. *Übersetzung und Erklärung der Bücher Deuteronomium und Josua und Allgemeine Einleitung in den Hexateuch* (Handkommentar zum Alten Testament 3), Göttingen: Vandenhoeck & Ruprecht.
Sweeney, Marvin A., 2010. *Form and Intertextuality in Prophetic and Apocalyptic Literature*, Oregon: Wipf & Stock.
Talmon, Shemaryahu, 1981. "Polemics and Apology in Biblical Historiography: 2 Kings 17:24–41," in *The Creation of Sacred Literature. Composition and Redaction of the Biblical Text*, ed. Richard Elliot Friedman, Berkeley: University of California Press, 57–68.
Tigay, Jeffrey H., 1982. *The Evolution of the Gilgamesh Epic*, Philadelphia: University of Philadelphia Press.
Tigay, Jeffrey H., 1985. *Empirical Models for Biblical Criticism*, Philadelphia: University of Pennsylvania Press.
Thackeray, Henry St. John, 1909. *A Grammar of the Old Testament in Greek according to the Septuagint, Vol. 1*, Cambridge: University Press.
Thompson, Thomas L., 1974. *The Historicity of the Patriarchal Narratives: The Quest for the Historical Abraham* (BZAW 133), Berlin: de Gruyter.
Thornton, Timothy, 1998. "Anti-Samaritan Exegesis Reflected in Josephus' Retelling of Deuteronomy, Joshua and Judges." *JTS* 47: Oxford: Oxford University Press, 125–130.
Tov, Emanuel, 1998. "The Rewritten Book of Joshua as Found at Qumran and Masada," in *Biblical Perspectives: Early Use and Interpretation of the Bible in Light of the Dead Sea Scrolls* (STDJ 28), ed. Michael Stone and Ester G. Chazon, Leiden: Brill, 233–256.
Tov, Emanuel, 1999a. "Midrash-Type Exegesis in Joshua in the Septuagint of Joshua," in *The Greek and Hebrew Bible. Collected Essays on the Septuagint* (VTSup 72), Leiden: Brill, 153–163.
Tov, Emanuel, 1999b. "The Fifth Fascicle of Margolis' The Book of Joshua in Greek," in *The Greek and Hebrew Bible. Collected Essays on the Septuagint* (VTSup 72), Leiden: Brill, 21–30.

Tov, Emanuel, 1999c. "The Growth of the Book of Joshua in Light of the Evidence of the Septuagint," in *The Greek and Hebrew Bible. Collected Essays on the Septuagint* (VTSup 72), Leiden: Brill, 385–396.

Tov, Emanuel, 1999d. "Some Sequence Differences Between the Masoretic Text and the Septuagint and their Ramifications for Literary Criticism," in *The Greek and Hebrew Bible. Collected Essays on the Septuagint* (VTSup 72), Leiden: Brill, 411–418.

Tov, Emanuel, 1999e. "Glosses, Interpolations, and Other types of Scribal Additions in the Text of the Hebrew Bible," in *The Book of Joshua* (BEThL 250), ed. E. Noort, Leuven: Peeters, 53–74.

Tov, Emanuel, 1999f. "The Literary History of the book of Jeremiah in Light of its Textual History," in *The Greek and Hebrew Bible. Collected Essays on the Septuagint* (VTSup 72), Leiden: Brill, 363–384.

Tov, Emanuel, 2004. *Scribal Practices and Approaches Reflected in the Texts Found in the Judean Desert*, Leiden: Brill.

Tov, Emanuel, 2012. *Textual Criticism of the Hebrew Bible*, Third edition, revised and expanded, Minneapolis: Fortress Press.

Tov, Emanuel, 2015a. *The Text-Critical Use of the Septuagint in Biblical Research*. Third edition, Winona Lake: Eisenbrauns.

Tov, Emanuel, 2015b. "Literary Development of the Book of Joshua as Reflected in the MT, the LXX, and 4QJosh^a," in *Textual Criticism of the Hebrew Bible, Qumran, Septuagint. Collected Essays, Vol. 3* (VTSup 167), Leiden: Brill, 132–153.

Trebolle, Barrera Julio C., 2005. "The Text-Critical Value of the Old Latin and Antiochean Greek Texts in the Books of Judges and Joshua." in *Interpreting Translation: Studies on the LXX and Ezekiel in honour of Johan Lust* (BEThL 192), ed. Florentino García Martínez and Marc Vervenne, Leuven: Peeters, 401–413.

Trebolle, Barrera Julio C., 2008. "A Combined Textual and Literary Criticism Analysis: Editorial Traces in Joshua and Judges," in *Florilegium Lovaniense: Studies in Septuagint and Textual Criticism in Honour of Florentino García Martínez* (BEThL 224), eds. Hans Ausloos, Bénédicte Lemmelijn and Marc Vervenne, Leuven: Peeters, 437–463.

Trebolle, Barrera Julio C., 2014. "Textual Variants in Joshua – Kings Involving the Terms 'People' and 'Israel'," in *In the Footsteps of Sherlock Holmes: Studies in the Biblical Text in Honour of Anneli Aejmelaeus* (CBET 72), ed. Kristin De Troyer, Timothy Michael Law and Marketta Liljeström, Leuven: Peeters, 231–256.

Trebolle, Barrera Julio C., 2016. "Division Markers as Empirical Evidence for the Editorial Growth of Biblical Books," in *Empirical Models Challenging Biblical Criticism*, ed. Raymond F. Person and Robert Rezetko, Atlanta: SBL, 165–216.

Ulrich, Eugene, 1992. "4QPaleoParaJoshua," in *Qumran Cave 4.4: Palaeo-Hebrew and Greek biblical manuscripts* (DJD 9), ed. Patrick W. Skehan, Eugene Ulrich and Judith E. Sanderson, Oxford: Oxford University Press, 201–203.

Ulrich, Eugene, 1995. "4QJosh^a," in *Qumran Cave 4.9: Deuteronomy, Joshua, Judges, Kings* (DJD 14), ed. Eugene Ulrich, Frank M. Cross, Sidney W. Crawford, Julie A. Duncan, Patrick W. Skehan, Emanuel Tov and Julio Trebolle Barrera, Oxford: Oxford University Press, 143–152.

Ulrich, Eugene, 2008. "Deuteronomistically Inspired Scribal Insertions into the Developing Biblical Texts: 4QJudg^a and 4QJer^a," in *Houses Full of All Good Things: Essays in Memory of Timo Veijola*, ed. Juha Pakkala and Martti Nissinen, Helsinki: Finnish Exegetical Society, 489–506.

Ulrich, Eugene, 2010. *The Biblical Qumran Scrolls. Transcriptions and Textual Variants* (VTSup 134), Leiden: Brill.

Ulrich, Eugene, 2015. *The Dead Sea Scrolls and the Developmental Composition of the Hebrew Bible* (VTSup 196), Leiden: Brill.
Van der Meer, Michaël N., 2004. *Formation and Reformulation. The Redaction of the Book of Joshua in the Light of the Oldest Textual Witnesses* (VTSup 102), Leiden: Brill.
Van der Meer, Michaël N., 2015. "Joshua," in *T&T Clark Companion to the Septuagint*, London: Bloomsbury T&T Clark, 86–101.
Van der Kooij, Arie, 2016. "On the Use of ἀλλόφυλος in the Septuagint," in *XV Congress of the International Organization for Septuagint and Cognate Studies*, ed. Wolfgang Kraus, Michaël N. Van der Meer and Martin Meiser, Atlanta: SBL, 401–408.
Van der Toorn, Karel, 2007. *Scribal Culture and the Making of the Hebrew Bible*, Cambridge: Harvard University Press.
VanderKam, James C., 2001. *The Book of Jubilees*, Sheffield: Academic Press.
VanderKam, James C., 2010. *The Dead Sea Scrolls Today, Second Edition*, Grand Rapids: Eerdmans.
Van Seters, John, 1975. *Abraham in History and Tradition*, New Haven: Yale University Press.
Van Seters, John, 1983. *In Search of History: Historiography in the Ancient World and the Origins of Biblical History*, New Haven: Yale University Press.
Van Seters, John, 1984. "Joshua 24 and the Problem of Tradition in the Old Testament," in *In the Shelter of Elyon: Essays on Ancient Palestinian Life and Literature in Honour of G. W. Ahlström* (JSOTSup 31), ed. W. Boyd Barrick and John R. Spencer, Sheffield: JSOT Press, 139–158.
Van Seters, John, 2006. *The Edited Bible: The Curious History of the "Editor" in Biblical Criticism*, Winona Lake: Eisenbrauns.
Veijola, Timo, 1975. *Die ewige Dynastie: David und die Enstehung seiner Dynastie nach der deuteronomistischen Darstellung*, Helsinki: Suomalainen Tiedeakatemia.
Veijola, Timo, 1977. *Das Königtum in der Beurteilung der deuteronomistischen Historiographie: eine redaktionsgeschichtliche Untersuchung* (AASF 198), Helsinki: Suomalainen Tiedeakatemia.
Vetter, Dieter, 1976. "שמד," in *Theologisches Handwörterbuch zum Alten Testament*, Vol. 2, ed. Ernst Jenni and Claus Westermann, München: Kaiser, 963–965.
Vroom, Jonathan, 2016. "A Cognitive Approach to Copying Errors: Haplography and Textual Transmission of the Hebrew Bible," *JSOT* 40: 259–279.
Von Rad, Gerhard, 1938. *Das formgeschichtliche Problem des Hexateuchs* (BWANT 78), Stuttgart: Kohlhammer.
Von Rad, Gerhard, 1962. *Old Testament Theology. Vol 1: The Theology of Israel's Historical Traditions*, trans. D. M. G. Stalker, Edinburgh and London: Oliver and Boyd.
Ward, Thomas B. & Kolomyts, Yuliya, 2010. "Cognition and Creativity," in *The Cambridge Handbook of Creativity*, Cambridge: University Press, 93–112.
Wellhausen, Julius, 1871. *Der Text der Bücher Samuelis*, Göttingen: Vandenhoeck & Ruprecht.
Wellhausen, Julius, 1899. *Die Composition des Hexateuchs und der Historischen Bücher des Alten Testaments, Dritte Auflage*, Berlin: G. Reimer.
Wijngaards, John, 1967. "הוציא and העלה A Twofold Approach to the Exodus," *VT* 15: 91–102.
Wischmeyer, Oda, 2006. "Stephen's Speech Before the Sanhedrin Against the Background of the Summaries of the History of Israel (Acts 7)," in *Deuterocanonical and Cognate Literature Yearbook 2006: History and Identity: How Israel's Later Authors Viewed its Earlier History*, ed. Nuria Calduch-Benages and Jan Liesen, Berlin: de Gruyter, 341–358.

Witte, Markus, 2010. "'What Share Do We Have in David...?' – Ben Sira's Perspectives on 1 Kings 12," in *One God – One Cult – One Nation. Archaeological and Biblical Perspectives* (BZAW 405), ed. Reinhard G. Kratz and Hermann Spieckermann, Berlin: de Gruyter, 91–120.

Woudstra, Marten, 1981. *The Book of Joshua*. Grand Rapids: Eerdmans.

Wright, Jacob L., 2010. "Continuing These Conversations," in *Historiography and Identity (Re)formulation in Second Temple Historiographical Literature*, ed. Louis Jonker, London: T&T Clark, 149–165.

Würthwein, Ernst, 1977. *Das Alte Testament Deutsch: neues Göttinger Bibelwerk 11, 1. Die Bücher der Könige: das erste Buch der Könige, Kapitel 1–16*, Göttingen: Vandenhoeck & Ruprecht.

Würthwein, Ernst, 1994. *The Text of the Old Testament, Second Edition*, trans. Erroll F. Rhodes, Grand Rapids: Eerdmans.

Yahuda, Abraham S., 1908. "Über die Unechtheit des Samaritanischen Josuabuches," *Sitzungsberichte der Königlich Preußischen Akademie der Wissenschaften* 39: 887–914.

Zahn, Molly, 2011. "Talking About Rewritten Texts: Some Reflections on Terminology," in *Changes in Scripture: Rewriting and Interpreting Authoritative Traditions in the Second Temple Period*, ed. Hanne von Weissenberg, Juha Pakkala and Marko Marttila, Berlin: de Gruyter, 93–120.

Index of Ancient Sources

This index does not aim at being complete but mentions mostly passages that have been discussed beyond a brief mention or are related in a significant way to the argumentation. The verse numbering follows the MT.

Hebrew Bible / Old Testament

Genesis
11–13 173, 174
11:26–32 173
12:6–8 68, 176
12:6 67, 190
12:7 173
14:22 173
15:19–21 89
17 136
17:8 174
33:19 124
33:20 70
35:1–15 70, 175
35:2 99, 210
35:3 210
35:4 67, 99
48:22 174, 175
49:1–27 249
49:1 113
50:22 240
50:25 68

Exodus
4:24–26 136
12–14 173, 204
12:23 177
12:27 177
12:38 138
12:43–48 137
12:51 177
13:19 68
14 72, 177, 178, 233, 257
14:9 177, 178, 257
14:10 79, 177, 178, 257
14:20 78, 177, 178, 257
14:23 257
14:28 177, 257
14:31 178
15:10 257
18–24 74
20 83
20:2 105
20:4 110
20:5 117
23:23 89, 179
23:28 91, 179
34:14 117
34:16 43

Leviticus
26–27 248

Numbers
11:4 138
14:29 138
20:15–16 78, 79, 195
21–24 173, 180, 181
21:21–25 180
22:5 181
31:16 181
32:13 264

Deuteronomy
1:34–46 137
1:46 140, 178, 179
2:14–15 264
2:16 137
2:24 180
2:30 180
3:2 180
4:1 183
4:9 179
4:10 182
4:24 117
4:34 106, 164
4:45 183
5:6 105
5:8 110
5:9 117, 141
6:1 183

6:2 182
6:4 173, 183
6:10–13 173, 181, 182, 195, 196, 216
6:12 105, 183
6:13–14 173, 182
6:13 182
6:15 117
6:20–24 74, 87, 88
6:22 106, 183
6:24 182
7:1 89, 179
7:3 43
7:6 173, 182, 194
7:9 103, 104
7:19 106, 179
7:20 91
7:24 180
8:14 105
9:1–5 175
9:20 74
10:6 74
11:16–17 185–187
11:26 173, 182, 194
12:2 110
13:5 183
13:11 105
16:21 110
17:14–15 88
20:13 180
21:10 180
23:5–6 181
23:6 85–87, 180, 181
26:3 114
26:5–10 74, 87, 88, 173, 194, 195, 204
26:5–6 72, 73, 75–77
26:7 78–80, 83, 178, 257
26:8 106
27:1–8 173, 183, 185, 267
29:2 106, 179
29:20 184
29:24 123
29:26 57
29:29 65
30:15–20 173, 182, 194, 209
31:24–27 173, 183
31:28 65
31:29 113, 114

32 249
32:45 212
32:50 74
34:5–9 128, 160, 173, 235, 236, 270

Joshua
1 7, 36, 233
1:1 160, 235
1:2–9 82
1:7–9 223, 235
1:14 160
1:15 160
2:11 103
2:15 31
3:6 25
4:6 76
4:10 135, 160
5 28, 259, 260
5:2–13 7, 36
5:2–9 130–142, 145
5:2 35
5:4ff. 32, 34, 107, 143, 144, 159, 160, 215, 243, 262–264, 270, 272
5:6 26
5:9 136
6 28, 188, 233
6:26 28
7 28
7:5 30
7:12 84
7:15 185
8:1–35 7, 36
8:11–13 35, 41
8:30–35 66, 151, 152, 166, 173, 184, 185, 187, 188, 211, 235, 242, 265, 267
8:33 64–66, 162, 185, 203, 216
8:34–35 41, 135, 266
9:1–2 265
9:16 58
10 8, 9, 233
10:14–17 35
10:10 30
10:12 45
10:20 30
11:3 26
11:23 208, 213, 227
12:6 160

13–19 34, 184, 188, 216, 227, 231, 238
13:1–6 235
13:1 208, 216, 223, 227
13:7, 8 30
13:22 181
13:23 235
13:33 160
14:2 160
14:3 160
14:8 114
14:15 26
15:8 255, 256
15:13 26
16:10 28
18 28, 71, 261
18:1 67, 233, 234
18:7 146
18:12 26
18:13 255, 256
19 28
19:49–50 143
20 32, 33
20:4–6 45
20:7 176
21:2 67
21:11 26
21:21 176
21:42 28, 136, 142–144, 159, 160
21:43–45 223, 233
22 9, 26, 69, 70, 100, 123, 151, 152
22:4 160
22:9 67
22:10–34 26, 27
22:12 67, 69
22:13 124
22:18–19 100
22:27–28 9
22:29 69
23–24 47, 63, 64, 163, 168, 184–187, 197, 215–223, 231, 232, 242
23 84, 183, 226
23:1 164, 216, 223
23:2 63–66, 162, 184, 185, 203, 208, 216, 221, 270
23:3 164, 208, 216
23:4–16 231
23:6 187, 223
23:14 164
23:16 185–187
24:1–13 51–91, 105, 168, 172, 173, 176, 180, 194–197, 207–209, 212, 214–217, 219, 231, 241
24:1 36, 56, 63–71, 110, 111, 156, 161, 162, 164, 175, 176, 184, 185, 191, 193, 203, 207, 208, 216, 221, 233, 261, 270, 272
24:2 57, 99, 172–174, 190, 191, 203, 207, 208, 210, 216, 261, 272
24:3 57, 89, 90, 156, 162, 172–174, 195, 254, 255, 258, 261
24:4–7 71–73, 204
24:4 57, 75–77, 79, 90, 156, 172–174, 183, 195, 196, 214, 258, 261
24:5–13 57–58, 66, 80–88, 156, 157, 168, 207, 261, 262
24:5 24, 49, 58–60, 73–77, 79, 87, 145, 156, 160, 162, 176, 181, 189, 191, 192, 194–196, 214, 215, 251, 252, 254, 256–258, 262, 270, 273
24:6 59, 74, 75, 90, 104, 123, 156, 164, 176–179, 189–192, 194, 195, 205, 214, 215, 241, 254, 256–258
24:7 59, 77–80, 83, 84, 87, 156, 176–179, 189, 192, 195, 196, 214, 215, 241, 256–258, 262
24:8 59, 60, 80, 84–87, 156, 160, 180, 181, 196, 254, 262
24:9–10 60–61, 85–87, 180, 181, 214
24:9 30, 61, 90, 156, 162, 181, 254
24:10 61–62, 181
24:11 62, 87–89, 156, 176, 179, 181, 188, 214
24:12 62, 63, 84, 85, 91, 156, 172, 174–176, 179, 181, 195, 261
24:13 164, 168, 181, 182, 195, 196, 207, 216, 217
24:14–27 92–118, 173, 182, 183, 189, 193, 197, 198, 207–209
24:14 97, 115, 156, 164, 168, 172, 175, 180, 182, 190, 207–213, 215, 217, 224, 241, 254, 266, 272
24:15 97, 98, 101–103, 113, 115, 116, 156, 160, 165, 180, 182, 189, 196, 208–210, 212, 213, 215, 224, 241, 258, 272
24:16 99, 103, 165, 208, 213, 272

24:17 98, 103–107, 123, 156, 160, 162, 177, 180, 182, 183, 195, 205, 208, 212, 215, 217, 235, 241, 251, 252, 273
24:18 62, 98, 103, 116, 117, 157, 165, 208, 211–213, 215, 217, 241, 265, 272
24:19–21 115, 116, 208, 210–212, 217, 224, 241
24:19 115–117, 211, 259, 265
24:21 117, 165
24:22 98, 107–109, 117, 157, 165, 168, 192, 208, 209, 211–213, 272
24:23 98, 99, 107–109, 115, 175, 208, 210–212, 217, 224, 232, 241
24:24 99, 117, 118, 157, 208, 211, 212, 217, 224, 230, 241, 253, 254
24:25 36, 67–71, 99, 111, 112, 156, 157, 161, 165, 175, 176, 183, 185–187, 208, 211, 212, 224–225, 233, 241, 254, 261
24:26 69, 71, 99, 110–112, 129, 157, 161 , 165, 168, 176, 183, 191, 208, 211, 212, 224–225, 241, 254, 261, 270
24:27 49, 99–101, 107, 112–115, 157, 165, 166, 168, 183, 208, 211, 212, 224–225, 241, 254
24:28–33 68, 118–156, 160, 173, 188, 189, 198, 207, 232, 249
24:28 122, 146–148, 150, 153, 168, 207, 208, 212, 213, 215, 223, 227, 229–231, 235–237, 270, 272
24:29 122, 215, 227–231, 233, 235–237, 240, 270
24:30 122, 166, 215, 227–231, 235–237, 240, 270
24:31 28, 122, 123, 127–130, 142, 148, 149, 157, 159, 160, 166, 168, 217, 223, 227–232, 235–237, 240, 259, 262, 265–267, 270
24:32 68, 123, 124, 146, 166
24:33 28, 35, 45, 124, 149–158, 228, 232, 236, 237, 242, 248, 254, 259

Judges
1 227, 229, 231, 232, 237, 238
2:1–5 127, 227, 229–231, 237
2:6–9 125–130, 173, 188–190, 207, 226, 228–232, 235–237, 270
2:6 146–148, 154, 227, 229, 231

2:7 147–149, 231
2:8 129, 208, 213, 215, 223, 227, 231, 232, 240
2:9 208, 213, 215, 223, 227, 232, 240
2:10 223, 228, 230, 231, 236
2:11–13 154, 231
3:5 179
3:12–14 154
3:12 150
3:17 154
6:7–10 173, 188–190, 204, 242
9 173, 176, 188, 190–194, 198, 224, 272
9:6 67
10:11–12 204
10:16 99, 175, 210
17–21 248
20:2 184
20:10 184
20:12 184
20:27–28 150, 152, 153
21:5 184

Ruth
4:9–12 108, 191, 209

1 Samuel
1 67, 234
2:12–36 153
2:28 184
7:3 99, 175, 210
7:4 175, 210
10:1 61
10:17–27 147, 173, 191–194, 198, 203
10:18 204
10:19–20 184
10:25 147
12 72, 73, 104, 162, 173, 191–194, 204, 214, 241, 253, 270
12:5 108, 192, 209
12:6–17 194
12:8 73, 74, 78, 191, 192, 258
12:10–11 61, 19, 257
12:14 118

2 Samuel
7 170
15:15 97

21–24 248, 249
22 2, 276

1 Kings
2:4 241
2:27 153
8:25 241
9:4–5 241
12 70, 173, 176, 190, 191, 193, 194, 198, 224, 272
18:21 182

2 Kings
6:22 175
14:6 187
16:4 110
17 170
18 2
18:14–20:19 6
24:18–25:30 6

2 Chronicles
15:16 154

Nehemiah
8:8 211
8:18 211
13:2 181
9:6–37 173, 194, 195

Judith
5:5–21 173, 194, 196, 197

Esther
9 248

Job
42:11 124

Psalms
18 2, 276
44:3 175
78 173, 194, 195
78:60 71
105 173, 194–196
105:26 73, 74
106 173, 194, 195

135 173, 194, 195
136 173, 194, 195

Isaiah
36 2
36:1–39:8 6

Jeremiah
8:3 97
32:21 106
46–51 267
51:64 248
52 6, 248

Ezekiel
38:16 113
47:15ff. 45

Hosea
1:7 175
3:5 113

Micah
4:1 113
6:4 73, 74, 106, 162, 251, 252

Nahum
1:2 117

Malachi
3:22–24 248

Qumran
4QJosh^a 35, 40, 41, 134, 135, 187, 188, 266, 267
4QJosh^b 35, 40, 41
4QJudg^a 189, 190
Rewritten Joshua Scrolls 42–43, 46, 219, 260
11QTa 56.12–14 88
Damascus Document 35, 150, 151

Other
Acts of the Apostles
7 194, 197

Jubilees
12:1–12 174

Josephus: *Jewish Antiquities*
1.157 68
5.115–116 68
5.117–118 68
5.119 45, 152

Targum Jonathan
5:3 134

Samaritan Joshua Texts 43–48, 68, 102, 111, 112, 152, 163–169, 183, 216–219, 242

Index of Modern Authors

Abusch, Tzvi 2
Adler, Alan D. 45
Aejmelaeus, Anneli 5, 25, 193, 274
Albright, William F. 199
Alt, Albrecht 199
Anbar, Moshe 202
Anderson, A. A. 196
Arnold, Bill T. 197
Auld, A. Graeme 27, 33, 34, 65, 67–69, 86, 90, 91, 128, 148, 149, 171, 181, 188, 201, 227
Aurelius, Erik 67, 108, 115, 182, 200, 206–208, 210, 211, 213, 215, 221
Ausloos, Hans 5, 190

Becker, Uwe 2, 67, 68, 108, 179, 201, 206–208, 210, 211, 213, 214, 216, 248, 250
Begg, Christopher T. 152
Ben Zvi, Ehud 3
Bennet, William Henry 33
Bieberstein, Klaus 18, 19, 36, 107, 138, 139, 230
Blum, Erhard 202, 211
Bodine, Walter R. 127
Boling, Robert G. 58, 73, 74, 83–85, 105, 108, 112, 114, 117, 128, 130, 131, 134, 179, 214, 221
Brettler, Marc Z. 202, 203, 205, 211
Brooke, Alan E. 23, 24
Brooke, George 1, 269
Butler, Trent C. 66, 73, 82, 86, 88, 90, 101, 103, 105, 107, 108, 113–115, 117, 150, 176, 179, 181, 189, 207, 221

Callaway, Phillip R. 253
Carr, David 3, 73, 179, 181, 199, 209, 215, 249, 250
Cohen, Jeffrey M. 218
Cooke, George Albert 33
Crawford, Sidnie W. 106, 159, 251, 252
Crown, Alan D. 46

De Rossi, Giovanni Bernardo 17
De Troyer, Kristin 5, 8, 9, 16, 22, 23, 38, 39, 41, 171, 188, 253

Debel, Hans 260, 268
Den Hertog, Cornelis Gijsbert 18, 19, 23, 24, 26, 27, 49, 50, 56–62, 67, 68, 97, 105, 111, 115, 124
Dever, William G. 200
Dillmann, August 31, 32, 116
Dogniez, Cécile 127
Donner, Herbert 246
Dozeman, Thomas 8, 37, 38, 135–137, 141, 171, 198–200, 220–222, 235, 236
Driver, Samuel R. 112
Durham, John I. 178

Edelman, Diana 91
Edenburg, Cynthia 171, 222
Ehrlich, Arnold 33, 144
Engnell, Ivan 3

Farber, Zev 44
Feldman, Ariel 41–43, 46, 135, 188, 219
Fensham, Frank C. 196
Fernández Marcos, Natalio 21
Finkelstein, Israel 200
Finsterbusch, Karin 159–161, 203, 211
Fokkelman, Jan 3
Fox, Michael 17
Fritz, Volkmar 115, 215, 221, 222

Gaster, Moses 44–47, 152, 163
Gera, Deborah Levine 194, 196
Gertz, Jan Christian 195
Greenspoon, Leonard J. 19, 20, 28, 60–61, 67, 97, 98, 130, 133
Groß, Walter 230
Gryson, Roger 21
Guillaume, Philippe 152, 230
Gärtner, Judith 196

Haar Romeny, Bas ter 10, 33, 36, 202, 209, 248, 276
Hanhart, Robert 23, 24
Hautsch, Ernst 21
Hendel, Ronald S. 274
Hjelm, Ingrid 47, 68

Hoffman, Hans-Detlef 183, 200
Hollenberg, Johannes 30, 31, 68, 77, 85, 136
Holmes, Samuel 28, 31–33, 36, 77, 82, 85, 90, 102–104, 107, 111, 116, 117, 130, 131, 137, 140, 143, 144, 159, 186

Janzen, John Gerald 254
Jellicoe, Sidney 18
Jericke, Detlef von 128
Juynboll, Theodor W. J. 44

Kahle, Paul 45
Kaufman, James C. 268
Kauhanen, Tuukka 23
Kennedy, James 45
Kennicott, Benjamin 17
Klein, Anja 196
Knauf, Ernst Axel 67, 68, 70, 71, 111, 118, 173, 182, 201, 215, 220, 229, 230, 233–235, 240
Knoppers, Gary N. 148
Kolomyts, Yuliya 269
Koopmans, William T. 61, 63, 65, 67, 69, 73, 78, 80, 86, 88, 90, 101, 103–106, 112, 114–117, 147, 171, 172, 175–178, 180–182, 184, 185, 189–193, 199, 200
Kratz, Reinhard 5, 193–195, 206–208, 216, 222, 230–232, 237–239
Kreuzer, Siegfried 170, 195
Kuenen, Abraham 198
Köhler, Ludwig 179

Lange, Armin 41
Latvus, Kari 186, 187, 219, 226
Law, Timothy M. 23
Lemche, Nils 3
Lemmelijn, Bénédicte, 5
Levin, Christoph 108, 176, 184, 190, 191, 194, 200, 206, 209, 210, 213, 215, 216, 221, 224, 226–229
Lohfink, Norbert 195, 222, 223

Macdonald, John 43–47, 163, 167, 217, 218
Margolis, Max L. 18–24, 33, 49, 50, 56–62, 97–100, 123, 124
Mayes, Andrew D. H. 151, 203, 223
Mays, James L. 251

Mazor, Lea 36, 131, 135, 159
McCarter, Kyle P. Jr. 248, 249
McKenzie, Steven L. 37
McLean, Norman 23, 24
Mendenhall, George E. 200
Merrill, Eugene H. 3
Milstein, Sara 2, 10, 209, 244
Moatti-Fine, Jacqueline 28, 29
Mowinckel, Sigmund 199
Müller, Reinhard 10, 33, 36, 81, 108, 115, 179, 190, 192, 194, 202, 206, 209–216, 221, 224, 226, 240, 241, 248, 276
Mäkipelto, Ville 265
Möhlenbrinck, Kurt 69, 70, 81, 170

Nelson, Richard D. 67, 105, 111, 128, 131, 137, 144, 184, 186, 200, 221, 222, 233
Nentel, Jochen 221, 222
Nielsen, Eduard 6, 66, 67, 68, 73, 74, 79, 81, 86, 87, 90, 105, 108, 113, 115–117, 175, 185
Nihan, Christophe 177, 178, 192, 203, 221, 222
Nodet, Étienne 45
Noort, Ed 33, 129, 130, 171, 183, 188, 221
Noth, Martin 33, 34, 81, 83, 91, 115, 116, 178, 181, 199, 206, 210, 212, 219–223, 226, 230, 249, 264

O'Brien, Mark 128, 222, 223, 226
Odorico, Marco de 2
Olson, Dennis T. 181
Orlinsky, Harry 24, 27, 32–34
Otto, Eckart 184

Pakkala, Juha 3, 10–12, 33, 36, 67, 68, 102, 104, 110–111, 161, 167, 171, 195, 202, 209, 211, 222, 224, 246, 248–250, 258, 276, 277
Perlitt, Lothar 81, 179, 183, 184, 200, 206
Person, Raymond F. 6, 7, 12, 13, 14
Popović, Mladen 184
Pressler, Carolyn 221
Pretzl, Otto 19, 50, 98

Rahlfs, Alfred 18, 23, 24, 49, 50, 56–62, 97–100, 124, 126
Rake, Mareike 188, 226, 227, 238

Rewentlow, Henning Graf 248
Rezetko, Robert 12–14
Rofé, Alexander 36, 128, 129, 145, 146, 149–151, 154
Römer, Thomas 124, 128, 184, 187, 199, 202, 203, 205, 211, 224, 248
Rösel, Harmut 144, 145, 148–150, 152
Rösel, Martin 28, 36, 64, 74, 75, 91, 105, 107, 115, 151, 174, 175, 179, 182–184, 189, 214

Schenker, Adrian 5, 9, 21
Schmid, Konrad 194, 219, 224
Schmitt, Götz 101
Schreiner, Joseph 127
Sigismund, Marcus 21, 22
Silberman, Neil Asher 200
Simpson, Cuthbert Aikman 267
Sipilä, Seppo 20–24, 26, 134
Smend, Rudolph 223, 224
Smith, Gary Verlan 19
Soggin, Alberto 16, 91, 151, 173, 174, 185, 221, 248, 267
Soisalon-Soininen, Ilmari 25, 27
Sollamo, Raija 25, 26
Spencer, John 151
Sperling, David 74, 179, 182, 214
Spronk, Klaas 188, 230, 231
Steck, Odil Hannes 2, 5
Stenberg, Robert J. 268
Stenhouse, Paul 46, 47
Steuernagel, Carl 33, 131, 264
Sweeney, Marvin A. 189

Talmon, Shemaryahu 209
Tekoniemi, Timo 265
Thackeray, Henry 24, 25
Thompson, Thomas L. 174

Thornton, Timothy 68
Tigay, Jeffrey 2, 5, 6, 209, 246
Tov, Emanuel 5, 9, 23, 28, 35, 36, 41–45, 67, 76, 106, 133, 134, 150, 152, 167, 248, 250, 251, 255, 265
Trebolle Barrera, Julio 5, 9, 10, 154
Tucker, Miika 265

Ulrich, Eugene 9, 41, 43, 134, 189, 226

Van der Kooij, Arie 99
Van der Meer, Michaël 5, 7, 8, 13, 14, 18, 19, 24, 28, 30, 31, 36, 37, 39–41, 134, 136, 138–141
Van der Toorn, Karel 1, 275
VanderKam, James 88, 174
Van Seters, John 2, 3, 174, 202–206, 212
Veijola, Timo 175, 192, 224, 241
Vetter, Dieter 84
Von Rad, Gerhard 67, 74, 87, 187, 195, 200
Vroom, Jonathan 269

Ward, Thomas B. 269
Wellhausen, Julius 6, 33, 67, 198
Wijngaards, John 177
Wischmeyer, Oda 194, 197
Witte, Markus 193
Woudstra, Marten H. 16, 111, 128, 189
Wright, G. Ernest 58, 73, 74, 83–85, 105, 108, 112, 114, 117, 128, 130, 131, 134, 179, 214, 221
Wright, Jacob L. 231
Würthwein, Ernst 193

Yahuda, Abraham S. 45

Zahn, Molly 16

www.ingramcontent.com/pod-product-compliance
Lightning Source LLC
Chambersburg PA
CBHW031758220426
43662CB00007B/453